Something Old, Something New

Other *For Better or For Worse*® Collections

Just a Simple Wedding
Home Sweat Home
Seniors' Discount
Teaching Is a Learning Experience!
She's Turning Into One of Them!
Never Wink at a Worried Woman
Striking a Chord
Reality Check
With This Ring
Family Business
Graduation: A Time for Change
The Big 5-0
Sunshine and Shadow
Middle Age Spread
Growing Like a Weed
Love Just Screws Everything Up
Starting from Scratch
"There Goes My Baby!"
Things Are Looking Up . . .
What, Me Pregnant?
If This Is a Lecture, How Long Will It Be?
Pushing 40
It's All Downhill from Here
Keep the Home Fries Burning
The Last Straw
Just One More Hug
"It Must Be Nice to Be Little"
Is This "One of Those Days," Daddy?
I've Got the One-More-Washload Blues . . .

Retrospectives

Suddenly Silver: 25 Years of For Better or For Worse®
All About April
The Lives Behind the Lines: 20 Years of For Better or For Worse®
Remembering Farley: A Tribute to the Life of Our Favorite Cartoon Dog
It's the Thought that Counts . . . Fifteenth Anniversary Collection
A Look Inside . . . For Better or For Worse®: *The 10th Anniversary Collection*

With Andie Parton

I Love My Grandpa!
So You're Going to Be a Grandma!
Graduation: Just the Beginning!
Leaving Home
Wags and Kisses

Something Old, Something New

For Better or For Worse 1st Treasury
by Lynn Johnston

**Andrews McMeel
Publishing, LLC**

Kansas City • Sydney • London

Andrews McMeel Publishing, LLC
an Andrews McMeel Universal company
1130 Walnut Street, Kansas City, Missouri 64106

www.andrewsmcmeel.com

10 11 12 13 14 RR3 10 9 8 7 6 5 4 3 2 1

ISBN: 978-0-7407-9139-0

Library of Congress Control Number: 2010924496

www.FBorFW.com

Foreword

"Wouldn't it be great," we say, "if we could go back in time?" If we could go back in time, we would change so many things. It would all be so much better, if only we could go back in time. Well, I got to do just that and I can say with certainty that changing the past has its consequences.

For almost thirty years, I lived in a comic-strip world. People and places existed in my head and things happened on schedule according to dates and deadlines. I lived in the parallel world of *For Better or For Worse* until the saga ended with the marriage of the Pattersons' eldest daughter, Elizabeth, to her longtime friend Anthony Caine. Normally, one wraps up a story and it's done; but I was offered the opportunity to see my work appear a second time in the newspapers, and after the initial overwhelming surprise, a kind of panic set in.

Looking at the work I did in 1979–80, I was discouraged to see the tentative lines, the disjointed ideas, and the faltering first steps of a newcomer to an art form that showcases heroes of the industry—and I wanted to make changes. Before my work was seen again, by a new audience, I wanted to go back in time. With the approval of my editors, I proceeded to rewrite strips, expand topics I had only alluded to, and generally improve the work that originally ran.

In 2007, I had already included some flashbacks in the dailies, so I had some spaces to fill when the story ran again. Happy to be starting over, I decided to begin the story with the arrival of Farley the dog. This, I reasoned, would be fun to see and fun to add to. So in October of 2007, I began to add new stuff, move old stuff, and in so doing, I mixed everything up! What ran in one year now ran the following year, and as long as the kids' sizes and abilities were consistent, I figured—why not? I altered text, changed the size of the "classic" kids when their appearances differed too much from the new illustrations, and was given free rein to do so. I figured I could get away with doing this until I was well into the 1982 material, and then the work could stand on its own. By 1982, I was a better writer and a more confident artist—I could *LIVE* with this being seen again, untouched.

Well, I think I succeeded in making things better. I certainly had fun. Trying to draw the way I did back then was a challenge I enjoyed. It was fun to play with kids and the dog and slapstick adults. The serious story lines of the later years had made my work less fluid and less funny, and now I was drawing pratfalls, writing goofy sound effects, and doing domestic comedy again. I didn't think about making this revised and reworked form of *FBorFW* into a treasury.

When Dorothy O'Brien, my editor at Andrews McMeel Publishing, suggested we compile the early work into a larger keepsake form, we both wondered what to do with the new material. Purists would suggest that everything run exactly as it did but then what to do with all the new strips that now belonged in the story? "I'll put everything in sequence," I suggested, "and we'll run the first part of the story with the mix of classic and new." Here is where going back in time can have negative results. Considering the many diversions I'd made from the story and how I'd arbitrarily put things wherever they "fit," I had given myself the nightmarish task of piecing it all together in a reasonable manner.

In order to do this, my daughter Katie printed out all of the integrated works. Strips that ran from the fall of 1979 to the summer of 1981 were laid out in rows covering my kitchen floor, spilling into the dining room and living room as well. The new work was cut, literally, with scissors and then taped into the original story; and when continuity was interrupted, we moved things around until everything fit. Sort of. It took days. Kate, who likes puzzles, did most of it. We presented the resulting ominous pile of papers, with notes attached and "stickies" of every color protruding from the edges, to Kevin Strang, who managed to collate it into a manuscript. Kevin, who colors my Sunday pages and scans, screens, and sends the dailies, had the patience of Job as he added photographs and other info. Katie typed all the commentary and generally kept things on track. Without them, this first treasury would have been just a good idea. It has been a lot of hard work, and for the first time in years, I'll be late for a deadline!

What I've also done (besides mix up the beginning) is tell you why some of the strips were created, which ones are true, and who they are based on. I've included the family photographs I referred to when doing caricatures and I've tried to tell you more about myself as well. *For Better or For Worse* has been a challenging and exciting career. I've been truly blessed. Like everyone else, I do think about going back in time; but even though it has been filled with ups, downs, and crazy situations, I've had a most wonderful life. It's been a trip worth taking . . . and, even if I could, I wouldn't change a thing!

I used to like this song. One day I actually listened to the words. The resulting Sunday comic—my first—received some great comments, and come to think of it, I never heard the song played again!

Looking back, I don't know how I juggled kids and housework, job, community activities, and all that traveling! From Lynn Lake, Manitoba, I sent my work by bus to Winnipeg, from there to Kansas and often I took it myself. Business travel was mixed in with family events—and often, we all went together in our small, blue Cessna. It was a busy, stressful, wonderful time and although the primal scream was not far from happening, life was good.

An actual quote and an actual scenario.

I LOVED THE WAY YOU TOLD THEM THE DISHES WERE YOUR JOB!

AND HOW YOU FEEL IT'S ONLY FAIR THAT THE MAN DO HALF THE CHORES...

THANKS FOR NOT TELLING THEM THE TRUTH!

WHOA! IT'S BEEN SUCH A BUSY MORNING, I DIDN'T THINK I'D HAVE TIME FOR LUNCH!

GET THE SOUP— IT'S CHOWDER.

I DON'T KNOW ABOUT YOU, TED, BUT I NEED A BREAK. LIFE'S TOO SHORT.

YOU NEED "GUY TIME", JOHN.

YOU NEED TO GET OUT MORE, HAVE SOME LAUGHS, LET LOOSE A LITTLE.

WANNA GO TO THE PUB ON FRIDAY?

NAH...

I TOLD MY MOM I'D STAY HOME.

Ted seemed to drift in and out of the strip with no apparent connection to anyone, no roots. I inserted these dailies— evidence that he had a life outside the medical/dental center—providing some insight into his character.

HOW IS YOUR MOTHER THESE DAYS?

I DUNNO... SHE ALWAYS SEEMS TO HAVE "SOMETHING."

THAT'S WHY IT'S SO HARD FOR ME TO MOVE OUT OF THE HOUSE. SHE NEEDS ME, SHE WORRIES ABOUT ME— ALWAYS WANTS TO KNOW WHERE I AM.

FORGIVE ME FOR SAYING THIS, TED— BUT, YOU NEED SOMEONE ELSE IN YOUR LIFE!

HEY, I'M NO WALLFLOWER, JOHN!

I AM QUITE OK WITH THE LADIES. I HAVE NO TROUBLE ATTRACTING GIRL-FRIENDS!

—I JUST HAVEN'T FOUND ONE MY MOTHER LIKES.

* Throughout the book, an asterisk denotes a newly drawn strip.

Aaron often answered the phone. He was always polite and responsible. He couldn't resist this response to a call for his dad—from the pharmacist. Good thing we lived in a small town and knew Bob Clarke well!

Our dental clinic was just a few minutes' walk from our home. I was always interested in what went on—and recorded some of the best musings of the day.

You can see in the third panel, especially, that one of my heroes was Jules Feiffer!

Names like Snodwattle, Wimpblight, Fuddmulch, and Borf aren't just fun to make up—they allow you to poke fun at someone who doesn't exist. Now and then, however, people with a name you thought you'd made up will write to say they'd seen their name in the paper! Fortunately, these folks took it as a compliment and asked for a copy of the strip.

MAMA! I'M SCARED..

IT WAS AWFUL, MA.. I DREAMED THAT THE ATTIC WAS FULL OF CRAWLY BLACK SPIDERS AN' THEY WAS COMIN' DOWN THE STAIRS INTO OUR ROOMS... BIG ONES, MA-AND..

IT WAS ONLY A DREAM, HONEY. OUR HOUSE IS SAFE. NO SPIDERS.. NOW GO TO SLEEP. EVERYTHING'S ALL RIGHT

Slithering, crawling things have never creeped me out—but I do have unfriendly thoughts about spiders. Big, hairy ones thrived in our childhood basement and made webs in the corners where vertical studs met the cement wall. My brother and I would look for flies to put on the silky web blanket that spiraled down into the nest and watch as the eight-legged inhabitant grabbed lunch. One morning, I woke to the horrific sight of spiders rushing toward my face! My brother had coaxed three big ones into a glass canning jar and as I opened my eyes, he tilted the jar, making the spiders run down to the clear bottom. In my stupor, it looked like they were coming straight for me. I let out a holler that would wake the dead and I still shudder when I recall this childhood prank. It's hard not to pass our phobias on to our kids, but we try!

Aaron said this, too. At first, I took real quotes and used them liberally—but at the time, I had a creative contract and no big deadlines. I could afford to wait for gag ideas. I had been given six months in which to develop the strip. When it came time to be serious and "under the gun," I made stuff up. Some of it was pretty hard-hitting. My husband, especially, had to develop a thick skin.

This was the original strip.

I later changed it to this, giving the vignette a better beginning.

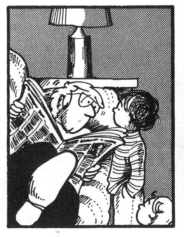

DADDY? EXACTLY HOW LONG WILL MOM BE GONE?

FOR SIX SLEEPS.

THAT'S A LONG TIME!

NO IT'S NOT, MICHAEL. IT'S GOING TO GO BY SO FAST!

YOU'VE GOT SCHOOL AND THINGS TO DO AT HOME.... WE'RE GOING TO GO OUT TO EAT AND SEE SOME MOVIES...

AN' THEN WHAT? - WHAT ARE WE GONNA DO **THEN!**

MA-NAAAA

SIX SLEEPS IS GOING TO BE A LONG TIME!

HEY THERE! HOW'S MR. MOM?

KNOCK IT OFF, TED.

JUST KIDDING! - SO, WHAT'S IT LIKE TO BE WITHOUT "THE LITTLE WOMAN"?

FINE, THANKS.

THERE'S NOTHING WRONG WITH TAKING ON A MORE NURTURING ROLE. MEN ARE SPENDING MORE TIME WITH THEIR KIDS, NOW. WE'RE ALL LEARNING HOW TO BE HANDS-ON PARENTS!

HEY, I'M IN FAMILY PRACTICE! - I KNOW THESE THINGS!

... AND, IF YOU DON'T PRACTICE ON YOUR FAMILY - WHO **CAN** YOU PRACTICE ON?!!

HEY, DAD! WHEN'S LUNCH! CAN WE GO SOMEPLACE? **DAD!**

RRRRRR

HOWCOME MA WENT OFF BY HERSELF, DAD? WHY'D SHE GO WITHOUT US!

YOUR MOTHER GETS THE URGE, NOW & THEN, TO GET AWAY FROM THE HOUSE. SHE SAYS SHE NEEDS TO BE HERSELF, TO BE FREE, I GUESS...

IS THAT WHAT THEY CALL WOMEN'S LIP?

Women's liberation, or "women's lib," was a big topic of conversation in the 1980s. When this strip came out, I was both criticized for this statement and complimented for raising the issue.

We had a lot of toys in our waiting room. Our kids never got into the supplies. The idea of blowing up all the gloves made me smile. Mike would never have been able to blow up this many in such a short time, but far-fetched is funny, and I enjoyed drawing the last panel. Don't the gloves all look like udders? This is the joy of being a cartoonist!

WHERE DOES MOM KEEP THE SPAGHETTI, MICHAEL?

WHERE DID MOM PUT LIZZIE'S CLEAN PANTS?

HOW AM **I** SUPPOSED TO KNOW WHERE HER BOTTLE IS!!

I JUST LIVE HERE...

DADDY - I DON'T WANNA EAT THIS.

IT'S BEANS. YOU LIKE BEANS!

MOM MAKES THEM WITH WIENERS.

WE DON'T HAVE ANY WIENERS. EAT YOUR BEANS.

DO I HAFTA EAT **ALL** OF THEM?

NO, YOU DON'T HAVE TO EAT ALL OF THEM, BUT EAT AT LEAST HALF. OK?

WHAT ON EARTH ARE YOU DOING, NOW?

COUNTING.

PUT YOUR PYJAMAS ON, MIKE.

I WANNA SLEEP IN MY CLOTHES.

I SAID, PUT YOUR PYJAMAS ON!

NO! THIS WAY I DON'T HAFTA GET DRESSED IN THE MORNING.

HERE. PUT THEM ON.

WHY? WHY DO I HAFTA? GIMME ONE GOOD REASON!!

WELL... I GUESS THERE IS NO GOOD REASON. THE WORLD WILL NOT END IF YOU DON'T WEAR PYJAMAS. - SLEEP IN YOUR CLOTHES! YOU'LL BE TOO HOT AND UN- COMFORTABLE. THEY'LL ITCH. BUT, THAT'S YOUR PROBLEM! OK... SLEEP IN YOUR CLOTHES!

I WANT MY PYJAMAS!

15

*

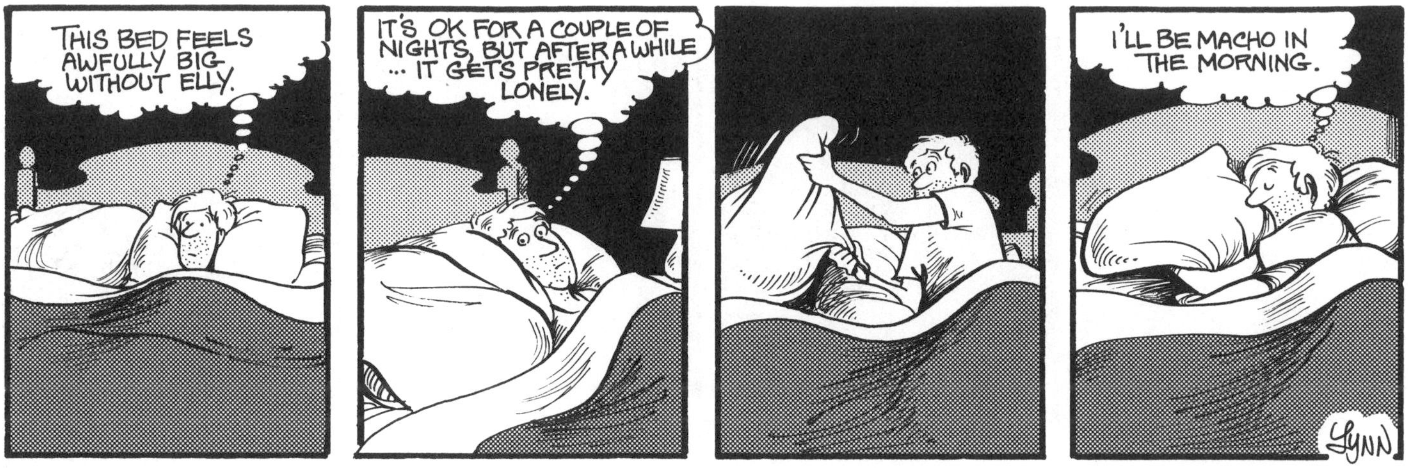

THIS BED FEELS AWFULLY BIG WITHOUT ELLY.
IT'S OK FOR A COUPLE OF NIGHTS, BUT AFTER A WHILE ... IT GETS PRETTY LONELY.
I'LL BE MACHO IN THE MORNING.
LYNN

*

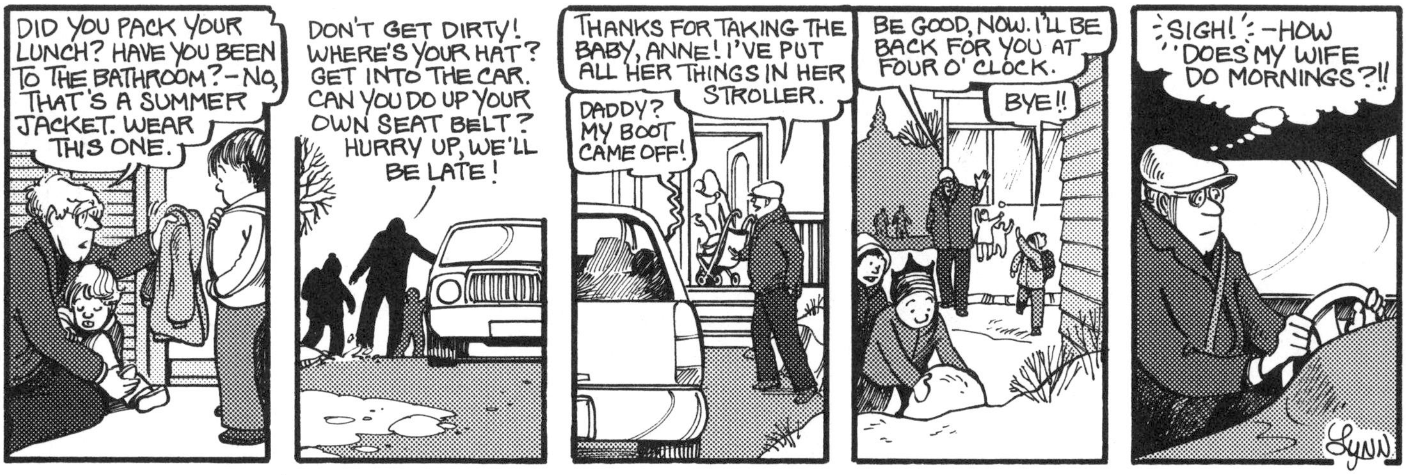

DID YOU PACK YOUR LUNCH? HAVE YOU BEEN TO THE BATHROOM? - NO, THAT'S A SUMMER JACKET. WEAR THIS ONE.
DON'T GET DIRTY! WHERE'S YOUR HAT? GET INTO THE CAR. CAN YOU DO UP YOUR OWN SEAT BELT? HURRY UP, WE'LL BE LATE!
THANKS FOR TAKING THE BABY, ANNE! I'VE PUT ALL HER THINGS IN HER STROLLER.
DADDY? MY BOOT CAME OFF!
BE GOOD, NOW. I'LL BE BACK FOR YOU AT FOUR O' CLOCK.
BYE!!
SIGH! -HOW DOES MY WIFE DO MORNINGS?!!
LYNN

*

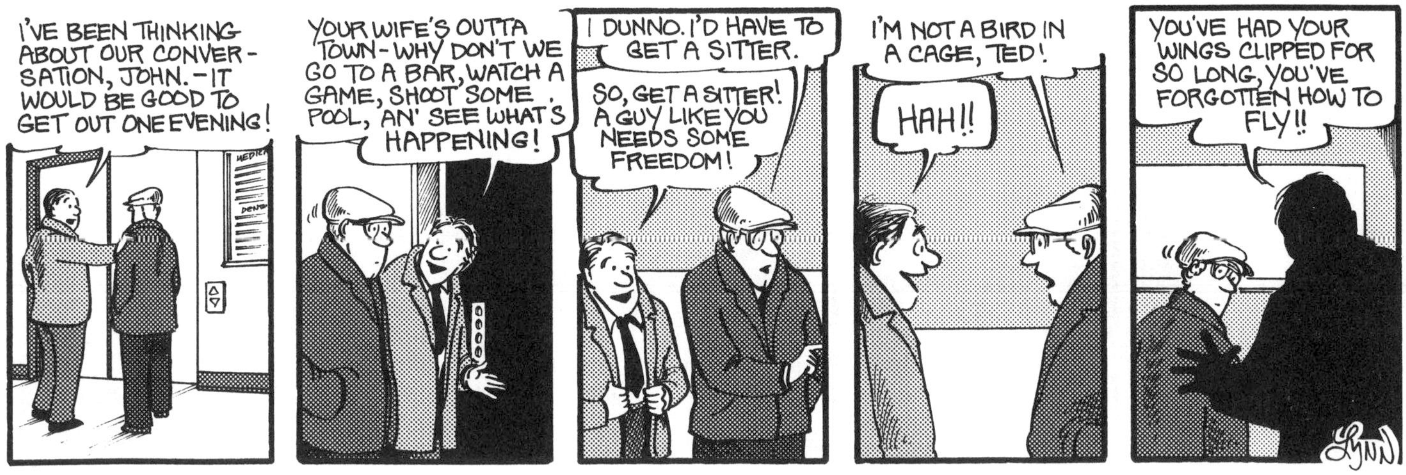

I'VE BEEN THINKING ABOUT OUR CONVERSATION, JOHN. - IT WOULD BE GOOD TO GET OUT ONE EVENING!
YOUR WIFE'S OUTTA TOWN - WHY DON'T WE GO TO A BAR, WATCH A GAME, SHOOT SOME POOL, AN' SEE WHAT'S HAPPENING!
I DUNNO. I'D HAVE TO GET A SITTER.
SO, GET A SITTER! A GUY LIKE YOU NEEDS SOME FREEDOM!
I'M NOT A BIRD IN A CAGE, TED!
HAH!!
YOU'VE HAD YOUR WINGS CLIPPED FOR SO LONG, YOU'VE FORGOTTEN HOW TO FLY!!
LYNN

We were lucky to have Rod's mom and dad close by. They lived a ten minutes' walk from our house and when I had to go out of town, Ruth and Tom would take the kids. Ruth had been an elementary school teacher and always had creative things for them to do. I don't think Rod ever had to "parent" on his own. In this vignette, I imagined what would happen if he had.

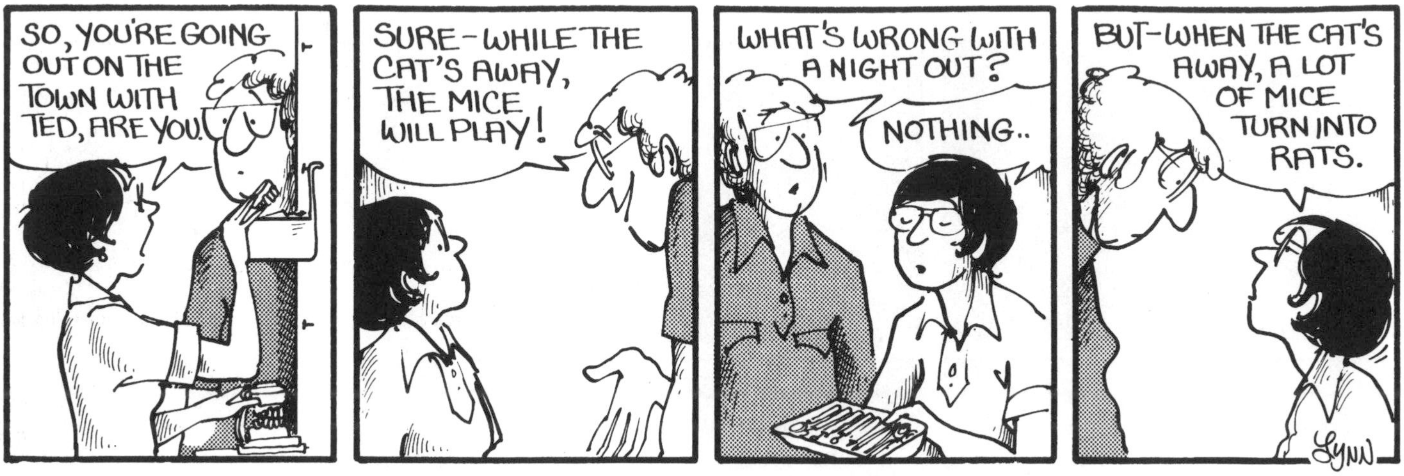
SO, YOU'RE GOING OUT ON THE TOWN WITH TED, ARE YOU.
SURE - WHILE THE CAT'S AWAY, THE MICE WILL PLAY!
WHAT'S WRONG WITH A NIGHT OUT?
NOTHING..
BUT - WHEN THE CAT'S AWAY, A LOT OF MICE TURN INTO RATS.
LYNN

*

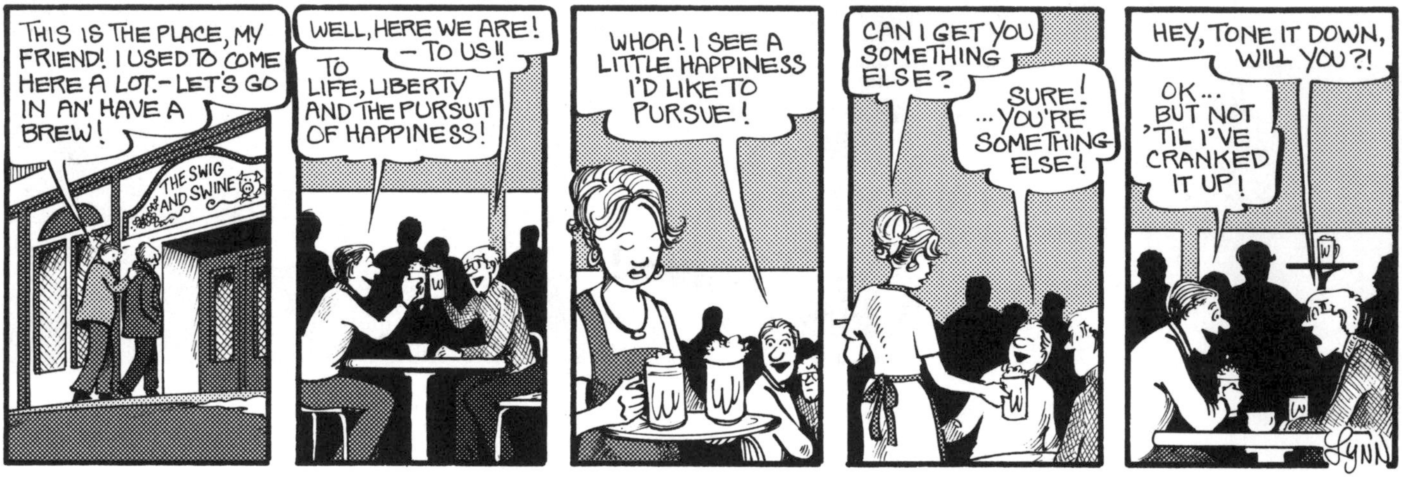
THIS IS THE PLACE, MY FRIEND! I USED TO COME HERE A LOT. - LET'S GO IN AN' HAVE A BREW!
THE SWIG AND SWINE
WELL, HERE WE ARE! - TO US!!
TO LIFE, LIBERTY AND THE PURSUIT OF HAPPINESS!
WHOA! I SEE A LITTLE HAPPINESS I'D LIKE TO PURSUE!
CAN I GET YOU SOMETHING ELSE?
SURE! ...YOU'RE SOMETHING ELSE!
HEY, TONE IT DOWN, WILL YOU?!
OK... BUT NOT 'TIL I'VE CRANKED IT UP!
LYNN

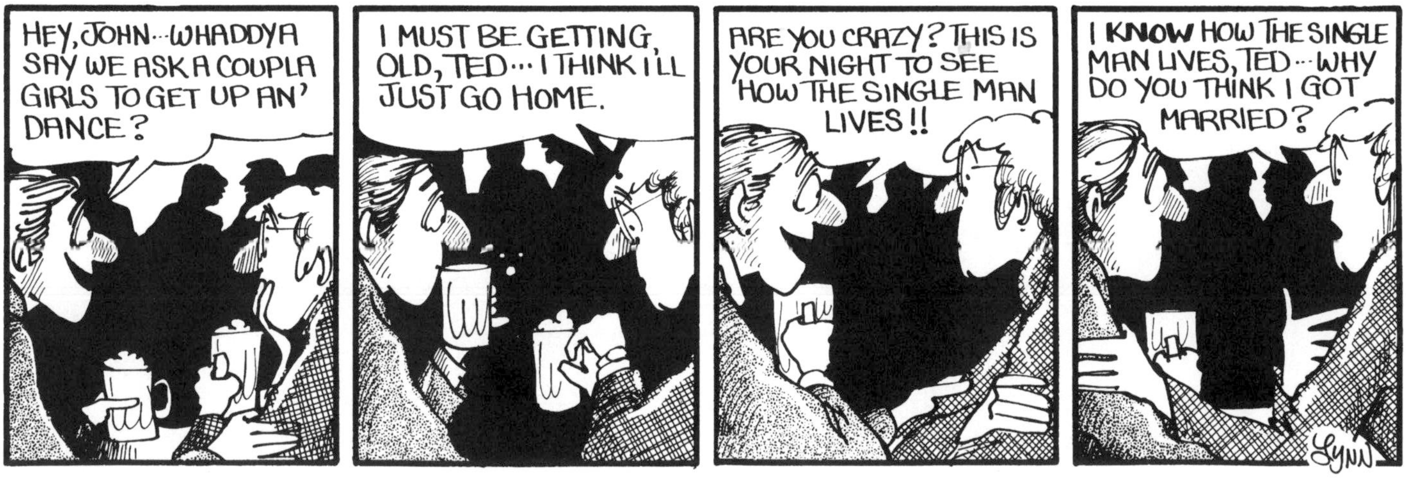
HEY, JOHN... WHADDYA SAY WE ASK A COUPLA GIRLS TO GET UP AN' DANCE?
I MUST BE GETTING OLD, TED... I THINK I'LL JUST GO HOME.
ARE YOU CRAZY? THIS IS YOUR NIGHT TO SEE HOW THE SINGLE MAN LIVES!!
I KNOW HOW THE SINGLE MAN LIVES, TED... WHY DO YOU THINK I GOT MARRIED?
LYNN

My second husband wasn't a sports fan. My friends all talked about "the guys" and "the game." This was never a part of our lives. Often other people's stories were integrated into *For Better or For Worse*.

My friend, Kevin (who does the coloring), wrote the text for the announcer's voice in the background. A serious hockey player, he wanted to read something that made sense! It's great to have help with my "research!"

My dad loved to change the lyrics in popular songs. His version of this one was, "Foam, foam on the range, in fear of Ma's cooking we pray . . ."

20

For years, there was tension between my mother and me. One of the things that affected our relationship was this job. Having gone through the Depression, she could not understand how or why we could afford to do the things we did. This story was done during a rather painful episode in our lives. When I saw it in print, I wished I hadn't done it. I thought, "Oh well, it's one day and one quote and it will be forgotten." But this strip has reappeared many times to haunt me, and here it is again!

My mom cleaned my face with spit on a Kleenex and I did the same to Aaron. Once! This quote cured me—and immediately went into the strip!

This was still the era of "the good swat." I didn't do it often—but I wanted to. It was the way I was brought up. Thankfully, I did learn to handle things differently.

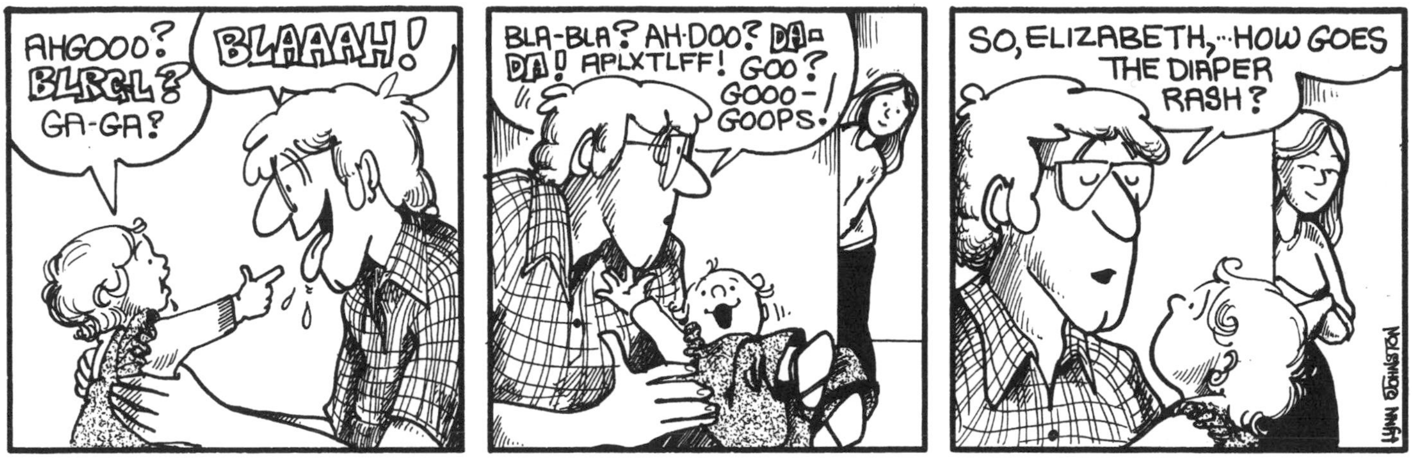
AHGOOO? BLRGL? GA-GA?
BLAAAH!
BLA-BLA? AH-DOO? DA-DA! APLXTLFF! GOO? GOOO-GOOPS!
SO, ELIZABETH,...HOW GOES THE DIAPER RASH?
LYNN JOHNSTON

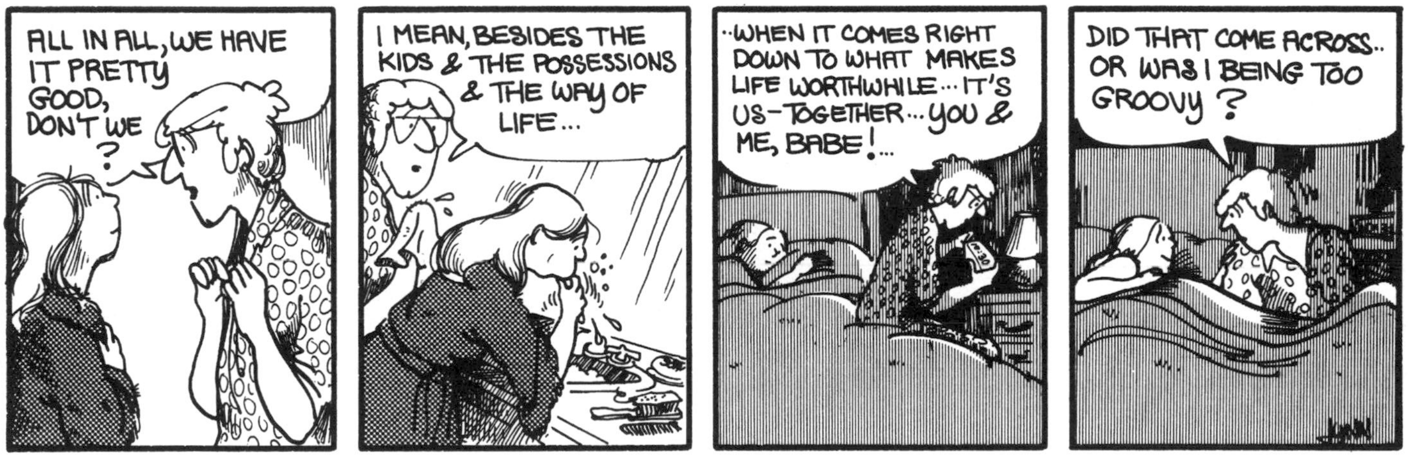
ALL IN ALL, WE HAVE IT PRETTY GOOD, DON'T WE?
I MEAN, BESIDES THE KIDS & THE POSSESSIONS & THE WAY OF LIFE...
...WHEN IT COMES RIGHT DOWN TO WHAT MAKES LIFE WORTHWHILE... IT'S US-TOGETHER... YOU & ME, BABE!...
DID THAT COME ACROSS.. OR WAS I BEING TOO GROOVY?
LYNN

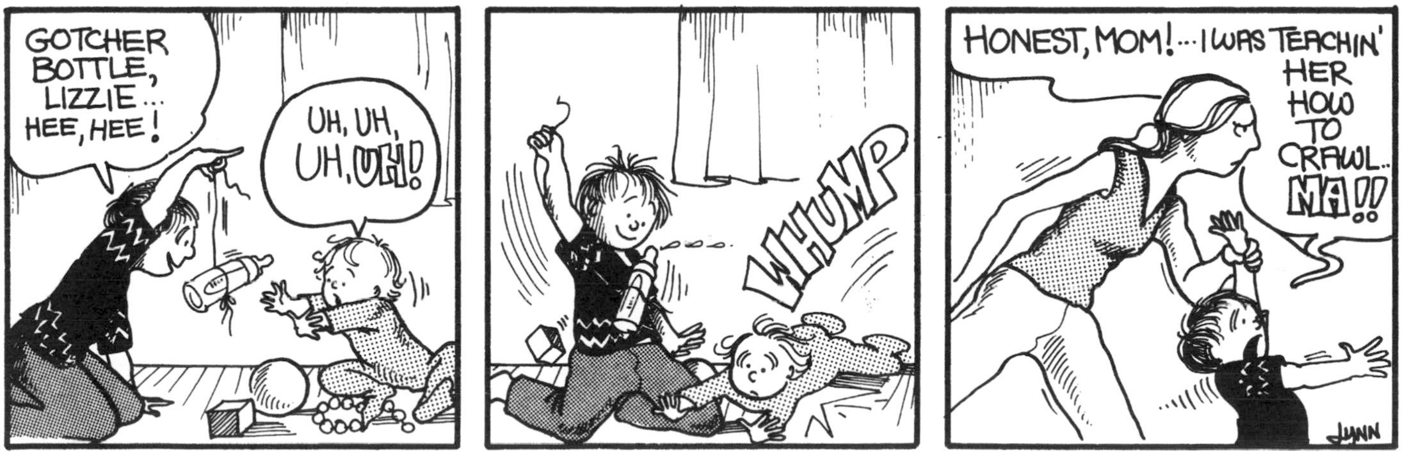
GOTCHER BOTTLE, LIZZIE... HEE, HEE!
UH, UH, UH, UH!
WHUMP
HONEST, MOM!...I WAS TEACHIN' HER HOW TO CRAWL.. MA!!
LYNN

When the kids were young, I yearned for new furniture. I'd look at our lumpy couch, the frayed cushions and the yellowing lampshades, wishing I had one of those fancy spaces you see in the "country living" magazines.

Now I have a tidy home, matching couches, my coffee tables are fingerprint free, . . . and I'm wishing I had little kids around me to color my world with their laughter and their wiles!

This is how we bought our first mattress. I didn't show here how Aaron had to jump on it as well.

 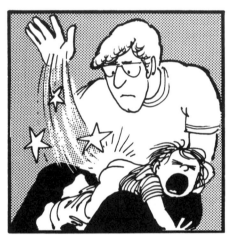 

When this true experience ran in the paper, people were outraged and I got my first real angry mail. We didn't repeat it when the classics began. It was just too controversial and, happily, passé.

We did think the other had it easier. Our days were filled, but with different demands.

This still irks me today. Delivery guys and repair men will tell you they'll be at your home on, say, "Tuesday." If you ask, "When?" they become evasive—"Sometime between noon and five," they might say—which means you're stuck at home waiting. Last time this happened to me, the FedEx guy came while I was in the can. He did leave a note, though— and it said, "Sign here if you want the package left at the door." Nice. Remember when there was a local number to call and a local person would answer? Now, it's "no service"—even if you are wearing socks, shirt, and shoes! Maybe, in time they'll figure out how to improve the "improvements."

Men Are from Mars, Women Are from Venus was a book I thoroughly enjoyed. They say that a good marriage begins with communication and I agree. You just have to understand each other's language!

This quote was so well received. It's true; moms don't get sick—we don't have time!

The fight to retain my figure has been an ongoing concern. I was never really overweight, but I've always felt that I needed to shed at least ten pounds. The trick is to shed twenty because you'll gain ten back. The trouble with this is—twenty is a daunting goal. It's much easier to stay the weight you are and complain about it!

This really happened. It's one of the many funny incidents that made a great Sunday strip.

This was our house in Dundas, Ontario. When we moved to Lynn Lake, Manitoba, I made the inside of the *FBorFW* house look like the inside of the house at Lynn Lake, thus creating an architectural nightmare for myself and later, for animators!

Aaron came home from kindergarten with this one-liner. Heaven only knows what they come home with now!

Quotes from Aaron regularly became punch lines.

Things he did were comic-strip fare.

32

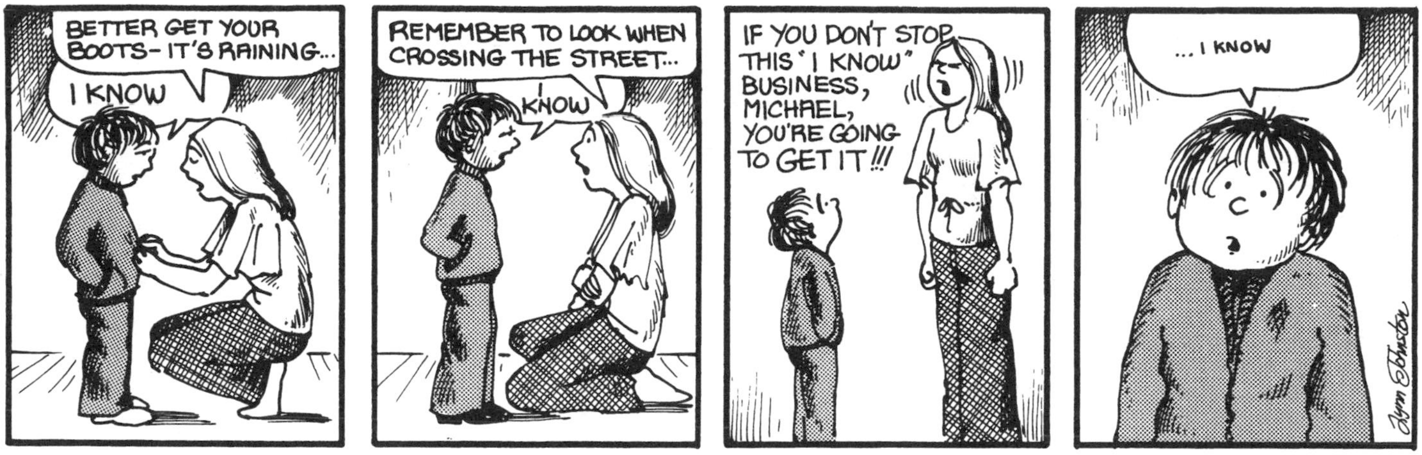
BETTER GET YOUR BOOTS- IT'S RAINING...
I KNOW
REMEMBER TO LOOK WHEN CROSSING THE STREET...
I KNOW
IF YOU DON'T STOP THIS "I KNOW" BUSINESS, MICHAEL, YOU'RE GOING TO GET IT!!!
...I KNOW
Lynn Johnston

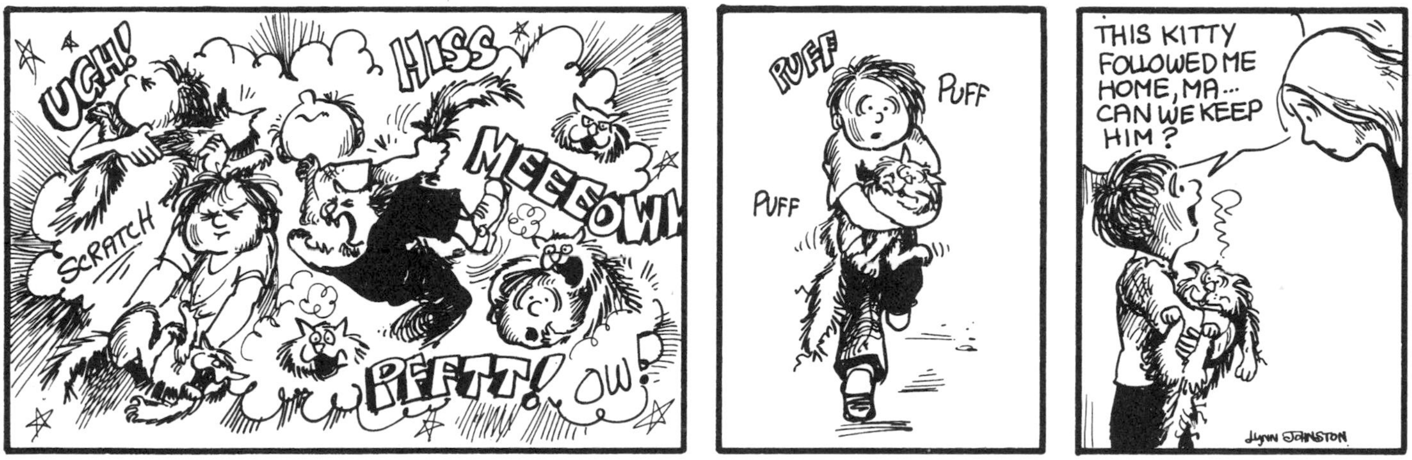
UGH!
HISS
MEEEOW!
SCRATCH
PFFTT!
OW!
PUFF
PUFF
PUFF
THIS KITTY FOLLOWED ME HOME, MA... CAN WE KEEP HIM?
LYNN JOHNSTON

This happened. Aaron fought to keep a kitten, but it turned him down.

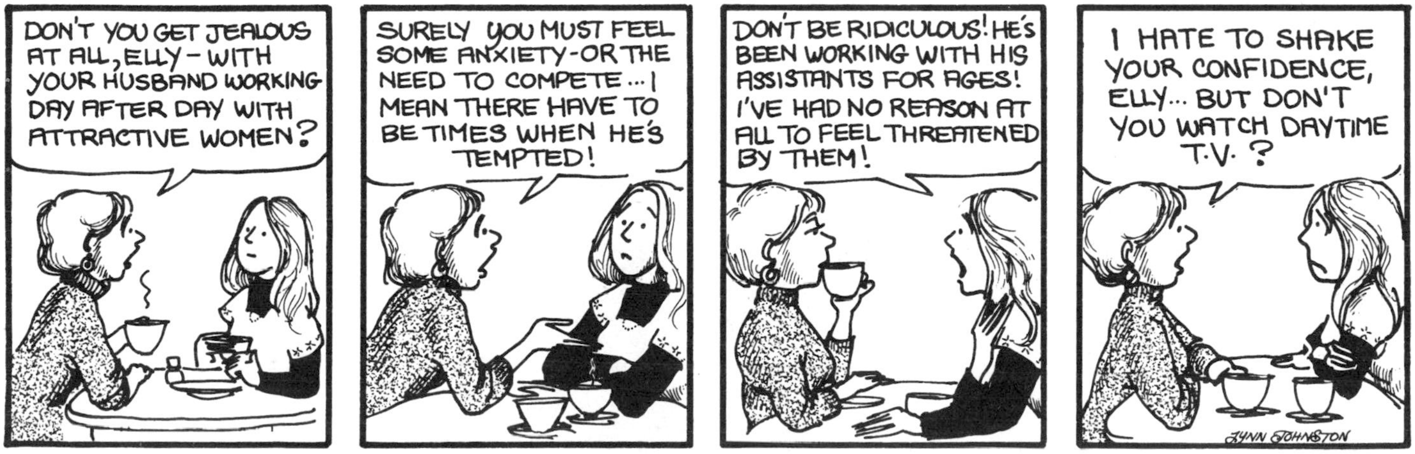
DON'T YOU GET JEALOUS AT ALL, ELLY - WITH YOUR HUSBAND WORKING DAY AFTER DAY WITH ATTRACTIVE WOMEN?
SURELY YOU MUST FEEL SOME ANXIETY - OR THE NEED TO COMPETE... I MEAN THERE HAVE TO BE TIMES WHEN HE'S TEMPTED!
DON'T BE RIDICULOUS! HE'S BEEN WORKING WITH HIS ASSISTANTS FOR AGES! I'VE HAD NO REASON AT ALL TO FEEL THREATENED BY THEM!
I HATE TO SHAKE YOUR CONFIDENCE, ELLY... BUT DON'T YOU WATCH DAYTIME T.V.?
LYNN JOHNSTON

Connie was supposed to be Elly's nemesis. Smart, savvy, career driven, and keen to compete with her insecure neighbor who wished she'd finished her education. This character soon evolved and the two became the best of friends. Strange how this happens—in life, too!

Trying on clothes is "trying" at the best of times, but when schlepping kids, it's all but impossible. I was either desperate to grab a cool sale item or in need of a headache when I shopped for this dress. Being able to vent my frustration in the strip saved my sanity!

Even though I had a challenging, satisfying job, I felt confined by my role as a mom and by the tiny remote community of Lynn Lake where we were living. Some of my women friends did not have jobs and many of their grievances made it into the strip. These women wanted careers outside the home and the cost of living was rapidly making two incomes a necessity.

I wanted Elly to love motherhood and resent it at the same time.

Elly felt she was getting old before she could reach her potential. Although I was fulfilled intellectually, the image in the mirror was changing, aging before I was ready. I'm still not there yet. Who is?

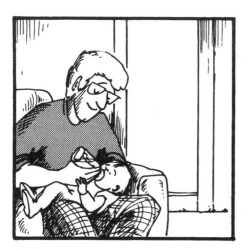

In the beginning, I jumped from topic to topic.

This is the first image of Lawrence—there in the last panel, with a cup in his hand. He was going to be "just a kid in the neighborhood." Like Connie, he was soon an integral part of the saga.

My mom should have been a doctor—heaven help you if you got sick; if the flu didn't kill you, her remedies would! The good thing was we had loads of medical supplies. Bandaging a squashed serpent is pretty easy—just wrap and wait for a miracle. This was my thinking as my dad stifled a smile and promised me the snake would appreciate my concern—even if he didn't make it.

Both Elly and I yearned for more adult conversation.

After a noisy fifth birthday party at home, I took Aaron and five friends (one for each year) to the local theater, which was a ten-minute walk from the house. It was like herding cats. This strip, and many more to come, was a "snapshot" from my mental album.

The Saturday matinee was always packed. It cost a dime to get in and you could sit through the cartoons twice, if they didn't catch you. Kissing scenes weren't just embarrassing to my buddies and me; they were boring. The "love interest" for kids is an unnecessary interruption between car chases, shootouts, and the scary stuff! It wasn't until we were teenagers that the kissing scenes were important—kind of like a "how-to" instruction video. Until then, we hissed and hollered through the hot spots and if it didn't make them go faster, it made them more fun.

Aaron insisted on walking the three blocks to his grandmother's house alone. I did follow him—and I felt silly for doing it, but I'd seen birds follow their fledglings, and so did I!

When I was writing strips or drawing them, my mind was not on the here and now. Kate and Aaron took advantage of this and would ask for cookies or a raise in their allowance—and I would automatically say yes.

In our small town, there was nowhere to go for an "evening out." We went to each other's homes for our entertainment (no invitation required), and one of the best things to happen was the arrival of the Avon or Tupperware salesperson. We ladies would dress up for the occasion, bring food and beverages to augment the hostess's offerings and dig in for a "night on the town." Since wine was an essential part of the event, sales went well and so did the evening. Fortunately, we could all walk home, having had a break from house, kids, and husband. I still own some of the not-so-essentials I bought: the price of entertainment!

What would I call this now . . . "Foreboding?"

Anne was based on a couple of women: one in Hamilton, Ontario, and one in Lynn Lake, Manitoba. We commiserated, shared our concerns, and babysat each other's kids. Neighbors like these are a godsend.

This punch line was delivered by my *FIRST* husband. A new baby fills your day—and what's left over is for organizing the house and *SLEEP*. When I really couldn't say what I had "done," I felt awful. A baby does take all your time.

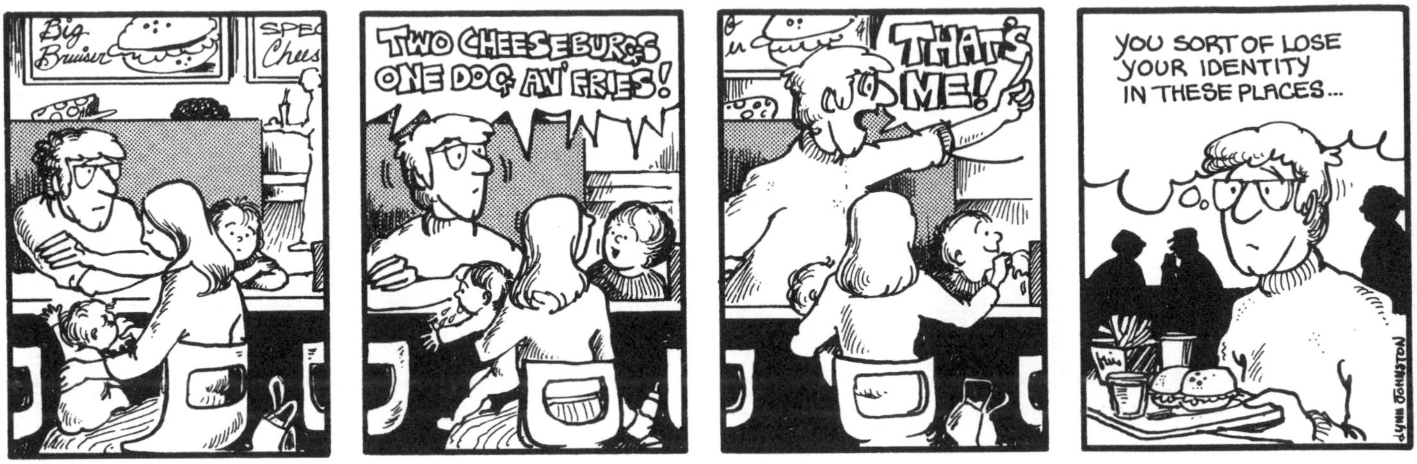
TWO CHEESEBURGS ONE DOG AN' FRIES!
THAT'S ME!
YOU SORT OF LOSE YOUR IDENTITY IN THESE PLACES...
LYNN JOHNSTON

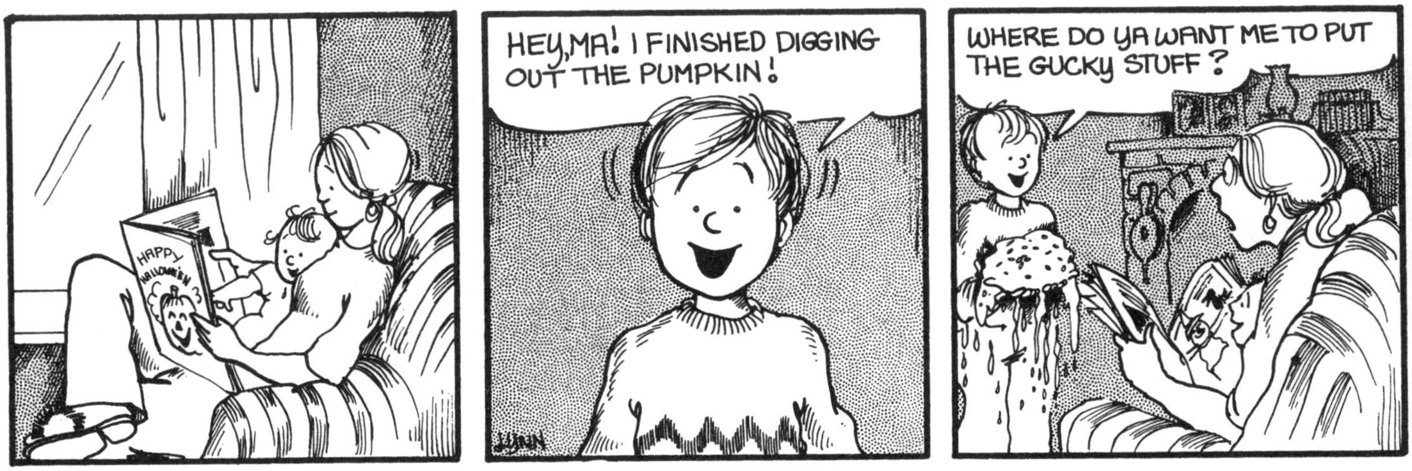
HAPPY HALLOWE'EN
HEY, MA! I FINISHED DIGGING OUT THE PUMPKIN!
LYNN
WHERE DO YA WANT ME TO PUT THE GUCKY STUFF?

*

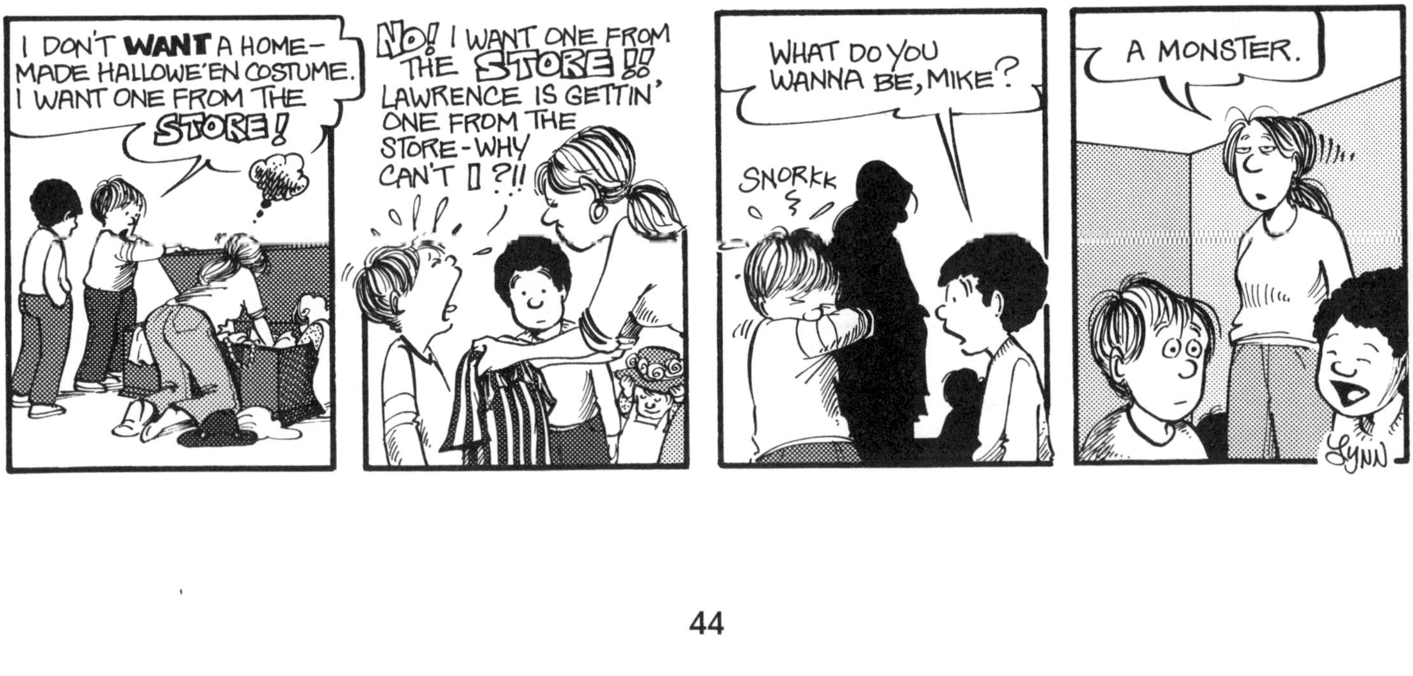
I DON'T WANT A HOME-MADE HALLOWE'EN COSTUME. I WANT ONE FROM THE STORE!
NO! I WANT ONE FROM THE STORE!! LAWRENCE IS GETTIN' ONE FROM THE STORE - WHY CAN'T I ?!!
WHAT DO YOU WANNA BE, MIKE?
SNORKK
A MONSTER.
LYNN

I have always loved Halloween. Perhaps this is why I've never had trouble thinking up Halloween cartoons. Things like Easter, Father's Day, and Mother's Day weren't so easy, but give me candy, costumes, and make-believe and my mind starts to spin. One holiday event I never really focused on was Thanksgiving. This is because it is celebrated in Canada and the States at two different times. Rather than confuse a large part of my reading audience, I left it out altogether—which, in turn, confused my audience.

HOMEMADE COSTUMES ARE NICE, EL- BUT, THIS IS SO MUCH EASIER.

YOU GO TO THE STORE, THE KID SEES WHAT HE WANTS, YOU GET IT AND GO HOME.

NO FUSS, NO MUSS-DONE!

SPACE GUY!!! YEAH!!

...I'VE CHANGED MY MIND!!!

46

Making costumes was an annual challenge—for my parents and later for me. Finding the right props, fabrics, glue, and gadgetry was half the fun and over the years we built an amazing assortment of goofy and creative get-ups.

One of the best costumes my parents made for me was a cowgirl riding a horse. The horse—with a skirt covering the sides—was attached to my waist. Stuffed fake legs made it look as though I was riding my steed. My outfit was pure Annie Oakley. I looked great! I only wore this outfit for a short time because I was soon targeted by kids who were much less fortunate. They threw firecrackers at me, igniting the frayed string mane on my horse. A neighbor put me out and sent me home. Sadly, I was safer as a paper store-bought ghost. I still enjoy making and wearing costumes, and I look forward to every opportunity.

Another real scenario. Because it was funny and made a great strip, I couldn't get angry.

Jealousy of a younger sibling is unavoidable. You try so hard to balance the scale and yet—it's there.

Rod often suffered from sarcastic punch lines that were quotes from another time in my life. He wouldn't have said this. The pressure to send something to the syndicate, however, was something he understood. He rarely objected to John being so chauvinistic, but I know he was hurt.

I once viewed stereo equipment the way I now look at computers and computerized machinery: I want it to say "on, off, high, low, fast, slow, volume" and so forth. I don't want a learning curve—I want to get straight to the point! When did complicated become cool? I'm not against progress—I just don't like change!

When Rod was a new dentist, he really did notice everyone's teeth first.

This is why wait staff habitually present a single dessert with two spoons. Either they've witnessed an unharmonious sharing or they're just primed for prevention. Either way, I support this movement and humbly suggest a larger serving.

Another element of "foreboding."

This strip garnered some angry letters from folks who thought I was making fun of people with speech problems—go figure.

Dentistry is a fidgety business. There are many opportunities for things to go wrong—nothing serious—just annoying little things like clamps not holding and materials setting too fast. Everything is done in such a wet, confined space—and backward, when using the mirror! Oblivious to this, I was once offended by the clinical and professional manner in which my husband was treating me. How could he treat me as if I was just another mouth? A friend, whose husband is a hairstylist, said, "You think that's rough; when Jack cuts my hair, he tells me what he did on the weekend as if I wasn't there!"

Rivalry between my kids wasn't as intense as it was between my brother and me. Aaron and Kate were almost five years apart, as were Mike and Lizzy, but it was always a challenge to make sure we treated them the same—if possible.

I have been sans kids for a while now. Both Katie and Aaron are adults with lives of their own. Still, I remember getting advice from folks who had no idea. Even the people who work with kids can't advise you unless they've been in the trenches of toddlerhood, too. After all these years, I've finally learned to keep my mouth shut. I don't give an opinion if I don't know what I'm talking about! That is . . . unless I'm asked.

Panel 1: I'D LOVE TO HAVE A DAUGHTER. LAWRENCE MEANS THE WORLD TO ME ...BUT, A DAUGHTER WOULD BE SO NICE!

Panel 2: DO YOU SEE YOURSELF GETTING MARRIED AGAIN, CONNIE?

PABLO AND I WERE NEVER MARRIED, EL. I JUST SAID WE WERE.

Panel 3: YEAH. I KNOW. ...YOU STILL THINK ABOUT HIM, DON'T YOU.

SURE. I DO. I TRY NOT TO, BUT HE'S WITH ME ALL THE TIME.

Panel 4: MOM? MIKE AN' I ARE GOIN' OUTSIDE, OK?

SURE.

Panel 5: HE'S JUST A LITTLE YOUNGER, THAT'S ALL.

Originally, there was no information given about Connie and Lawrence. They were mother and son and that's all. Eventually the story of her youthful trip to South America and falling in love with a Brazilian doctor appeared much later. I tried, here, to set it up.

Panel 1: I DON'T LIVE IN THE PAST, ELLY. I CAN SEE MYSELF WITH ANOTHER GUY. ...I MEAN - IF THE RIGHT ONE CAME ALONG.

Panel 2: IT'S NOT AS THOUGH I'M NOT LOOKING. I WORK IN A BUSY PLACE, I GO TO THE GYM...

Panel 3: I MEAN, I **AM** IN THE MARKET...

Panel 4: I JUST HAVE TO FIND THE RIGHT AISLE !

Panel 1: MICHAEL, LAWRENCE, COME IN, NOW - IT'S GETTING COLD.

AWW!

Panel 2: WE SHOULD BE GOING HOME, ELLY. THANKS FOR THE TEA.

WAIT! TAKE SOME COOKIES ...WE CAN'T EAT THEM ALL.

Panel 3: YES, WE CAN !!

MICHAEL! DON'T BE RUDE!

Panel 4: THAT'S OK, WE HAVE STUFF AT HOME. I'LL SEE YOU LATER.

Panel 5: THE RUDE DUDE GETS THE FOOD !

58

I think Katie's first words were "no" and "candy."

As we put this book together, we discovered a number of archiving irregularities. These two strips were missing from our files entirely. We mentioned this on our website and a reader responded by sending us these two images from his local paper. He'd kept them in a scrapbook! Having no original art to work from, I traced the fuzzy images, which gave us a clean, black line—and Kevin coloured them. We're more than grateful to our observant and very helpful readers!

This happened. Aaron even checked my head for extra eyes—but then again, I *had* lied about having them.

This was one I enjoyed drawing, and Rod—well, he thought it was too close to home.

We had a mailbox like this in my childhood home. I loved to tease the mailman and he came to expect everything from finger puppets to squirt guns coming through the slot!

I was never one to share the housework. Born in the "woman's work is never done" era, I did all the cleaning, kid raising, and related stuff. Today's moms would never feel guilty seeing their spouse scrub a floor—they'd feel they were partners in grime!

One thing I felt as a young mother was unappreciated. I wanted to hear more compliments, more thank-yous, and more affirmation that the menial chores I performed were noticed and commented on. In reality, the detailed preparation of a good meal is a labor of love—an offering, a gift. That it should be slugged down the hatch without fanfare (a belch doesn't cut it) was unforgiveable. Amazing, isn't it, how a small gesture, a little appreciation, can make such a difference.

It was so hard to talk about life insurance. "Life" seemed like a "sure" thing!

This decision was difficult—when you're young, preparing for death seems premature and planning seriously is a downer. Still, we were smart and got our wills in order—thanks, in part, to Rod's mom, who insisted we do it for the sake of the children.

An actual conversation, punch line and all.

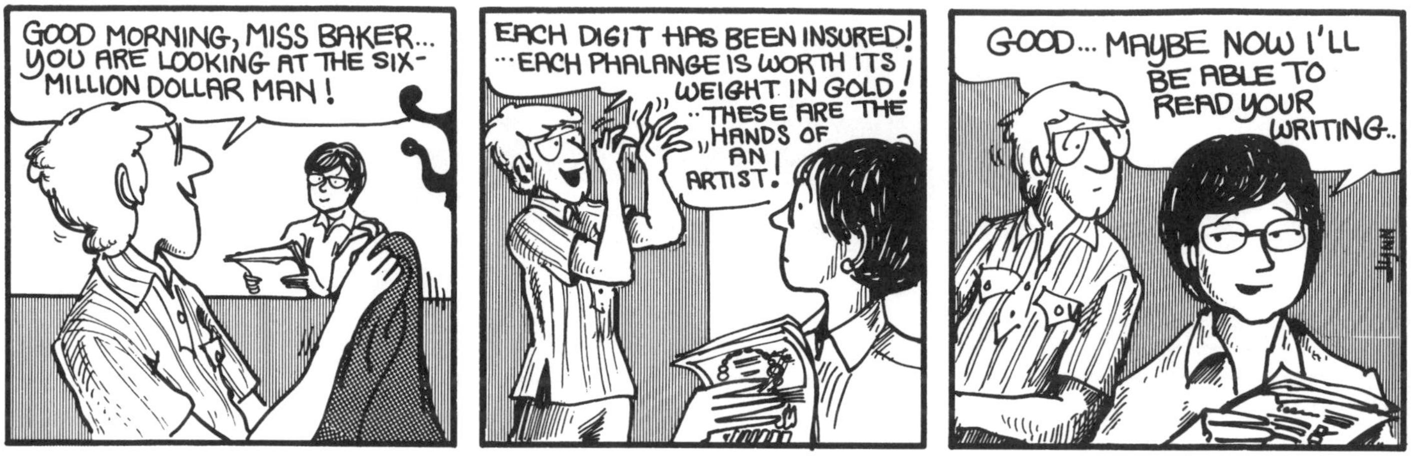
GOOD MORNING, MISS BAKER... YOU ARE LOOKING AT THE SIX-MILLION DOLLAR MAN!
EACH DIGIT HAS BEEN INSURED! ...EACH PHALANGE IS WORTH ITS WEIGHT IN GOLD! ..THESE ARE THE HANDS OF AN ARTIST!
GOOD... MAYBE NOW I'LL BE ABLE TO READ YOUR WRITING..
LYNN

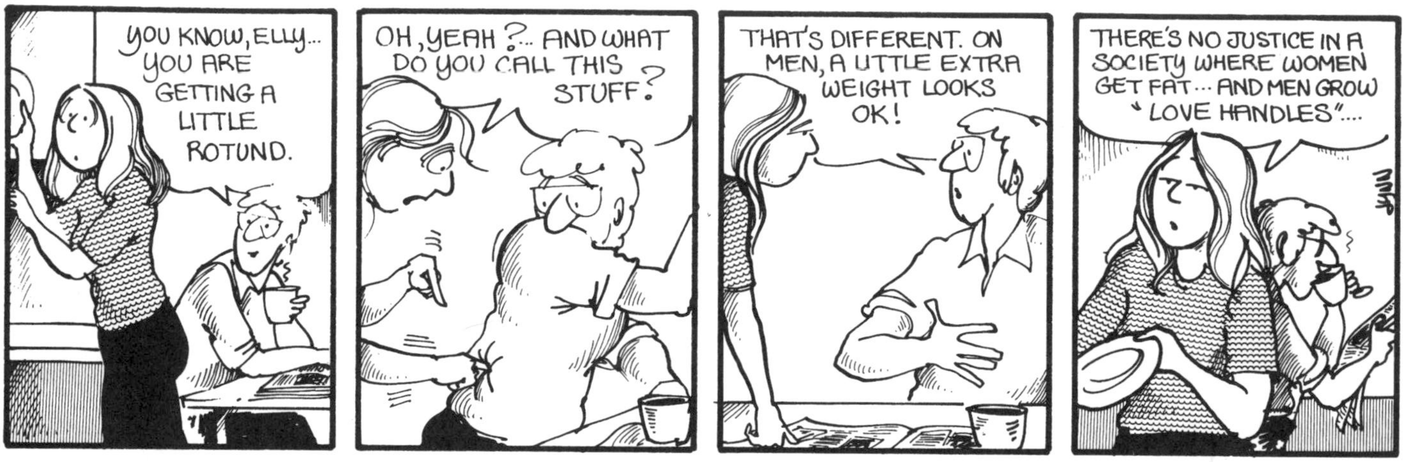
YOU KNOW, ELLY... YOU ARE GETTING A LITTLE ROTUND.
OH, YEAH?... AND WHAT DO YOU CALL THIS STUFF?
THAT'S DIFFERENT. ON MEN, A LITTLE EXTRA WEIGHT LOOKS OK!
THERE'S NO JUSTICE IN A SOCIETY WHERE WOMEN GET FAT... AND MEN GROW "LOVE HANDLES"....
LYNN

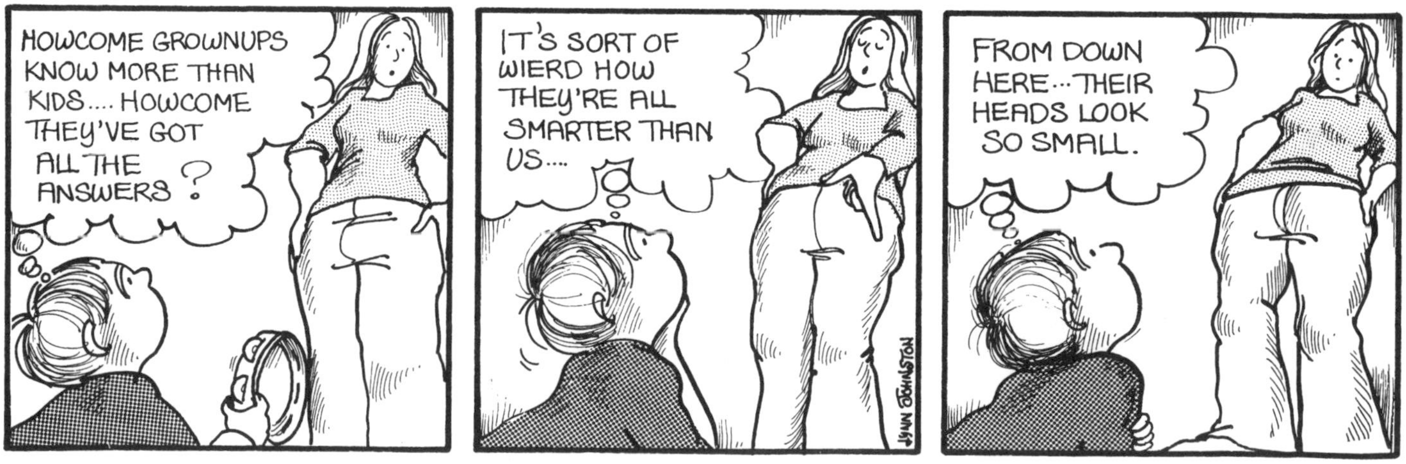
HOWCOME GROWNUPS KNOW MORE THAN KIDS.... HOWCOME THEY'VE GOT ALL THE ANSWERS?
IT'S SORT OF WIERD HOW THEY'RE ALL SMARTER THAN US....
LYNN JOHNSTON
FROM DOWN HERE... THEIR HEADS LOOK SO SMALL.

Getting out of the house, going somewhere alone, is something a young mom really looks forward to. Even grocery shopping becomes an event wherein the parolee may pause, reflect, even have an uninterrupted conversation. The downtown core of Lynn Lake, Manitoba, was two blocks long. I would peruse every store, get what I needed, and enjoy the walk home. Altogether, this might have taken an hour and a half, but it was ninety minutes of peaceful me-time and enough to prepare once again for the perils of parenthood.

*

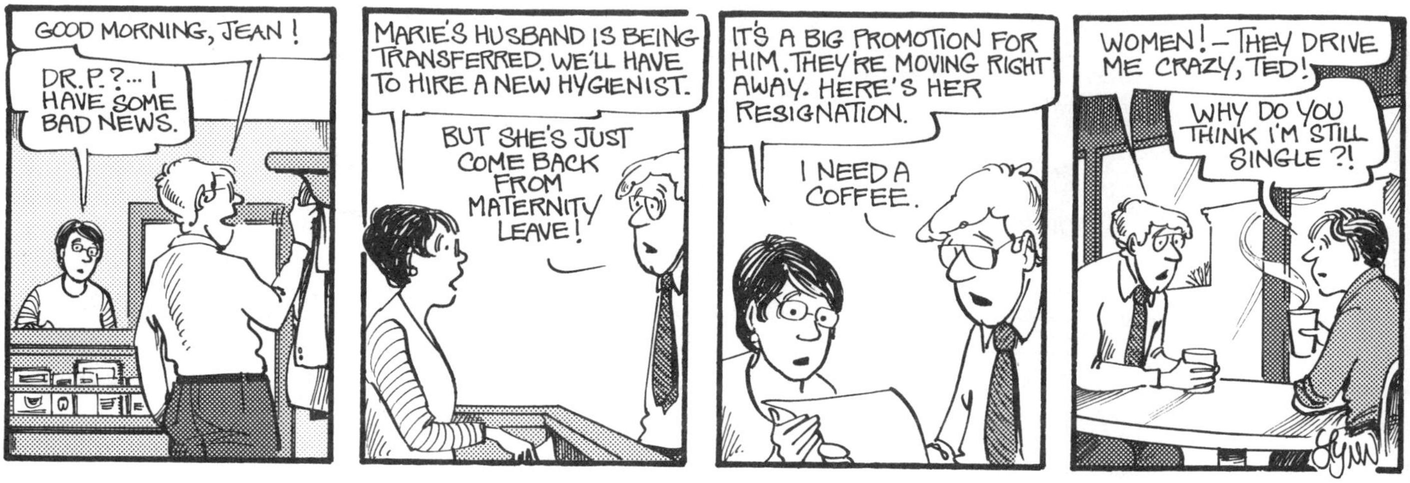
GOOD MORNING, JEAN!
DR. P.?... I HAVE SOME BAD NEWS.
MARIE'S HUSBAND IS BEING TRANSFERRED. WE'LL HAVE TO HIRE A NEW HYGIENIST.
BUT SHE'S JUST COME BACK FROM MATERNITY LEAVE!
IT'S A BIG PROMOTION FOR HIM. THEY'RE MOVING RIGHT AWAY. HERE'S HER RESIGNATION.
I NEED A COFFEE.
WOMEN! – THEY DRIVE ME CRAZY, TED!
WHY DO YOU THINK I'M STILL SINGLE?!
LYNN

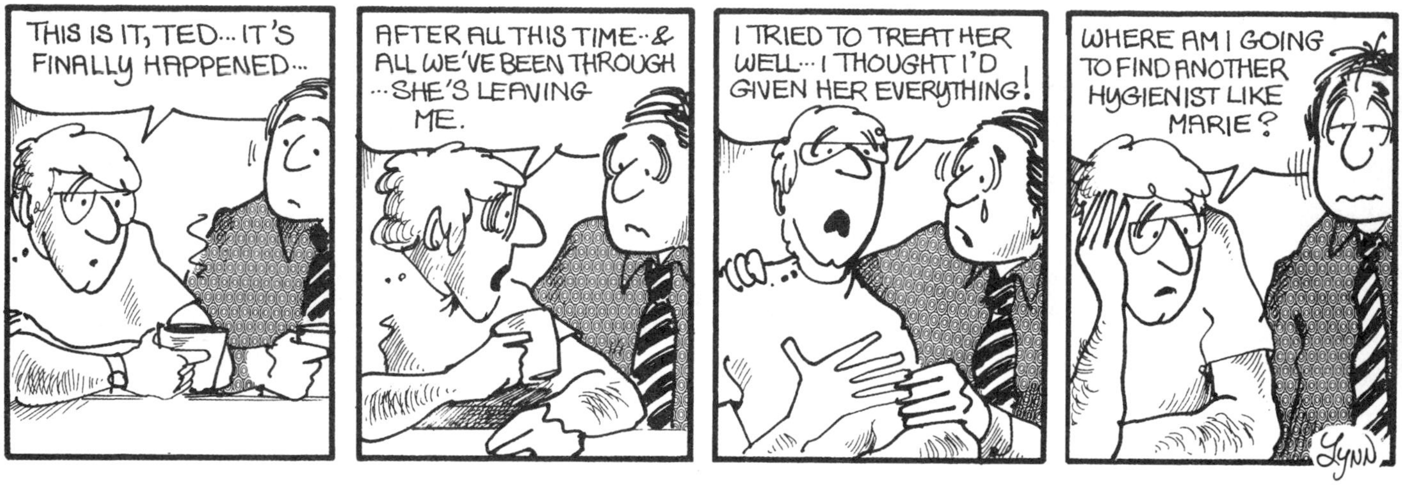
THIS IS IT, TED... IT'S FINALLY HAPPENED...
AFTER ALL THIS TIME.. & ALL WE'VE BEEN THROUGH ... SHE'S LEAVING ME.
I TRIED TO TREAT HER WELL... I THOUGHT I'D GIVEN HER EVERYTHING!
WHERE AM I GOING TO FIND ANOTHER HYGIENIST LIKE MARIE?
LYNN

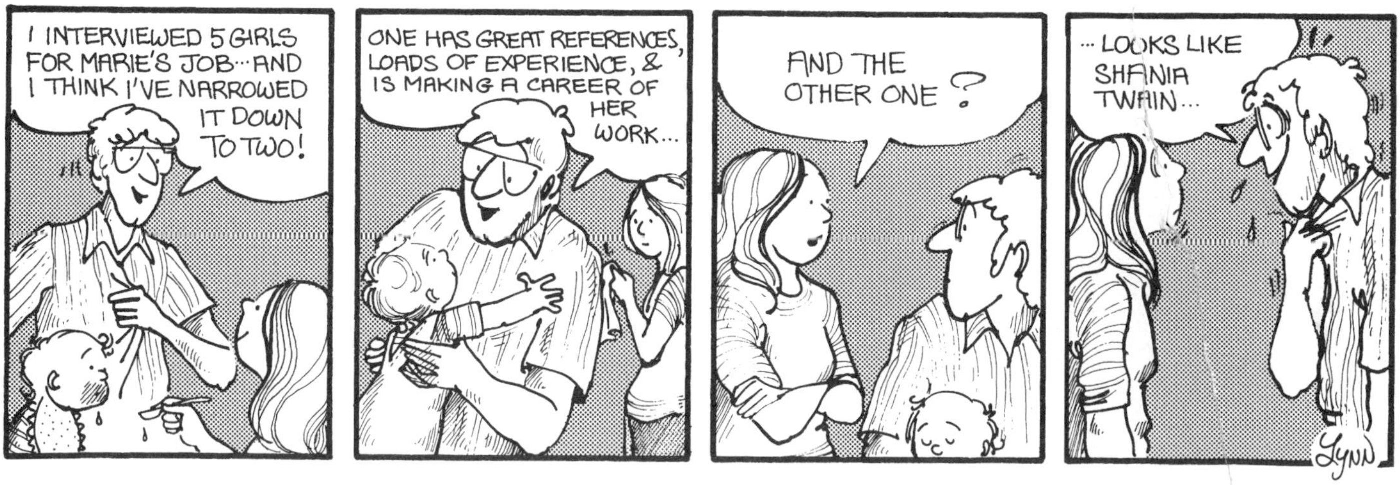
I INTERVIEWED 5 GIRLS FOR MARIE'S JOB... AND I THINK I'VE NARROWED IT DOWN TO TWO!
ONE HAS GREAT REFERENCES, LOADS OF EXPERIENCE, & IS MAKING A CAREER OF HER WORK...
AND THE OTHER ONE?
... LOOKS LIKE SHANIA TWAIN...
LYNN

This is a real quote. At a dental party, I once made the comment, "There's no such thing as an ugly hygienist." The wives laughed—without smiling.

69

Superteddy was Aaron's invention. His teddy became a missile and was soon on the "no-fly list." He was a nifty character though, and readers wanted to see more of him!

*

The saying "Silence is golden" was not written by the parent of a toddler.

71

I think I can count the times my husband(s) changed a diaper on the fingers of one washed, anointed, and powdered hand.

It was so exciting to see my first collection book!

This quote became the title of my first collection book. There's nothing more exciting than seeing your first book of cartoons in print!

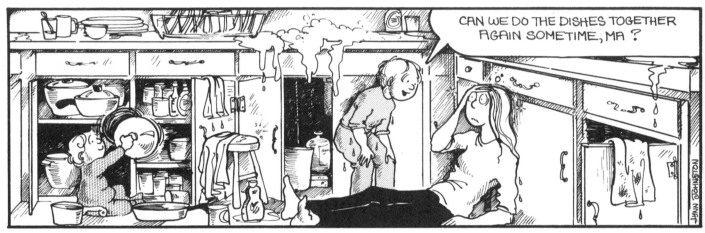

Letting the kids "help" seems like more trouble that it's worth—but it's done with the hope they'll be willing, eager, and efficient helpers when they're older. Dream on!

Here is an example of the inconsistency that sometimes crept into the mix of new and retro strips. In the daily strip above, Elizabeth is quite the baby. In the following Sunday strip, she's grown!

My mother told me I'd spoil the kids if I kept getting up when they cried. It was hard to ignore them, but I needed my sleep. When Aaron was a baby, a good friend gave me an egg timer with the advice to set it for ten minutes. "They won't die in ten minutes!" she told me—and this advice was a lifesaver. When I had made sure he was safe, warm, dry, fed, and cared for but continued to cry, I'd set the timer for ten minutes. I'd relax, breathe deeply, and prepare myself for another audience with "the kid." My favorite gift to new parents is an egg timer and the sage advice to "turn it on when you have to—and let 'em cry!"

This idea has been done by every cartoonist on the planet—even the ones who don't have kids! We do it because it's so true!

This was one of our family Christmas cards, circa 1980.

My folks had very little left over from Dad's weekly paycheck. He made $47 a week, and if there were no dental bills or shoes to buy, we could put something aside for Christmas, birthdays, and family treats. My folks could make anything, so store bought gifts were rare. We had handmade clothing and handmade toys—things I'd cherish now, if I still had then. At the time, my brother and I couldn't understand why some of our friends had so much more than we did, and we wondered why Santa Claus was so unfair. We, in turn, had much more than other people. The unfairness in the world still puzzles me and as much as I enjoy tradition, I wonder why life can be so unfair.

The teenage babysitters I hired often seemed more like peers than children, and I felt I should treat them with the same respect I had for adults.

Putting these Sunday and daily strips together turns Elly and John into "quick-change artists." But as we sorted through the artwork trying to create continuity, we did some juggling. I could have redrawn their outfits, but you're seeing this collection—warts and all!

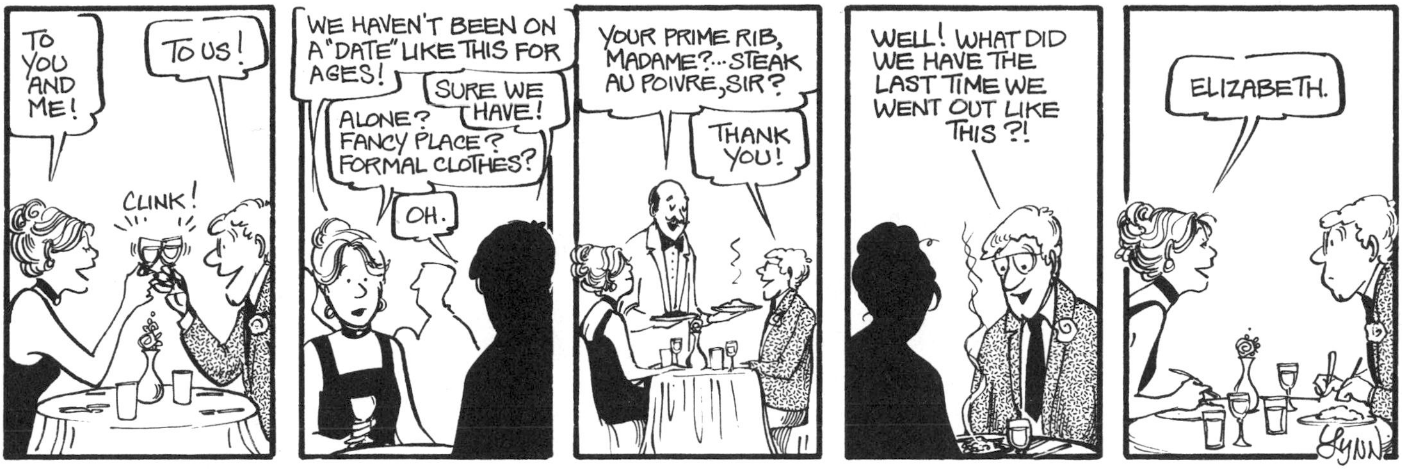
TO YOU AND ME!
TO US!
CLINK!
WE HAVEN'T BEEN ON A "DATE" LIKE THIS FOR AGES!
SURE WE HAVE!
ALONE? FANCY PLACE? FORMAL CLOTHES?
OH.
YOUR PRIME RIB, MADAME?...STEAK AU POIVRE, SIR?
THANK YOU!
WELL! WHAT DID WE HAVE THE LAST TIME WE WENT OUT LIKE THIS?!
ELIZABETH.
LYNN

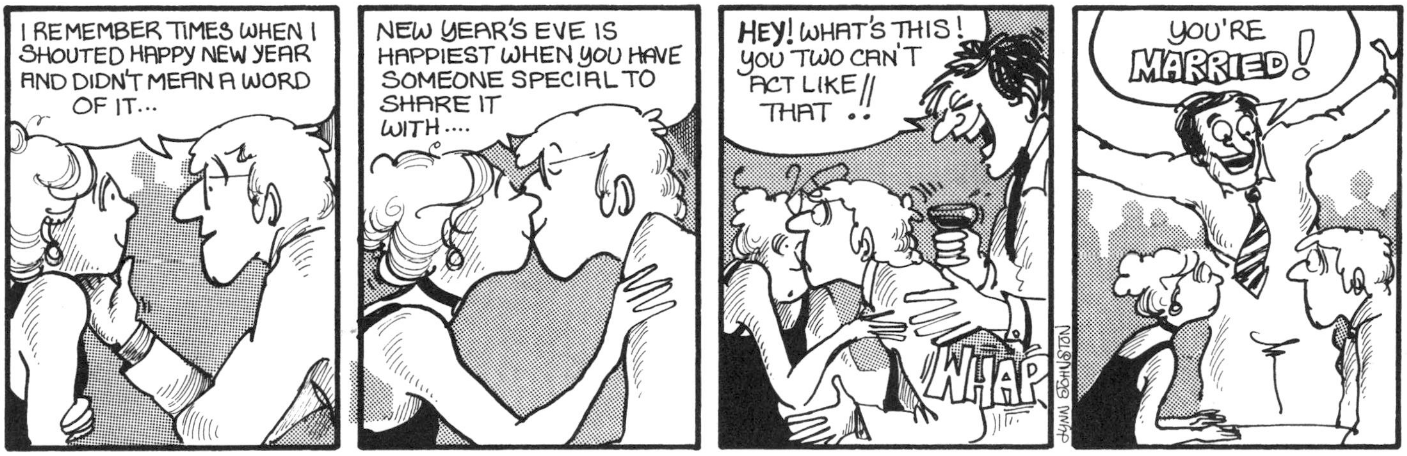
I REMEMBER TIMES WHEN I SHOUTED HAPPY NEW YEAR AND DIDN'T MEAN A WORD OF IT...
NEW YEAR'S EVE IS HAPPIEST WHEN YOU HAVE SOMEONE SPECIAL TO SHARE IT WITH....
HEY! WHAT'S THIS! YOU TWO CAN'T ACT LIKE THAT!!
WHAP
LYNN JOHNSTON
YOU'RE MARRIED!

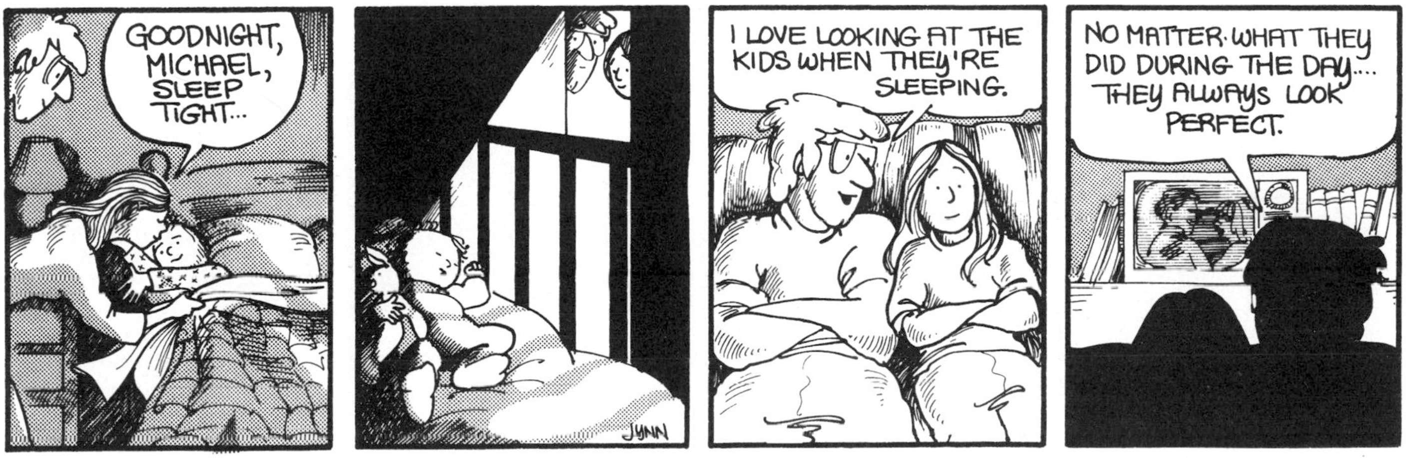
GOODNIGHT, MICHAEL, SLEEP TIGHT...
LYNN
I LOVE LOOKING AT THE KIDS WHEN THEY'RE SLEEPING.
NO MATTER WHAT THEY DID DURING THE DAY.... THEY ALWAYS LOOK PERFECT.

Connie was to Elly what Ted was to John—something of a negative balance. She, however, had a lot more potential as a character. Perhaps it's because, as a woman, I could identify with her more.

CONNIE IS SO DEPRESSED. EVERY TIME I SEE HER I FEEL GUILTY. COMPARED TO HER··· I HAVE EVERYTHING!

I HAVE A STABLE HOMELIFE, A FINE FAMILY, A RELIABLE, LOVING HUSBAND AND FATHER;··· HOW COULD I EVER COMPLAIN?!

YEAH. TOO BAD THERE AREN'T MORE OF US TRULY GREAT GUYS TO GO AROUND····

LOOK, I SAID I WASN'T MAD, MICHAEL··· IT WAS AN ACCIDENT.

SO DON'T STAND THERE LOOKING MISERABLE BECAUSE I AM **NOT** ANGRY.

I AM ANNOYED, I AM PUT OUT, BUT I AM NOT **ANGRY.**

Lynn

THEN HOWCOME YOU HAVE ALL THOSE WRINKLES UP HERE?

PICK THIS UP ¡SNIVEL! PUT THAT AWAY SNIFF ¡SNIFF! DO THIS··· DO THAT!···

WORK! WORK! WORK!··· NOBODY LOVES MEEEE···!!

DO THIS! ¡SNIVEL! DO THAT! ¡OOOOH. NOBODY LOVES MEEEE···

Lynn Johnston

My dad would fall asleep on his big, yellow recliner chair. It didn't take long for my brother and me to figure out that a good shove on the footrest would vault Dad into a sitting position, with an expression on his face that meant war. It was worth the punishment.

I was raised by a neat freak. I am a neat freak and living in a world of toys, food, noise, and constant chaos wasn't easy. This strip was a way to complain—positively.

As a young dentist in the 1980s, Rod had to overcome a sad bit of history. Today, dentistry is almost painless, but the remarks continue and they hurt.

There was a book on the market a few years ago called *Children: The Challenge*. It was given to me by a social worker who knew I could use some kindly advice. The thing I remember about the book was it said that anxiety, frustration, resentment, and doubt were all normal feelings. Wanting to dropkick Junior off the closest overpass *crosses all our minds*—wishing we were single again with no responsibilities *crosses our minds*. "Married with children" should be a degree, not a description, for in truth it's the toughest course and takes about thirty years to graduate! Thank heaven for good teachers and good books!

As Canadians, we often felt that the USA had it all. When Aaron said he was learning about the anointed states, I laughed out loud. I don't know if there was a similar response south of the border!

I introduced Deanna Sobinski as Michael's elementary school love interest, but never really focused on her or his feelings for her. I wanted to revisit this time in their lives—as she later unexpectedly played a much larger role!

*

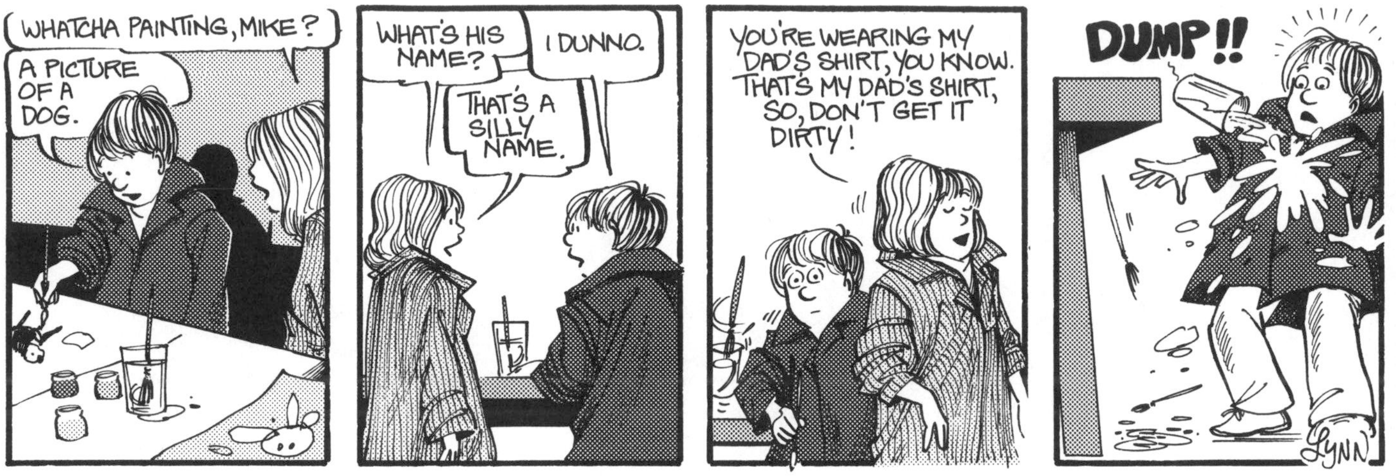
WHATCHA PAINTING, MIKE?
A PICTURE OF A DOG.
WHAT'S HIS NAME?
I DUNNO.
THAT'S A SILLY NAME.
YOU'RE WEARING MY DAD'S SHIRT, YOU KNOW. THAT'S MY DAD'S SHIRT, SO, DON'T GET IT DIRTY!
DUMP!!
LYNN

*

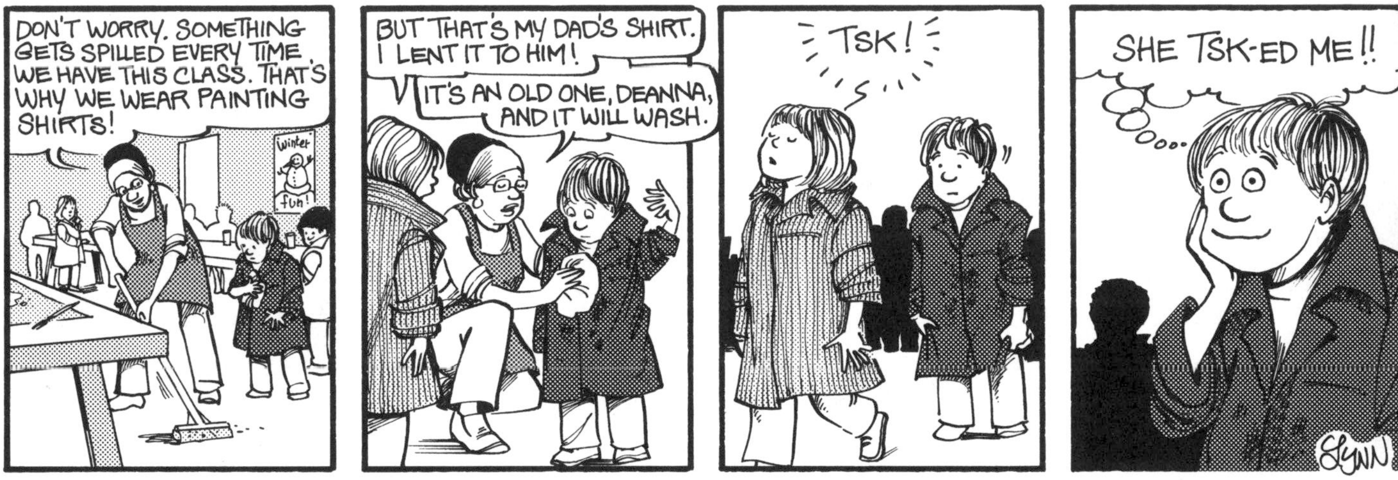
DON'T WORRY. SOMETHING GETS SPILLED EVERY TIME WE HAVE THIS CLASS. THAT'S WHY WE WEAR PAINTING SHIRTS!
Winter fun!
BUT THAT'S MY DAD'S SHIRT. I LENT IT TO HIM!
IT'S AN OLD ONE, DEANNA, AND IT WILL WASH.
TSK!
SHE TSK-ED ME!!
LYNN

*

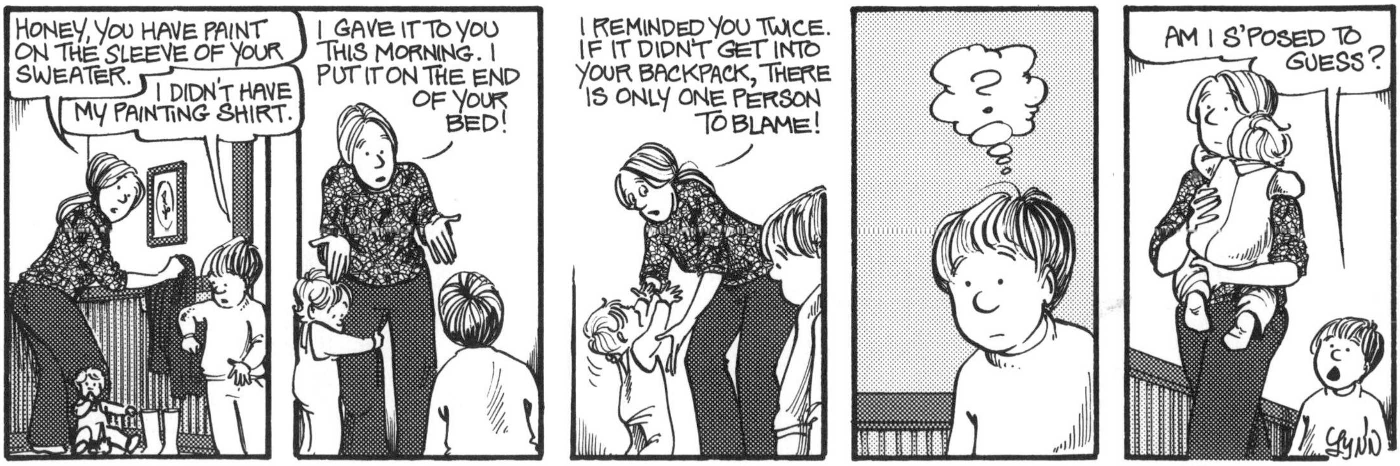
HONEY, YOU HAVE PAINT ON THE SLEEVE OF YOUR SWEATER.
I DIDN'T HAVE MY PAINTING SHIRT.
I GAVE IT TO YOU THIS MORNING. I PUT IT ON THE END OF YOUR BED!
I REMINDED YOU TWICE. IF IT DIDN'T GET INTO YOUR BACKPACK, THERE IS ONLY ONE PERSON TO BLAME!
?
AM I S'POSED TO GUESS?
LYNN

My two played "good kid–bad kid." When one was in trouble, the other became angelic. The angel role was consistently played by Kate, who hid her "devil's side" well.

The word "meany" always cut to the bone. You try so hard to be fair and kind and understanding and then *this*! I said it to my mom. My kids said it to me.

This was a mean comment and not something Rod would have said. I guess I was in a negative mood when I wrote this one. I think he put up with a lot of this kind of thing in the early years.

I DON'T WANT TO GO TO WORK THIS MORNING....

—NOW, WOMEN ARE LUCKY BECAUSE THEY DON'T HAVE A STRUCTURED DAY. THEY HAVE A CHOICE...

YEAH. GOOD POINT. NOW... SHOULD I SCOUR THE TOILETS BEFORE I FOLD THE LAUNDRY... OR VICE VERSA?

HOW CAN I WALK TO KINDERGARTEN, MA — IT'S FREEZING OUT THERE!

IT'S THREE WHOLE BLOCKS AWAY!... I'LL DIE!

MICHAEL, WHEN I WAS YOUR AGE, I WALKED 6 BLOCKS TO SCHOOL AND WE DIDN'T EVEN OWN A CAR!

...AND I SWORE I'D NEVER SOUND LIKE MY MOTHER.

UGH!...IT'S ABOUT TIME I CLEANED OUT THIS FRIDGE!

ONE CUP NONDESCRIPT GRAVY, A BOWL OF (SNIFF) CUSTARD, ONE SLICE BOLOGNA, A MUSHY GREEN PEPPER...

I FEEL GUILTY THROWING OUT ALL THIS STUFF....

MY MOTHER WOULD HAVE MADE IT INTO A CASSEROLE.

Many of the sour expressions and violent actions that I drew were over the top. Screaming and throwing objects was not our way of behaving; rather, it was the way I was feeling at the time. Raw emotion came out on the comics page while I quietly burned inside—"many a truth is said in jest," and there was a lot of truth in my drawing.

YEAH, I KNOW WHAT YOU MEAN, ANNE. JOHN DOESN'T KNOW WHERE THE LAUNDRY ROOM IS EITHER...

AS FAR AS HE'S CONCERNED, YOU DROP YOUR SOCKS BEHIND THE DRESSER AND IN TWO DAYS, THEY MAGICALLY REAPPEAR IN THE BUREAU DRAWER!

ARE YOU KIDDING? THE LAST TIME HE REMEMBERED MY BIRTHDAY WAS —

ELLY!

YOU COULD AT LEAST HAVE THE DECENCY TO CRITICIZE ME BEHIND MY BACK!

LYNN JOHNSTON

JOHN, THIS IS THE 4TH TOWEL YOU'VE USED IN TWO DAYS.... AND THE SINK IS FULL OF WHISKERS!

I KNOW THESE ARE HABITS YOU HAVE DEVELOPED OVER THE YEARS... BUT SURELY YOU CAN CHANGE!

WHY, DARLING... AND LET YOUR TALENT FOR NAGGING GO TO WASTE?

lynn

YOU'RE RIGHT, ELLY... I SHOULD HELP OUT... SO I NOT ONLY PUT MY CLOTHES IN THE LAUNDRY ROOM...

I PUT A WHOLE LOAD IN THE WASHER, AND FOLDED ALL THE SHEETS!

FOAMO

THEN, I ORGANIZED THE LIVINGROOM AND PUT AWAY THE DISHES!

I THINK I'LL WAIT BEFORE TELLING HIM HE'S DONE IT ALL WRONG...

OOOOO...

lynn

Deanna was my friend Nancy Lawn's youngest daughter. Sobinski was the last name of an art school chum. I liked the sound of the two names together, so I called Michael's first crush "Deanna Sobinski."

97

*

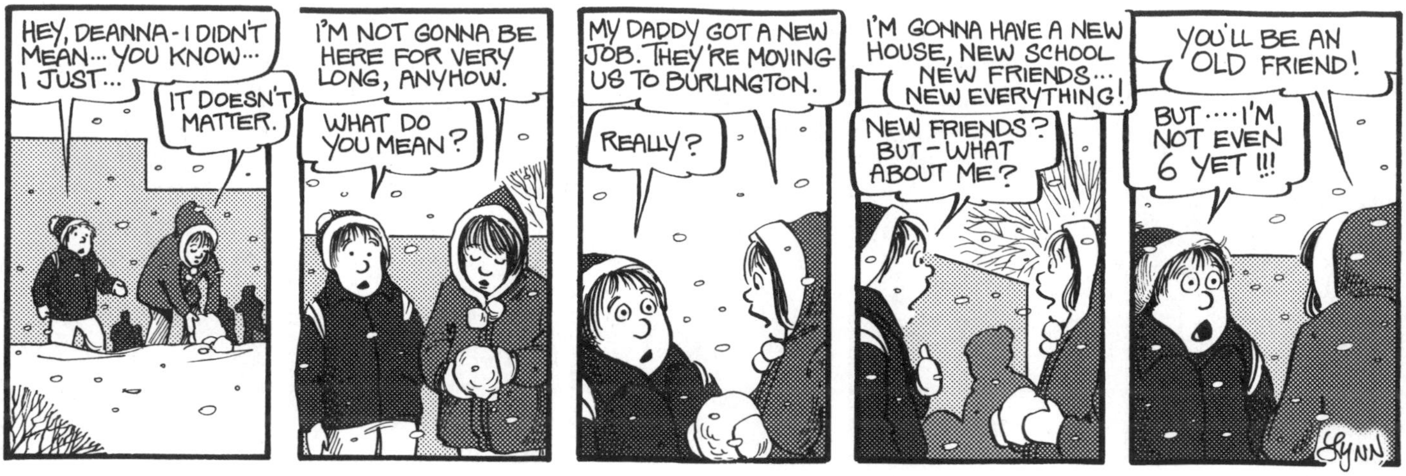
HEY, DEANNA- I DIDN'T MEAN... YOU KNOW... I JUST...
IT DOESN'T MATTER.
I'M NOT GONNA BE HERE FOR VERY LONG, ANYHOW.
WHAT DO YOU MEAN?
MY DADDY GOT A NEW JOB. THEY'RE MOVING US TO BURLINGTON.
REALLY?
I'M GONNA HAVE A NEW HOUSE, NEW SCHOOL NEW FRIENDS... NEW EVERYTHING!
NEW FRIENDS? BUT- WHAT ABOUT ME?
YOU'LL BE AN OLD FRIEND!
BUT....I'M NOT EVEN 6 YET!!!
LYNN

*

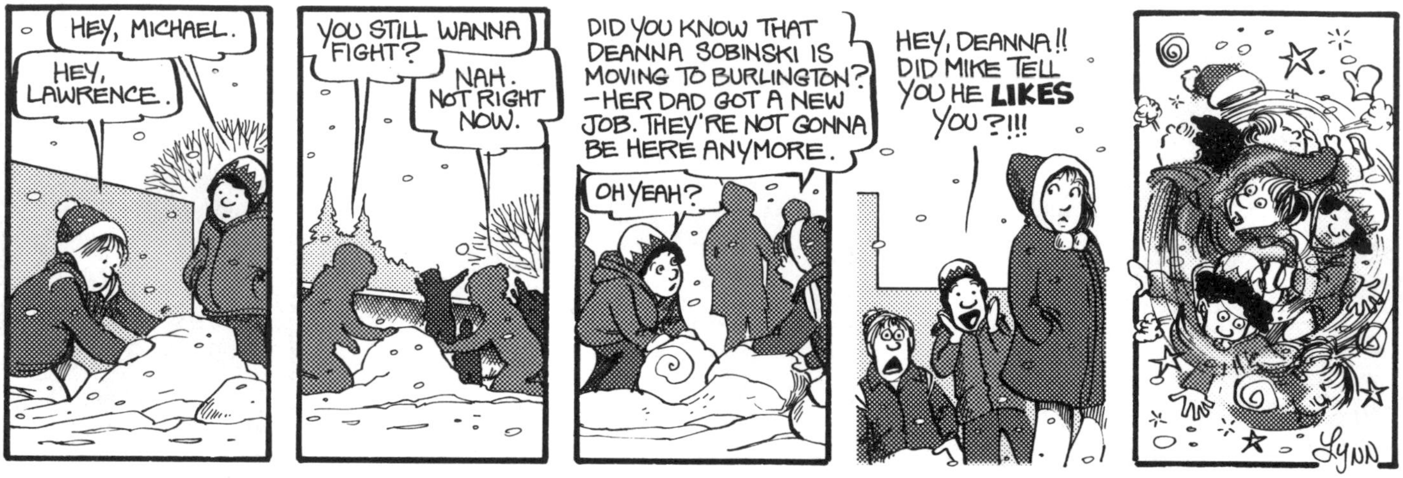
HEY, MICHAEL.
HEY, LAWRENCE.
YOU STILL WANNA FIGHT?
NAH. NOT RIGHT NOW.
DID YOU KNOW THAT DEANNA SOBINSKI IS MOVING TO BURLINGTON? -HER DAD GOT A NEW JOB. THEY'RE NOT GONNA BE HERE ANYMORE.
OH YEAH?
HEY, DEANNA!! DID MIKE TELL YOU HE **LIKES** YOU?!!!
LYNN

*

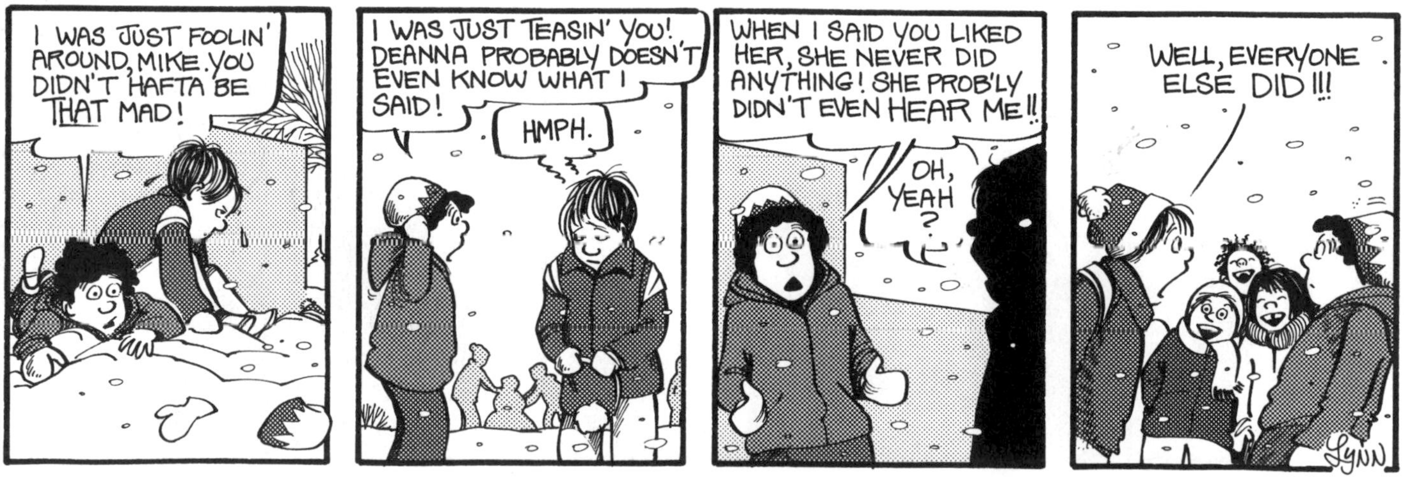
I WAS JUST FOOLIN' AROUND, MIKE. YOU DIDN'T HAFTA BE THAT MAD!
I WAS JUST TEASIN' YOU! DEANNA PROBABLY DOESN'T EVEN KNOW WHAT I SAID!
HMPH.
WHEN I SAID YOU LIKED HER, SHE NEVER DID ANYTHING! SHE PROB'LY DIDN'T EVEN HEAR ME!!
OH, YEAH?
WELL, EVERYONE ELSE DID!!!
LYNN

LOOK, MA.. I GOT DEANNA SOBIN-SKI'S PICTURE!

WELL, SHE IS A PRETTY LITTLE GIRL, MICHAEL.

YOU SEEM VERY PLEASED WITH THAT PICTURE. IT MUST BE SOMETHING VERY SPECIAL!

YEAH. I HAD TO BEAT UP LAWRENCE FOR IT.

MOM - COULD YOU DRIVE ME TO DEANNA'S HOUSE?

NO!

BUT, MOM!! I PROMISED I'D GO OVER- AN' YOU KNOW DEANNA IS SPECIAL... *REAL* SPECIAL, MA!

DEANNA LIVES JUST 4 BLOCKS AWAY, MICHAEL. YOU CAN WALK OR RIDE YOUR BIKE!

NAH. SHE'S NOT *THAT* SPECIAL.

My first "crush" was in grade one. Jimmy was so handsome I couldn't stand it. He lived on Third Street; I lived on Fifth. I used to follow him down to St. Andrews Road before he turned down the hill towards home and pretend we were together. Puppy love was real to me, and in grade two, when his dad was transferred to Alberta, it broke my heart . . . until I fell for Terry in grade three!

JOHN, YOU CAN'T WEAR THAT SHIRT AND PANTS TOGETHER!

LISTEN, NOBODY CARES ABOUT THE CLOTHES ONE WEARS, ELLY.. IT'S THE MAN INSIDE.

EVEN IF THE MAN INSIDE LOOKS LIKE A BOZO?

I'VE HAD IT, I'VE REALLY HAD IT!

YOU CRITICIZE THE WAY I DRESS, THE WAY I EAT, THE WAY I COMB MY HAIR!

...JOHN, IT'S JUST THAT SOME THINGS COULD BE IMPROVED...

WHY DO YOU WANT A MISERABLE NEW AND IMPROVED WHEN YOU'VE GOT A HAPPY OLD AND PREDICTABLE?

LOOK, I DON'T PICK ON YOU, DO I?

I MIGHT SAY YOU'RE PICKY OR UNPREDICTABLE... OR A LITTLE INSECURE, BUT THAT'S NOT CRITICISM...

I LIKE TO THINK THAT I ACCEPT YOU JUST THE WAY YOU ARE...

A CHALLENGE.

I often travel with women friends. Sometimes we share very "cozy" spaces. Snoring and talking in one's sleep are not such delicate subjects, now. We shove, bark at and answer each other, and I am about to invest in professionally crafted earplugs. The good thing about sleeping in a room with women who snore is we admit we do it!

I admit to being hooked on soap operas. The ones made in Latin America run for about six months and are over. Watching them improves my Spanish and has taught me that a story has to have a happy ending and it has to be plausible. Wouldn't it be nice if we could craft our own finale?

102

For five years, I was a medical artist for McMaster University, so this environment is familiar. Having both Connie and Ted working at a hospital made it easier for me to identify with them and to place them somewhere outside their relationships with John and Elly.

103

* I LOOK AT MYSELF IN THE MIRROR, AND I WONDER... WHO WOULD BE INTERESTED IN ME?!!

LOOK AT MY HAIR. IT'S AWFUL.

YOU'RE JUST DOWN IN THE DUMPS, THAT'S ALL.

LET'S DO A MAKE-OVER! WE'LL DO YOUR ROOTS, PUT ON SOME MAKEUP, DO YOUR NAILS...

IS THAT GONNA MAKE ME FEEL BETTER?

I DUNNO...

BUT IF NOT, AT LEAST YOU'LL BE BEAUTIFUL IN YOUR MISERY.

PETE'S BEEN GONE A YEAR NOW, CONNIE - YOU'VE GOT TO ACCEPT THAT.

I KNOW. STILL - WHEN YOU'RE ALONE LIKE THIS IT'S HARD TO FORGET.

- OUR MARRIAGE WAS LIKE THE AGONY AND THE ECSTASY...

- I JUST WISH I COULD FORGET THE ECSTASY.

Here, I tried to change Connie's hair color to separate her from Anne.

* MOM, CAN LAWRENCE AN' I MAKE A SANDWICH?

WAIT 'TIL I'M FINISHED, OK?

BEAUT MASC

BUT, WE'RE HUNGRY NOW!

I'LL ONLY BE A FEW MINUTES.

WHIP WHAP SPLAPP TWAPP WHIP

HEY!... CAN WE WATCH?

HA HA HA HA HA HA HA HA HA HA HA HA

GO MAKE YOURSELVES A SANDWICH!!

104

This Sunday page brought in so much mail! It's hard to predict the subjects that will hit home, but this one did on several levels. Busy working parents admitted to having no patience when they got home. Stay at home parents agreed. Dentists wrote to say their jobs were often too stressful, and some kids wrote to commiserate with kids who also saw themselves in this strip. We shared our realities with so many others!

When I was divorced the first time, I entered the dating game as a single mother. All of these observations were from my own experience.

My two years as a single mom came into this. It wasn't an easy time.

ONCE YOU'RE NOT PART OF A COUPLE, MOST OF YOUR MARRIED FRIENDS DRIFT AWAY...

WELL, NOTHING'S CHANGED FOR ME, CONNIE... WE'VE KNOWN EACH OTHER FOR 10 YEARS!

THANKS, ELLY. YOU'RE ONE OF THE FEW HAPPILY MARRIED FRIENDS I'VE GOT.

...IT SORT OF MAKES YOU WONDER... WHICH ONE OF US IS IN THE MINORITY GROUP.

I decided to pair Lawrence up with Connie. It was impossible to make her all bad—in fact, she was becoming another of Elly's confidantes. So, Connie became a single mom and Lawrence became a regular member of the cast.

CONNIE IS RIGHT— I'VE BEEN TAKING OUR MARRIAGE FOR GRANTED!

MAYBE I NEED A CHANGE OF IMAGE...

COSMETICS

...SHOW HIM THAT I'M STILL THE WANTON, EXCITING, LUSCIOUS WENCH HE MARRIED!—I SHALL EFFECT THE ULTIMATE TRANSFORMATION

BUT FIRST I MUST DO THE IMPOSSIBLE —GET A COUPLE OF HOURS TO MYSELF!

YOU CAN SEE I'M BUSY, JOHN...THE LEAST YOU COULD DO IS UN- PLUG THE KETTLE!

YEAH, DAD... YOU SURE ARE LAZY!

...AND, MICHAEL, IT IS NOT YOUR PLACE TO CRITICIZE YOUR FATHER!

...YOU'RE INFRINGING ON YOUR MOTHER'S TERRITORY.

I have been "watching" my weight since I was twelve. I haven't been dieting, necessarily—just watching. I have enjoyed thin as much as I have enjoyed eating my way out of my wardrobe. The hardest thing is to cut back while your partner is chowing down. If you can, save a large snack until bedtime. If you hit the sack hungry, the hum of the refrigerator will drive you crazy. Don't give in: Something happens to leftovers at night; they improve. The only way to avoid rapid ingestion is to freeze them first. This works for me. At least it slows me down.

These are the true images of parent-child interaction that brought in positive mail. Moms always thought I had a camera in their kitchen.

When you have to produce something funny every day, you sometimes resort to an old gag. We all do it; the trick is to put a different spin on it. Ultimately, the reason cartoonists do this one so often is for the fun of drawing the third panel!

This was our bedroom. The furniture was modified, but much of what you see was in Elly and John's bedroom, too!

ANNE! YOU'RE HANGING OUT THE LAUNDRY!

IT'S A GOOD DAY FOR IT, EL!

WITH THE FRESH AIR BLOWING, I THOUGHT "WHY USE THE DRYER WHEN MOTHER NATURE CAN DO THE JOB?"

AND, THE CLEAN, SWEET SCENT MAKES ALL THE HARD WORK WORTH- WHILE!

GOOD ENOUGH.

WHIFF O' SPRING ★★★★

Lynn

NO, I DON'T SEE CONNIE TOO OFTEN... SHE'S ON DAYSHIFT AGAIN.

TO TELL YOU THE TRUTH, I'M AVOIDING HER BECAUSE I DECIDED NOT TO GET A JOB YET.

ELLY, IF YOU'RE NOT READY FOR A JOB, DON'T WORRY ABOUT IT. YOU HAVE ENOUGH TO DO!

...ANNE—DO YOU SUPPOSE THAT BEING A HOUSEWIFE WILL EVER COME BACK IN STYLE?

Lynn

I had trouble, at first, drawing Connie and Anne. Because they were "out of my head" and I had no model, they tended to look far too similar. Connie had glasses and curlier hair; Anne was heavier and had straight hair. It wasn't until I had to draw sheets for animation that I really defined their looks. If I'm ever asked for advice from young cartoonists, I'll tell them to draw the model sheets *first*!

ELLY, BEING A HOMEMAKER HAS NEVER BEEN MORE IN STYLE!

LOOK AT THE KITCHEN AIDS, THE GOURMET FOODS, THE BOOKS ON PARENTING!

WOK'S COOKING

NO WOMAN SHOULD FEEL INADEQUATE BECAUSE SHE WORKS AT HOME !

...TAKEN FOR GRANTED, MAYBE... BUT NEVER INADEQUATE.

Lynn

Panel 1: SO, HOW'S CONNIE THESE DAYS?..STILL DEPRESSED? ..STILL MANHUNTING?

Panel 2: WELL, ANNE..CONNIE IS A CLOSE FRIEND AND I COULD NEVER, EVER TALK ABOUT HER BEHIND HER BACK...

Panel 3: I HATE GOSSIP! I REFUSE TO BE A GOSSIP!

Panel 4: BUT IF YOU CALL IT HUMAN INTEREST..I'LL TELL YOU EVERYTHING!

*

Panel 1: CONNIE CAN'T LET GO OF THE PAST. SHE THINKS ABOUT LAWRENCE'S FATHER A LOT. HE'S STILL IN SOUTH AMERICA SOMEWHERE. HE'S NEVER SEEN OR CONTACTED HIS SON.

Panel 2: PABLO WAS THE LOVE OF HER LIFE. HE PROMISED TO MARRY HER, BUT SHE CAME BACK TO CANADA ALONE... AND EXPECTING LAWRENCE.

Panel 3: WHEN SHE MARRIED PETER, SHE THOUGHT LIFE WOULD BE GOOD, BUT HE NEVER REALLY WANTED A FAMILY— AND, HE WAS SO MEAN TO HER.

Panel 4: IT WAS AN AWFUL DIVORCE. I KNOW. YOU AND I WERE THERE TO HELP PICK UP THE PIECES.

Panel 5: AND, SHE'S STILL TRYING TO GLUE THEM ALL BACK TOGETHER.

*

Panel 1: DAD?..ARE WE EVER GONNA MOVE AWAY? I DON'T THINK SO. NO PLANS, MIKE.

Panel 2: WHY DO YOU ASK? I DUNNO...JUST WONDERING.

Panel 3: A KID AT SCHOOL IS MOVING ...AN'...WELL— IT'S GONNA BE WEIRD.

Panel 4: IS IT SOMEONE SPECIAL? NAH. JUST A GIRL IN MY CLASS. IT'S NOTHIN' IMPORTANT. I DON'T REALLY CARE

Panel 5: ...MUCH.

112

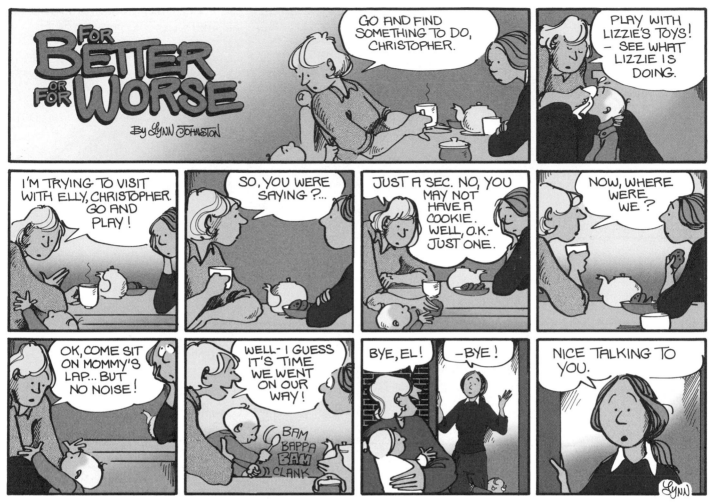

Mothers can carry on complete, coherent conversations with other moms despite distraction, interruption, and tears. This is only possible, however, if both mothers' offspring are present. Another parenting peculiarity.

When I was six, I made a will. I made one again when I was sixteen. At the time, I thought it was a good idea. Now I wonder, "What in the world was I thinking?!!"

FOR BETTER OR FOR WORSE®
BY Lynn Johnston

MOM... I KNOW... I JUST KNOW YOU'RE GOING TO BE MAD AT ME.

WHAT HAPPENED, HONEY? TELL ME WHAT IT IS.

I'M SCARED TO TELL YOU- MA... I KNOW YOU'RE GOING TO BE MAD! YOU'RE GOING TO HATE ME, MA!! PLEASE DON'T HATE ME, PLEASE!

MICHAEL...I WANT YOU TO BE ABLE TO TRUST US WITH YOUR PROBLEMS...

YOU'RE EXPECTING ME TO BE ANGRY & I DON'T EVEN KNOW WHAT'S HAPPENED. TELL ME, SWEETHEART...

I DREW ALL OVER THE NEW COUCH WITH FELT PENS.

Aaron did not draw on the couch with felt pens. He took an X-Acto knife and poked it into the cushions . . . many times. Fortunately, it was an old couch and my brother-in-law is a weaver. The couch was repaired somewhat and life went on. Parents have the ability to see the positive side of a situation like this. It ensures the survival of the species.

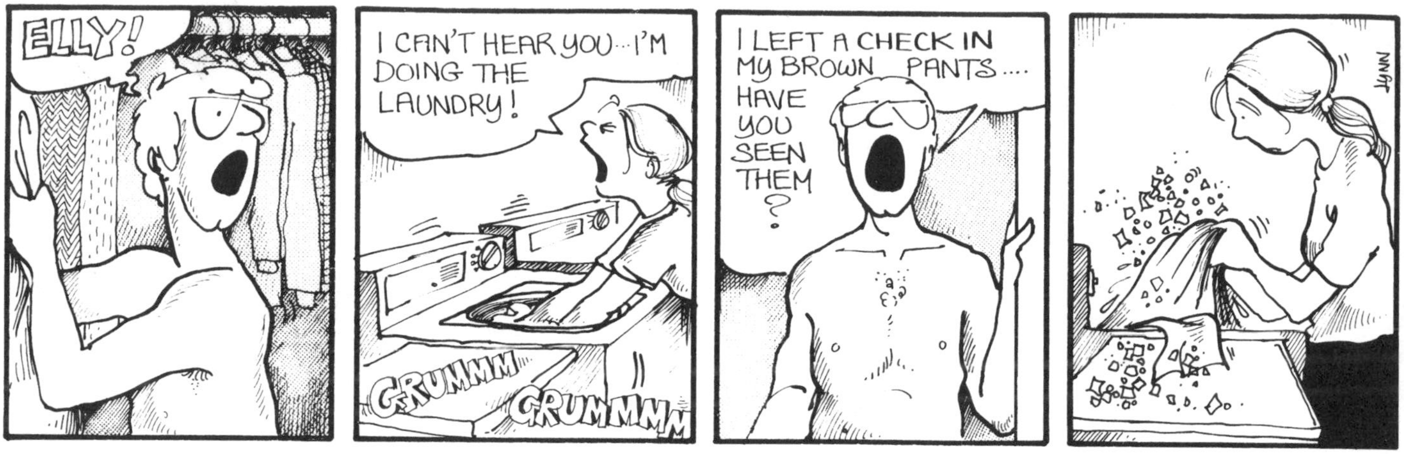
ELLY!
I CAN'T HEAR YOU...I'M DOING THE LAUNDRY!
GRUMMM
GRUMMMM
I LEFT A CHECK IN MY BROWN PANTS.... HAVE YOU SEEN THEM?
LYNN

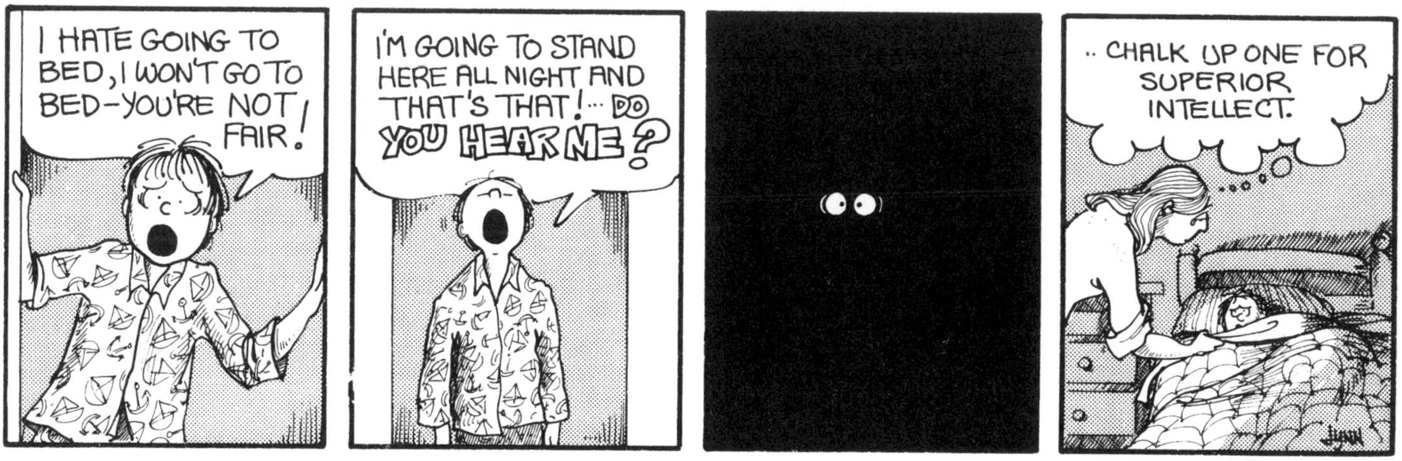
I HATE GOING TO BED, I WON'T GO TO BED-YOU'RE NOT FAIR!
I'M GOING TO STAND HERE ALL NIGHT AND THAT'S THAT!... DO YOU HEAR ME?
.. CHALK UP ONE FOR SUPERIOR INTELLECT.
LYNN

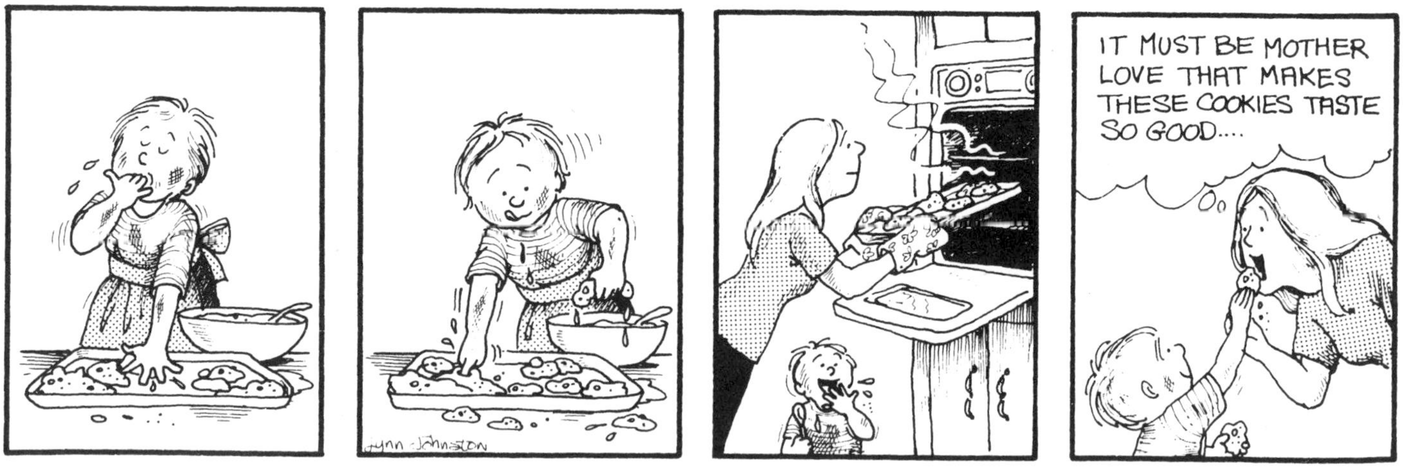
LYNN JOHNSTON
IT MUST BE MOTHER LOVE THAT MAKES THESE COOKIES TASTE SO GOOD....

I wasn't allowed to have gum. My mother hated it, and keeping a wad of gum secret meant creative hiding places. My gum often had paint chips in it or the faint flavor of rust.

Cutting the gum out of a pocket is something I did. We weren't allowed to chew gum, so after I found a wad stuck in my jeans, I took the scissors to it so my mom wouldn't find out.

YOU WERE A DIFFERENT PERSON WHEN YOU WERE MARRIED, CONNIE...

YOU WERE A DEFEATEST... WHERE DID YOUR INFERIORITY COMPLEX GO?

HE LEFT ME WITH A HOUSE, A CAR, THE BILLS, TWO SIAMESE CATS AND A FIVE YEAR OLD KID.

If I had checked this strip before I wrote about Connie's early years (later in the saga), I'd have remembered to put in the cats. But I didn't. Alert readers have spotted errors in my thirty-year story and this is one of them!

MOM, I DON'T FEEL VERY WELL. I THINK I GOT A FEVER.

OH, NO! WELL, TRY NOT TO SPREAD IT AROUND, OK? LET'S KEEP THIS THING UNDER CONTROL.

WASH YOUR HANDS, MICHAEL. COUGH INTO A TISSUE AND STAY AWAY FROM EVERYONE. DON'T GO TOUCHING PEOPLE.

COUGH COUGH COUGH

WAAAH!

HACK CHOKE COUGH HACK KOFF HACK WHEEZE GARGLE HACK HACK

MA! KOFF WHEEZE COUGH HACK SNIVEL

I REMEMBER MY MOTHER COMING TO ME WHEN I WAS SICK AT NIGHT...

... AND I ALWAYS SAW HER AS A VISION OF LOVELINESS.

I was a relatively healthy person until I had kids. Forget the infectious dangers of exotic pets. Kids bring more bacteria into the house than a host of howler monkeys high on black bananas!

120

I'll let you in on a secret: I thought that all references to Deanna ended here. In the newly inserted strips, I had her move to Burlington to resolve the question of what happened to Deanna. But a friend who was very familiar with the story pointed to a later reference and so I had to bring her back. After thirty years, you can forget what you wrote, so it pays to research your own material.

"Do you love me?" I guess we need to be in the right mood to answer that question. We need the right time, the right place and the right mood. Trouble is, when the setting is perfect, it's often far too late.

Burps and toots are funny. Have been since humans crawled out of the swamp and claimed the first cave. I know this because no language is required, no illustration, no preparation, no ability to do "stand-up" is necessary. (Standing up might be helpful, come to think of it.) If required, we are all capable of breaking wind—which breaks the ice, on most occasions. And since another ice age is sure to follow global warming, it's good to know there's hope for the future.

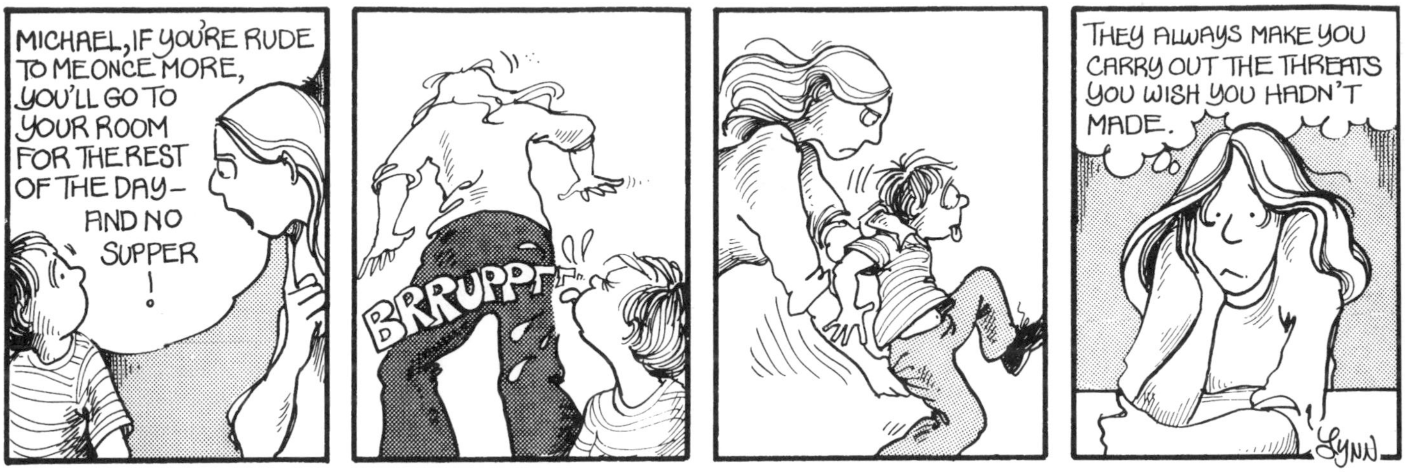
MICHAEL, IF YOU'RE RUDE TO ME ONCE MORE, YOU'LL GO TO YOUR ROOM FOR THE REST OF THE DAY– AND NO SUPPER!
BRRUPPT
THEY ALWAYS MAKE YOU CARRY OUT THE THREATS YOU WISH YOU HADN'T MADE.
LYNN

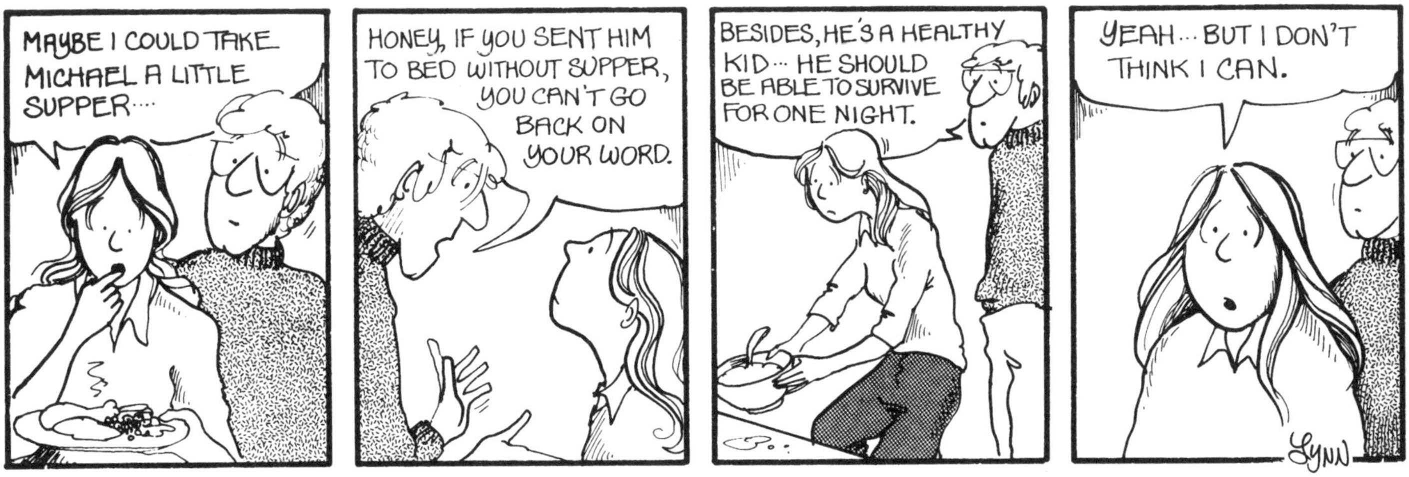
MAYBE I COULD TAKE MICHAEL A LITTLE SUPPER....
HONEY, IF YOU SENT HIM TO BED WITHOUT SUPPER, YOU CAN'T GO BACK ON YOUR WORD.
BESIDES, HE'S A HEALTHY KID... HE SHOULD BE ABLE TO SURVIVE FOR ONE NIGHT.
YEAH... BUT I DON'T THINK I CAN.
LYNN

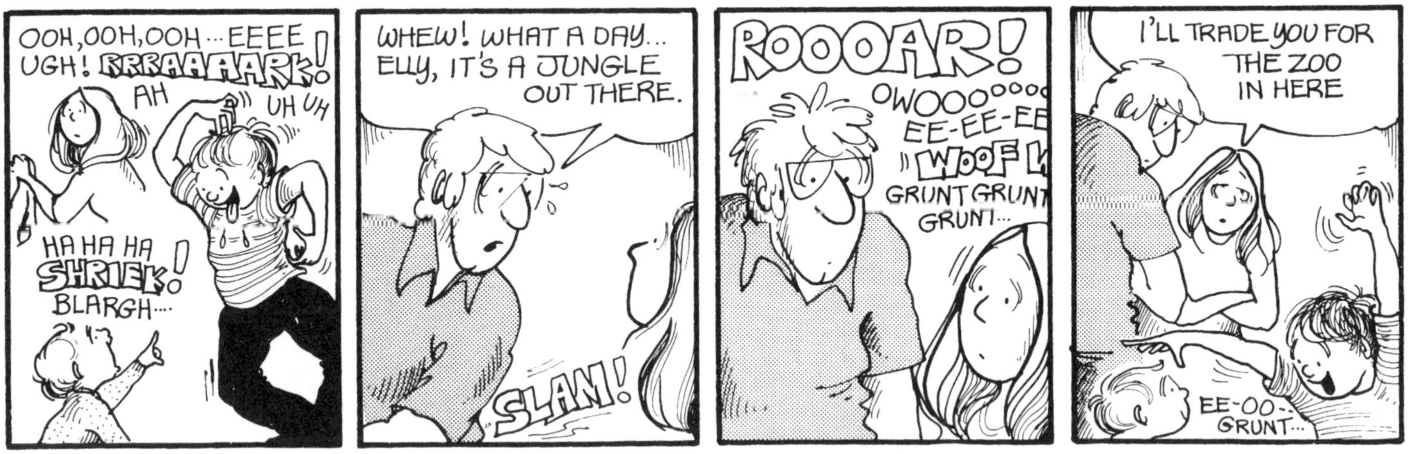
OOH, OOH, OOH... EEEE UGH! RRRAAAARK!
AH
UH UH
HA HA HA SHRIEK!
BLARGH....
WHEW! WHAT A DAY... ELLY, IT'S A JUNGLE OUT THERE.
SLAM!
ROOOAR!
OWOOOoooo
EE-EE-EE
WOOF
GRUNT GRUNT GRUNT...
I'LL TRADE YOU FOR THE ZOO IN HERE
EE-OO-GRUNT...

My dad used to embarrass me beyond words. He was a comic at heart, a genius with word play, and a born entertainer. He could mimic and mime. He did pratfalls and made sound effects, which was wonderful until we went out. I remember cringing at the zoo as Dad mugged at the monkeys, wishing I was a million miles away. What he did was to lay the foundation for my future career as a cartoonist. He also, in his wisdom, taught me how to embarrass my own kids when they came along.

This wasn't the best punch line in the world, but it said what many of us think as we pass through the supermarket checkout. All those "women's" magazines. All those perfect faces, figures, and coifs. All those perfect kitchens and bedrooms, living rooms and dens, are an unattainable dream when you've got kids. Oh, sure, there are magazines for parents, full of info and articles and helpful hints, but check out the kids on the covers. They are all too perfect!

GOOD GRIEF, WOULD YOU LOOK AT THE ADS IN THIS PAPER, ELLY!

IT'S ALL SWINGING COUPLES LOOKING FOR PARTNERS!

GOSH, I COULD NEVER IMAGINE DOING A THING LIKE THAT... COULD YOU, ANNE?

OF COURSE NOT!... I'D HAVE TO LOSE AT LEAST 20 POUNDS!

TUG PULL

TUG-TUG PULL PULL TUG PULL

KRACK!

INCOME TAX TIME AGAIN?

THE FUEL COMPANY DIDN'T OVER-CHARGE US, ELLY - YOU PAID THEIR BILL TWICE! -THIS IS A CREDIT BALANCE.

NO WONDER THEY DIDN'T UNDER-STAND YOUR COMPLAINT. - IT SAYS RIGHT HERE: "DO NOT PAY."

- I JUST PAY THE BILLS.... I'M NOT EXPECTED TO READ THEM!

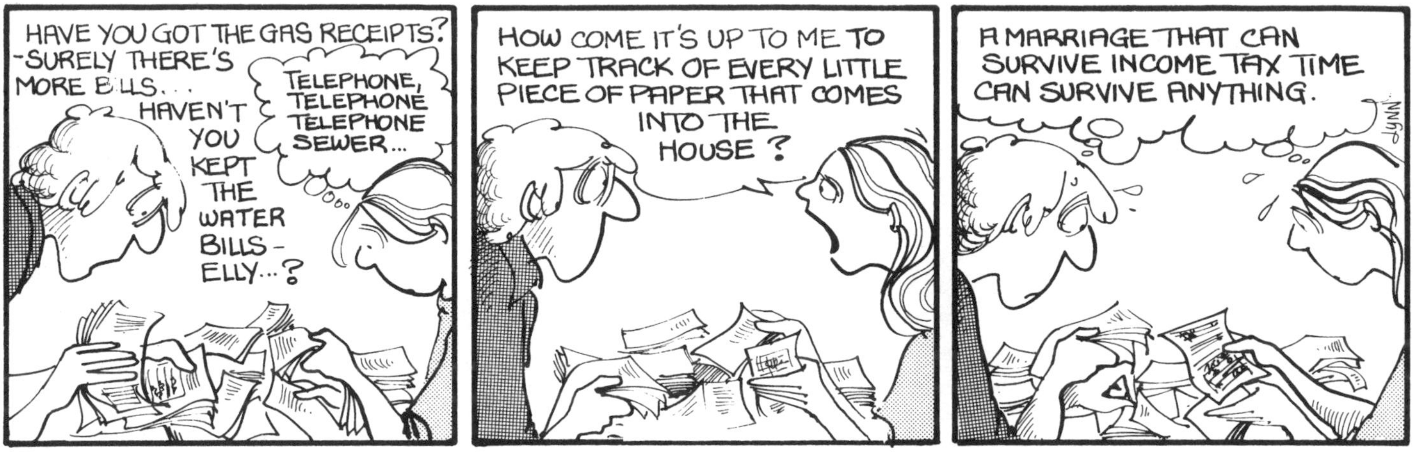
HAVE YOU GOT THE GAS RECEIPTS? -SURELY THERE'S MORE BILLS...
HAVEN'T YOU KEPT THE WATER BILLS - ELLY...?
TELEPHONE, TELEPHONE TELEPHONE SEWER...
HOW COME IT'S UP TO ME TO KEEP TRACK OF EVERY LITTLE PIECE OF PAPER THAT COMES INTO THE HOUSE?
A MARRIAGE THAT CAN SURVIVE INCOME TAX TIME CAN SURVIVE ANYTHING.
LYNN

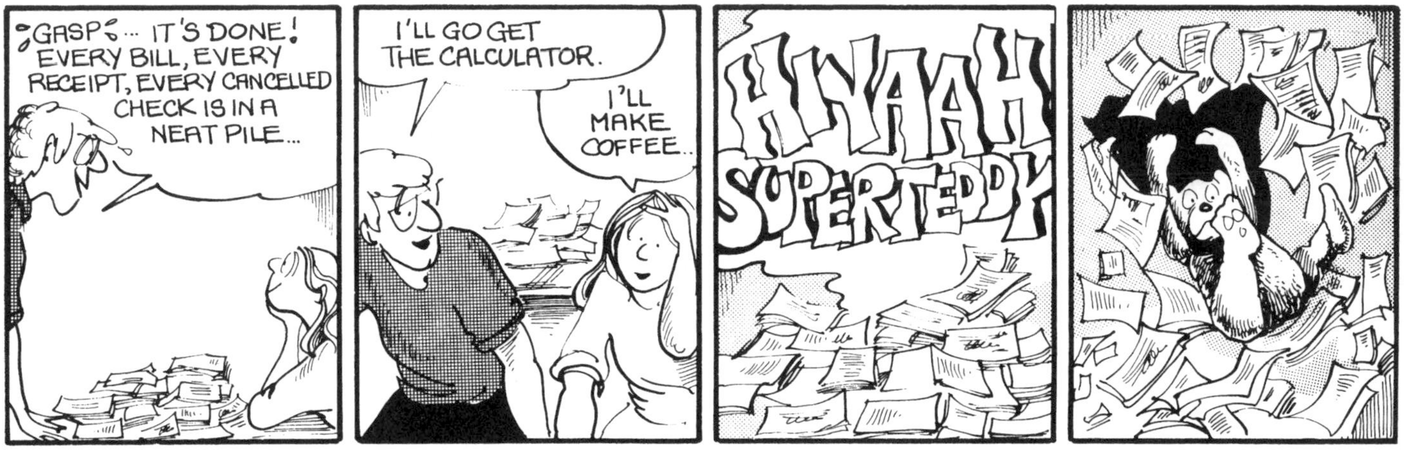
GASP... IT'S DONE! EVERY BILL, EVERY RECEIPT, EVERY CANCELLED CHECK IS IN A NEAT PILE...
I'LL GO GET THE CALCULATOR.
I'LL MAKE COFFEE..
HIYAAH SUPERTEDDY

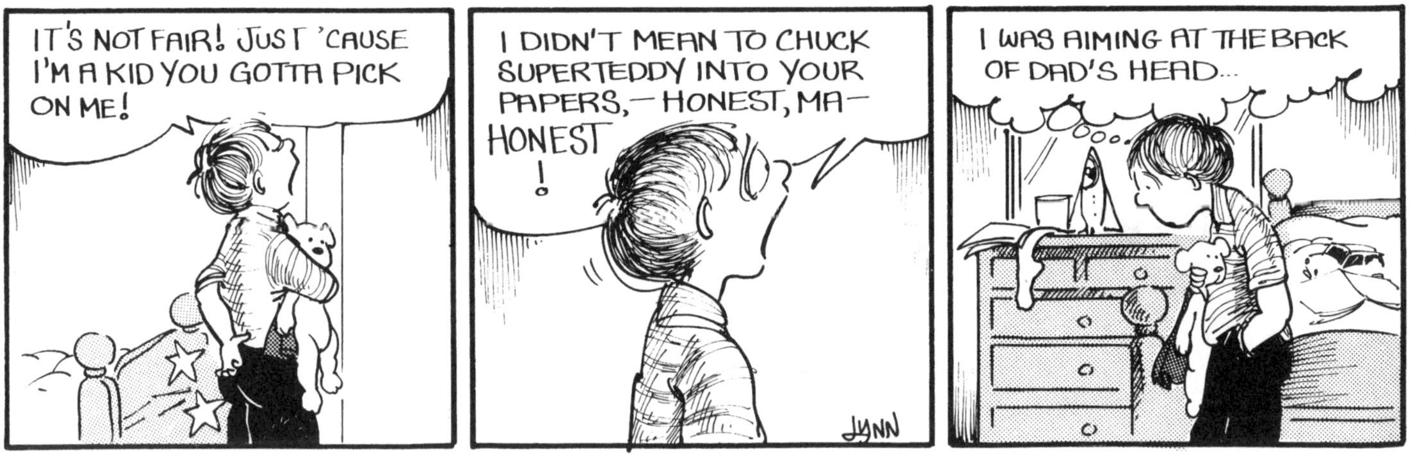
IT'S NOT FAIR! JUST 'CAUSE I'M A KID YOU GOTTA PICK ON ME!
I DIDN'T MEAN TO CHUCK SUPERTEDDY INTO YOUR PAPERS, — HONEST, MA — HONEST!
LYNN
I WAS AIMING AT THE BACK OF DAD'S HEAD...

I credit Aaron, again, for a punch line I didn't make up.

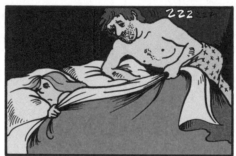

My friend Nancy Lawn called to tell me her husband had done this very thing. Jim had left their daughter, Deanna, in the kitchen, in the dark. It was one of my favorite strips and the Lawns have the original.

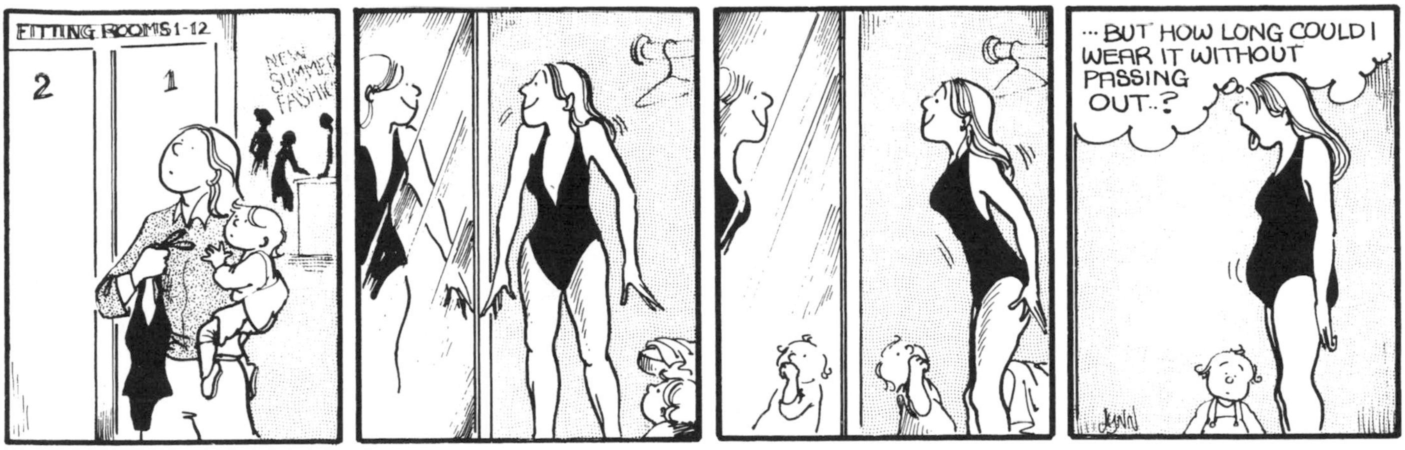
FITTING ROOMS 1-12
2
1
...BUT HOW LONG COULD I WEAR IT WITHOUT PASSING OUT..?
Lynn

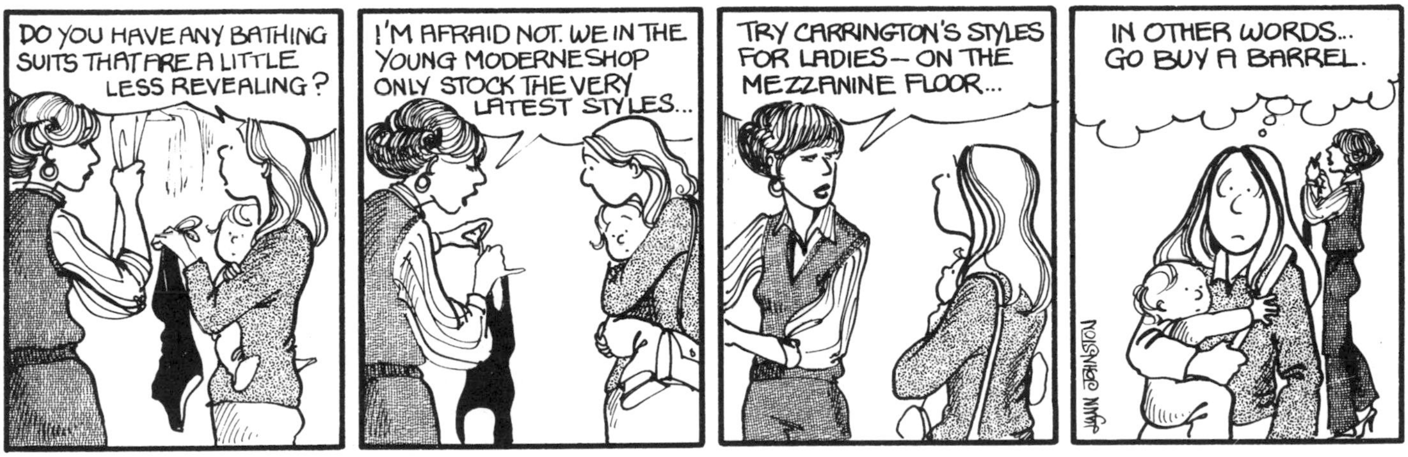
DO YOU HAVE ANY BATHING SUITS THAT ARE A LITTLE LESS REVEALING?
I'M AFRAID NOT. WE IN THE YOUNG MODERNE SHOP ONLY STOCK THE VERY LATEST STYLES...
TRY CARRINGTON'S STYLES FOR LADIES — ON THE MEZZANINE FLOOR...
Lynn Johnston
IN OTHER WORDS... GO BUY A BARREL.

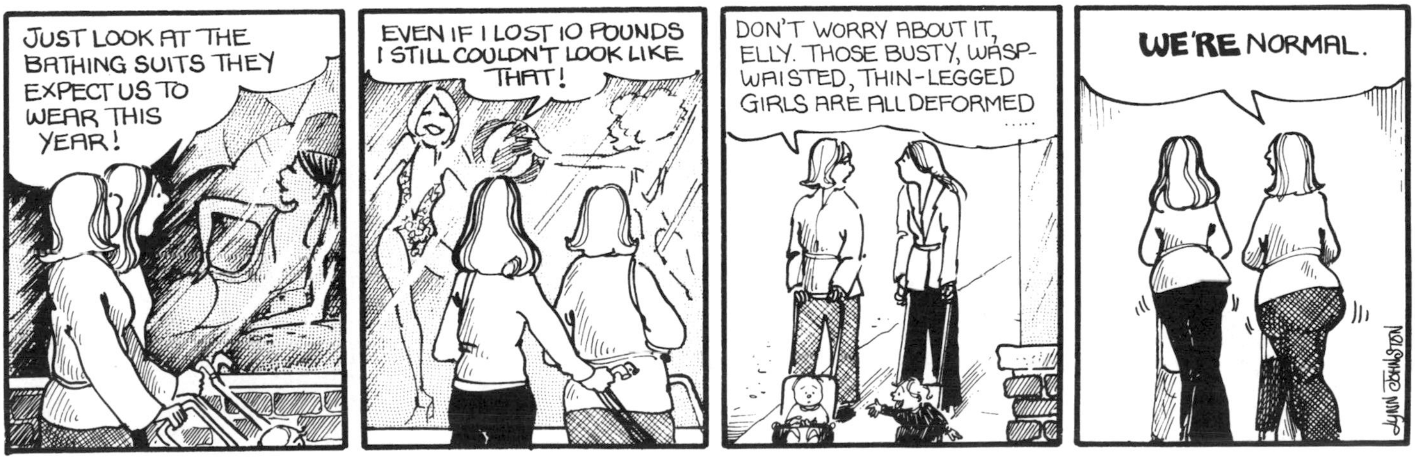
JUST LOOK AT THE BATHING SUITS THEY EXPECT US TO WEAR THIS YEAR!
EVEN IF I LOST 10 POUNDS I STILL COULDN'T LOOK LIKE THAT!
DON'T WORRY ABOUT IT, ELLY. THOSE BUSTY, WASP-WAISTED, THIN-LEGGED GIRLS ARE ALL DEFORMED .....
WE'RE NORMAL.
Lynn Johnston

At the time, I didn't think I looked like my mother at all, but as the years roll by, every time I pass a mirror, there she is looking back at me. Now, this is an actual quote. I remember being at a loss for words, which was often a sign that I was thinking "punch line!"

I like the expression "muffin top." As soon as the hip-hugging pants met the mini shirt, it was bound to happen. Whoever coined the expression "victims of fashion" was right on the money. It's expensive to look bad! A young woman shells out a bundle these days to bulge out of her blue jeans. And hey, why not add a navel ring and a tattoo? Decorate your dewlaps!

In this era of "expand and expose," when cleavage—at both ends is (gaggg!) acceptable, I'm glad I'm a fogey. Give me comfortable undies and a bulky knit sweater and I'm ready for the road. It says something doesn't it? When a woman would rather be wrinkled than fashionably fooled.

ALL I HAVE TO DO IS LOOK AT MY MOM AND SHE GETS MAD!

HONEST, MIKE? YOU WERE JUST LOOKIN' AT HER?

YEAH. SHE WAS IN THE BATH AT THE TIME.

WHAT'S THE MATTER, JOHN... WHAT ARE ALL THESE PAPERS?

EVERY YEAR!—IT NEVER FAILS!—AS SOON AS YOU SEND OFF YOUR INCOME TAX FORMS..

—AS SOON AS IT'S TOO LATE...

YOU FIND ANOTHER DRAWER FULL OF DEDUCTIONS!!

GIAFELLDDPP?

YAH!

KACHUNG!

WHAT DO YOU MEAN—IT'S ONLY DOLLY PARTON!!

These days, they leave CDs and DVDs where stoves can melt them, shoes can scratch them, and things can wipe them out—at least they can still be used as coasters!

FOR BETTER OR FOR WORSE
BY LYNN JOHNSTON
ZZZZ
TURN, TOSS, TURN, TOSS..
2:45 A.M.
SIGH
TOSS, TURN, TOSS
WHAT ARE YOU DOING UP, MOM?... IT'S WAAAAY PAST YOUR BEDTIME.
COULDN'T SLEEP, HUH. YEAH... SOME-TIMES THAT HAPPENS TO ME, TOO.
ARE YOU WORRIED ABOUT SOMETHING? DO YOU NEED SOMEONE TO TALK TO?
'CAUSE, IF YOU DO, I'M RIGHT HERE.
I'M FINE, HONEY. THANK YOU.
AND, THIS MORNING, I WAS SO MAD AT HIM... I WANTED TO GIVE HIM AWAY.
LYNN

Remember when we carried checkbooks and gas was pumped by an attendant? Is life easier or more impersonal?

In our tiny, isolated community, neighborhood dogs often had free rein. Some were nice and some were nasty. We were one of the few nonpet families and Aaron really wanted a puppy. It was hard to say no to a stray, but there was always someone in town willing to adopt one more.

Before seat belts were in every car and the law was set, kids moved freely around on the back seat. One day, I wondered why a man stuck his tongue out at me. He was returning the "salute" coming from my kids in the car's rear window.

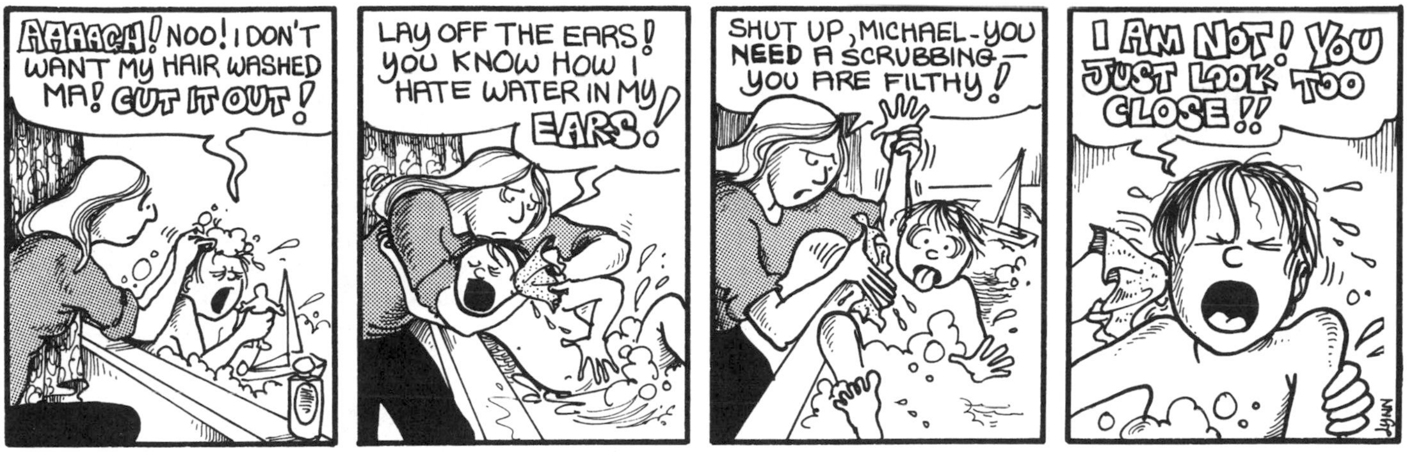
AAAAGH! NOO! I DON'T WANT MY HAIR WASHED MA! CUT IT OUT!
LAY OFF THE EARS! YOU KNOW HOW I HATE WATER IN MY EARS!
SHUT UP, MICHAEL-YOU NEED A SCRUBBING-YOU ARE FILTHY!
I AM NOT! YOU JUST LOOK TOO CLOSE!!
LYNN

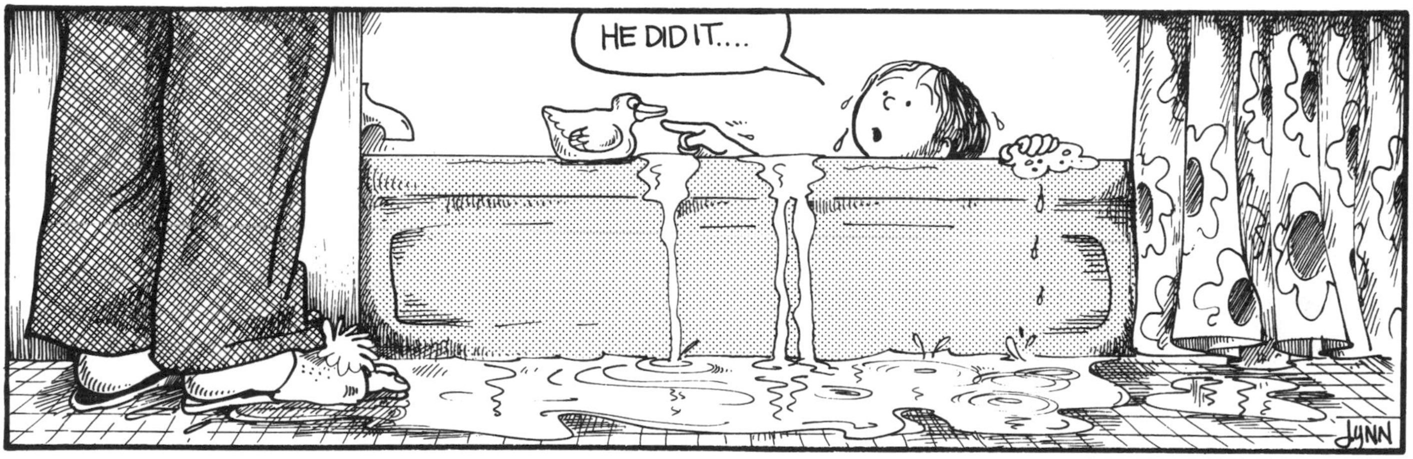
HE DID IT....
LYNN

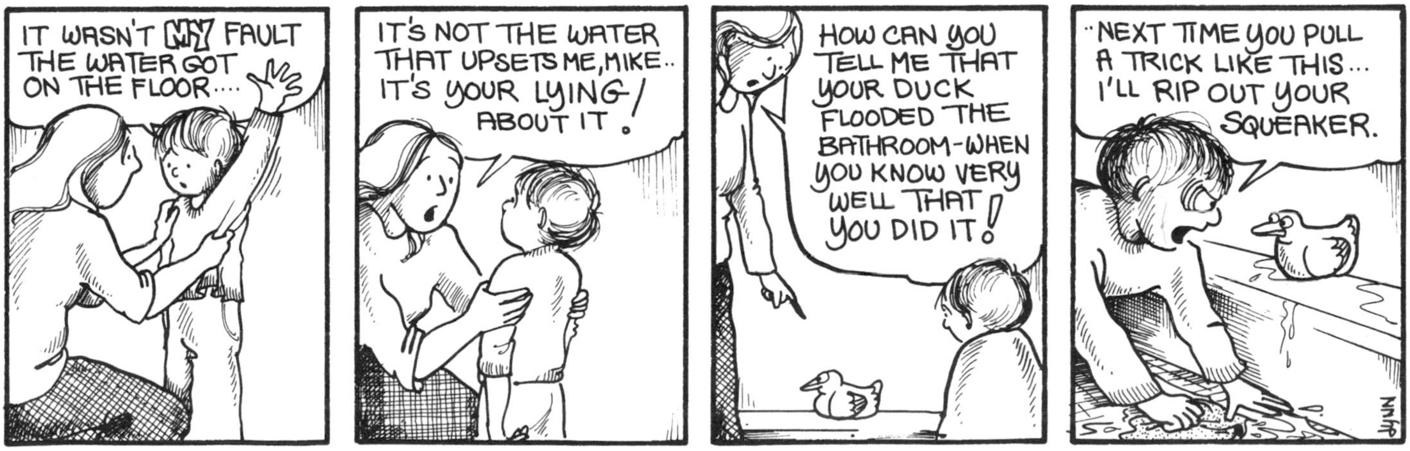
IT WASN'T MY FAULT THE WATER GOT ON THE FLOOR....
IT'S NOT THE WATER THAT UPSETS ME, MIKE.. IT'S YOUR LYING ABOUT IT!
HOW CAN YOU TELL ME THAT YOUR DUCK FLOODED THE BATHROOM-WHEN YOU KNOW VERY WELL THAT YOU DID IT!
..NEXT TIME YOU PULL A TRICK LIKE THIS... I'LL RIP OUT YOUR SQUEAKER.
LYNN

I sent this Sunday strip to Robin Williams after receiving a nice note from his wife. She graciously thanked me in a second note. I eventually met him in a comedy club in Toronto. This job has connected me to a number of my heroes!

We ordered this exercise gizmo from a magazine, thinking that the size and simplicity would guarantee its use. Fortunately, it went the way of all such things—into the crawlspace of good intentions before the doorknobs had a chance to break.

There was a time when four-letter words were learned from the kids in the alley behind the house. Now, they're liberally supplied through song, film, and television. Freedom of speech or fouling it?

I'M GLAD YOU DON'T MIND MY TAKING OFF LIKE THIS, EL. I WON'T BE GONE FOR LONG!

YOU COULD HAVE COME, BUT THAT WOULD MEAN FINDING SOMEONE TO TAKE THE KIDS.

BESIDES, CONVENTIONS ARE JUST A LOT OF STANDING AROUND, SITTING THROUGH BORING LECTURES AND CHIT-CHAT.

YOU WOULDN'T ENJOY IT ANYWAY.

BLFPTTT !!

I'M GLAD YOU'RE SO UNDERSTANDING, ELLY...

SOME OF THE GUYS' WIVES ARE REALLY UPSET ABOUT THIS BUSINESS TRIP.

PASSENGERS ONLY ⇨

HE'D BETTER NOT HAVE A GOOD TIME.

I WISH DADDY WOULD HURRY UP AN' COME HOME...

I MISS DADDY, TOO, MICHAEL. WE'RE JUST NOT A FAMILY WITHOUT HIM.

WE DON'T REALIZE HOW MUCH WE NEED OUR DADDY UNTIL HE'S NOT HERE.

IS THAT WHY HE GOES AWAY SOMETIMES?

This is my mother's story. During the Depression, she bought a chocolate rabbit as a gift for her sister, but she couldn't resist tasting it. Monica received her rabbit minus the ears.

I was raised in the Anglican faith and went to church every Sunday until I was old enough to rebel. The day I stopped going was an Easter Sunday. It was a spectacular, clear, sunny morning. Daffodils and crocus were in bloom. I walked with my mother to St. John's church in a blue and white outfit she'd made for me. In the cool interior of St. John's, everyone looked forward to a message of hope and joy. Instead, we were told we were all sinners; we were all responsible for the torture and death of a holy man. I was eight years old. I hadn't killed anyone. We went out into the sunshine and I vowed never to go back. That night, I prayed to God to let me marry a minister so I could write his sermons. I wanted to say positive things instead of negative. I wanted people to smile. I still attend services, but at the United Church—and only twice a year.

In our situation, I was the one who traveled. Hotel rooms were often too big, too lonely, and I'd wonder what I was doing so far from home.

146

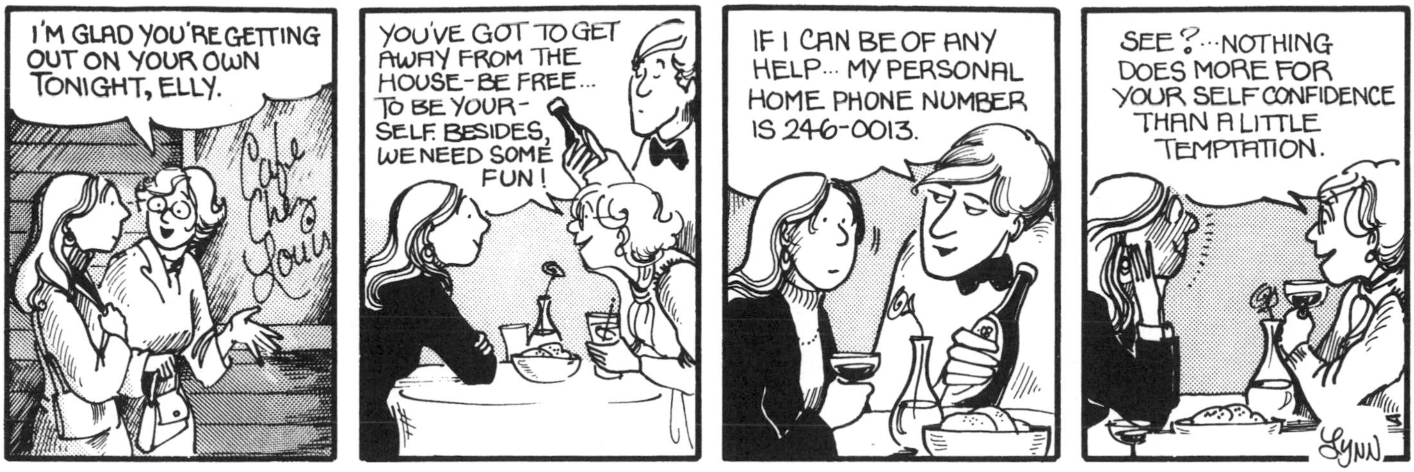
I'M GLAD YOU'RE GETTING OUT ON YOUR OWN TONIGHT, ELLY.
Cafe Chez Louis
YOU'VE GOT TO GET AWAY FROM THE HOUSE– BE FREE... TO BE YOURSELF. BESIDES, WE NEED SOME FUN!
IF I CAN BE OF ANY HELP... MY PERSONAL HOME PHONE NUMBER IS 246-0013.
SEE?...NOTHING DOES MORE FOR YOUR SELF CONFIDENCE THAN A LITTLE TEMPTATION.
LYNN

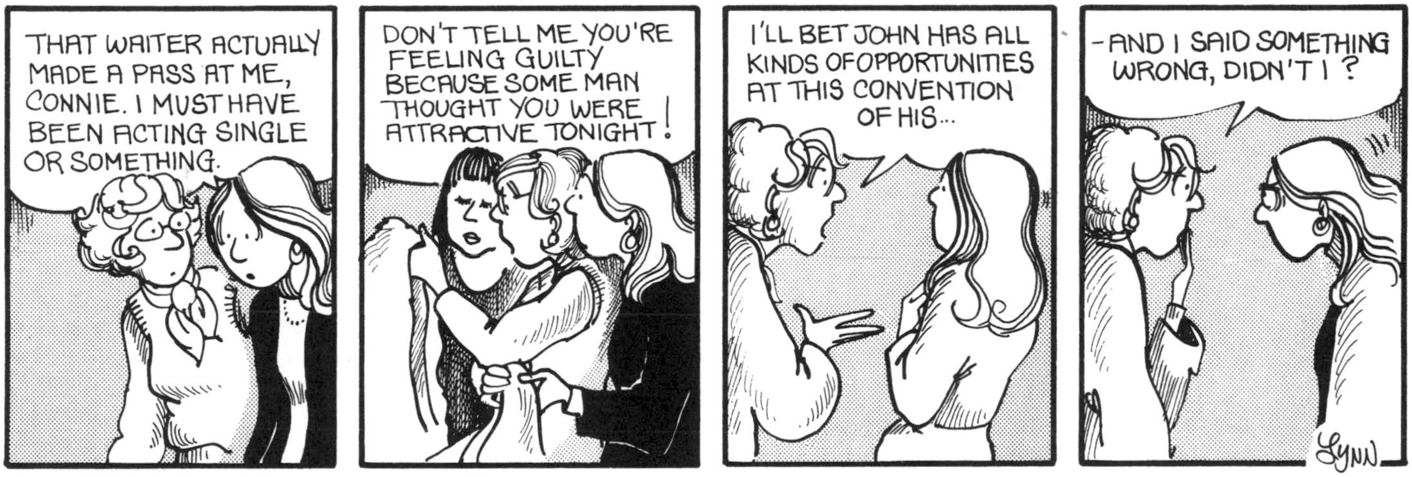
THAT WAITER ACTUALLY MADE A PASS AT ME, CONNIE. I MUST HAVE BEEN ACTING SINGLE OR SOMETHING.
DON'T TELL ME YOU'RE FEELING GUILTY BECAUSE SOME MAN THOUGHT YOU WERE ATTRACTIVE TONIGHT!
I'LL BET JOHN HAS ALL KINDS OF OPPORTUNITIES AT THIS CONVENTION OF HIS...
–AND I SAID SOMETHING WRONG, DIDN'T I?
LYNN

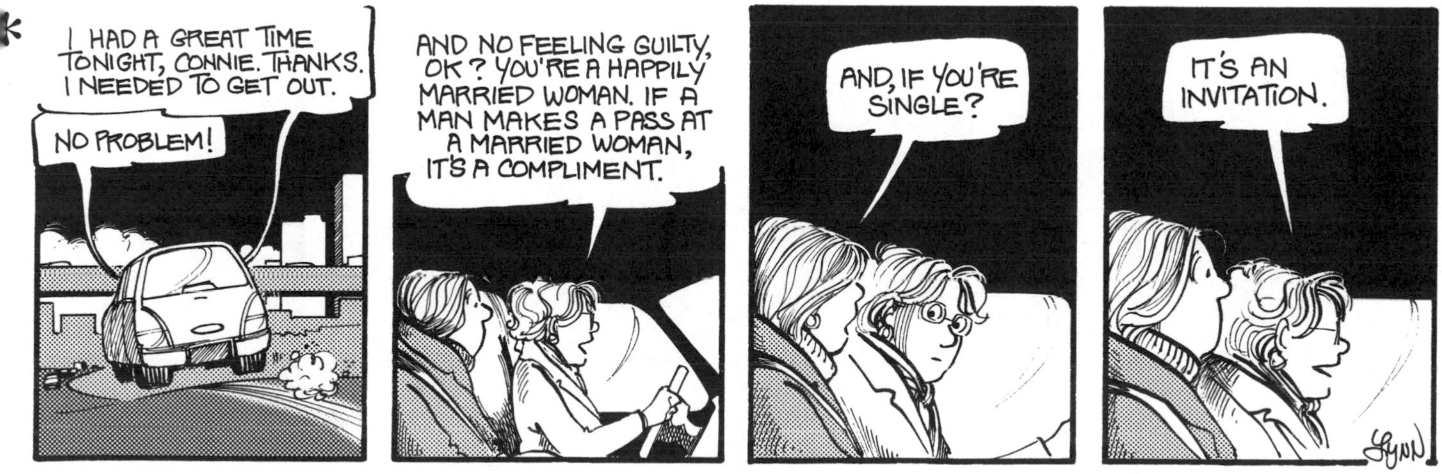
I HAD A GREAT TIME TONIGHT, CONNIE. THANKS. I NEEDED TO GET OUT.
NO PROBLEM!
AND NO FEELING GUILTY, OK? YOU'RE A HAPPILY MARRIED WOMAN. IF A MAN MAKES A PASS AT A MARRIED WOMAN, IT'S A COMPLIMENT.
AND, IF YOU'RE SINGLE?
IT'S AN INVITATION.
LYNN

In grade four, my friend Cathy had to use the bathroom in her own house. This made for awkward moments and fast bike rides—but we always got there in time.

One of the things I enjoyed most about traveling for work was shopping for small gifts to take home. I still do this, even though my kids are grown. I know, deep inside, there's a small voice saying, "What did you bring me?"

Living in rainy North Vancouver, my brother, Alan, and I created our own cache of indoor games. One was called "Socko." By putting one sock inside another, we had a fairly harmless, but effective weapon. After a few hours of furiously swinging and pummeling each other with a Socko, the outer part of the weapon would become long and extended. This game was even better if the socks were wet!

The disco craze was everywhere then. It's considered hopelessly out of date now . . . but it will come back!

The omnipresent, invisible mess. How could they live in such chaos? Maybe when one's mind is innocent, one's surroundings can be filled to the brim with junk!

152

REMEMBER OUR TALK ABOUT WASTING FOOD, JOHN?...IT'S YOUR TURN TO FINISH OFF THE KIDS' LEFTOVERS.

EAT!

SO, LET'S SEE THIS THING YOU'VE BEEN WORKING ON AT ANNIE'S PLACE ALL MONTH...

HEY, ELLY—THAT'S GREAT! I THINK YOU'VE REALLY GOT SOMETHING THERE...DON'T YOU?

I GUESS SO...IT STARTED OUT AS A PLACEMAT.

ANNIE'S TEACHING ME HOW TO DO FIBER ART, JOHN—JUST WAIT TILL YOU SEE THIS!

IT DISPLAYS TENSION AND ANTI-TENSION IN FREE-FORM POSITIVE SPACE USING NATURAL MEDIA!

I HAVE UTILIZED THE WARMTH OF EARTH TONES TO INSTILL THE SENSE OF SPONTANEOUS GROWTH...LIKE IT?

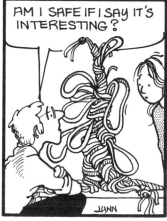

AM I SAFE IF I SAY IT'S INTERESTING?

My mom-in-law was a weaver whose several huge looms beckoned me to try my hand at something. The repetition required to produce a piece of cloth, or even a place mat, was too much for me and I turned my first (and only) project into a work of art.

153

I once set a bird trap just like this. Convinced it would work, I sat hidden behind a tree for most of an afternoon—chalk one up for bird brains!

I'm relatively unfazed by public speaking, but I fall apart in a crowd. Conventions and other gatherings that surround me with strangers leave me, well, wanting to leave. Once, at a large deluge of dentists and office personnel, I went in search of something nonalcoholic to keep me from running out into the night and discovered a parrot in the foyer of the building. It belonged to the janitor and also the security guy. As the parrot and I commiserated in silence, it occurred to me that I, too, was in a cage, one of my own making.

As these strips ran, irate letters came in from people who were horrified by John's "alcoholism." Mostly women, these readers felt I was sending the wrong message. I took their criticism to heart and didn't repeat this theme.

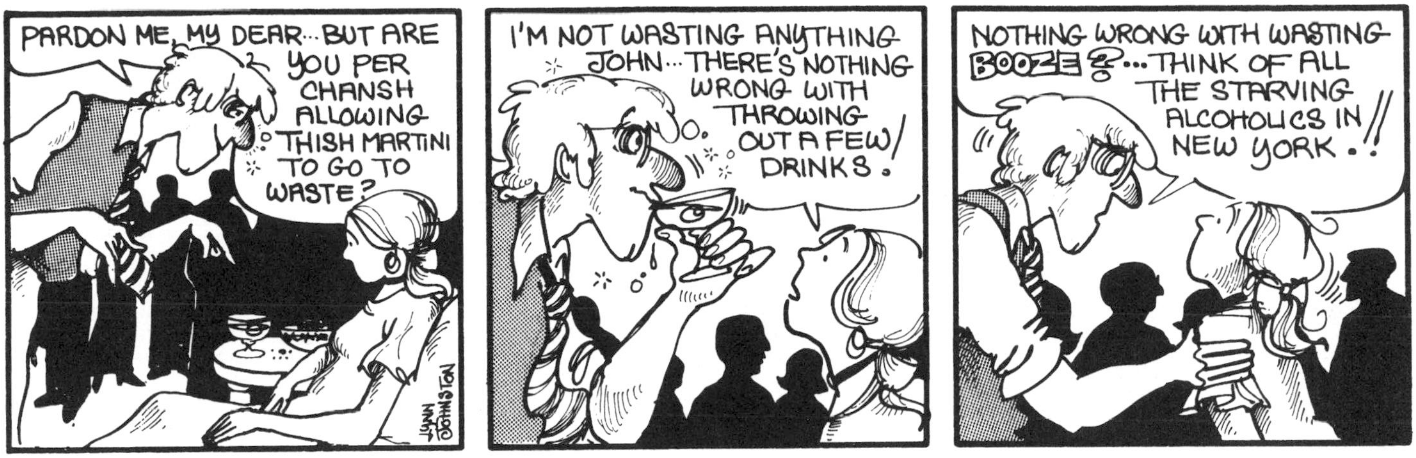
PARDON ME, MY DEAR... BUT ARE YOU PER CHANSH ALLOWING THISH MARTINI TO GO TO WASTE?
I'M NOT WASTING ANYTHING JOHN... THERE'S NOTHING WRONG WITH THROWING OUT A FEW DRINKS!
NOTHING WRONG WITH WASTING BOOZE?... THINK OF ALL THE STARVING ALCOHOLICS IN NEW YORK.!!
LYNN JOHNSTON

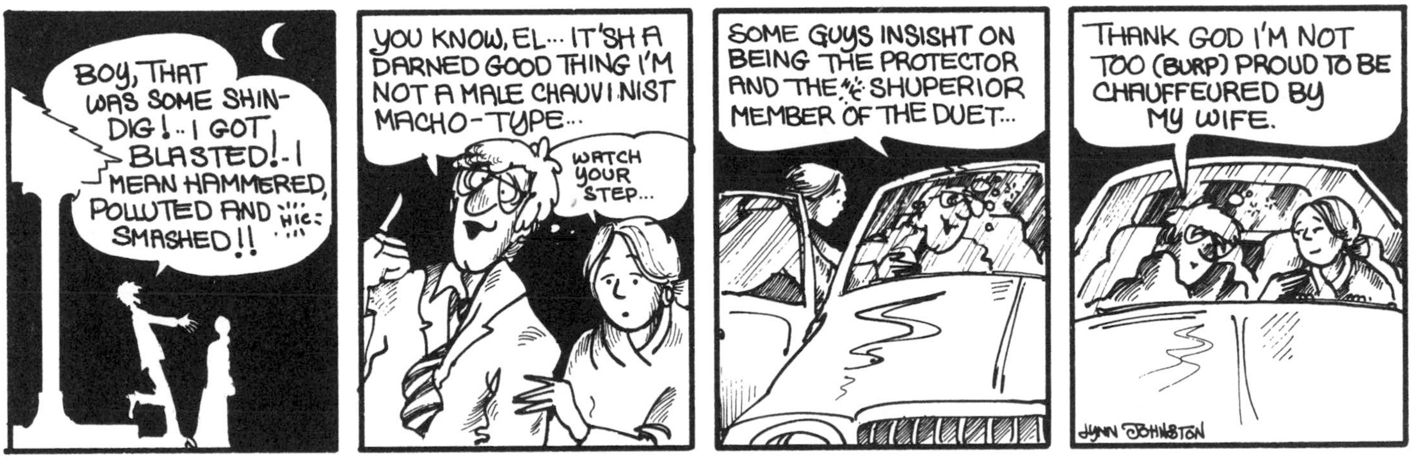
BOY, THAT WAS SOME SHIN-DIG!.. I GOT BLASTED!.. I MEAN HAMMERED, POLLUTED AND SMASHED!!
HIC
YOU KNOW, EL... IT'SH A DARNED GOOD THING I'M NOT A MALE CHAUVINIST MACHO-TYPE...
WATCH YOUR STEP...
SOME GUYS INSISHT ON BEING THE PROTECTOR AND THE SHUPERIOR MEMBER OF THE DUET...
THANK GOD I'M NOT TOO (BURP) PROUD TO BE CHAUFFEURED BY MY WIFE.
LYNN JOHNSTON

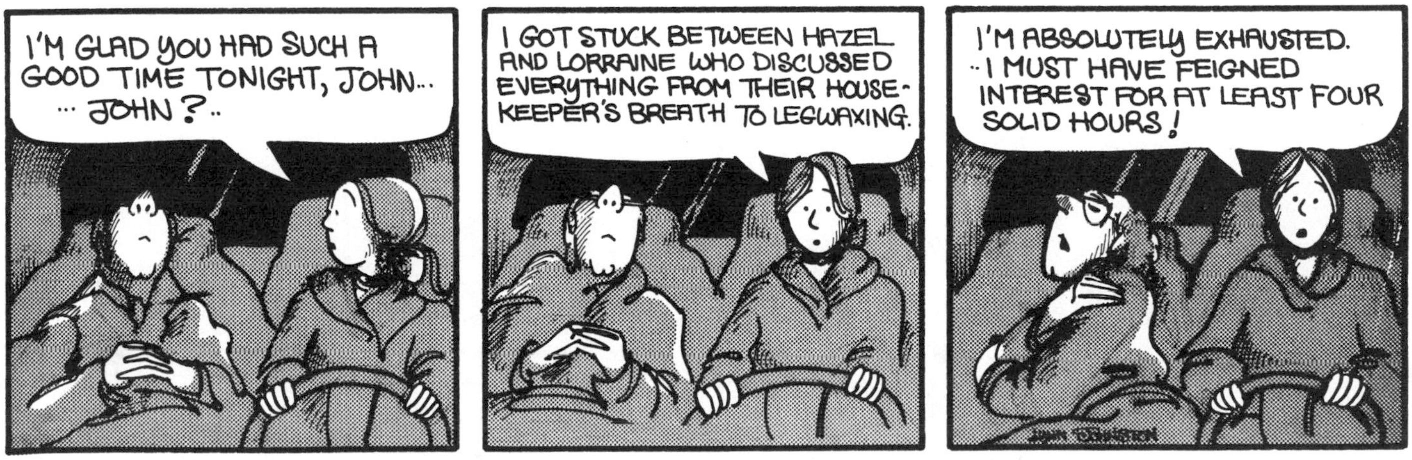
I'M GLAD YOU HAD SUCH A GOOD TIME TONIGHT, JOHN... ... JOHN?..
I GOT STUCK BETWEEN HAZEL AND LORRAINE WHO DISCUSSED EVERYTHING FROM THEIR HOUSE-KEEPER'S BREATH TO LEGWAXING.
I'M ABSOLUTELY EXHAUSTED. ..I MUST HAVE FEIGNED INTEREST FOR AT LEAST FOUR SOLID HOURS!
LYNN JOHNSTON

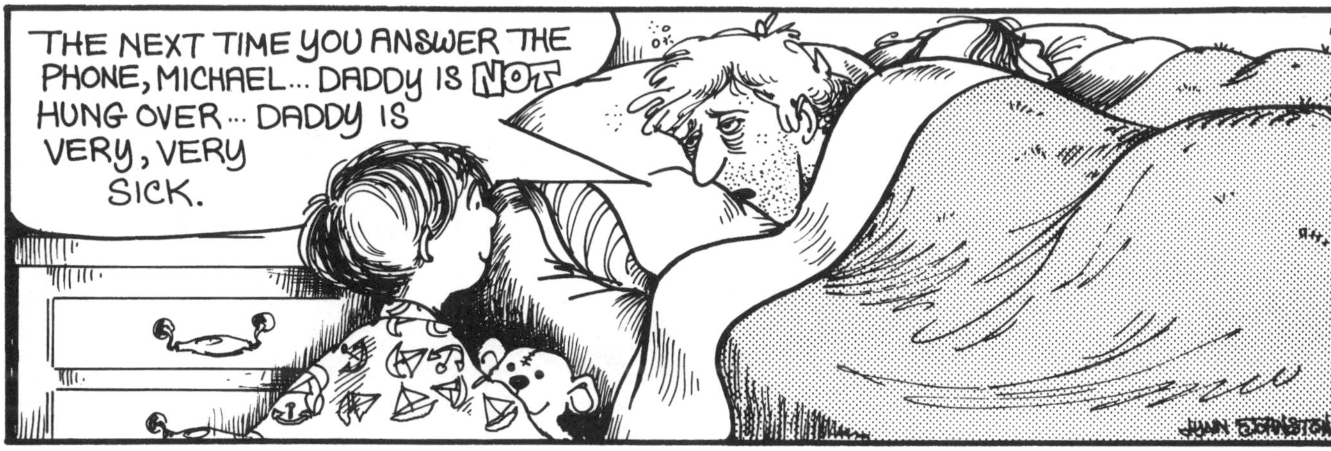
THE NEXT TIME YOU ANSWER THE PHONE, MICHAEL... DADDY IS NOT HUNG OVER... DADDY IS VERY, VERY SICK.
LYNN JOHNSTON

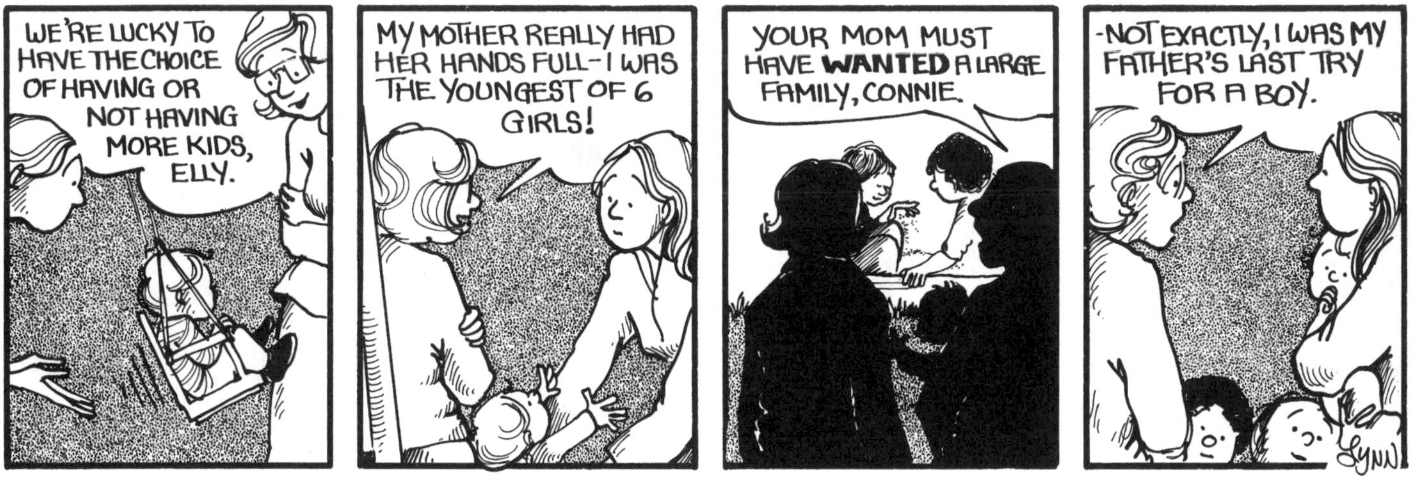
WE'RE LUCKY TO HAVE THE CHOICE OF HAVING OR NOT HAVING MORE KIDS, ELLY.
MY MOTHER REALLY HAD HER HANDS FULL - I WAS THE YOUNGEST OF 6 GIRLS!
YOUR MOM MUST HAVE WANTED A LARGE FAMILY, CONNIE.
-NOT EXACTLY, I WAS MY FATHER'S LAST TRY FOR A BOY.
LYNN

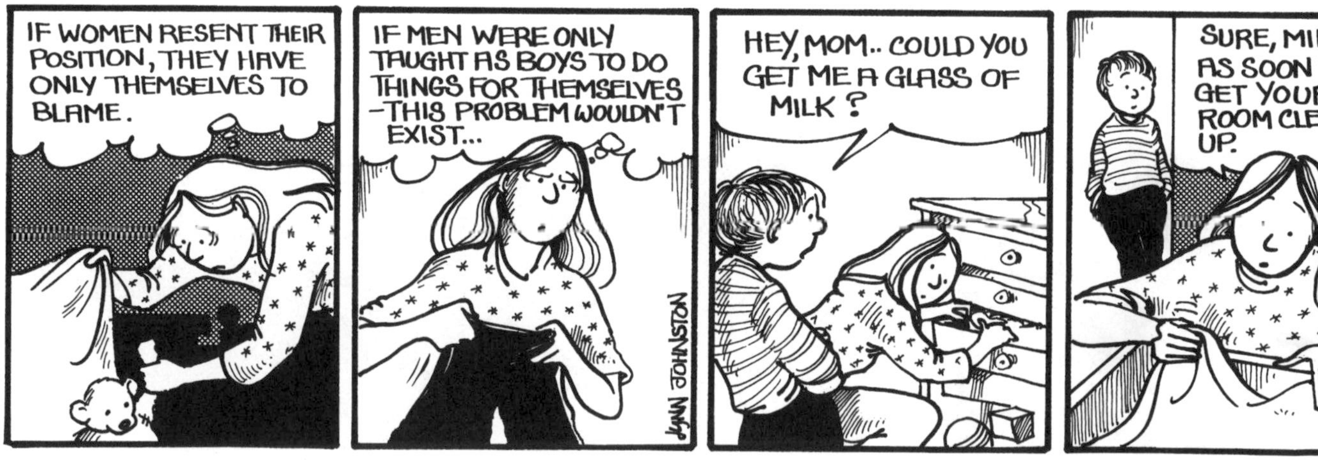
IF WOMEN RESENT THEIR POSITION, THEY HAVE ONLY THEMSELVES TO BLAME.
IF MEN WERE ONLY TAUGHT AS BOYS TO DO THINGS FOR THEMSELVES -THIS PROBLEM WOULDN'T EXIST...
LYNN JOHNSTON
HEY, MOM.. COULD YOU GET ME A GLASS OF MILK?
SURE, MIKE... AS SOON AS I GET YOUR ROOM CLEANED UP.

-SO YOU WENT OUT AND JOINED A WEIGHT CONTROL CLINIC!

YEAH. I GO ONCE A WEEK AND I PAY $10.00 EACH TIME 'TIL I REACH MY GOAL.

I HOPE STEVE'S GIVING YOU SOME ENCOURAGE- MENT, ANNE.

-HE FIGURES - AT $10.00 A WEEK, WITH MY WILL- POWER... I'M WORTH AT LEAST $500.00 A POUND.

WELL-HOW WAS YOUR COFFEE KLATCH WITH ANNE AND HER CRONIES?

WAIT A MINUTE-YOU THINK OUR COFFEE KLATCHES ARE A WASTE OF TIME, DON'T YOU!

I DIDN'T EXACTLY MEAN IT LIKE THAT! ...BUT WHAT ELSE WOULD YOU CALL IT!

HUMAN CONTACT.

WHAT THE HECK ARE YOU PUTTING ALL OVER YOUR FACE?

I HOPE YOU'RE NOT PLANNING TO WEAR THAT STUFF TO BED!

SURE! - DON'T YOU WANT ME TO HAVE A HEALTHY, YOUTHFUL COMPLEXION ALL DAY?

NOT IF I HAVE TO SLEEP NEXT TO THAT ALL NIGHT.

*

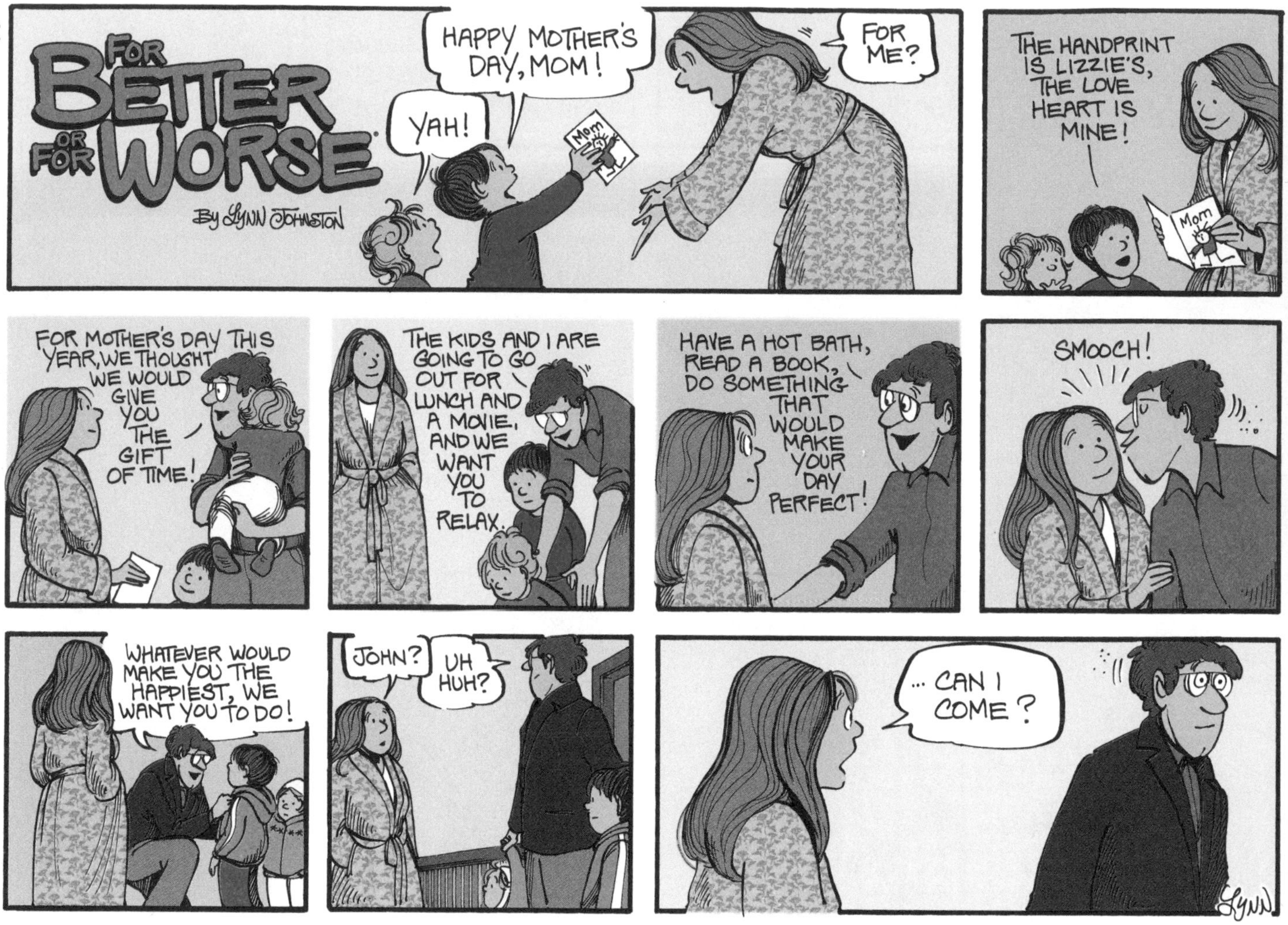
FOR BETTER OR FOR WORSE
BY LYNN JOHNSTON
HAPPY MOTHER'S DAY, MOM!
YAH!
MOM
FOR ME?
THE HANDPRINT IS LIZZIE'S, THE LOVE HEART IS MINE!
MOM
FOR MOTHER'S DAY THIS YEAR, WE THOUGHT WE WOULD GIVE YOU THE GIFT OF TIME!
THE KIDS AND I ARE GOING TO GO OUT FOR LUNCH AND A MOVIE, AND WE WANT YOU TO RELAX.
HAVE A HOT BATH, READ A BOOK, DO SOMETHING THAT WOULD MAKE YOUR DAY PERFECT!
SMOOCH!
WHATEVER WOULD MAKE YOU THE HAPPIEST, WE WANT YOU TO DO!
JOHN?
UH HUH?
...CAN I COME?
LYNN

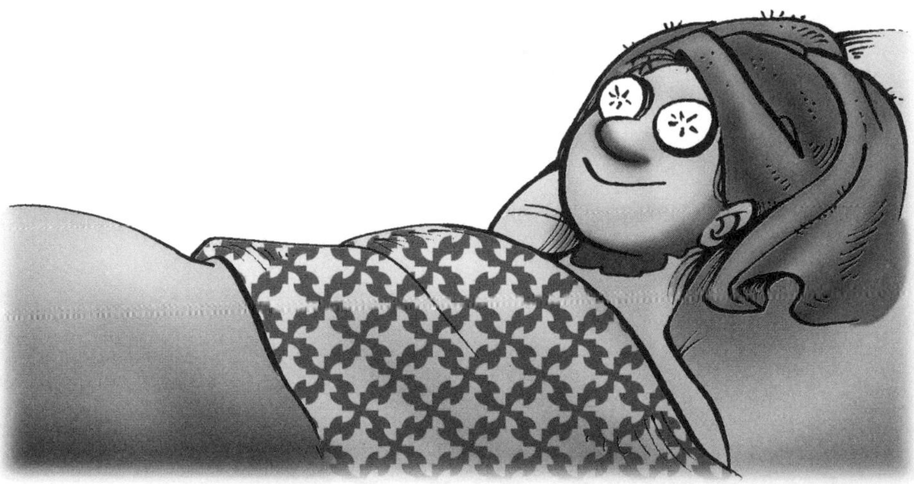

Because the new material was added for more than a year, duplicate "event" Sundays were created. Here are two Mother's Day strips done for the same week of dailies.

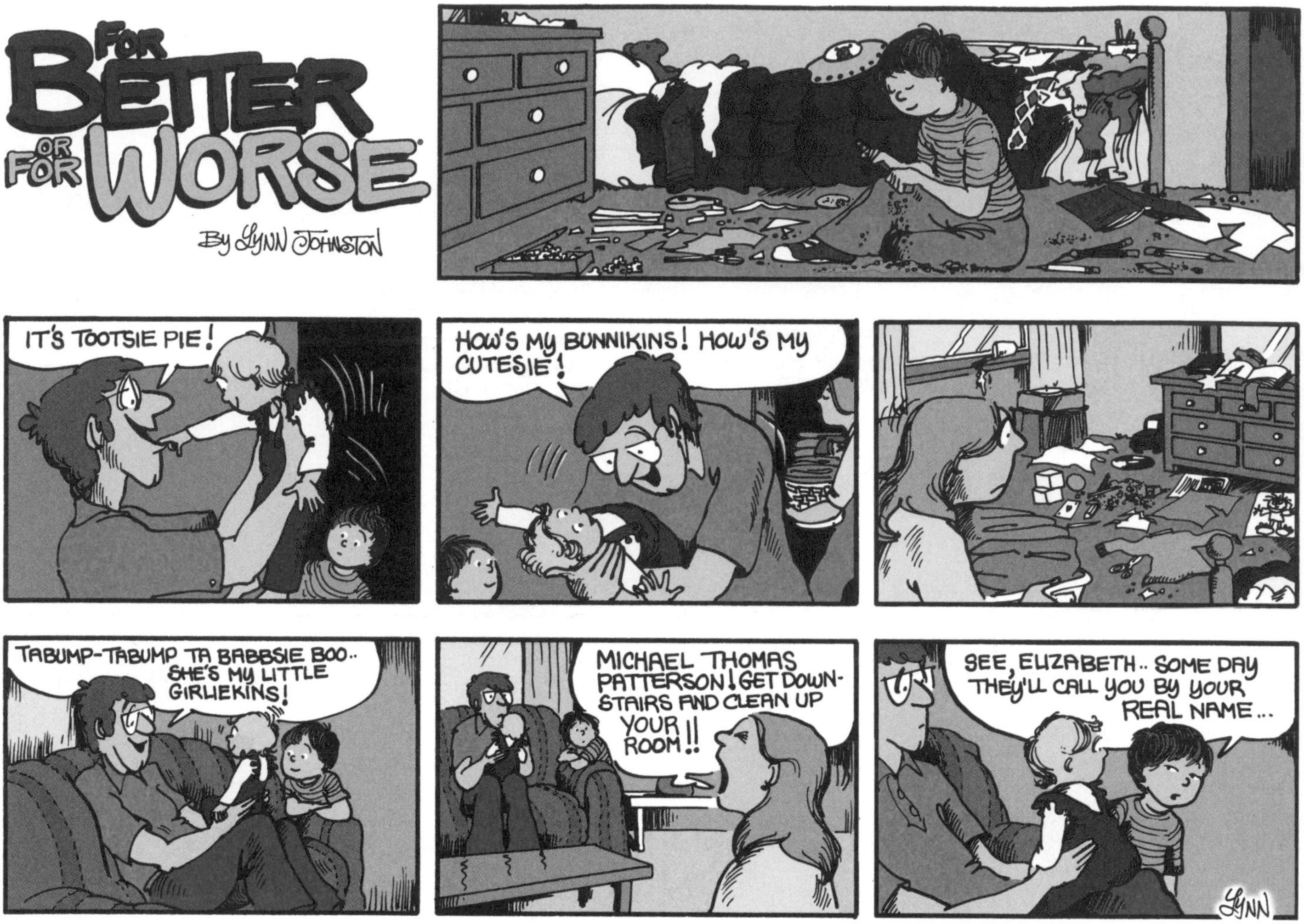
FOR BETTER OR FOR WORSE
BY LYNN JOHNSTON
IT'S TOOTSIE PIE!
HOW'S MY BUNNIKINS! HOW'S MY CUTESIE!
TABUMP-TABUMP TA BABBSIE BOO.. SHE'S MY LITTLE GIRLIEKINS!
MICHAEL THOMAS PATTERSON! GET DOWN-STAIRS AND CLEAN UP YOUR ROOM!!
SEE, ELIZABETH.. SOME DAY THEY'LL CALL YOU BY YOUR REAL NAME...
LYNN

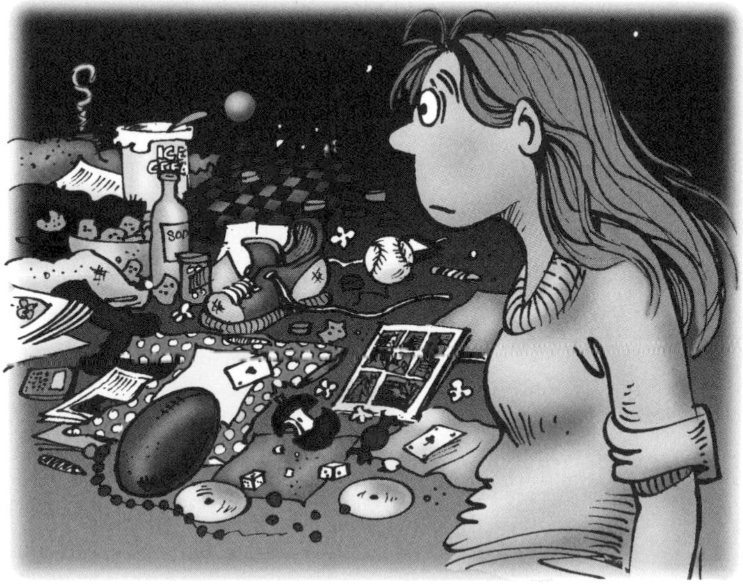

ALLRIGHT...JUST EAT THE VEGETABLES, MICHAEL.

I'LL BE HAPPY IF YOU'LL JUST EAT A *FEW* CARROTS, THEN.

OK...I GUESS IF YOU CAN'T EAT, YOU CAN'T EAT.

HEY! WHAT ABOUT DESSERT?

JYNN JOHNSTON

:SIGH:—THERE ARE SO MANY WOMEN WHO ARE MAKING THEIR MARK ON HISTORY THESE DAYS!

HERE I SIT WHILE OTHERS ARE FIGHTING FOR EQUAL RIGHTS AND AN END TO POVERTY.

WHY SHOULD YOU WANT TO GO OUT AND RAISE CONSCIOUSNESS, ELLY?...

—WHEN WE STILL NEED PEOPLE WHO CAN RAISE KIDS!

LYNN

...I WAS WONDERING IF YOU COULD TELL ME HOW MUCH I HAVE IN ACCOUNT NO. 01-632?

CHECKS WRITTEN?...OH, I'VE SPENT—SAY $280.00 GIVE OR TAKE $10.00 SINCE THE LAST STATEMENT.

YES—BUT I KEEP FOR-GETTING TO WRITE THEM DOWN. OH. YEAH, SURE, OK... THANKS. 'BYE.

DUMB BANKS.

This was just plain honesty. Keeping my accounts in order has never been something I have enjoyed. Bookkeeping was always left to my husband and my father-in-law. I've since learned to pay attention when I pay the bills!

163

It rained a lot in North Vancouver—if the morning sky was heavily overcast, guaranteed it would rain for a week. My mother had endless rainy-day activities for us. We drew and painted, sculpted with Plasticine and papier-mâché. The kitchen, living, and dining rooms would be cluttered with crafts. As long as we were happy, she allowed "art school" to proceed as her spotless house deteriorated. I have much to thank her for.

The day we moved into our house in Lynn Lake there were boxes everywhere. When Rod decided to burn some packing material in the fireplace, Aaron wanted to help by putting a large wad of newspaper on the fire. A huge macramé wall hanging, done by my mother, had been hastily hung on the wall over the fireplace earlier that day. The hanging went unnoticed. The newspaper caught fire and flames leaped up past the mantle, igniting the hanging; fire immediately burst up to the ceiling. There was a fire extinguisher mounted on the side of a kitchen cupboard. In our panic to get it down, we pulled so hard we broke the side of the cupboard, almost pulling the whole thing off the wall! In the end, we did more damage to the kitchen than the fire had done to the living room. Later, we made sure that we knew how to undo the clip that held the fire extinguisher, hung flammables well away from the fireplace, and only burned small amounts of paper at a time.

They're teaching babies sign language these days. I wonder what the action is for, "I'm clean, fed and comfortable; I'm just ticked off."

166

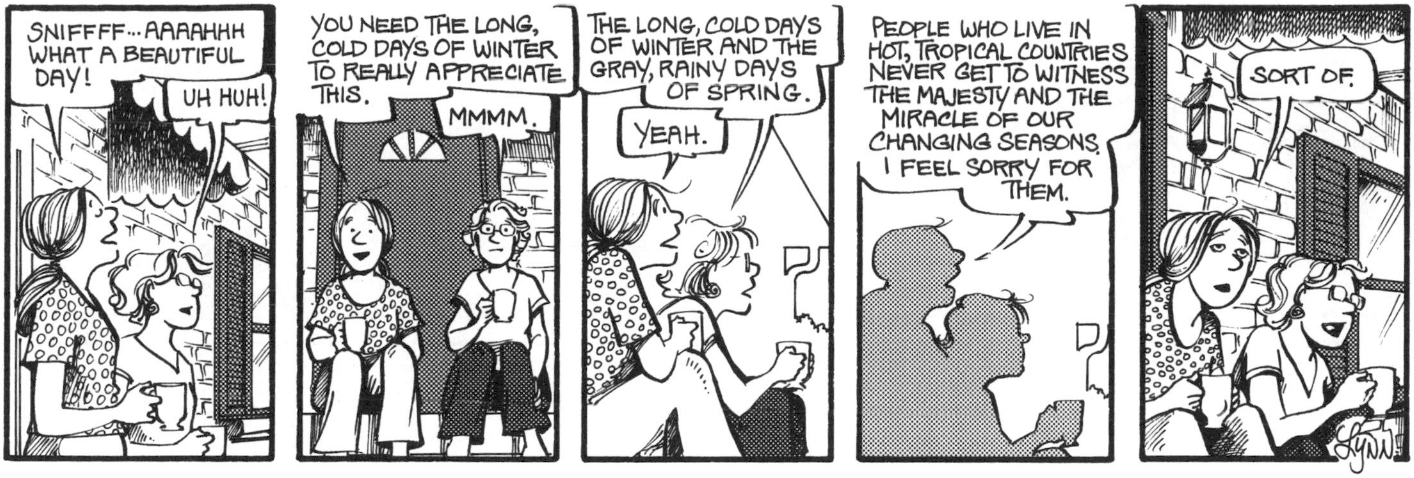
SNIFFFF...AAAAHHH WHAT A BEAUTIFUL DAY!
UH HUH!
YOU NEED THE LONG, COLD DAYS OF WINTER TO REALLY APPRECIATE THIS.
MMMM.
THE LONG, COLD DAYS OF WINTER AND THE GRAY, RAINY DAYS OF SPRING.
YEAH.
PEOPLE WHO LIVE IN HOT, TROPICAL COUNTRIES NEVER GET TO WITNESS THE MAJESTY AND THE MIRACLE OF OUR CHANGING SEASONS. I FEEL SORRY FOR THEM.
SORT OF.
LYNN

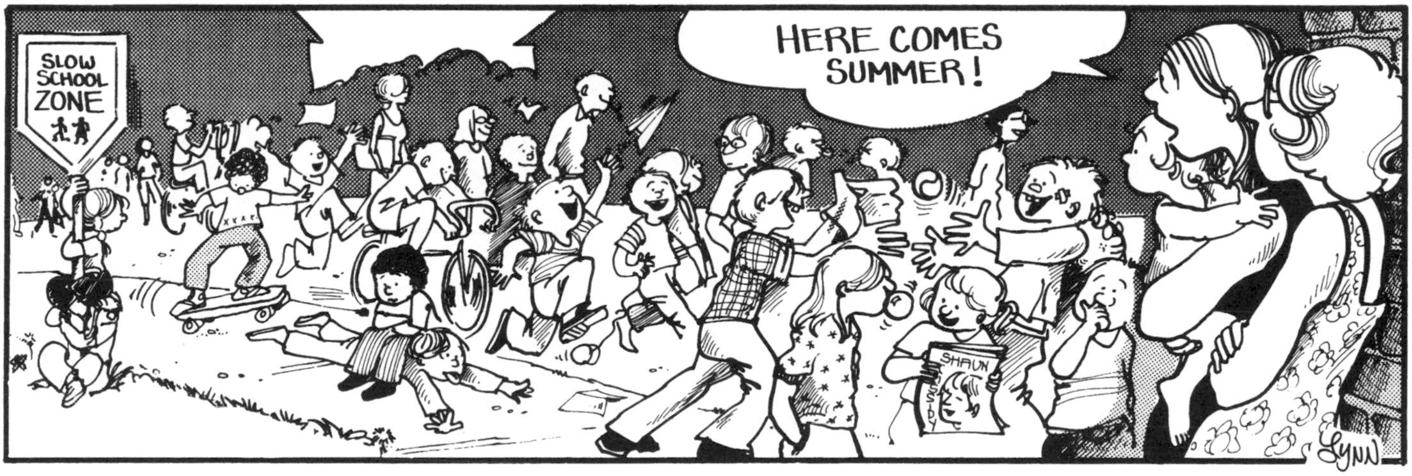
SLOW SCHOOL ZONE
HERE COMES SUMMER!
SHAUN
LYNN

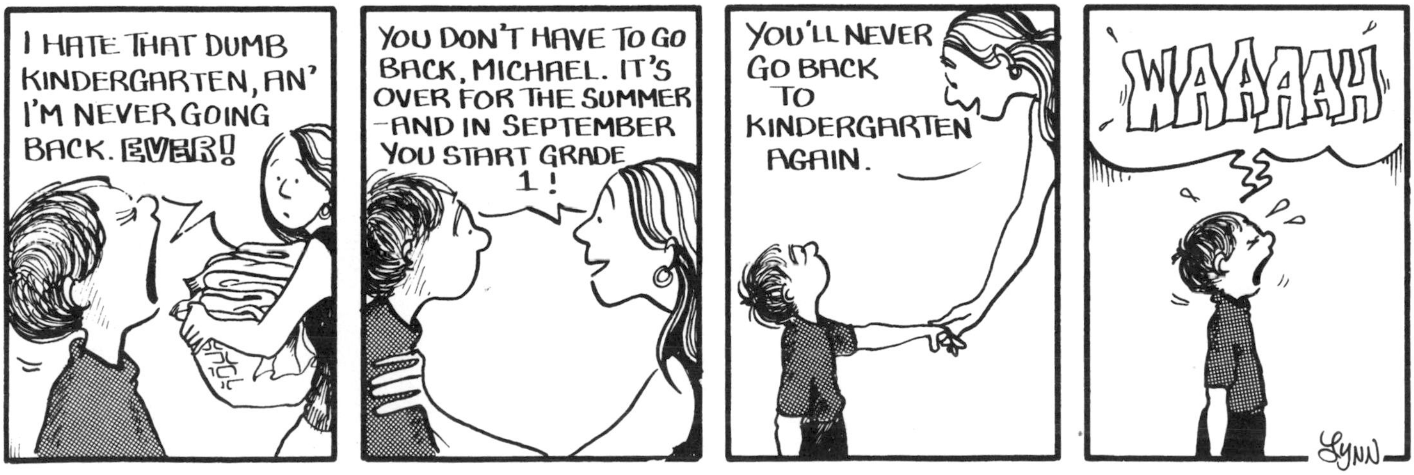
I HATE THAT DUMB KINDERGARTEN, AN' I'M NEVER GOING BACK. EVER!
YOU DON'T HAVE TO GO BACK, MICHAEL. IT'S OVER FOR THE SUMMER -AND IN SEPTEMBER YOU START GRADE 1!
YOU'LL NEVER GO BACK TO KINDERGARTEN AGAIN.
WAAAAH
LYNN

This was an earnest plea for forgiveness. By writing and drawing this, I was exposing a serious truth. Reading it again, I'm grateful for children's ability to see the best in you—even when you're at your worst.

OH! NO... I'VE GOT A WRINKLE!

SO.. WHAT'S ONE WRINKLE?

THIS IS THE BEGINNING! THIS IS IT! SOME DAY I'LL BE COVERED WITH LINES!!!

I'LL ALWAYS BE ABLE TO READ BETWEEN THEM...

JOHN, I'VE BEEN THINKING. THE KIDS AND I COULD USE A CHANGE!

I KNOW IT'S IMPRAC--TICAL...BUT, I'D REALLY LIKE TO TAKE THEM TO SEE MY FOLKS!

MICHAEL HASN'T SEEN MOM FOR 6 MONTHS - AND LIZZIE WILL LOVE GOING ON A PLANE!

ELLY... ARE YOU LOOKING FOR A CHANGE - OR AN ORDEAL?

SO - YOU'RE TAKING A TRIP WITH THE KIDS. - JUST LIKE THAT!

SURE MUST BE NICE BEING MARRIED TO A RICH DENTIST, ELLY.

THAT'S CRAZY! - WE'RE NOT RICH, CONNIE! - WE'RE THE SAME AS EVERYONE ELSE!

WE'RE LIVING TO THE EXTENT OF OUR INCOME.

My hair is a hassle, lifeless and dull brown. I've done everything to it but shave it off. My daughter recently suggested I grow it long again so I wouldn't look like all the other older women out there. I thought about it, but decided to stay flatus quo. It's not the hair that makes me look 60+, it's the whole @*#! package!

On a summer trip to Manitoulin Island, we left Aaron's teddy behind at a motel. On the ferry he cried all the way to the mainland. A week later, the kind people at the motel sent it back to us. At the age of thirty-seven, Aaron still has this precious teddy (made by my mother) sitting on his bedroom dresser.

I took the kids on my own to Vancouver from Lynn Lake, Manitoba. Anytime I see a mom schlepping kids like this, I *feel* for her!

An encounter with a stranger on a crowded plane became an appreciated Sunday strip.

Using photographs of my parents, I did these caricatures. They never said too much, but I think they enjoyed being comic-strip characters—especially my dad. A cartoonist at heart, my dad was a wonderful slapstick model.

My parents, Ursula and Mervyn Ridgway, on their fortieth wedding anniversary.

DO I REALLY GET TO SLEEP IN THE SAME BED MOM SLEPT IN WHEN SHE WAS LITTLE, GRAMPA?

YEP! -YOUR MOM SLEPT HERE, DREAMED HERE, DID HER THINKING HERE...

-SiGH-

...FOR AN OLDEN DAYS BED, IT FEELS PRETTY GOOD!

MOM, WHEN I WAS HERE BEFORE CHRISTMAS, YOU SPENT A WEEK LECTURING ME...

THIS TIME, WITH THE KIDS ··· OUR RELATION-SHIP IS SO DIFFERENT!

MAYBE THAT'S BECAUSE ALONE- YOU'RE MY DAUGHTER...

-BUT WITH THE KIDS- WE'RE BOTH MOMS.

GA-GA!

STOP IT, YOU TWO! YOU'VE BEEN TORMENTING AND JUMPING ON GRAMPA ALL DAY!

BUT, MOM! ...THAT'S WHAT GRAMPAS ARE FOR!

This scenario, of course, would be followed by a mad panic to pick up and disinfect the "guy space" before the wife and kids got home.

As I write this, I am sixty-three years old. Do I feel mature? I think so. The best thing about being over sixty is that I've learned to keep my mouth shut! And, for me, that's a major accomplishment.

This was so close to home. I was glad to be back in Ontario when these strips ran.

178

My mom didn't spoil the kids (much), but my father did. He was a pushover. It didn't take Kate and Aaron long to figure the game out and soon we were playing "he said, she said, I said" and so on. Much as I enjoyed a visit with the folks, I knew that serious deprogramming would take place as soon as we hit home turf. The cry, "But Grampa said . . ." was countered with, "But we're in our house now." This worked until the in-laws came to stay, and the whole process began again.

Guys aren't supposed to whistle at girls anymore—it is considered sexist. Too bad. I kind of appreciated a good whistle!

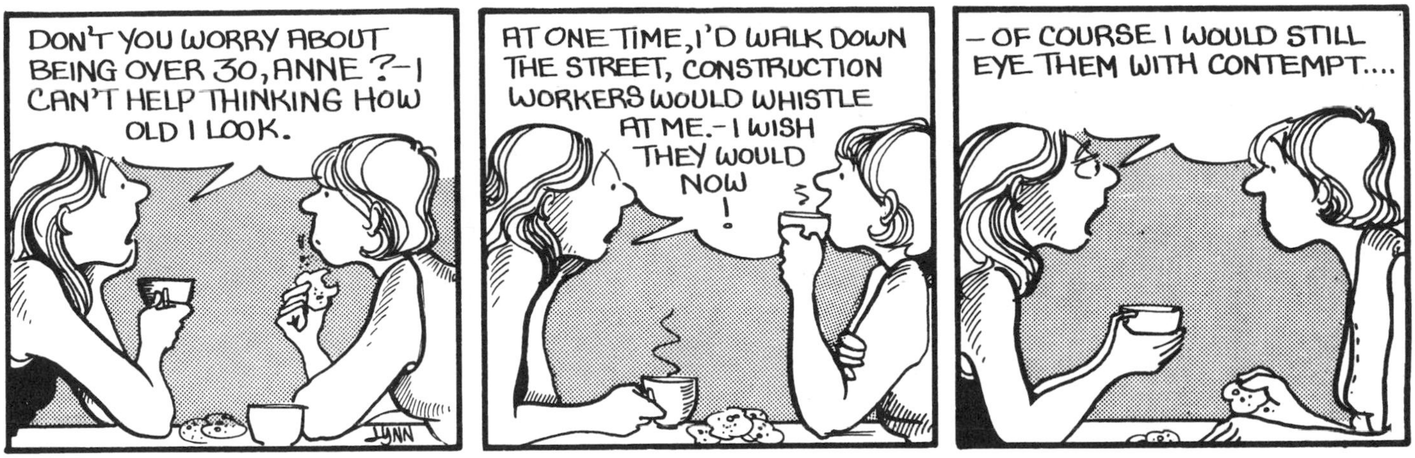
DON'T YOU WORRY ABOUT BEING OVER 30, ANNE ?- I CAN'T HELP THINKING HOW OLD I LOOK.
AT ONE TIME, I'D WALK DOWN THE STREET, CONSTRUCTION WORKERS WOULD WHISTLE AT ME.- I WISH THEY WOULD NOW !
- OF COURSE I WOULD STILL EYE THEM WITH CONTEMPT....
LYNN

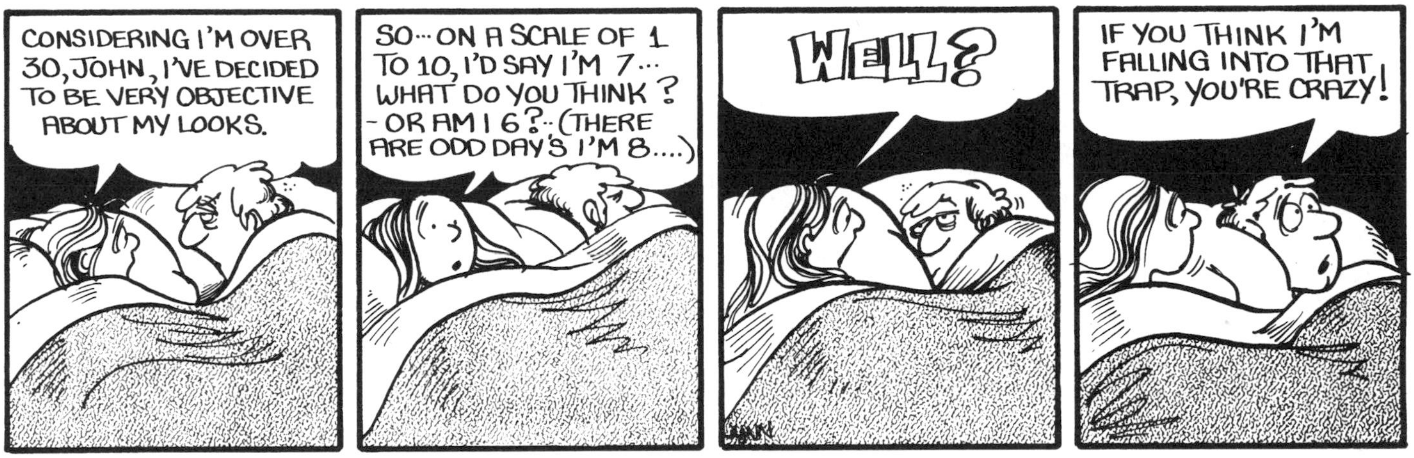
CONSIDERING I'M OVER 30, JOHN, I'VE DECIDED TO BE VERY OBJECTIVE ABOUT MY LOOKS.
SO... ON A SCALE OF 1 TO 10, I'D SAY I'M 7... WHAT DO YOU THINK ? - OR AM I 6?.. (THERE ARE ODD DAY'S I'M 8....)
WELL?
IF YOU THINK I'M FALLING INTO THAT TRAP, YOU'RE CRAZY!
LYNN

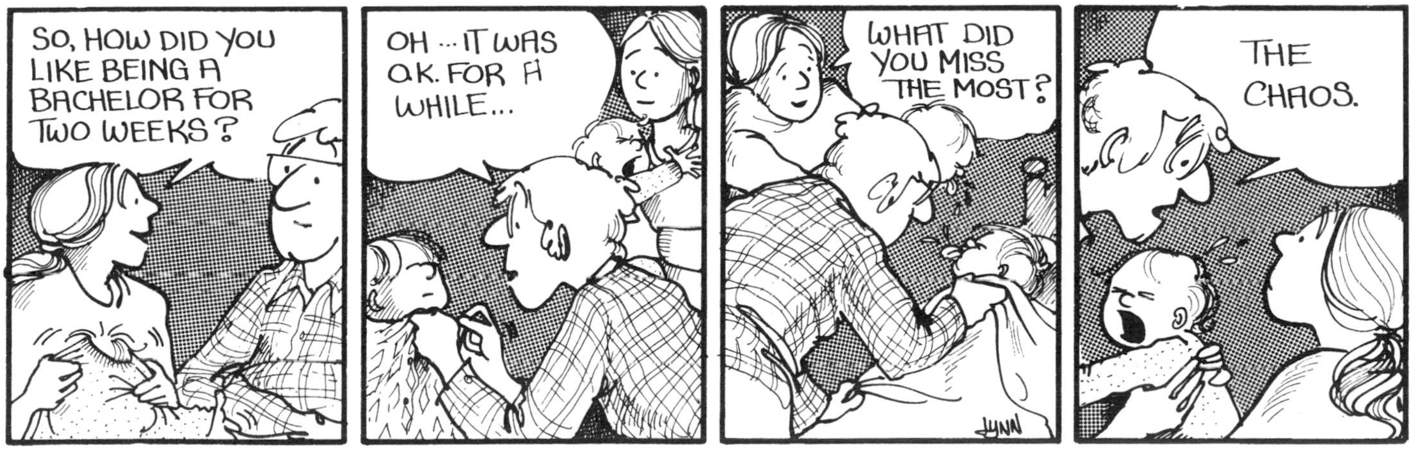
SO, HOW DID YOU LIKE BEING A BACHELOR FOR TWO WEEKS ?
OH ... IT WAS O.K. FOR A WHILE...
WHAT DID YOU MISS THE MOST ?
THE CHAOS.
LYNN

In the 1980s, digital watches and clocks of all kinds flooded the market—it was almost impossible to find an analog watch at the time. This exchange took place on the dance floor after the National Cartoonists Society's Reuben Awards.

As single moms, my friend Andie and I wondered what the response to billboard advertising would be—we were that desperate to find true love. These days you put your specs on the Internet. Either way, it's a crapshoot. We decided that with three kids in diapers (between us) and years left to live, we'd leave it to karma and time.

I tried to imagine how a child would feel if he overheard his mom say she was lonely—not understanding that she was lonely for adult companionship. I thought Lawrence would feel hurt. I would!

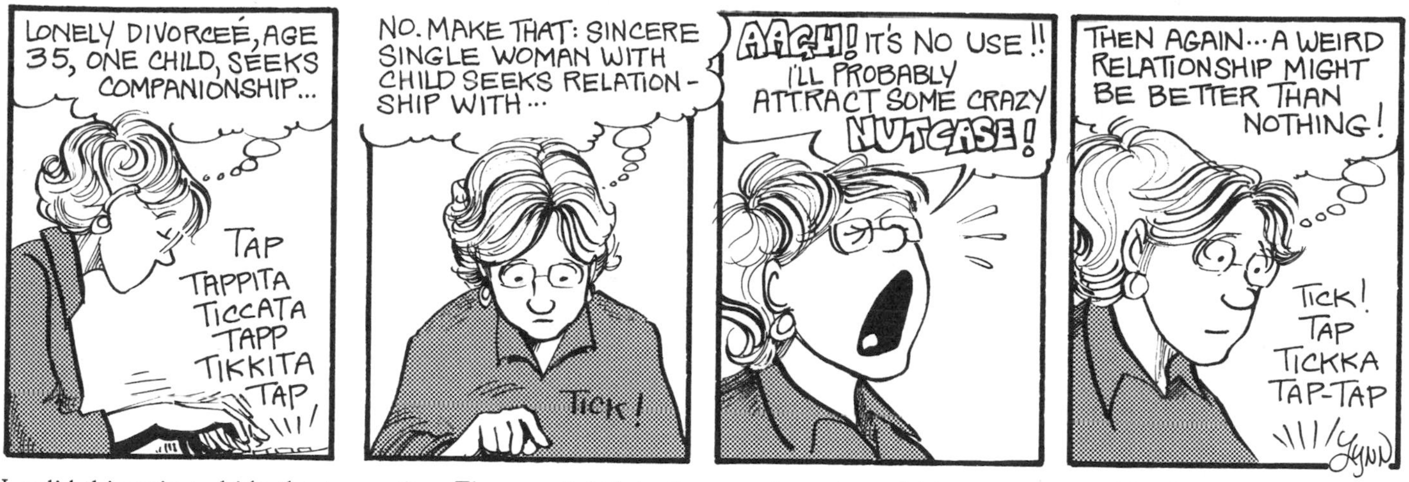
LONELY DIVORCEÉ, AGE 35, ONE CHILD, SEEKS COMPANIONSHIP...
TAP TAPPITA TICCATA TAPP TIKKITA TAP
NO. MAKE THAT: SINCERE SINGLE WOMAN WITH CHILD SEEKS RELATION-SHIP WITH...
TICK!
AAGH! IT'S NO USE!! I'LL PROBABLY ATTRACT SOME CRAZY NUTCASE!
THEN AGAIN... A WEIRD RELATIONSHIP MIGHT BE BETTER THAN NOTHING!
TICK! TAP TICKKA TAP-TAP
LYNN

I redid this strip to hide the typewriter. The way it fit into the new format would have made anything but a computer look odd. Best to leave the machinery hidden, I thought. *I did want* to run this strip again, though; *I did answer* a personal ad once and I met a nice man who was not for me. It's amazing what you will do when you're lonely.

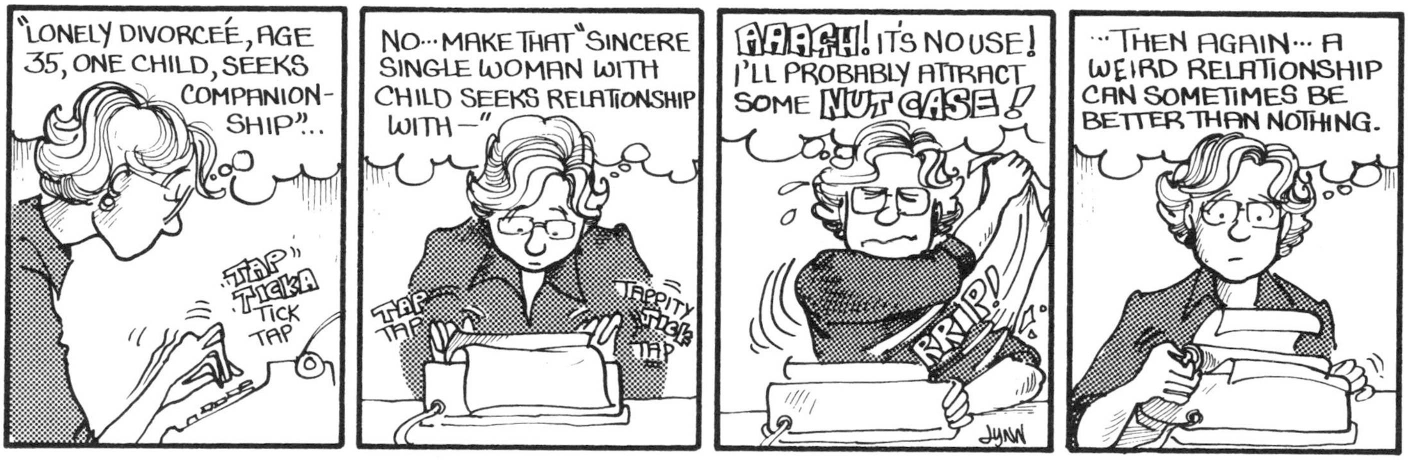
"LONELY DIVORCEÉ, AGE 35, ONE CHILD, SEEKS COMPANION-SHIP"...
TAP TICKA TICK TAP
NO... MAKE THAT "SINCERE SINGLE WOMAN WITH CHILD SEEKS RELATIONSHIP WITH —"
TAP TAP TAPPITY TICKA TAP
AAAGH! IT'S NO USE! I'LL PROBABLY ATTRACT SOME NUT CASE!
RRIP!
LYNN
...THEN AGAIN... A WEIRD RELATIONSHIP CAN SOMETIMES BE BETTER THAN NOTHING.

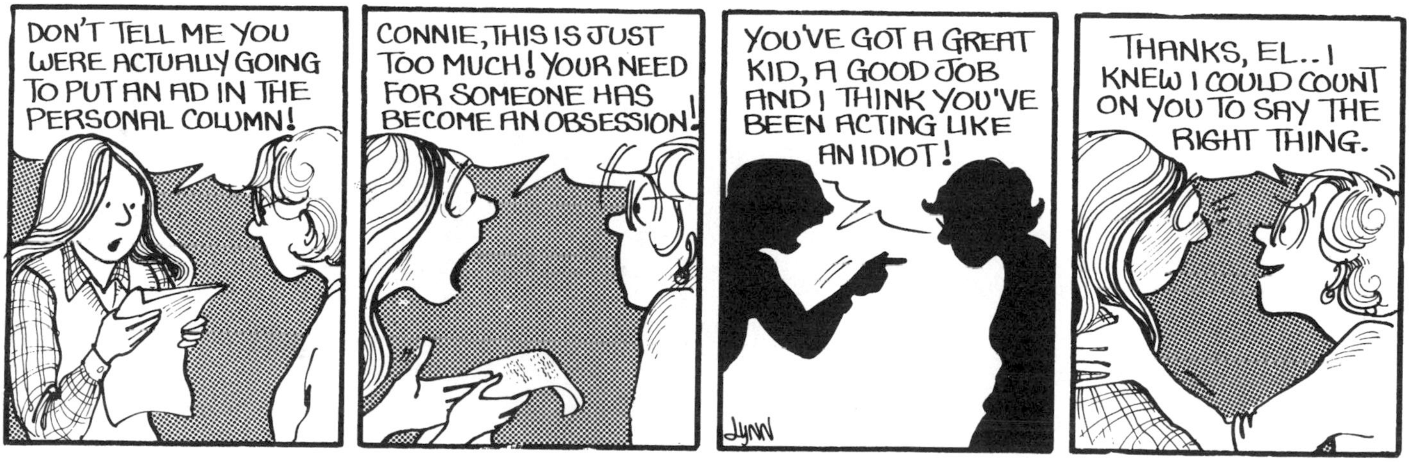
DON'T TELL ME YOU WERE ACTUALLY GOING TO PUT AN AD IN THE PERSONAL COLUMN!
CONNIE, THIS IS JUST TOO MUCH! YOUR NEED FOR SOMEONE HAS BECOME AN OBSESSION!
YOU'VE GOT A GREAT KID, A GOOD JOB AND I THINK YOU'VE BEEN ACTING LIKE AN IDIOT!
LYNN
THANKS, EL.. I KNEW I COULD COUNT ON YOU TO SAY THE RIGHT THING.

FOR BETTER OR FOR WORSE BY Lynn Johnston

HAPPY FATHER'S DAY...

DADDY!!

LET'S MAKE PANCAKES!

YAH!!

IT'S YOUR DAY, HONEY! WHAT WOULD YOU LIKE TO DO?

WELL... I THOUGHT I'D GO DOWN TO THE HARDWARE STORE.

GOOD!

...WOULD YOU PICK UP THE GROCERIES? AND THERE'S SOME STUFF TO GET FROM THE DRY CLEANER.

THEN, I THOUGHT I'D PUTTER AROUND IN MY WORKSHOP.

NICE!

COULD YOU SHARPEN THE KNIVES, PLEASE? AND THE STAIRS INTO THE GARAGE NEED REPAIRING.

THEN, I'D REALLY LIKE A STEAK DINNER.

I'LL GET THE BARBECUE READY FOR YOU.

AND, THEN, I'LL TAKE A BATH.

THAT SOUNDS PERFECT. YOU DO THAT.

AFTER ALL... IT **IS** YOUR DAY!!!

Remember "The House Brigade?" It was a commercial for Endust or some other cleaning product. A group of critical biddies enter your home to inspect it for cleanliness. Their disdain for disorder was "grime and punishment," leaving the hapless female householder disgraced and demoralized.

We all knew it was a stupid ad, a sexist scenario and an unlikely situation, but it stuck. To this day, I panic when the doorbell rings. I pump the Febreeze, hide the dishes, and apologize for the mess.

Christopher was my friend Andie's youngest child. I liked the name.

Strange how uncomfortable it feels to be wearing the wrong thing. Really, who cares? And it's only for one evening, one gathering, one event. I have often envied the wildlife—which shows up to every occasion dressed in the coat they were born in. Not only that—each species wears the exact same thing! Odd that humans are so particular—to the point of angst, embarrassment, and paranoia. In the next life, I want to be a bird. I want to be a parakeet . . .but I've got to be blue!

Girls' night out. It's a necessity. Ladies—if you haven't done this for a while, make plans now to bring together your perfect pod of pals. Go to a decent beanery, dress in your best, drink something sparkly, and hire a cab home. Put it all down as a medical expense because from start to end, it's therapy—and that's the honest truth!

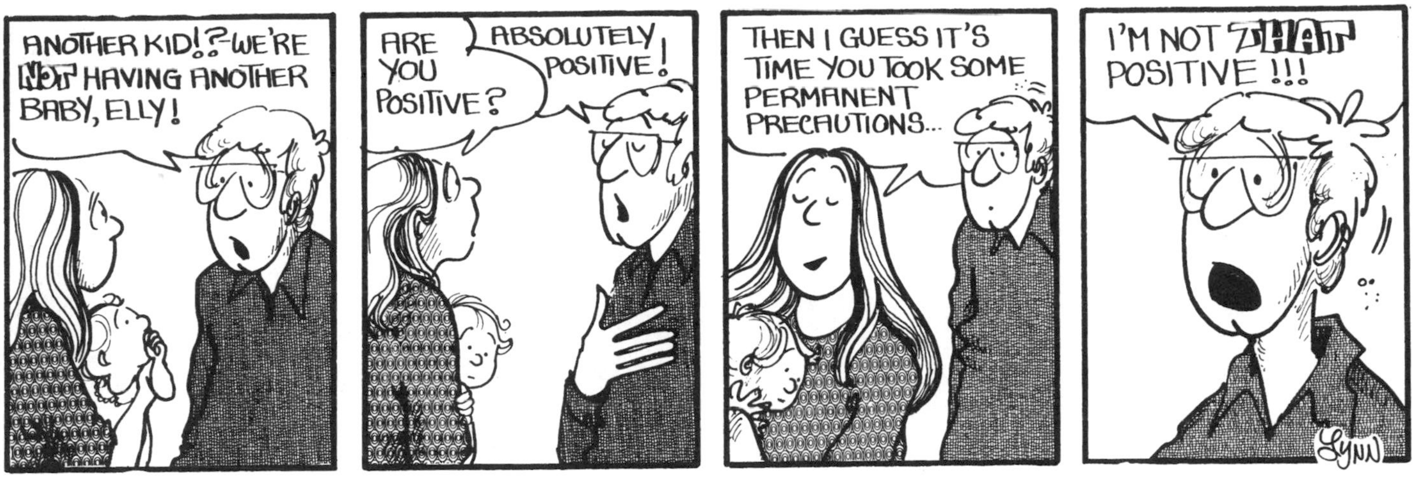

ANOTHER KID!?-WE'RE NOT HAVING ANOTHER BABY, ELLY!
ARE YOU POSITIVE?
ABSOLUTELY POSITIVE!
THEN I GUESS IT'S TIME YOU TOOK SOME PERMANENT PRECAUTIONS...
I'M NOT THAT POSITIVE!!!

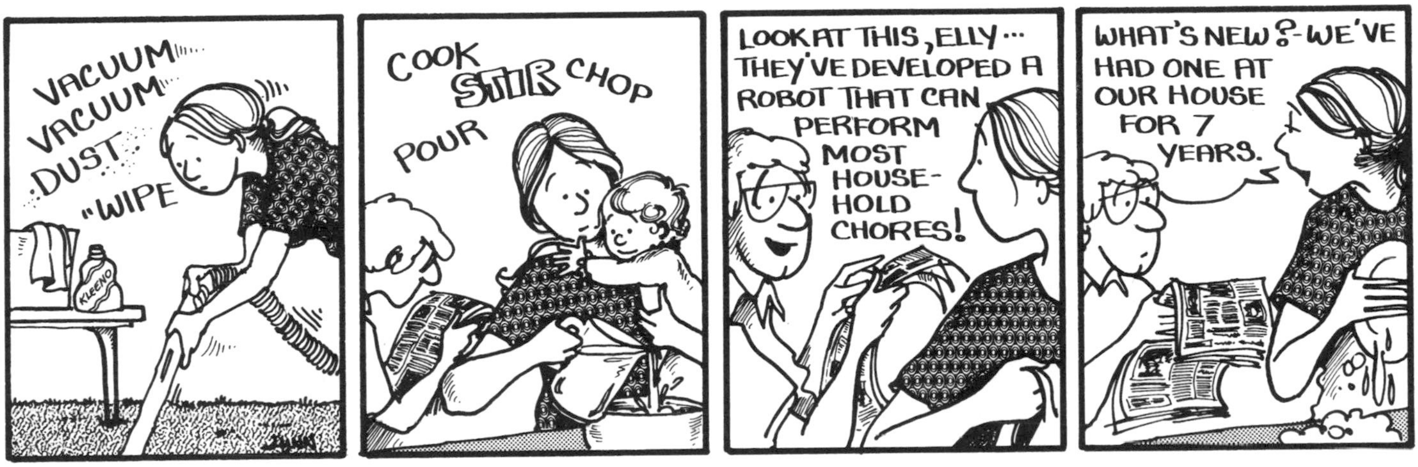

VACUUM
VACUUM
DUST
WIPE
COOK
STIR
CHOP
POUR
LOOK AT THIS, ELLY... THEY'VE DEVELOPED A ROBOT THAT CAN PERFORM MOST HOUSE-HOLD CHORES!
WHAT'S NEW?-WE'VE HAD ONE AT OUR HOUSE FOR 7 YEARS.

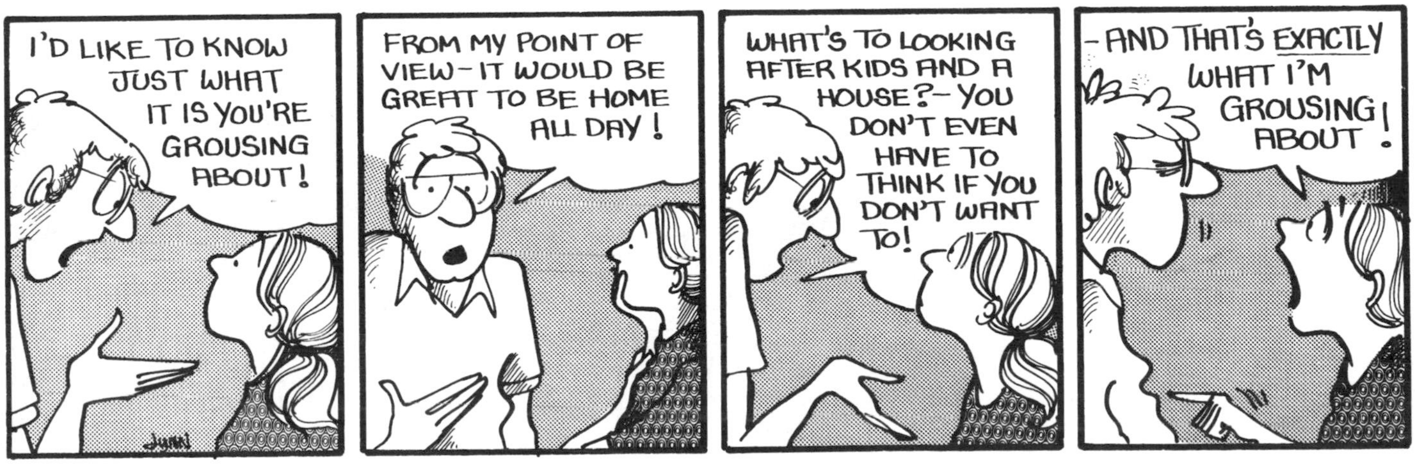

I'D LIKE TO KNOW JUST WHAT IT IS YOU'RE GROUSING ABOUT!
FROM MY POINT OF VIEW-IT WOULD BE GREAT TO BE HOME ALL DAY!
WHAT'S TO LOOKING AFTER KIDS AND A HOUSE?-YOU DON'T EVEN HAVE TO THINK IF YOU DON'T WANT TO!
-AND THAT'S EXACTLY WHAT I'M GROUSING ABOUT!

I have always been embarrassed by my lack of "higher education."

*

LOOK, JOHN! - SHE'S WALKING! ELIZABETH'S WALKING! THAT'S IT, BABY... ONE MORE STEP!

SHE'S WALKING! ISN'T THAT WONDERFUL?! SHE'S TAKING HER FIRST STEPS TODAY!

LOOK AT THAT! SHE'S REALLY GETTING INTO IT!

SHE'S GETTING INTO IT ALL RIGHT!

...AND, TOMORROW - SHE'LL BE GETTING INTO EVERYTHING!

Aaron and Katie, who was just learning to walk.

HELLO, MOM? LIZZIE TOOK HER FIRST STEPS TODAY! - SHE'S **WALKING!**

THOSE LITTLE RAIN BOOTS YOU SENT ARE GOING TO BE PUT TO GOOD USE.

YES, THE BOOTS, THE HAT AND COAT... SHE'S ABLE TO WEAR THEM ALL!

This punch line pleased me a great deal. I wonder, now that I've stopped doing the strip, what will happen to these ideas? Time will tell.

Another true story. A friend in Lynn Lake made a huge batch of bread for a church sale, forgot the salt, and buried the results in her garden. When her kids came home from school, they found the biggest "puffball" (a kind of fungus) growing in the back yard. You can't make this stuff up!

195

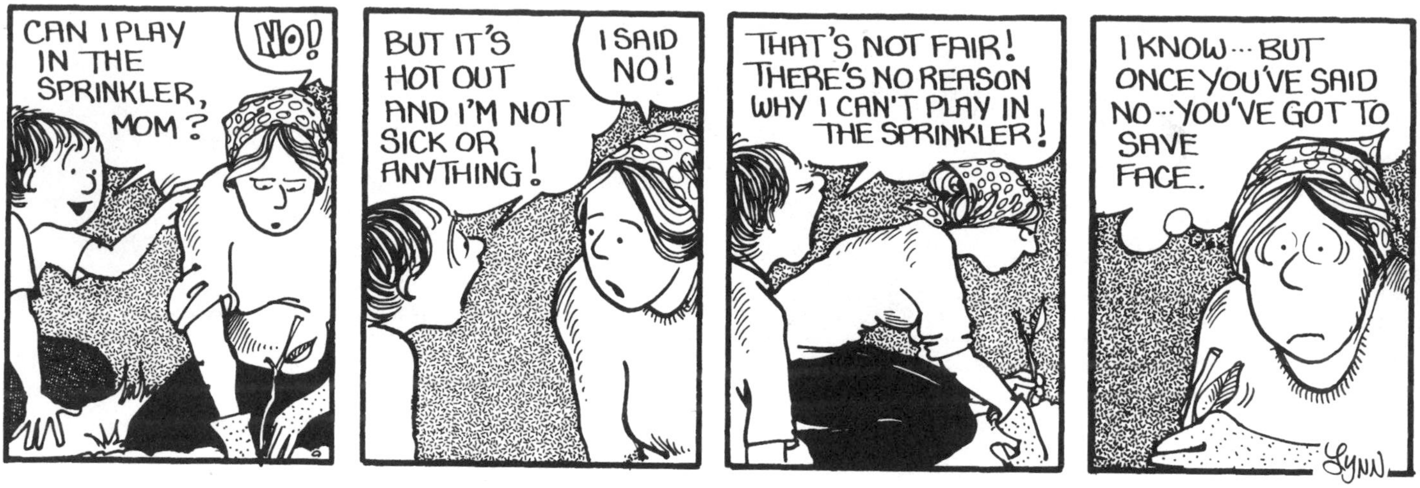
CAN I PLAY IN THE SPRINKLER, MOM?
NO!
BUT IT'S HOT OUT AND I'M NOT SICK OR ANYTHING!
I SAID NO!
THAT'S NOT FAIR! THERE'S NO REASON WHY I CAN'T PLAY IN THE SPRINKLER!
I KNOW... BUT ONCE YOU'VE SAID NO... YOU'VE GOT TO SAVE FACE.
LYNN

*

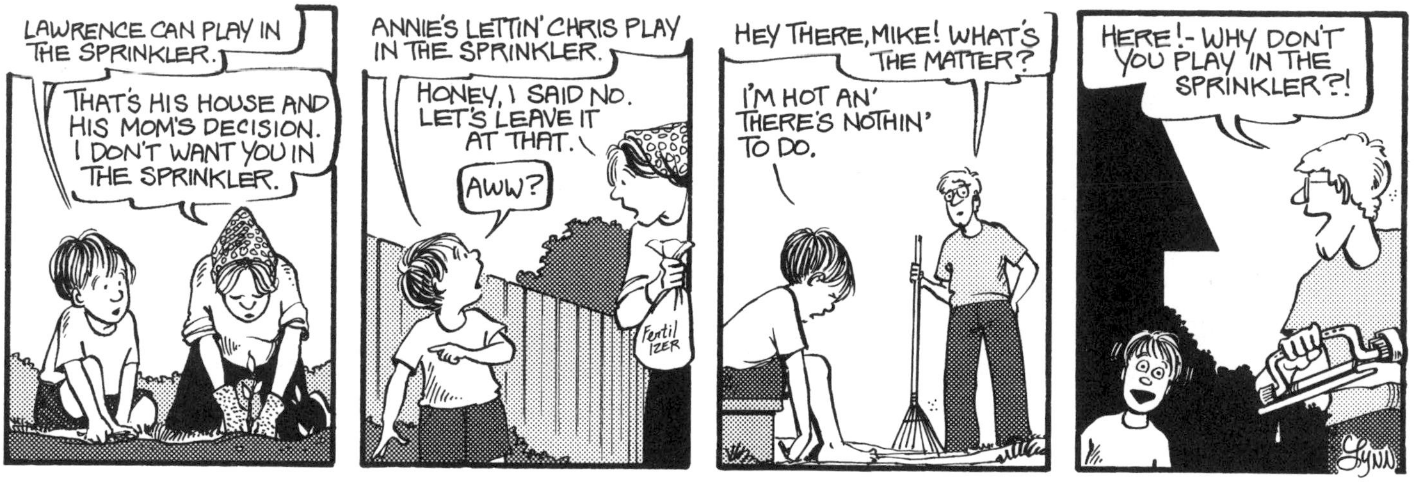
LAWRENCE CAN PLAY IN THE SPRINKLER.
THAT'S HIS HOUSE AND HIS MOM'S DECISION. I DON'T WANT YOU IN THE SPRINKLER.
ANNIE'S LETTIN' CHRIS PLAY IN THE SPRINKLER.
HONEY, I SAID NO. LET'S LEAVE IT AT THAT.
AWW?
FERTILIZER
HEY THERE, MIKE! WHAT'S THE MATTER?
I'M HOT AN' THERE'S NOTHIN' TO DO.
HERE! - WHY DON'T YOU PLAY IN THE SPRINKLER?!
LYNN

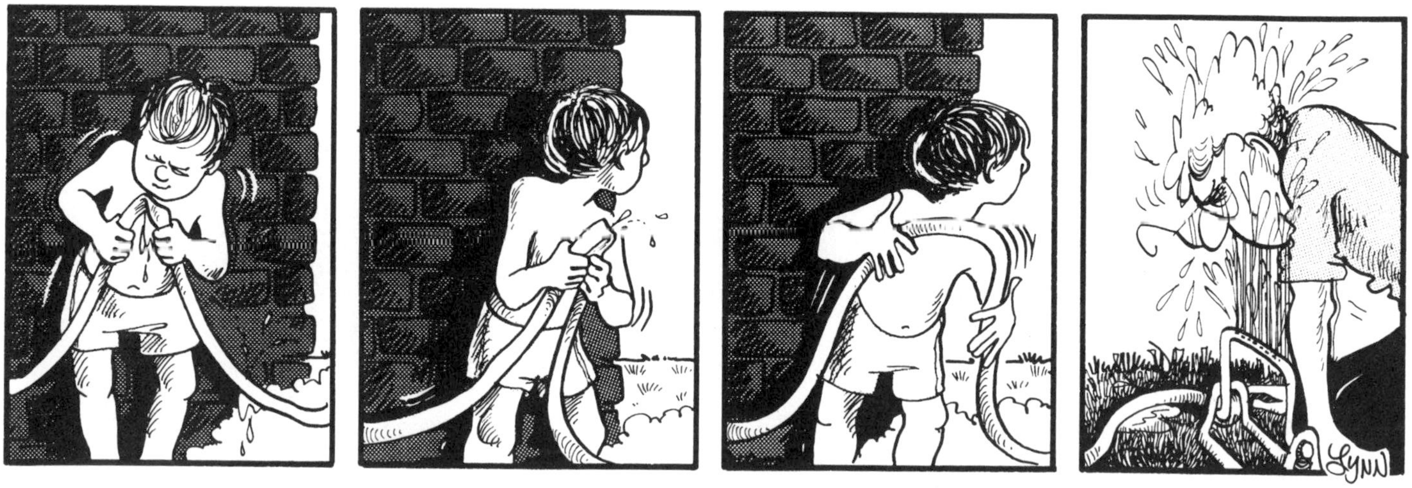
LYNN

The good, the bladder, and the ugly. I always liked the word "incontinent." It implies that the problem is worldwide.

*
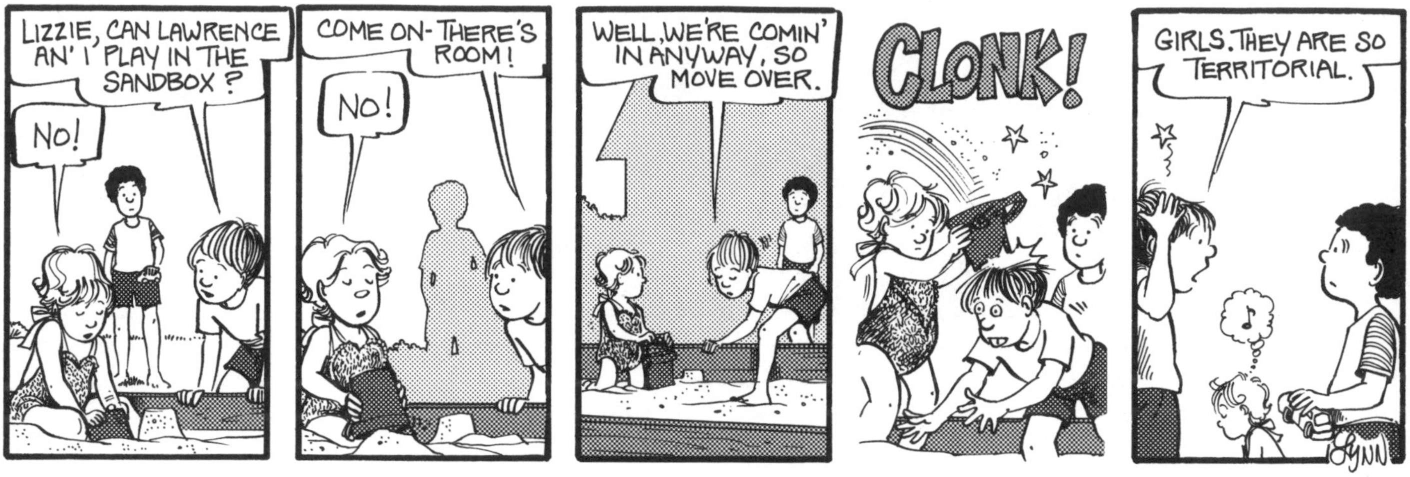
LIZZIE, CAN LAWRENCE AN' I PLAY IN THE SANDBOX?
NO!
COME ON- THERE'S ROOM!
NO!
WELL, WE'RE COMIN' IN ANYWAY, SO MOVE OVER.
CLONK!
GIRLS. THEY ARE SO TERRITORIAL.
LYNN

*
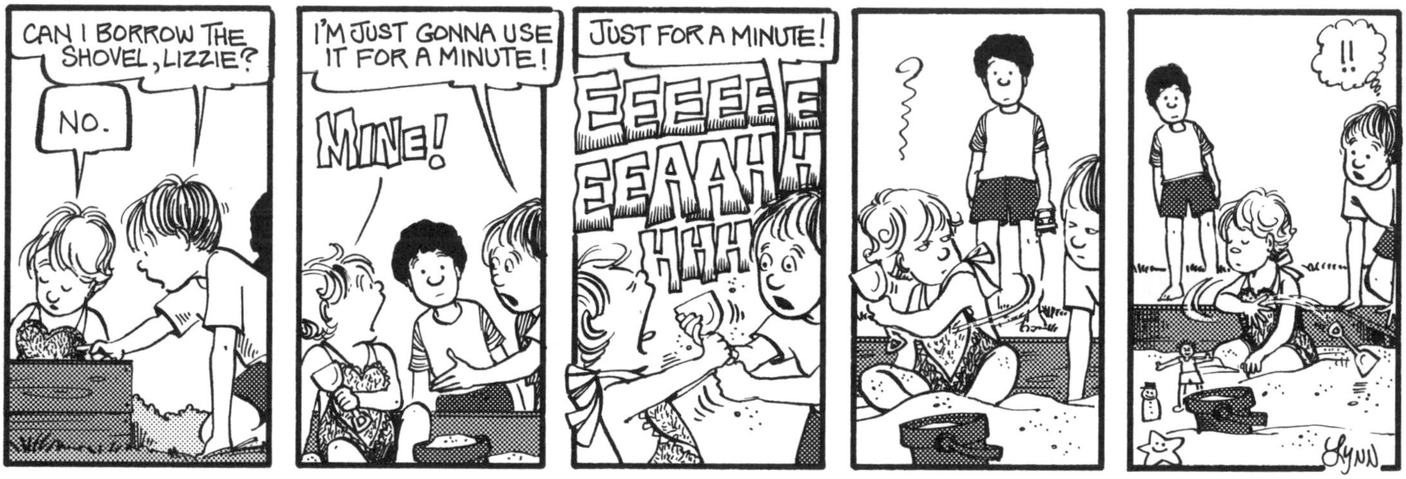
CAN I BORROW THE SHOVEL, LIZZIE?
NO.
I'M JUST GONNA USE IT FOR A MINUTE!
MINE!
JUST FOR A MINUTE!
EEEEEEE EEAAHHH HHH
?
!!
LYNN

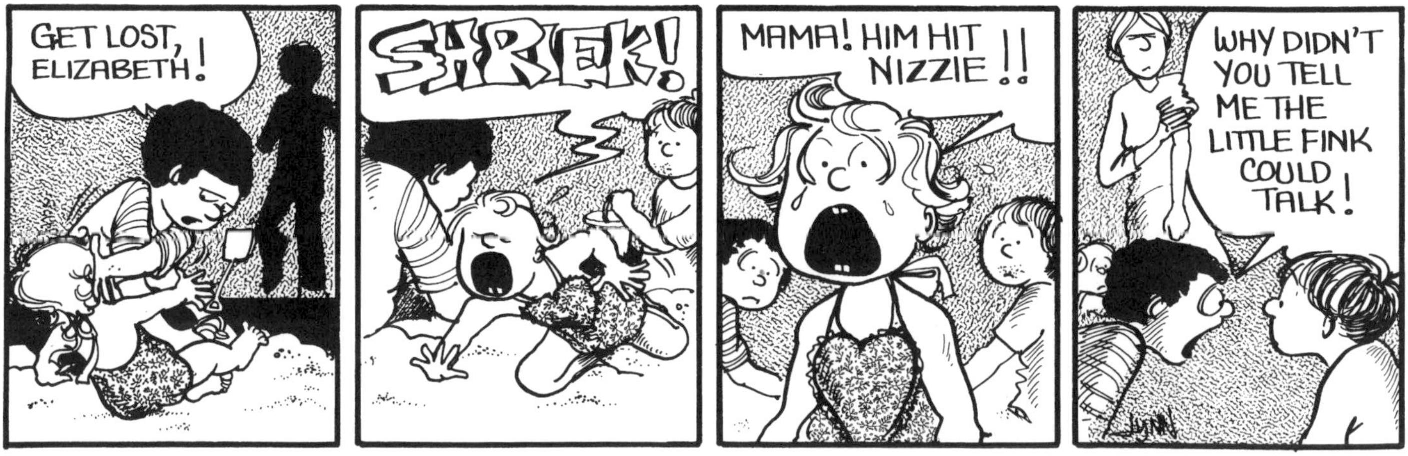
GET LOST, ELIZABETH!
SHREK!
MAMA! HIM HIT NIZZIE!!
WHY DIDN'T YOU TELL ME THE LITTLE FINK COULD TALK!
LYNN

DON'T YOU EVER HIT LIZZIE AGAIN, LAWRENCE!

HONEST, MIKE... IT WASN'T HARD... I JUST ER-SORT OF PUSHED...

WELL JUST YOU WATCH IT. OR ELSE.

NOBODY PICKS ON MY BABY SISTER... —BUT ME.

My brother had this philosophy. We pounded the snot out of each other, but each would have defended the other to the death!

YOUR SISTER IS A PAIN IN THE NECK.

SHE'S A PAIN IN THE EVERYTHING!

WE'RE BORED. THERE'S NOTHIN' TO DO.

WHY DON'T YOU GO DOWN TO THE PARK?

NAH. I DUNNO.

HIDE AND SEEK WOULD BE A GREAT IDEA.

GRUNT.

NAH. NO WAY.

BECAUSE IF I SEE YOU GUYS MOPING AROUND WHEN I COME OUT OF THE HOUSE, I'LL PUT YOU BOTH TO WORK.

I'LL COUNT TO TWENTY.

ABSOLUTELY NOT!-YOU TWO CAN WALK TO THE PARK FROM HERE!

IF YOU KIDS DON'T START USING YOUR LEGS, THEY'LL SHRIVEL UP AND FALL OFF FROM LACK OF USE!!!

FEEL ANYTHING YET?

199

Again, the sound effects make illustrations like this one so much fun to do. I think my favorite written sound is the one made by the toilet plunger: "Ka-FLOOMPA-gush, ka-FLOOMPA-gush" seemed to do it for me. I can only guess how these sounds would be written in other languages!

200

Sometimes Rod said things that were so funny—he had a natural sense of humor that cracked me up. It was one of the things about him that I found so endearing.

I started noticing boys in grade one. I noticed boys starting to notice girls in grade four. They noticed the girls in grade eight and the grade eight girls noticed the boys in grade twelve. When I have grandchildren and they're "that age," I must remember to "notice!"

This was actually progressive for its day. Living in the far north, we had just one TV station (the CBC from Winnipeg) and we got the newspaper a day late! Nobody had cable; it was a southern phenomenon. When films were available on VHS, we rented the units from the Hudson's Bay Store and eagerly watched whatever was in stock. Times have changed. I think they have high-speed Internet and Wi-Fi up there now!

Right. And if Elly was paying a king's ransom for this thing, it would be a size three. Go figure.

*

Rod often came home with stories about his patients, and I found that some could be embellished for the strip.

I have eaten some disgusting leftovers so they wouldn't go to waste. Mothers have been recycling since babies were invented. Going green is nothing new. I've been going green just thinking about the crud I've consumed!

These were flowers from my garden that grew in a place where summer only lasted four weeks. Aaron eventually learned to include the stems.

Another Aaronism.

It's the old cycle—"Do unto me, and I'm likely to take it out on someone else." I'm guilty. I admit it. And, I'm sorry . . . pass it on.

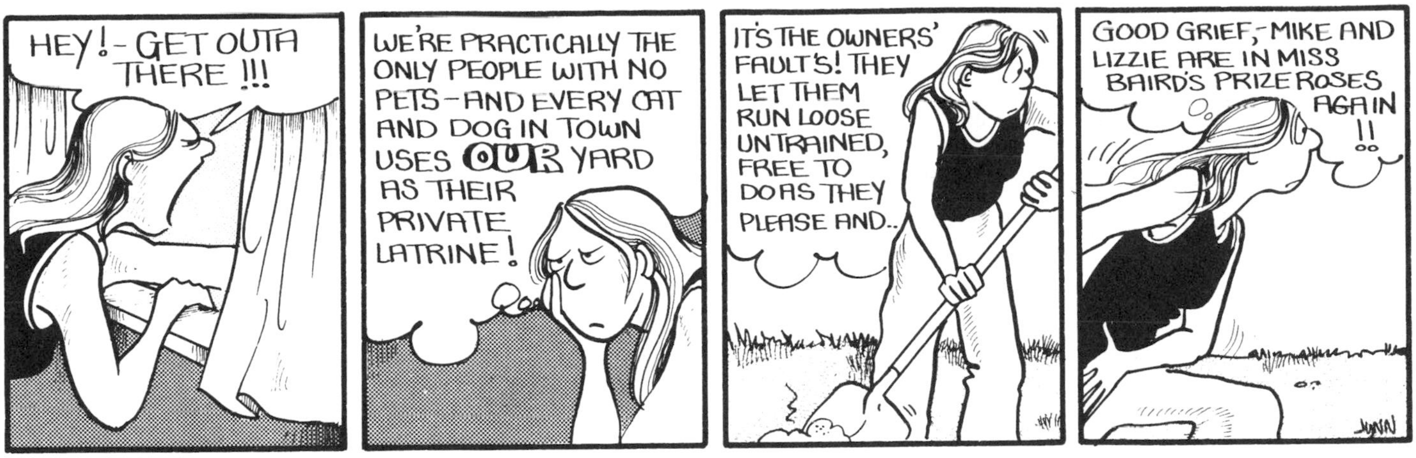
HEY! - GET OUTA THERE !!!
WE'RE PRACTICALLY THE ONLY PEOPLE WITH NO PETS - AND EVERY CAT AND DOG IN TOWN USES OUR YARD AS THEIR PRIVATE LATRINE!
IT'S THE OWNERS' FAULTS! THEY LET THEM RUN LOOSE UNTRAINED, FREE TO DO AS THEY PLEASE AND..
GOOD GRIEF, - MIKE AND LIZZIE ARE IN MISS BAIRD'S PRIZE ROSES AGAIN !!
LYNN

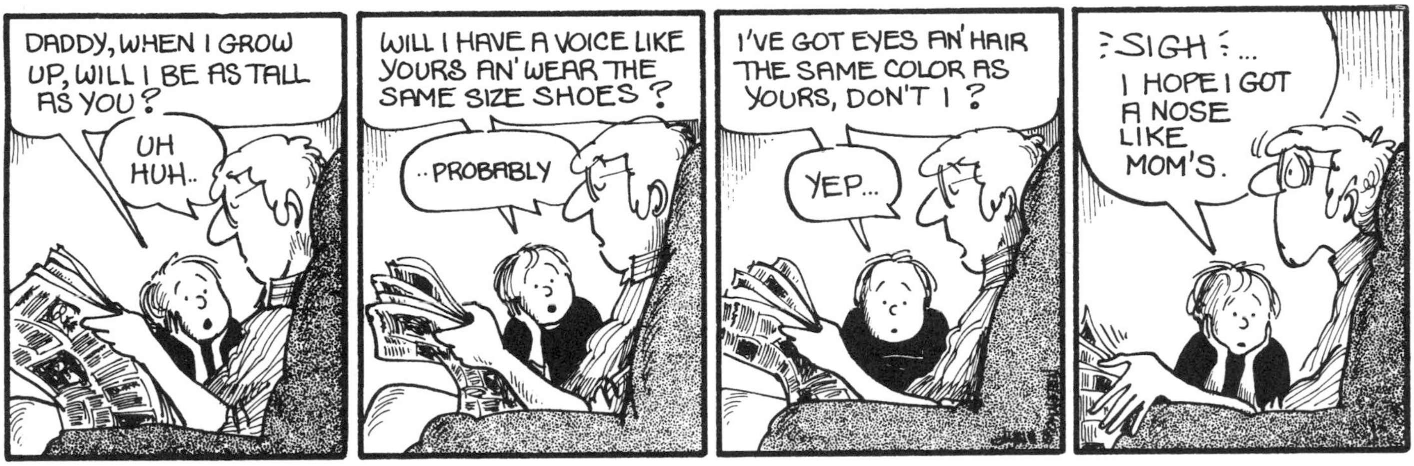
DADDY, WHEN I GROW UP, WILL I BE AS TALL AS YOU?
UH HUH..
WILL I HAVE A VOICE LIKE YOURS AN' WEAR THE SAME SIZE SHOES?
..PROBABLY
I'VE GOT EYES AN' HAIR THE SAME COLOR AS YOURS, DON'T I?
YEP...
SIGH ...
I HOPE I GOT A NOSE LIKE MOM'S.

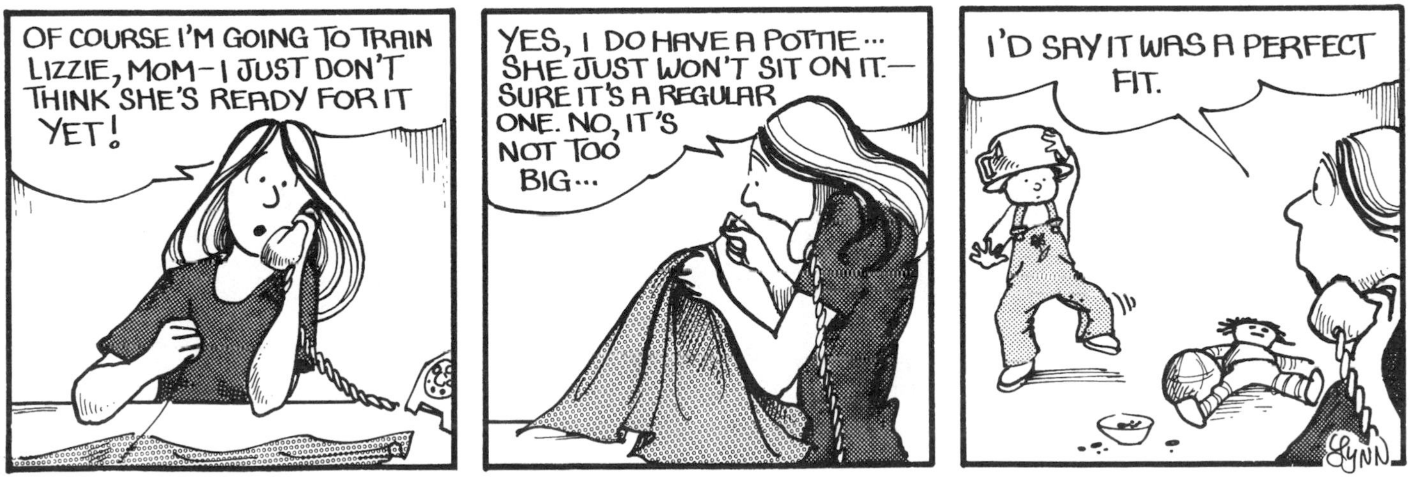
OF COURSE I'M GOING TO TRAIN LIZZIE, MOM - I JUST DON'T THINK SHE'S READY FOR IT YET!
YES, I DO HAVE A POTTIE... SHE JUST WON'T SIT ON IT. — SURE IT'S A REGULAR ONE. NO, IT'S NOT TOO BIG...
I'D SAY IT WAS A PERFECT FIT.
LYNN

*
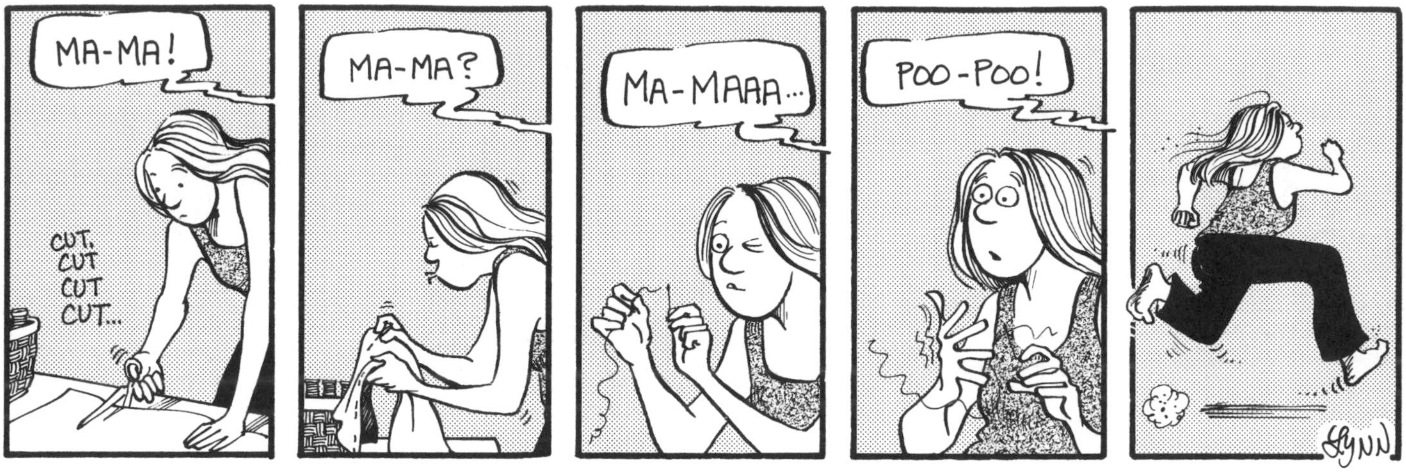
MA-MA!
CUT. CUT CUT CUT...
MA-MA?
MA-MAAA...
POO-POO!
LYNN

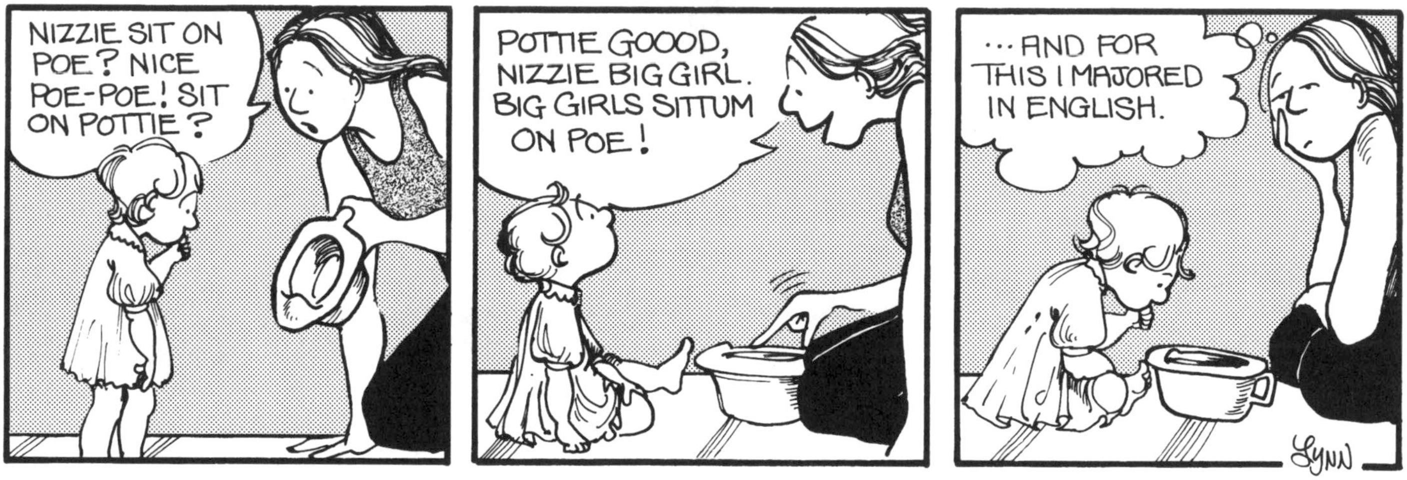
NIZZIE SIT ON POE? NICE POE-POE! SIT ON POTTIE?
POTTIE GOOOD, NIZZIE BIG GIRL. BIG GIRLS SITTUM ON POE!
...AND FOR THIS I MAJORED IN ENGLISH.
LYNN

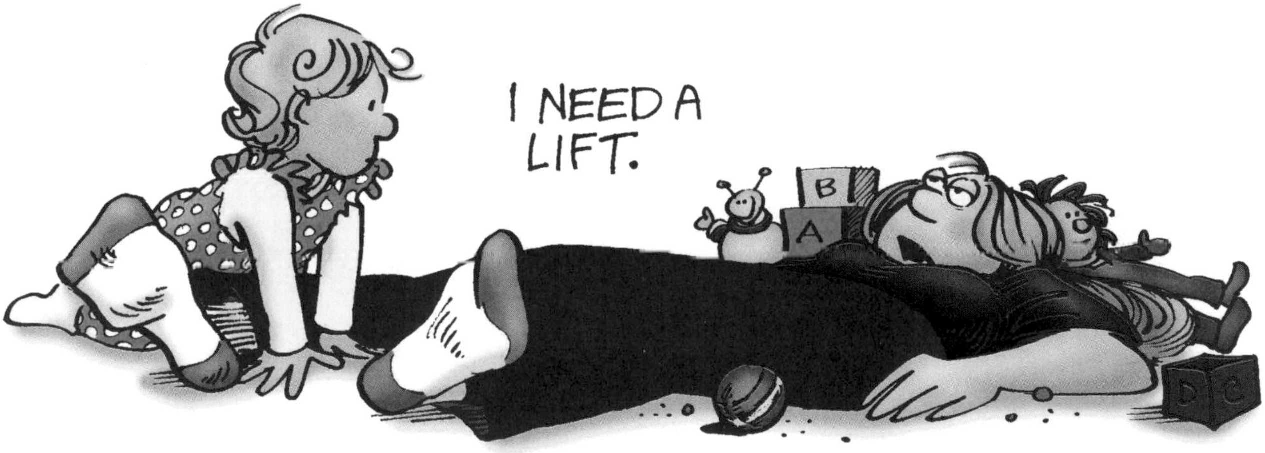
I NEED A LIFT.

I did this strip after telephone solicitors called repeatedly—and right at suppertime. When the phone rang the following night—at the same time, I let the kids answer it, hoping it was another solicitor and they'd give her the runaround. It was and they did. Now, I'm on the no call list—but they still call. Kids . . . they're never around when you need them!

We encouraged both our kids to express themselves artistically. Some of Aaron's most creative efforts were portraits of us—and not all flattering.

I'M NOT GOING TO BOTHER COOKING TONIGHT. I'M GOING TO PUT ALL THE LEFTOVERS OUT ON THE COUNTER, AND EVERYONE CAN FEND FOR THEMSELVES.

ELLY? TED'S HERE! I'VE INVITED HIM HOME FOR DINNER!

AN IMPOSITION? NO WAY! BESIDES, IF YOU WEREN'T HERE, WE'D PROBABLY BE HAVING LEFTOVERS!

YOU DON'T KNOW WHAT HASSLES ARE, TED.

ALTOGETHER, I'VE GOT 9 GIRLS WORKING FOR ME!

4... 5... 6... 7... 8...

YOU FINK!!! YOU COUNTED **ME**!

ELLY, YOU ARE FAR TOO SENSITIVE!

IF I KID YOU ABOUT YOUR ROLE AT HOME, YOU'RE IMMEDIATELY ON THE DEFENSIVE!

CONTRARY TO POPULAR BELIEF— I AM **NOT** A MALE CHAUVINIST PIG!

— I JUST BRING HOME THE BACON.

THERE'S ONE DONUT IN THE FRIDGE.... I CAN'T STOP THINKING ABOUT IT.

I'VE GOT TO KEEP AWAY FROM IT. I DON'T NEED IT. I MUST HAVE **WILL POWER!**

I CAN'T TAKE IT ANYMORE. **I GIVE UP!!**

¡GASP!... ONE LAST DESPERATE BURST OF RESISTANCE.

Lynn

I'M BREAKING DOWN. AGAIN. I'M GOING TO OPEN THE FRIDGE DOOR.

THIS IS IT. I'M TOO WEAK TO RESIST TEMPTATION!

I'VE THROWN OUT MY DIGNITY AND MY SELF-RESPECT FOR A LOUSY DONUT...

AND IT'S **GONE!**

Lynn

It was hard to get angry when a situation made a good strip.

SIGH I DON'T WANT TO GO TO WORK.

I COULD CANCEL MY PATIENTS AND SPEND THE DAY RELAXING AT HOME WITH THE KIDS.... MA!

MAA! — LIZZIE'S DONE SOMETHIN' AWFUL ON THE RUG AN' I KNOCKED OVER THE PLANTER GETTIN' AWAY FROM IT!

ON SECOND THOUGHT, I HATE BEING LATE.

Lynn

214

This one didn't quite work. I wanted to show Elly worried to death that something bad had happened to her husband. Instead of being relieved and happy that he is home, she barks at him. If I'm showing you the warts and all . . . this is another wart.

I once caught Kate crawling into the dryer—hoping for a ride. Fortunately, her bro was elsewhere. He might have helped her do it!

"Decorations" was my mom's word for the differences between guys and girls, too, until the *real* questions began.

For my dad-in-law's birthday, we put 80 candles on the cake. It became a furnace. He was terrified. It took three of us to blow them out. Obviously this drawing was done before this took place—while we still thought it was a great idea!

Somebody gave us this very toy. If I knew who it was, I'd have bought their kids a drum set!

This hall stairway appears in so many *FBorFW* illustrations, I had to include a photo of it.

THAT'S **WONDERFUL**, LIZZIE!

I must have received ten letters from parents who had experienced this themselves. I loved the company.

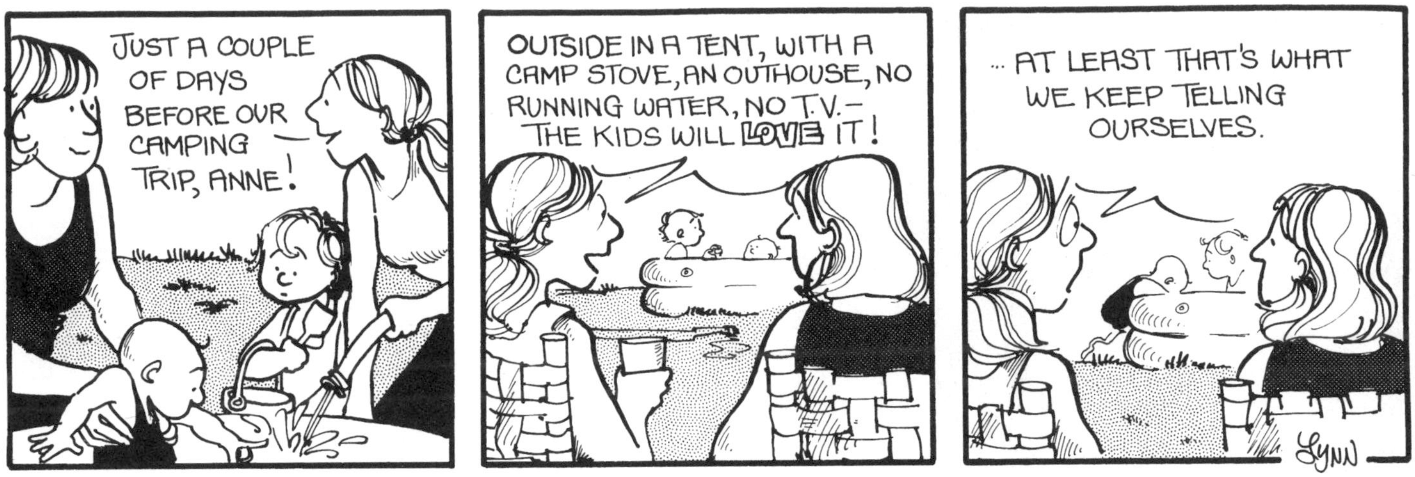
JUST A COUPLE OF DAYS BEFORE OUR CAMPING TRIP, ANNE!
OUTSIDE IN A TENT, WITH A CAMP STOVE, AN OUTHOUSE, NO RUNNING WATER, NO T.V.— THE KIDS WILL LOVE IT!
... AT LEAST THAT'S WHAT WE KEEP TELLING OURSELVES.
LYNN

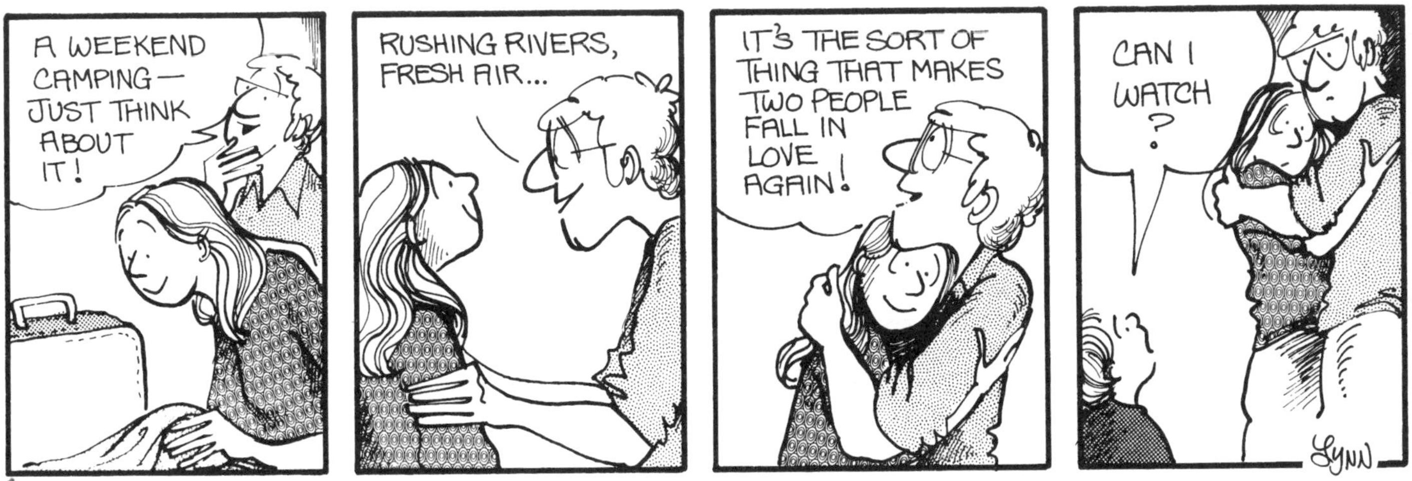
A WEEKEND CAMPING— JUST THINK ABOUT IT!
RUSHING RIVERS, FRESH AIR...
IT'S THE SORT OF THING THAT MAKES TWO PEOPLE FALL IN LOVE AGAIN!
CAN I WATCH?
LYNN

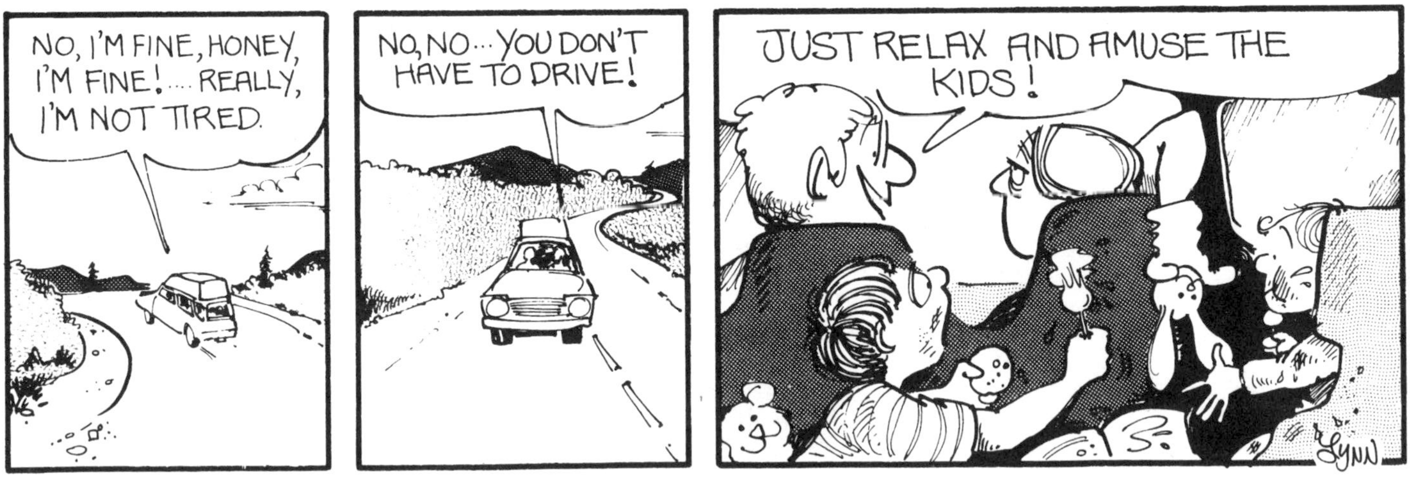
NO, I'M FINE, HONEY, I'M FINE!.... REALLY, I'M NOT TIRED.
NO, NO... YOU DON'T HAVE TO DRIVE!
JUST RELAX AND AMUSE THE KIDS!
LYNN

Another actual event. After admonishing the kids for throwing trash out of the car window, we went back and made them pick it up—only to find all kinds of litter on the roadside. I'd hoped the litterbugs would see themselves in this small attempt at social commentary.

I remember, "Watch me." I remember hollering out to my parents, and my kids hollered out to me. "Watch me!!!" "Watch me jump, watch me splash, watch me swim—watch me!!!" And, I did. I might have been reading or relaxing or talking to someone—but I was watching. Kids are too precious to let out of your sight!

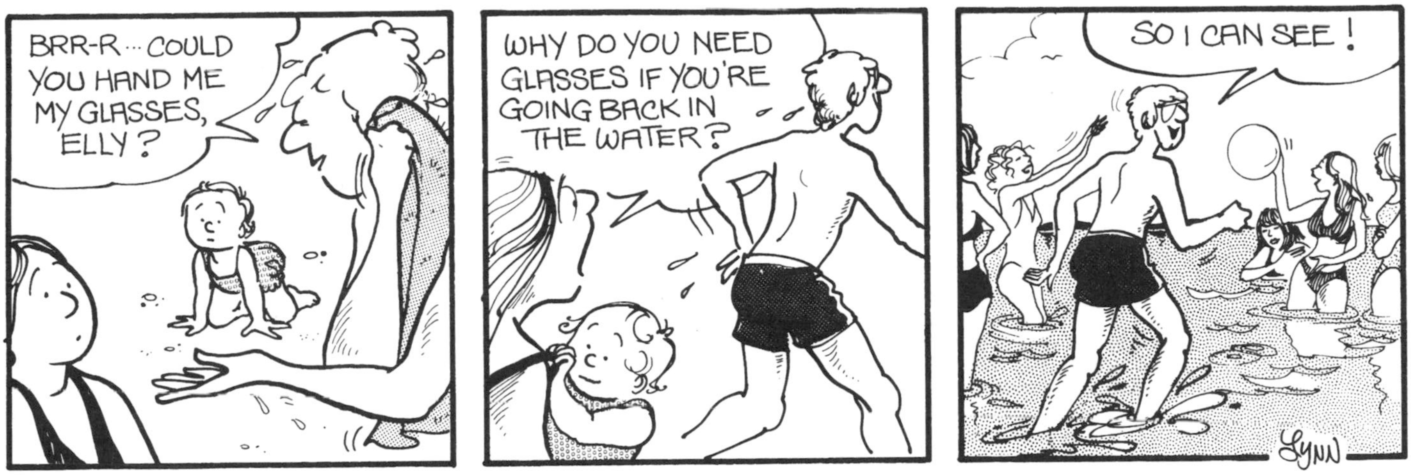
BRR-R... COULD YOU HAND ME MY GLASSES, ELLY?
WHY DO YOU NEED GLASSES IF YOU'RE GOING BACK IN THE WATER?
SO I CAN SEE!
LYNN

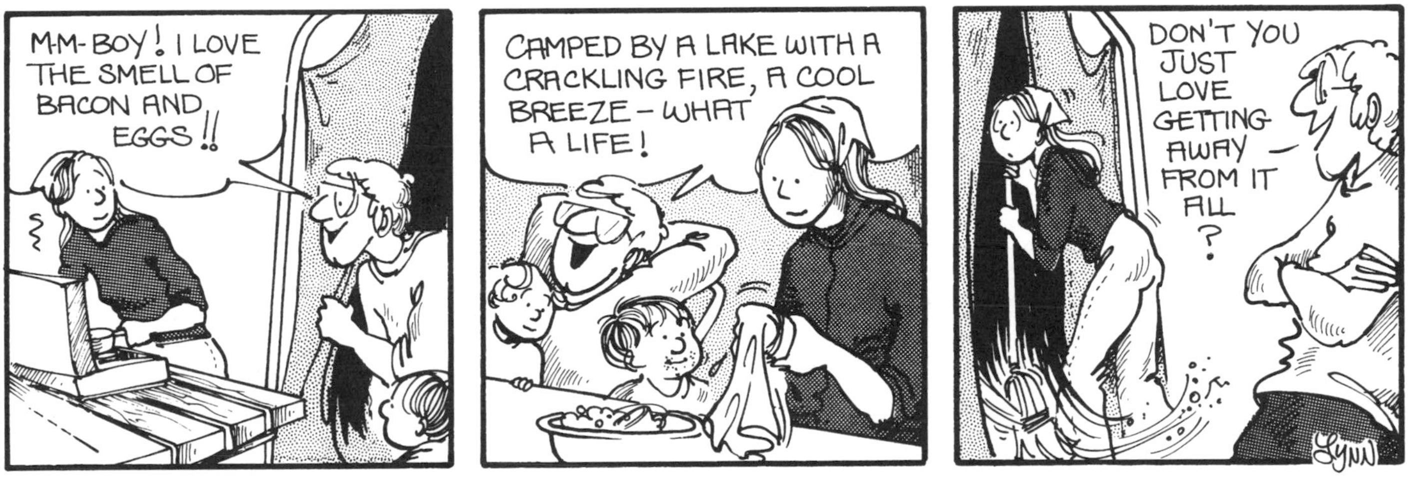
M-M-BOY! I LOVE THE SMELL OF BACON AND EGGS!!
CAMPED BY A LAKE WITH A CRACKLING FIRE, A COOL BREEZE - WHAT A LIFE!
DON'T YOU JUST LOVE GETTING AWAY FROM IT ALL?
LYNN

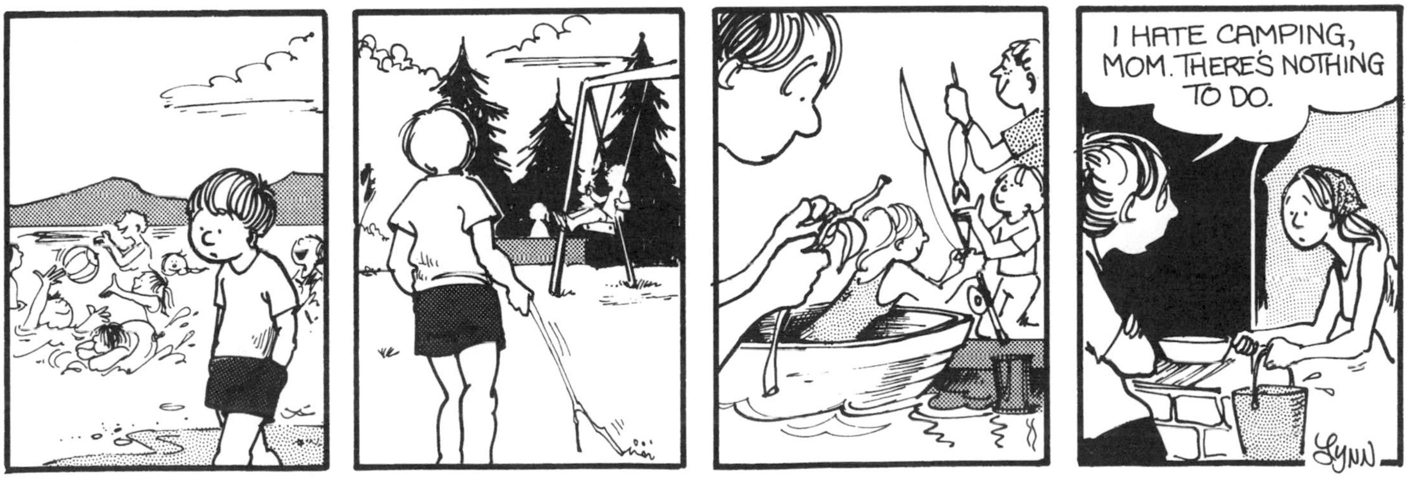
I HATE CAMPING, MOM. THERE'S NOTHING TO DO.
LYNN

The guy in the background is reminiscent of a friend from school who got a job at a roadside burger shack. Out of boredom, he started putting flies into the burgers. Following this revelation, my eating habits changed considerably.

When I was a kid, I used to hug my house whenever we came home from an overnight trip. When they later tore down that house to build apartments, I wished I'd been able to hug it one more time.

BOY, MOM – HOW COME YOUR HAMBURGERS DON'T TASTE LIKE THIS?

I DON'T KNOW, MICHAEL... I GUESS I NEVER HIT ON THE RIGHT BLEND OF SAWDUST!

IT'S OUR BIG, BIG BACK-TO-SCHOOL BARGAIN BLITZ!! EVERYTHING, YES, EVERYTHING YOU NEED FOR "BACK TO SCHOOL" IS HERE AT HINKLEY'S HANDY HAVEN!

FOR ONE-STOP SHOP-PIN' GET HOPPIN'! GOT KIDS? BRING 'EM! GOT THE MUNCHIES? EAT HERE! FAST! FUN! FRIENDLY! FIND IT ALL AT HINKLEY'S HANDY HAVEN!

WE SLICE PRICES! WE GIVE YOU DEALS! TOP BRANDS, LABELS –YOU NAME IT, WE GOT IT FOR **LESS!** YES! COME ON IN TO HINKLEY'S HANDY HAVEN!!!

I NEVER SHOP THERE.

WHY NOT?

I HATE THEIR ADVERTISING.

SEE, ELLY? THE PRICES ARE AMAZING. HANDY HAVEN IS A GREAT PLACE TO SHOP.

IT'S TACKY.

HINKLEY'S HANDY HAVEN

SO? WHAT YOU LOSE IN CLASS, YOU GAIN IN CASH! CHECK OUT THE BACK-TO-SCHOOL CLOTHING.

HMM...

SAVE

SALE

50% OFF

IT'S NOT VERY GOOD QUALITY, ANNE.

EXACTLY!

I FIGURE THAT BY THE TIME IT FALLS APART, THEY'LL HAVE GROWN OUT OF IT ANYWAY.

SALE

LOOK, DAD! I GOT MY SCHOOL STUFF! I GOT A BATMAN PENCIL CASE AN' SPIDER-MAN PENCILS...

I GOT A RULER AN' TAPE AN' SCISSORS AN' NOTE-BOOKS AN' CRAYONS AN' ERASERS AN' GLUE!

AN' I GOT CONSTRUCTION PAPER IN ALL DIFFERENT COLORS!

WELL! —THIS IS JUST LIKE CHRISTMAS!

YAH!

EXCEPT, **YOU** DIDN'T GET ANYTHING!

MICHAEL, THAT WAS A MEAN THING TO SAY!

SORRY.

DON'T SAY YOU'RE SORRY TO ME... SAY IT TO YOUR SISTER.

SORRY.

THAT WASN'T A SINCERE "SORRY." SAY YOU ARE SORRY - AND, MEAN IT!

SIGH

SORRY!

BUT, THAT WAS THE BEST I COULD DO !!!

ELIZABETH - WHAT'S WRONG?

MICHAEL WAS SHOW-ING ME HIS SCHOOL SUPPLIES AND SHE FEELS LEFT OUT.

WELL, I HAVE SCHOOL SUPPLIES FOR YOU TOO, HONEY. I HAVE PAPER AND COLORED PENCILS AND ALL KINDS OF THINGS.

WHAT WOULD YOU LIKE? PENCILS?

SHRIEK!

OK, YOU CAN HAVE PAPER AND PENCILS.

GRUNCH

226

Both of my kids drew on the walls. Once. After that, they peeled the wallpaper.

Consistency. Saying what you mean and meaning what you say. Setting out the rules and following them. This all sounds good on paper and works quite well at home—but things change when you're out in public and "Go to your room" won't fly. Note (of course) the lack of seat belts in panel one. I think they were enforced as much to keep kids separated as they were to keep them safe.

I visited my old elementary school recently. Much had changed, but for the most part, things were familiar. I was immediately shot back in time to grades 4, 5, 6, 7—and if anyone had called my name sharply, I would have gone straight to the office.

229

*

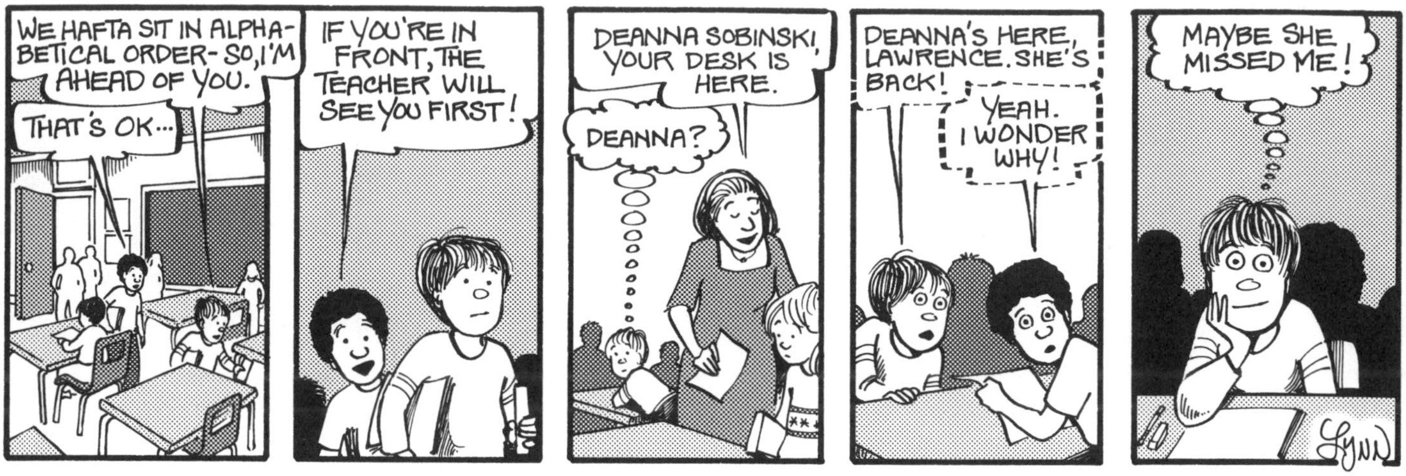
WE HAFTA SIT IN ALPHA-BETICAL ORDER- SO, I'M AHEAD OF YOU.
THAT'S OK...
IF YOU'RE IN FRONT, THE TEACHER WILL SEE YOU FIRST!
DEANNA SOBINSKI, YOUR DESK IS HERE.
DEANNA?
DEANNA'S HERE, LAWRENCE. SHE'S BACK!
YEAH. I WONDER WHY!
MAYBE SHE MISSED ME!
LYNN

*

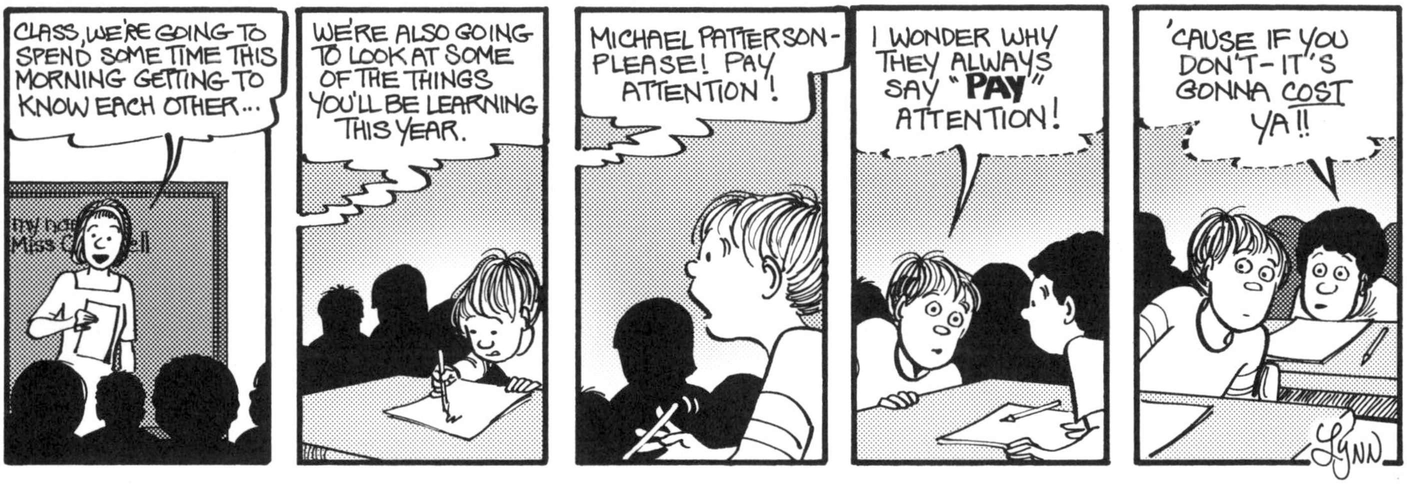
CLASS, WE'RE GOING TO SPEND SOME TIME THIS MORNING GETTING TO KNOW EACH OTHER...
WE'RE ALSO GOING TO LOOK AT SOME OF THE THINGS YOU'LL BE LEARNING THIS YEAR.
MICHAEL PATTERSON - PLEASE! PAY ATTENTION!
I WONDER WHY THEY ALWAYS SAY "PAY" ATTENTION!
'CAUSE IF YOU DON'T - IT'S GONNA COST YA!!
LYNN

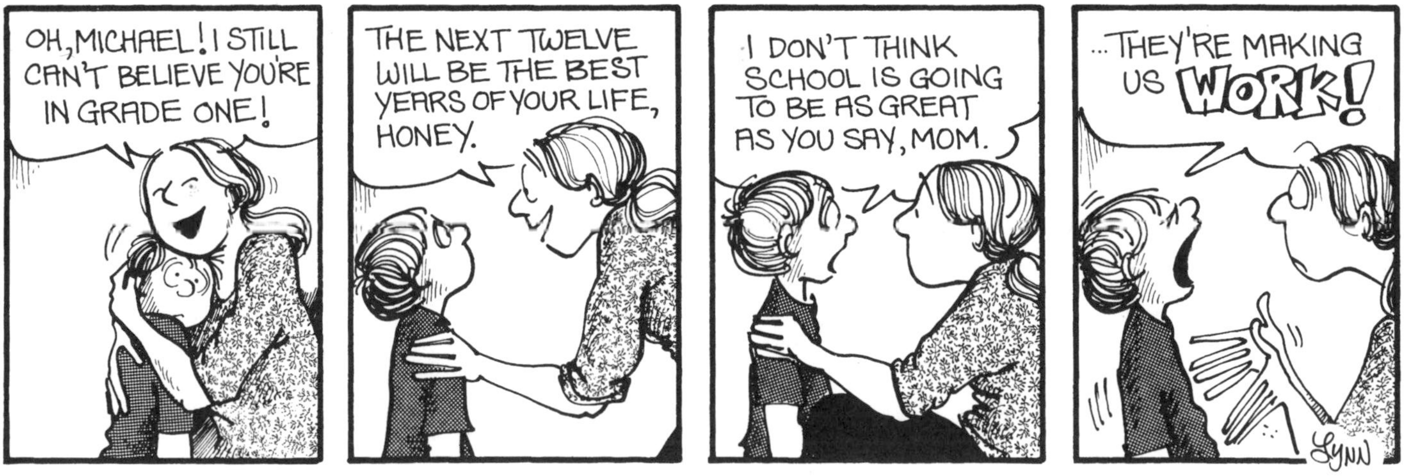
OH, MICHAEL! I STILL CAN'T BELIEVE YOU'RE IN GRADE ONE!
THE NEXT TWELVE WILL BE THE BEST YEARS OF YOUR LIFE, HONEY.
I DON'T THINK SCHOOL IS GOING TO BE AS GREAT AS YOU SAY, MOM.
...THEY'RE MAKING US WORK!
LYNN

Actually, it was cheddar.

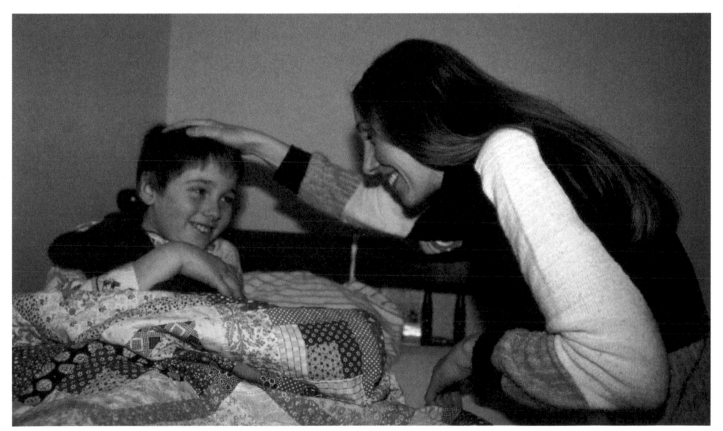

Aaron's roost on the top bunk was a bed and a refuge. He was king of the world up there and enjoyed seeing me climb a ladder to kiss him good night.

This was my incentive to clean the house. Now, inviting someone to dinner is an incentive to cook!

BUMP!

OOPS!

SORRY.

WELL... I TALKED TO HER.

WE HAD AN OK HOUSE IN BURLINGTON, BUT WE COULDN'T SELL THE ONE HERE.

THEN, MY DAD'S OLD BOSS SAID HE MISSED HIM AN' ASKED HIM IF HE WANTED TO BE THE MANAGER OF A BIG, NEW HARDWARE STORE AN' MY MOM SAID "YES"!

SO, WE'RE BACK IN OUR OLD HOUSE, WHICH IS COOL BECAUSE I WANTED TO BE WITH ALL OF MY FRIENDS AGAIN!

BLARPFF FFTTT!

JOHN! - YOU'RE NOT GOING OUTSIDE LIKE THAT!

ORANGE AND BLUE PLAID WITH GREEN HOUNDS-TOOTH CHECK—AAACK!!

HONESTLY! WHAT WILL PEOPLE THINK?

WITH LUCK, THEY'LL THINK I'M A MAN FIXING A FENCE.

Would it have been better to be honest and say I did mind? I don't know. Sometimes generosity and goodwill come back to bite you in the tush.

Ted, like Connie, was a negative influence introduced to create some tension in John's world. He, also like Connie, eventually became human—that is, he had his reasons for being the way he was.

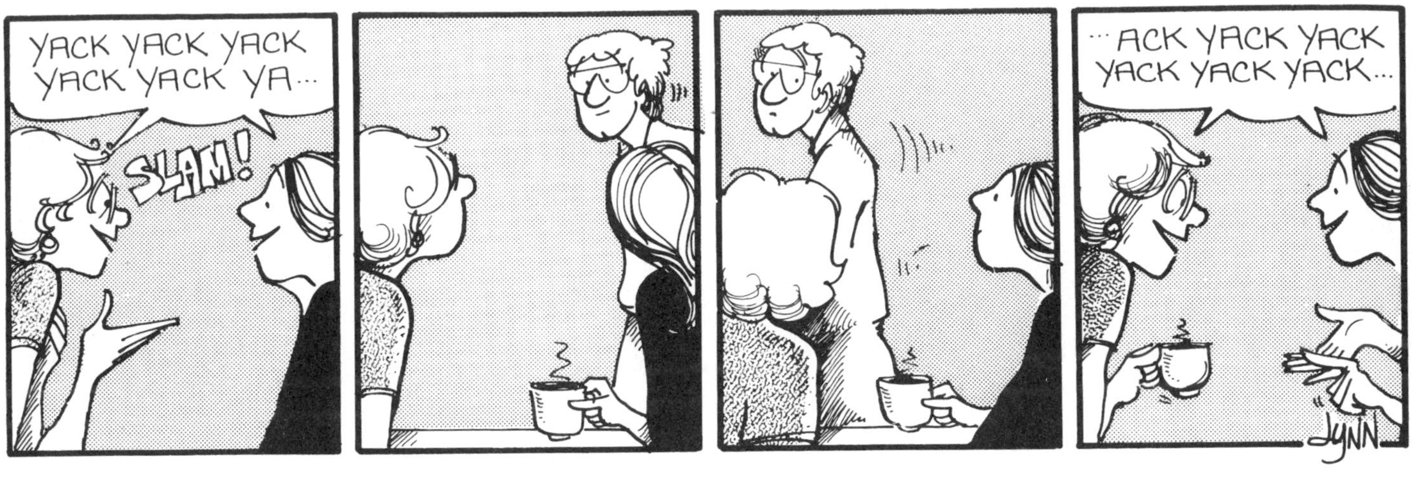
YACK YACK YACK YACK YACK YA...
SLAM!
...ACK YACK YACK YACK YACK YACK...
LYNN

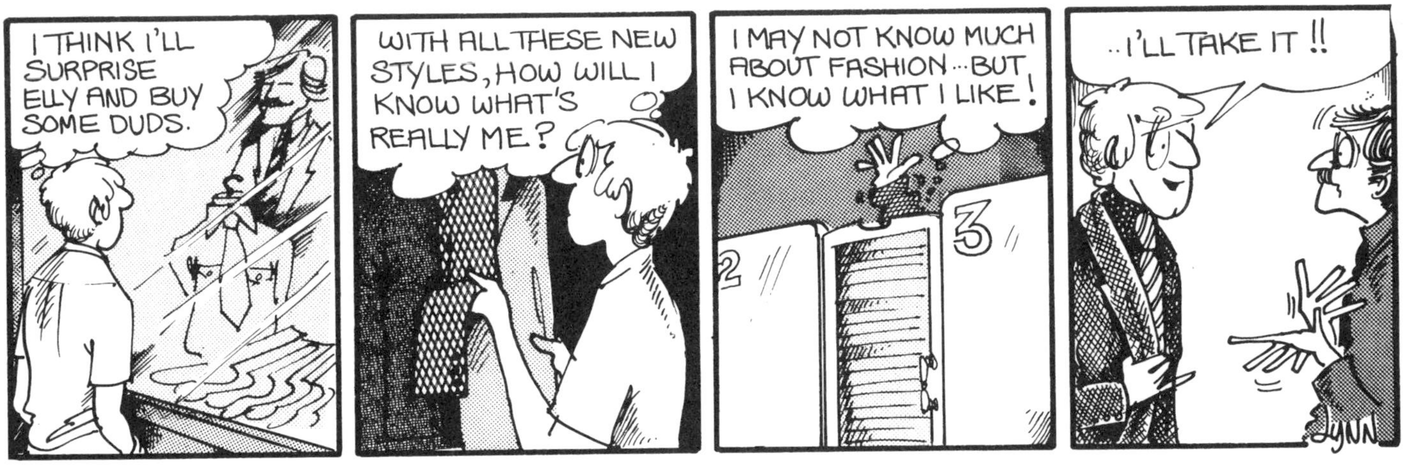
I THINK I'LL SURPRISE ELLY AND BUY SOME DUDS.
WITH ALL THESE NEW STYLES, HOW WILL I KNOW WHAT'S REALLY ME?
I MAY NOT KNOW MUCH ABOUT FASHION...BUT I KNOW WHAT I LIKE!
2
3
..I'LL TAKE IT!!
LYNN

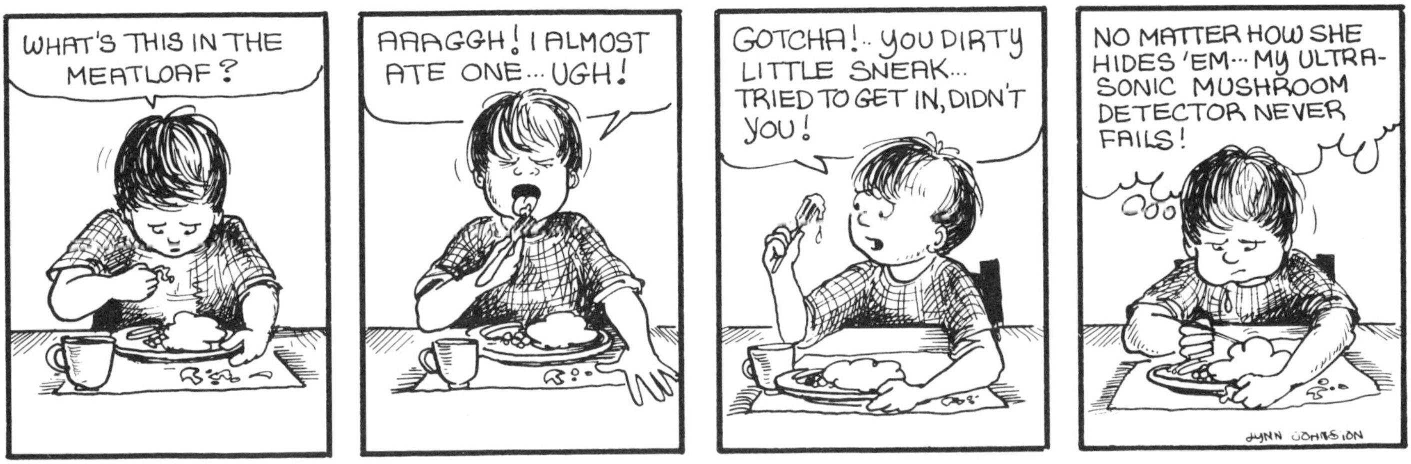
WHAT'S THIS IN THE MEATLOAF?
AAAGGH! I ALMOST ATE ONE...UGH!
GOTCHA!.. YOU DIRTY LITTLE SNEAK... TRIED TO GET IN, DIDN'T YOU!
NO MATTER HOW SHE HIDES 'EM...MY ULTRA-SONIC MUSHROOM DETECTOR NEVER FAILS!
LYNN JOHNSTON

On rare occasion, I've used the strip to make a point. I love good humor and often wonder why smut continues to play such a big role in stand-up comedy when folks should have been over it by the time they're twelve.

237

My dad worked in Vancouver and we lived on the north shore. Sometimes Mom would take Alan and me down to meet him at the ferry after work and the four of us would walk home. There was always a large number of male passengers—all wearing much the same thing: dark suits, trench coats, fedora. My brother was in a carriage; I must have been around three. Dad greeted us and in the crush of folks on the platform, I grabbed the wrong leg. I remember looking up into a stranger's face and the panic I felt was awful. This sweet man lifted me up so my parents could find me and I can still feel the relief today.

HI, ANNE! HOW'S IT GOING?

OK, I GUESS.

STEVE'S AWAY AGAIN, RICHARD'S GOT A COLD, MY DRIER'S BROKEN AND I'M OUT OF DIAPERS.

I THINK YOU NEED A BREAK. BRING THE KIDS AND COME TO MY PLACE!

A CHANGE IS AS GOOD AS A REST!

YEAH?

— WHO GETS A REST?!!

YES, STEVE'S AT ANOTHER CONVENTION. IF HE'S NOT ON THE ROAD SEEING CLIENTS, HE'S AT SOME KIND OF MEETING.

IT'S NOT AS THOUGH HE **WANTS** TO BE AWAY FROM THE KIDS AND ME.

I MEAN, EVERYTHING'S WORK-RELATED! IT'S ALL WORK-RELATED!

I KNOW.

HE WORKS... AND YOU'RE RELATED.

CHRISTOPHER, SHARE YOUR RAISINS WITH MICHAEL.

NO!

DON'T BE SELFISH. GO AND SHARE.

BLAHPP!

HE DIDN'T WANT ANY.

By Lynn Johnston

RICHARD! – PLAY NICELY WITH MICHAEL!

HE HIT ME FIRST!

I DIDN'T SEE HIM HIT YOU.

WELL, HE DID!

MICHAEL, DID YOU HIT RICHARD?

NO–IT WAS A PAT!–I PATTED HIM, THAT'S ALL.

WAS IT A HARD PAT?

IT WAS A MEDIUM PAT. MAYBE A STRONG MEDIUM PAT. SORT OF A HIT... – BUT, A SOFT HIT.

SO, YOU DID HIT HIM FIRST!

MOM, IT WAS AN ACCIDENT! I DIDN'T MEAN TO TOUCH HIM, BUT I DID!!

THE KIDS SEEM TO BE HAPPY, NOW, ELLY– WHY DON'T WE JUST CALL IT "CASE CLOSED".

OK

SIGH ...MOMS NEVER SEEM TO GET TO THE TRUTH, THE WHOLE TRUTH AND NOTHING BUT THE TRUTH!

It's often hard to get to the truth. Tears make a kid look so innocent!

"Green with envy" is an interesting expression. Not much will grow in a bitter, cold environment.

THE HOUSE IS SURE QUIET WITHOUT MICHAEL. THE WHOLE PLACE SEEMS STRANGE!

WITH HIM IN SCHOOL ALL DAY, LIFE IS DIFFERENT... EASIER........ PEACEFUL...

HOW LONG AM I GOING TO FEEL GUILTY FOR ENJOYING IT?

—WITH MICHAEL IN SCHOOL, I GUESS ELLY WILL BE GETTING A JOB!

WELL, I HOPE THE SUBJECT DOESN'T COME UP.

I'M NOT HOLDING HER BACK, MIND YOU— SHE CAN BE AS LIBERATED AS THE REST OF THEM!

...AS LONG AS SHE DOES IT AT HOME.

JOHN, I'VE BEEN THINKING...

NOW THAT I HAVE MORE TIME, WHAT WOULD YOU SAY TO MY GETTING A PART-TIME JOB?

COME ON!—I CAN'T SPEND MY LIFE BAKING COOKIES AND PICKING UP SOCKS!

MY MOTHER DID!

242

I KNOW IT'S SELFISH, BUT I LIKE MY WIFE TO BE WHERE SHE IS.

I DON'T LIKE THE IDEA OF WORKING MOTHERS. A HOUSE SHOULD BE A HOME.

CALL ME NARROW-MINDED... CALL ME OLD-FASHIONED...

BUT OINK AT ME ONCE MORE AND YOU'RE FIRED!

John was different from Rod. Rod didn't mind where I worked as long as I was happy. I was lucky to be able to work from home. I had a good job, and yet I often wished I could go somewhere else and keep my home separate. Friends who were stay-at-home moms envied me—and still, I wanted something else. It's human nature, I guess, to never be satisfied, which is why I think that heaven must be a strange place; perpetual perfection is not possible when the inhabitants naturally want *more*!

YOUR MOM SAYS WE'VE GOT TO GO OUTSIDE, MIKE.

SHE SAID TO TURN OFF THE T.V. RIGHT NOW - SO HOWCOME YOU'RE STILL WATCHIN' THIS STUFF?

SHE'S NOT MAD YET.

I'M BORED. **ME, TOO.**

I WISH IT WAS SUMMER AGAIN. **ME, TOO.**

I WISH WE COULD GO SWIMMING AN' HAVE PICNICS AN' HANG OUT AN' HAVE FUN ALL THE TIME. **YEAH.**

MOM? THERE'S NOTHIN' TO DO. LAWRENCE AN' I ARE BORED, BORED BORED!!

WHAT DID SHE SAY? **..."ENJOY."**

WHAT'S THIS BOTTLE OF CHANGE FOR, ELLY?

CHINKA CLUNK

ER, WELL...I SAVE IT FROM THE GROCERIES SO I CAN SPEND IT ON...OH...LITTLE THINGS I NEED.

BUT, HONEY, YOU KNOW THAT I'LL GIVE YOU MONEY FOR WHATEVER IT IS YOU NEED. ALL YOU HAVE TO DO IS ASK!

I KNOW...BUT THIS WAY I FEEL I'VE EARNED IT.

Before I had my job doing comic strips, I earned a small living as a freelance graphic artist. Paying my own way has always been a priority. My friends who were homemakers often felt strange about accepting "handouts" from their husbands.

* HI, ELLY! I BROUGHT IN YOUR PAPER.

THANKS, CONNIE.

JUST PUT IT OVER THERE. JOHN WILL READ IT WHEN HE GETS HOME.

WHAT ABOUT YOU?

I DON'T HAVE TIME. AFTER HE'S DONE, I JUST READ THE HEADLINES.

HOW COME HE HAS TIME TO READ THE PAPER AND YOU DON'T?

HIS JOB ENDS AT FIVE.

* I THINK JOHN'S A GOOD GUY, EL. HE'S HONEST, RELIABLE...A GOOD DAD—

I KNOW.

I JUST WISH I COULD GET HIM TO DO MORE OF THE CHORES.

LIKE WHAT?

I DUNNO...DISHES, LAUNDRY—

BUT, YOU **HATE** THE WAY HE DOES DISHES AND LAUNDRY!

YEAH—BUT, I APPRECIATE THE GESTURE!

244

CONNIE SAYS I DON'T APPRECIATE YOU ENOUGH, JOHN...

SHE SAYS I DWELL ON PETTY PERSONAL PROBLEMS & OVERLOOK THE REALLY WORKING PARTNERSHIP WE HAVE...

WHUMPH

BUT I GUESS I'D KNOW IF OUR MARRIAGE WAS SUFFERING...

SNIFFF... AAAHHHH— WHAT A WONDERFUL TIME OF YEAR!

CRISP, COOL WINDS, COLORFUL LEAVES..... NO PLANTING, NO WEEDING NO MOWING, NO BUGS, NO...

THANKS.

NO PROBLEM.

Fall is my favorite time of the year. Where I live, the trees become spectacular. Hillsides fairly pulse with color and the air smells so sweet. It's also the time that kids go back to school. Yes—Fall is definitely my favorite season.

THIS IS FUN, MIKE... IT FEELS GREAT! —I'D LET YOU TRY BUT I DON'T THINK YOU COULD HANDLE IT!

YESSIR·· NOTHING LIKE RAKING LEAVES! TOO BAD YOU'RE NOT BIG ENOUGH...

IF YOU'RE GOOD, I'LL LET YOU DO SOME OF THIS, MICHAEL!

NAH·· I'LL SEE YA, DAD.

THE OL' TOM SAWYER METHOD HAS HAD ITS DAY...

Why do kids like to play at war? Are we programmed to destroy one another? Every time I hear a symphony, watch a play, see a painting or enjoy the thrill of the Olympic games I think of the talent we possess—and I wonder how many brilliant, wonderful people have been lost to war.

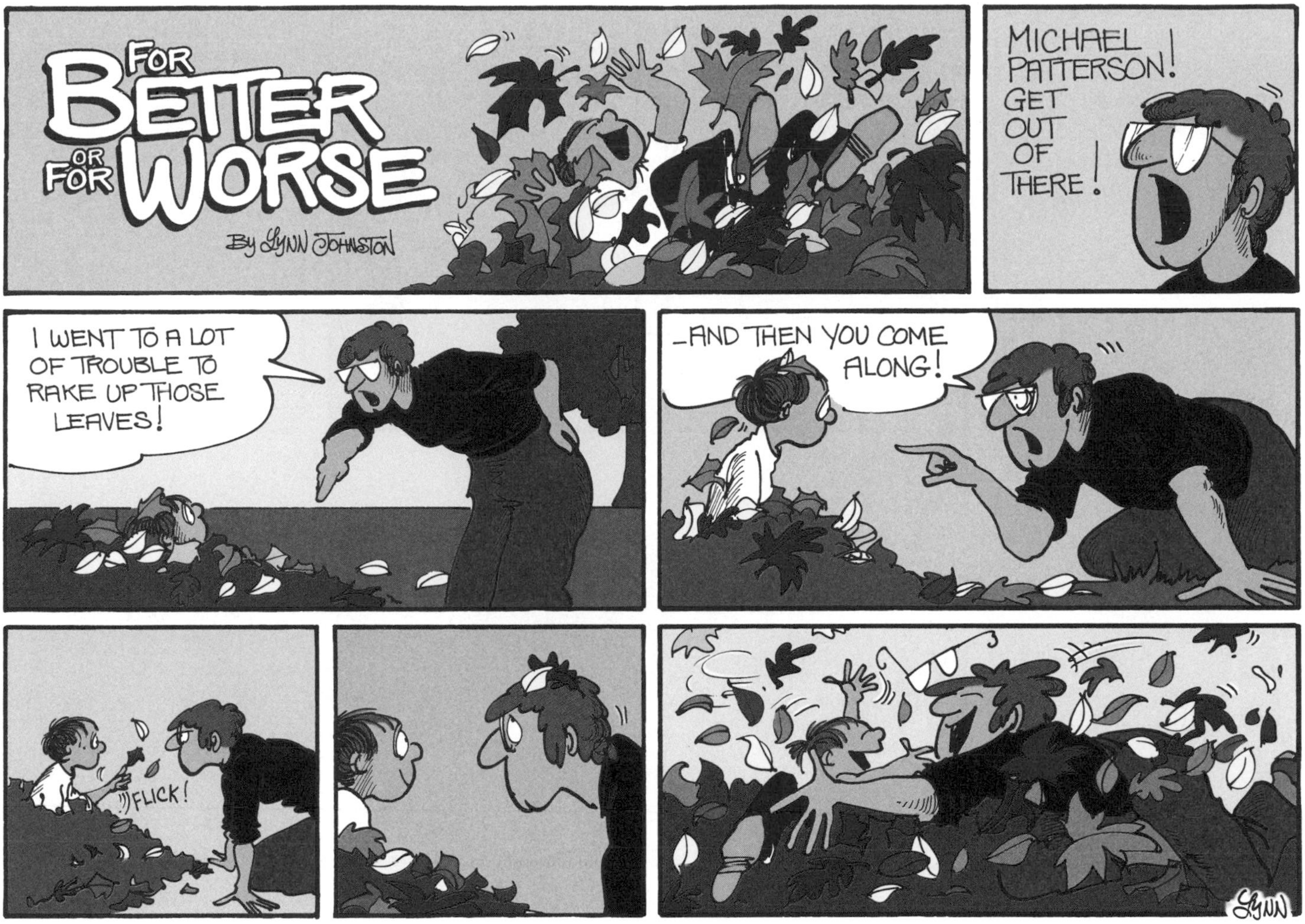
FOR BETTER OR FOR WORSE
BY LYNN JOHNSTON
MICHAEL PATTERSON! GET OUT OF THERE!
I WENT TO A LOT OF TROUBLE TO RAKE UP THOSE LEAVES!
-AND THEN YOU COME ALONG!
FLICK!
LYNN

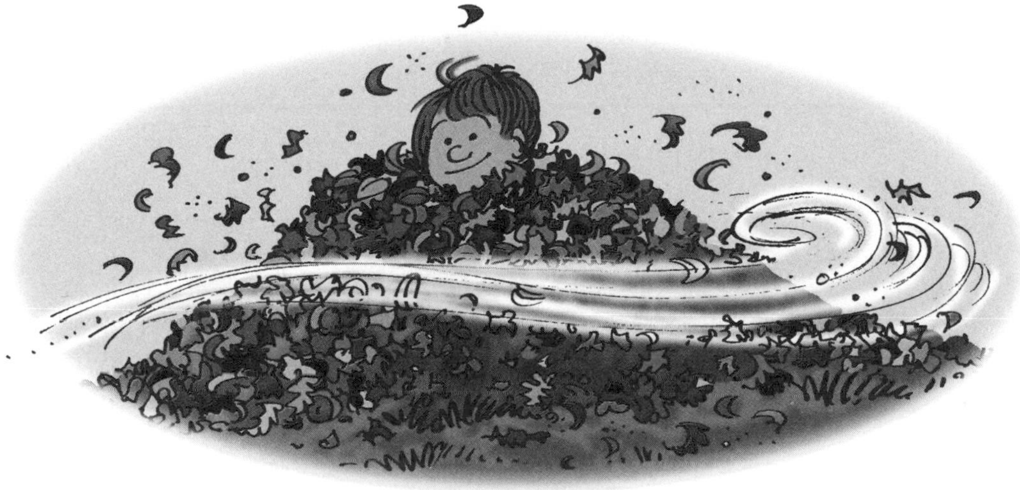

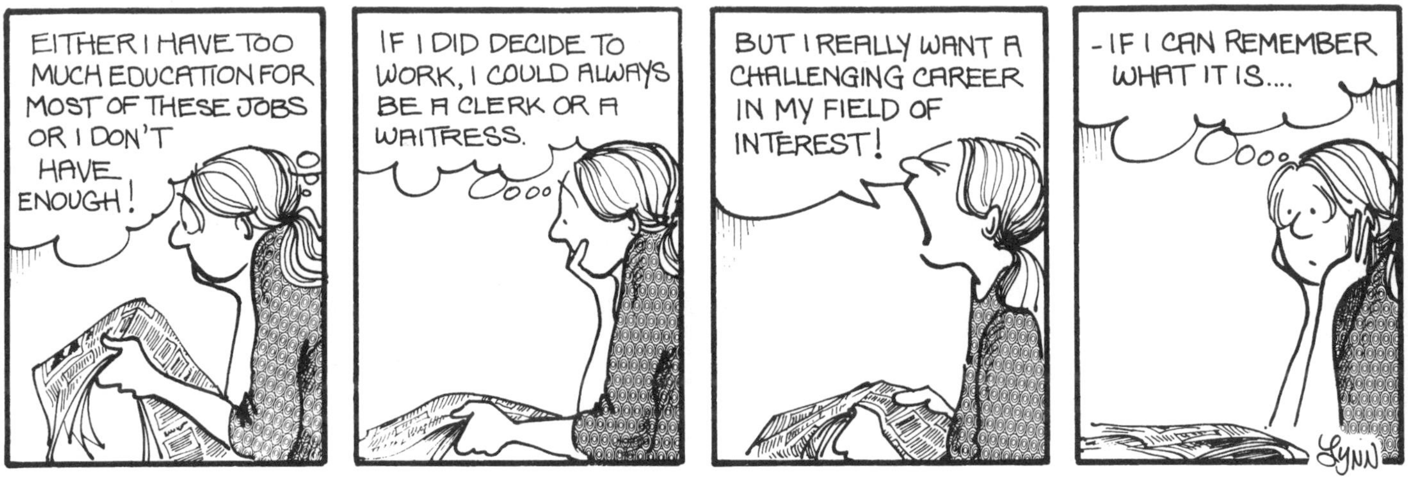
EITHER I HAVE TOO MUCH EDUCATION FOR MOST OF THESE JOBS OR I DON'T HAVE ENOUGH!
IF I DID DECIDE TO WORK, I COULD ALWAYS BE A CLERK OR A WAITRESS.
BUT I REALLY WANT A CHALLENGING CAREER IN MY FIELD OF INTEREST!
-IF I CAN REMEMBER WHAT IT IS....
LYNN

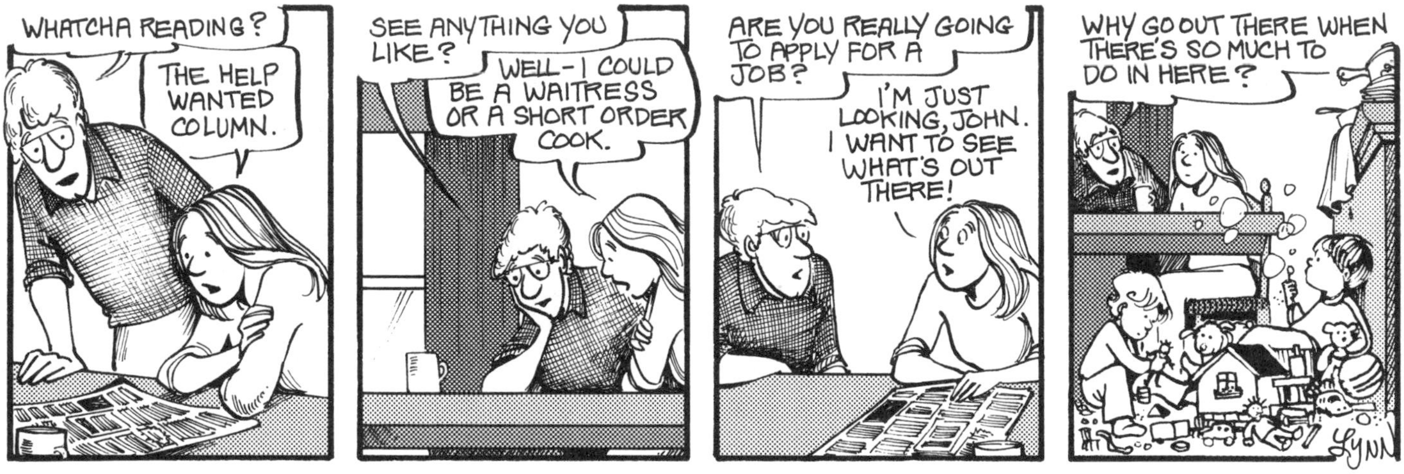
WHATCHA READING?
THE HELP WANTED COLUMN.
SEE ANYTHING YOU LIKE?
WELL- I COULD BE A WAITRESS OR A SHORT ORDER COOK.
ARE YOU REALLY GOING TO APPLY FOR A JOB?
I'M JUST LOOKING, JOHN. I WANT TO SEE WHAT'S OUT THERE!
WHY GO OUT THERE WHEN THERE'S SO MUCH TO DO IN HERE?
LYNN

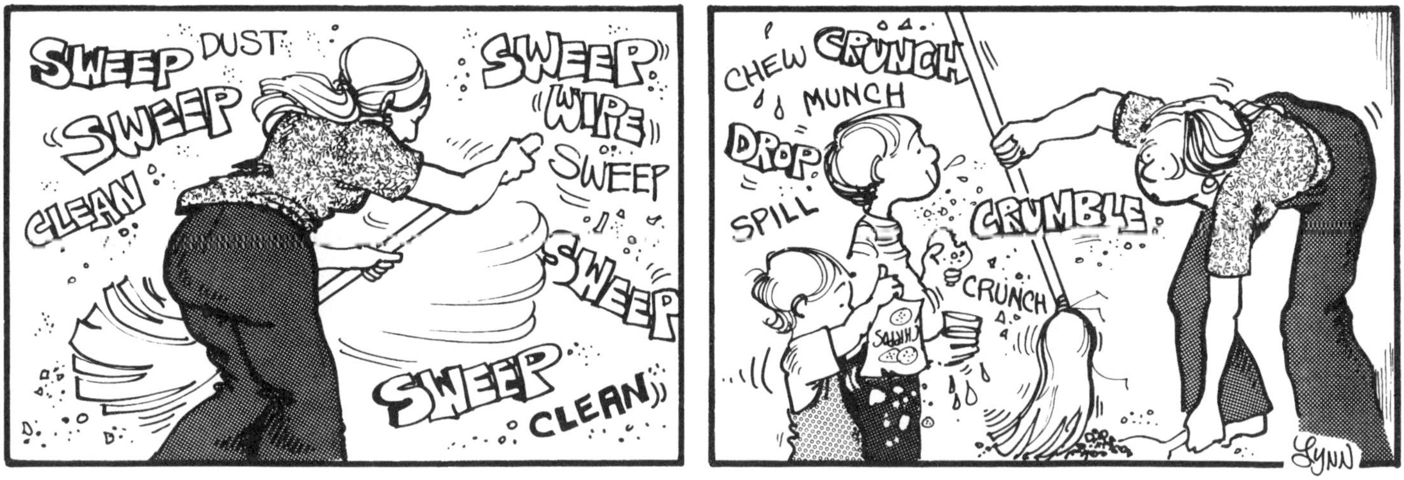
SWEEP
DUST
SWEEP
CLEAN
SWEEP
WIPE
SWEEP
SWEEP
SWEEP
CLEAN
CHEW
CRUNCH
MUNCH
DROP
SPILL
CRUMBLE
CRUNCH
CHIPS
LYNN

Every year my folks would drive to the Oakanagan Valley to buy fruit and veggies. We bought fresh apples, corn, pumpkins, and squash before winter; peaches and plums in summer; strawberries in spring. It was always so much fun for us—and later, so much work for my mother.

We were fortunate to have canned fruit and frozen pies all winter. We were fortunate to have such a talented, hard-working mom. I never thanked her enough for this—and now she's gone.

SINCE YOU WANT TO WORK, HONEY... I HAVE A SUGGESTION.

JEAN IS TAKING A WEEK OFF - SO I NEED SOMEONE AT THE FRONT DESK.

IT'S NOT EXCITING, BUT IT WOULD BE A CHANGE.

WHAT HAVE I DONE?

TEACHER DRAWS A WHOLE LOT BETTER THAN YOU, MOM.

YEAH... AN' SHE PRINTS BETTER THAN YOU TOO!

HOW COME YOU CAN'T READ AS WELL AS TEACHER?

..I'VE BEEN DEMOTED.

UH! COOKIE! NUM-NUM! COOKIE GOOD. NIZZIE EAT COOKIE!

SHE'S GROWING UP, ELLY... SHE'S WALKING AND TALKING AND TURNING INTO A REAL LITTLE GIRL.

LET'S HOPE I'VE GOT A FEW YEARS BEFORE SHE FINDS ANOTHER BOYFRIEND!

One of the women in town constantly made me feel guilty about having a babysitter. She made me feel guilty about many things, but perhaps it was just me. Guilt seems to play a big role in the life of a mom.

Every week, my dear friend Janet comes to help me with the house. After many years, I confess, I still clean the place before she gets here!

I'M GLAD YOU'RE ABLE TO HELP ME OUT LIKE THIS, ELLY.

NO PROBLEM!

WHEN THE GIRL I HIRED TO TAKE JEAN'S PLACE CANCELLED AT THE LAST MINUTE, I THOUGHT I WAS UP THE CREEK!

MMM.

SIGH: ....IT'S ALWAYS SOMETHING: MATERNITY LEAVE, PMS, FAMILY ISSUES, PERSONAL STUFF..... TSK!

...WOMEN!

THIS IS GOING TO BE FUN, JOHN, - I HAVEN'T HELPED IN THE CLINIC FOR YEARS!

YOU WERE JUST OUT OF DENTAL SCHOOL .... DOESN'T THIS BRING BACK FOND MEMORIES?

SURE. THAT WAS WHEN I STILL ENJOYED WORKING.

I worked in the clinic with Rod for about a week. It was not a good thing for either of us and I soon gave up my second career as a dental assistant!

DR. PATTERSON'S OFFICE, PLEASE HOLD...

PLEASE TAKE A SEAT, HE'LL BE WITH YOU IN A MINUTE.

YES, MAY I SPEAK TO SOMEONE IN ACCOUNTING, PLEASE?

OK, THEN - PLEASE HAVE HER RETURN MY CALL.

PLEASE COME IN AT 2:00 TOMORROW.

WOULD YOU SIGN THIS, PLEASE?

ARE YOU READY FOR A BREAK, EL?

OH... PLEASE!!

WOW! — WHERE'D YA GET THE CUTE LITTLE ASSISTANT, JOHN?

BET YOU CAN'T KEEP YOUR HANDS OFF THIS ONE, HA! HA! HA!

YOU SHOULD LET ELLY OUT OF THE KITCHEN MORE OFTEN, GUY!

SOME COMPLIMENTS ARE SO INSULTING.

JOHN, I CAN'T FIGURE OUT WHY YOU LIKE TED McCAULEY.

HE'S OK WHEN YOU GET TO KNOW HIM.

FOR A FAMILY PHYSICIAN, WHO WORKS WITH THE PUBLIC ALL THE TIME, HOW CAN HE BE SO.... SOCIALLY INEPT?

YOU JUST DON'T GET HIS SENSE OF HUMOR, ELLY.

SENSE OF HUMOR?!.... HE'S DOWNRIGHT RUDE!

NAH. HE JUST CAN'T CONTROL HIS MOUTH.

THAT'S BECAUSE THERE'S A FOOT IN IT.

MICHAEL CAME RIGHT HERE AFTER SCHOOL, JUST LIKE HE WAS SUPPOSED TO. THEN, HE FED AND WALKED FARLEY...

ELIZABETH WAS SUCH A GOOD GIRL. SHE ATE ALL HER LUNCH, HAD A NICE NAP AND PLAYED WELL WITH CHRISTOPHER.

YOU'RE A SWEETHEART, ANNE. I'M SO GRATEFUL TO YOU. I FEEL GUILTY, THOUGH... LETTING ANOTHER MOM TAKE CARE OF MY CHILDREN.

WHY?!

...NOT ONLY DO I GET PAID FOR WHAT I DO... I GET **THANKED** FOR IT!

Panel 1: WHEW! THAT WAS QUITE A DAY, JOHN. GETTING THE KIDS READY IN THE MORNING AND RUSHING DOWNTOWN IS A REAL EFFORT.

Panel 2: THEN, GETTING USED TO OFFICE ROUTINES, PHONES RINGING, PATIENTS COMING AND GOING, FILING CHARTS ... IT WAS EXHAUSTING!

Panel 3: AFTER THAT—COMING HOME, FIXING DINNER AND GETTING THE KIDS TO BED ALMOST KNOCKED ME OUT!

Panel 4: SO, BEING A WORKING WOMAN ISN'T THAT GREAT, I GUESS.

Panel 5: ARE YOU KIDDING? ....IT'S **WONDERFUL!!**

Panel 1: HELÈNE, WOULD YOU SHOW ELLY THE PROPER WAY TO MOUNT X-RAYS.

Panel 2: NO, I WANT THE CARVER AND THEN THAT OTHER "GADGET."

Panel 3: HURRY UP, YOU CAN'T TAKE ALL DAY FOR HEAVEN'S SAKE!

Panel 4: IT'S OK, MR SHADBOLT ... SHE'S MY WIFE.

Jack Shadbolt was a well-known Canadian artist who lectured at the Vancouver School of Art when I was a student there. We were lucky to have been taught by such an accomplished professional . . . and I always liked his name!

Panel 1: ELLY, DENTISTRY IS AN EXACTING BUSINESS.—I GET VERY TENSE.

Panel 2: SO I GOT IMPATIENT. MAYBE I BARKED AT YOU A FEW TIMES...

Panel 3: SO WHAT IF I SAID YOU WERE A KLUTZ AND A DUMMY!

Panel 4: DO YOU HAVE TO TAKE IT PERSONALLY?

Dentistry is a fidgety and sometimes frustrating business. While I was assisting at the clinic, Rod would often ask me for instruments in a curt manner—it was hard not to take it personally. It was definitely easier on the marriage to leave the assisting to a trained professional from outside the family.

OOPS! – I'D BETTER CLEAN THAT PLASTER OFF THE FLOOR OR JOHN WILL THROW A FIT!

YOUR HUSBAND IS FANATIC ABOUT KEEPING THIS PLACE CLEAN AND TIDY. – HE GOES NUTS IF WE LEAVE A MESS ANYWHERE!

ELLY, THIS IS NO TIME TO DISCUSS WHERE I THREW MY SOCKS THIS MORNING!

LYNN

BOY, WHAT A DAY! I'M GLAD THE WEEK'S OVER.

YEAH! I'M ABSOLUTELY EXHAUSTED!

WORKING FULL TIME REALLY TAKES IT OUT OF YOU. IT'S SO GOOD TO BE HOME.

WELL... WHAT'S FOR SUPPER?

LYNN

For a while, I worked as Rod's dental assistant.

256

FOR BETTER OR FOR WORSE
BY LYNN JOHNSTON
CLINGG
MOM! LIZZIE JUST LOCKED HERSELF IN THE BATH-ROOM!
LIZZIE? JUST TURN THE KNOB, HONEY!
WAAH!
COME TO THE DOOR, BABY, THAT'S IT... NO - THE DOOR...
THE *!@ WINDOW IS STUCK!
COME TO MOMMY, LIZZIE... TURN THE HANDLE!
SNIFFL
CLICK!
IT'S ALRIGHT, JOHN - SHE'S OUT NOW!
GOOD. -WHERE IS SHE?
MOM! LIZZIE JUST LOCKED HERSELF IN THE BATH-ROOM!
LYNN

A drawer in our bathroom would block the door when it was open. Katie often "locked" herself in the can where she happily unrolled the tissue and scratched layers off the soap. Twice we had to climb through the window to get her out. Architecturally, this was a definite design flaw!

Angry mail came whenever I showed any violence at all—even the killing of a spider.

SHE MADE ME A PUMPKIN.

DEANNA IS A WITCH AN' LAWRENCE IS A GHOST-BUT I GOTTA BE A DUMB **PUMPKIN!**

MAYBE MISS CAMPBELL THOUGHT YOU'D BE THE VERY <u>BEST</u> PUMPKIN IN THE WHOLE CLASS!

SNIVEL

I LOVE PSYCHOLOGY ····WHEN IT WORKS.

WEE WITCHES, GHOSTS AND PUMPKINS TOO HAVE DONE A HARVEST PLAY FOR YOU! THIS IS THE END, THE FINAL SCENE — WE WISH YOU HAPPY HALLOWEEN!

HE DIDN'T DO ANYTHING (SNIFF) -BUT HE DID IT SO WELL!

CLAP CLAP

AND··ER··· I FIGURED THAT SINCE I ····UM···· WORKED FOR YOU, I SHOULD GET····

PAID?-SURE, HONEY IF YOU'D LIKE A PAYCHECK, THAT'S FINE!

GREAT! — AND YOU CAN CALL IT A BUSINESS EXPENSE!

I THINK I'LL CALL IT AN OUNCE OF PREVENTION.

I had originally written "Pay Cheque," but because so many of my papers were in the United States, one of my editors was determined to see American spelling. I insisted on the Canadian spelling and suggested that the changes be left up to the individual newspaper editors—if they objected. When this editor went on to other things, my Canadianisms were left alone. I received a few comments from readers, but otherwise there was no objection. After all, as the beer ad goes, "I AM CANADIAN!"

I confess. In an effort to save my children from potentially tampered treats, I've eaten some of the best loot in their goodie bags. With all of us having "sweet teeth," it was good to be living with a dentist.

Again, producing new material and adding to the number of strips extended work into the following year. Confusing? Well, it confused me! This 2009 Sunday page ran with 1980 material . . . but it worked. The best part was reliving a time I so enjoyed. Just drawing Mike with his mouth full in panel four made my day!

I'M EMBARRASSED ABOUT ACCEPTING THIS CHECK FROM YOU, JOHN....

WIVES USUALLY WORK FOR THEIR HUSBANDS WITHOUT EVEN THINKING ABOUT AN HOURLY WAGE!

I ASKED FOR A SALARY ON PRINCIPLE ....JUST TO MAKE A POINT!

MIND YOU....I'M SURE MY GUILT WILL SUB-SIDE WHEN THIS IS CASHED.

I COULDN'T ACCEPT PAYMENT FOR TAKING THE KIDS, ELLY!

I'M JUST ONE OF THOSE MOMS WHO LOVES BEING WITH CHILDREN! — IT WAS A PLEASURE.

WHILE YOU WERE GONE, LIZZIE AND MIKE HAD A WARM, STABLE HOME ENVIRON-MENT HERE!

—SO RELAX!—SOME OF US ENJOY PARENTING... SOME OF US DON'T!

ELLY, THE TROUBLE WITH YOU IS THAT YOU'RE TOO EASILY INFLUENCED BY OTHER PEOPLE!

DON'T LET ANNE AND JOHN MAKE YOU FEEL GUILTY FOR DOING WHAT YOU WANT TO DO!

WOMEN WITH FAMILIES ARE ALWAYS MADE TO FEEL GUILTY—AND GUILT IS A USELESS WASTE OF TIME!

... I'VE ALWAYS CONSIDERED IT A WAY OF LIFE.

Even though I look like both my parents and inherited their skills, I asked them repeatedly if I was adopted. Not because I wanted to know for sure—I just liked the way it irked them!

NO, MICHAEL, WE ARE NOT GOING TO BUY A DOG -AND THAT'S THAT!

BUT, WHY, MOM! WHY CAN'T WE GET A DOG? WHY?

FOR ONE THING...I CAN'T EVEN RAISE A PLANT.

Originally, Michael had no pets before Farley arrived. It seemed to me that Elly, being aware of his strong desire to have one, would test his level of responsibility by getting him something smaller (and flushable!). This series was an entirely new addition to the story.

YOU BOUGHT MICHAEL A FISH? HE WANTS A DOG, JOHN... A FISH IS EASIER.

BESIDES, HE HAS TO LEARN HOW TO BE RESPONSIBLE FOR A PET.

IF HE DOES WELL WITH THE FISH, WE CAN TRY MOVING UP THE FOOD CHAIN.

DOES THAT MEAN YOU'LL GET ME SOMETHING THAT COULD EAT FRED?

MOM GOT ME A FISH, LAWRENCE. HIS NAME'S FRED.

WHAT DOES HE DO? NOTHIN' MUCH.

THAT MUST BE PRETTY BORING. YEAH.

WE SHOULD STIR HIM UP A BIT!

265

*
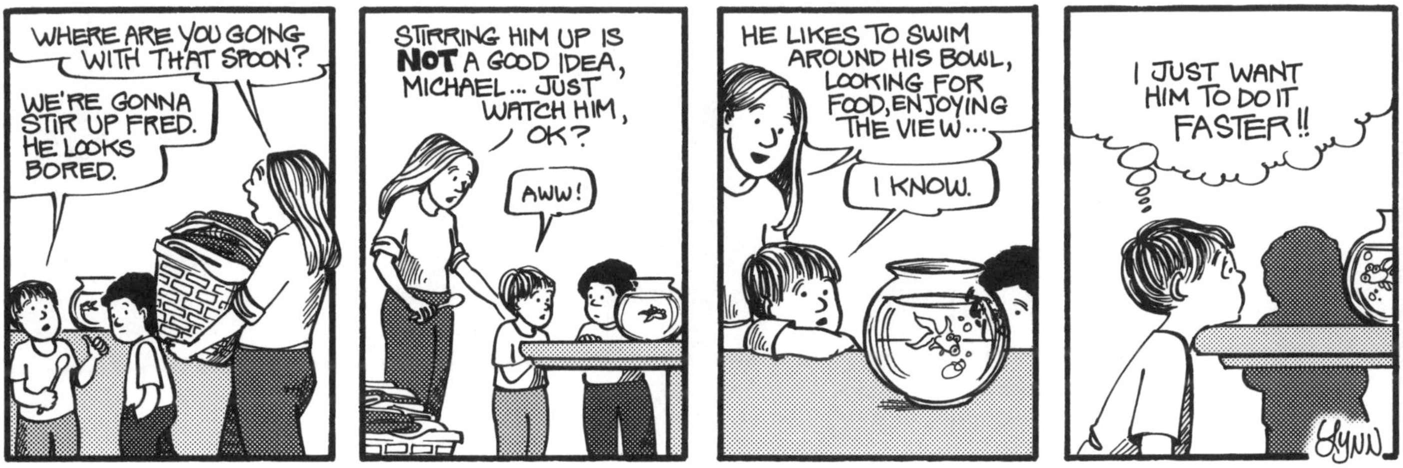
WHERE ARE YOU GOING WITH THAT SPOON?
WE'RE GONNA STIR UP FRED. HE LOOKS BORED.
STIRRING HIM UP IS **NOT** A GOOD IDEA, MICHAEL... JUST WATCH HIM, OK?
AWW!
HE LIKES TO SWIM AROUND HIS BOWL, LOOKING FOR FOOD, ENJOYING THE VIEW...
I KNOW.
I JUST WANT HIM TO DO IT FASTER!!
LYNN

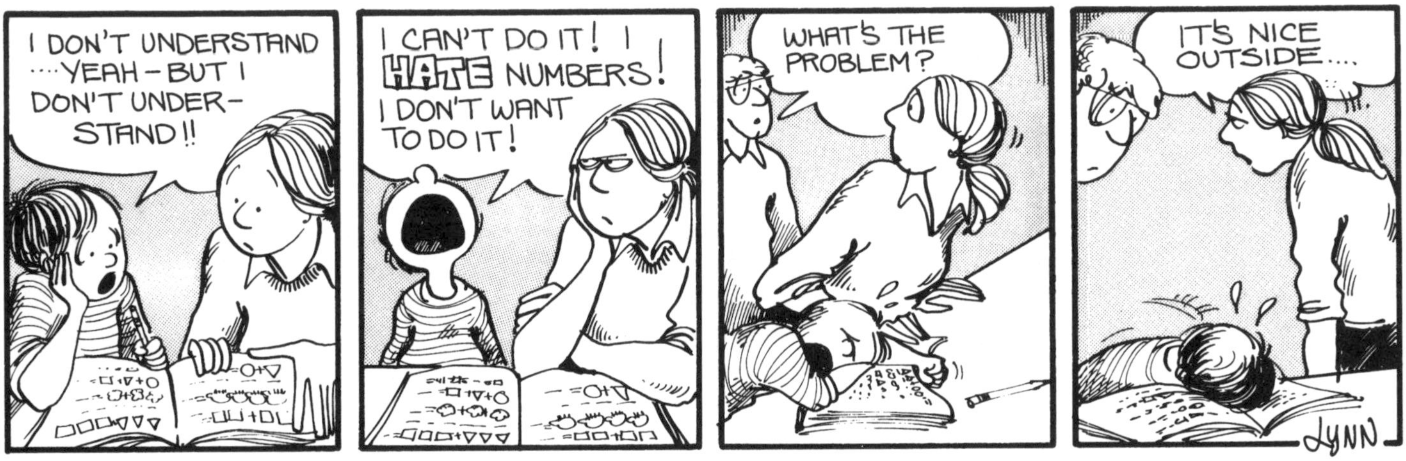
I DON'T UNDERSTAND ....YEAH - BUT I DON'T UNDER-STAND!!
I CAN'T DO IT! I HATE NUMBERS! I DON'T WANT TO DO IT!
WHAT'S THE PROBLEM?
IT'S NICE OUTSIDE....
LYNN

*
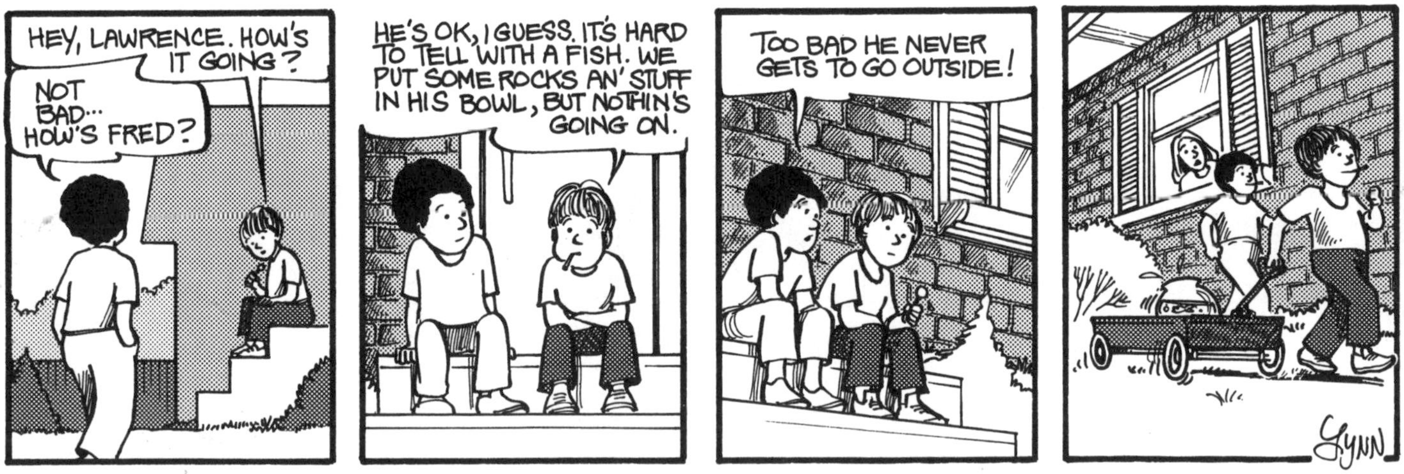
HEY, LAWRENCE. HOW'S IT GOING?
NOT BAD... HOW'S FRED?
HE'S OK, I GUESS. IT'S HARD TO TELL WITH A FISH. WE PUT SOME ROCKS AN' STUFF IN HIS BOWL, BUT NOTHIN'S GOING ON.
TOO BAD HE NEVER GETS TO GO OUTSIDE!
LYNN

People have criticized me for leaving my son in the bathtub alone. By the time Aaron was the age shown above (six?) he could swim well, and my only worry was that he'd dump out the shampoo. I was always so careful with both my children—but accidents happen and most letters of concern and advice were accepted with sincere appreciation.

Actually, my husband never wanted a dog. I did!

268

Even the most level-headed parents will lose their cool. The most caring and thoughtful folks can fly off the handle when pushed just a hair too far. This strip was not well received by many readers . . . and I suspected the most negative ones were *sans enfants*.

I SURE ENJOYED WORKING AT THE CLINIC, CONNIE.

YEAH?

I LIKED GETTING OUT EVERY DAY, WORKING WITH THE PUBLIC, USING MY BRAINS...

I LIKED WEARING NICE CLOTHES AND PUTTING MY HAIR UP AND LOOKING PROFESSIONAL FOR A CHANGE.

AND, NOW THAT IT'S OVER?

IT FEELS LIKE MY COACH TURNED INTO A PUMPKIN.

YOU NEED A CAREER, EL.

I KNOW.

IF YOU COULD SNAP YOUR FINGERS AND BE ANYTHING — WHAT WOULD YOU BE?

HMMM...

WELL, I LOVE BOOKS. I LOVE LITERATURE AND POETRY AND DRAMA. I WOULD BE SOMEONE WHO DID SOMETHING THAT INVOLVED BOOKS.

TROUBLE IS ··· I RARELY HAVE TIME TO READ.

MOM? CAN I PLAY OUTSIDE IN THE RAIN BY MYSELF FOR A WHILE?

SURE, HONEY.

DON'T GO GETTING WET!!

Growing up in Vancouver, the sound, smell, and feel of gumboots was just part of life. There's great satisfaction in splashing through puddles and running outside in the rain. I enjoyed the memory as much as I enjoyed drawing this strip.

A few years ago, I began to show symptoms of a neurological disorder. It's well under control now, but at the time, it was awful. The one thing that kept me from feeling sorry for myself was that it happened to me and not to either of my children.

My first husband, Doug, and I made the mistake of looking at Old English sheepdog puppies. We brought one home and named him Farley (for author Farley Mowat). He was such a character. Years later, Farley the dog made a great addition to the Patterson family. At the time, we did not have a dog, so drawing and writing about one was a challenge. My memories were not enough to keep the dog growing at the proper speed and doing all of the things that dogs do. He was much easier to cartoon when we finally got Willy, our cocker spaniel, who became a wonderful comic resource. In the *new* strips, I tried to fill out the early part of the story and tell more about the arrival of the new puppy.

Our Farley dog as a puppy!

*

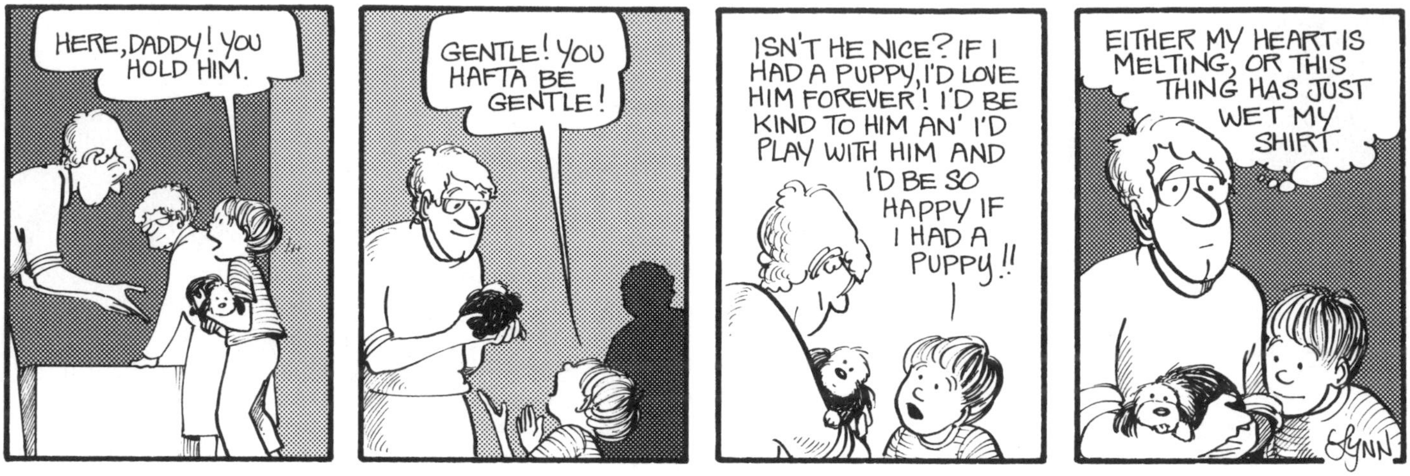
HERE, DADDY! YOU HOLD HIM.
GENTLE! YOU HAFTA BE GENTLE!
ISN'T HE NICE? IF I HAD A PUPPY, I'D LOVE HIM FOREVER! I'D BE KIND TO HIM AN' I'D PLAY WITH HIM AND I'D BE SO HAPPY IF I HAD A PUPPY!!
EITHER MY HEART IS MELTING, OR THIS THING HAS JUST WET MY SHIRT.
LYNN

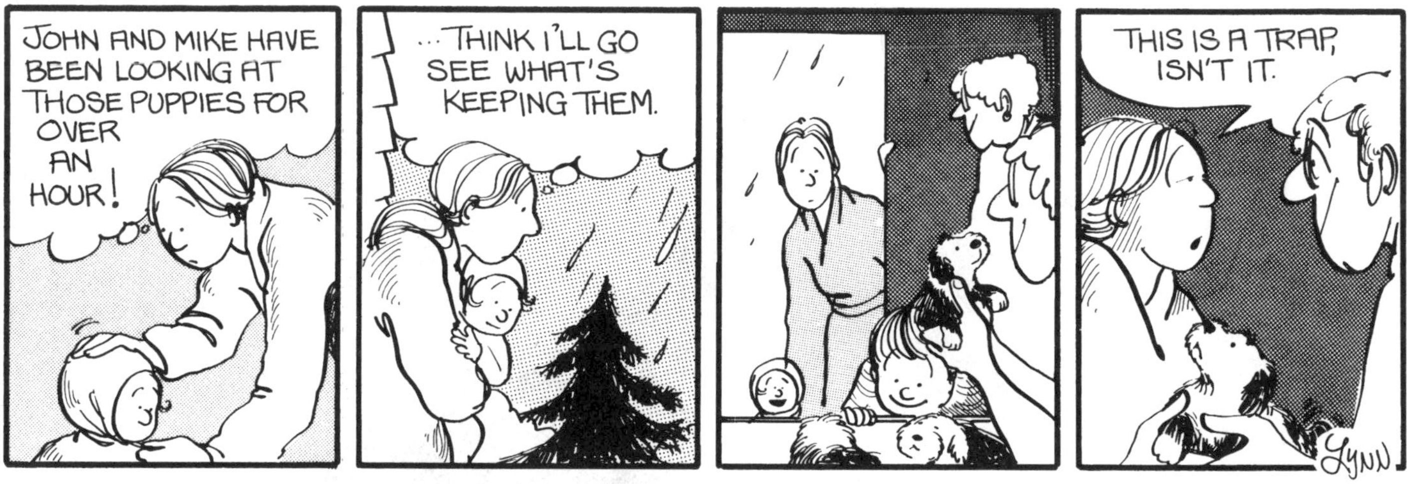
JOHN AND MIKE HAVE BEEN LOOKING AT THOSE PUPPIES FOR OVER AN HOUR!
...THINK I'LL GO SEE WHAT'S KEEPING THEM.
THIS IS A TRAP, ISN'T IT.
LYNN

*

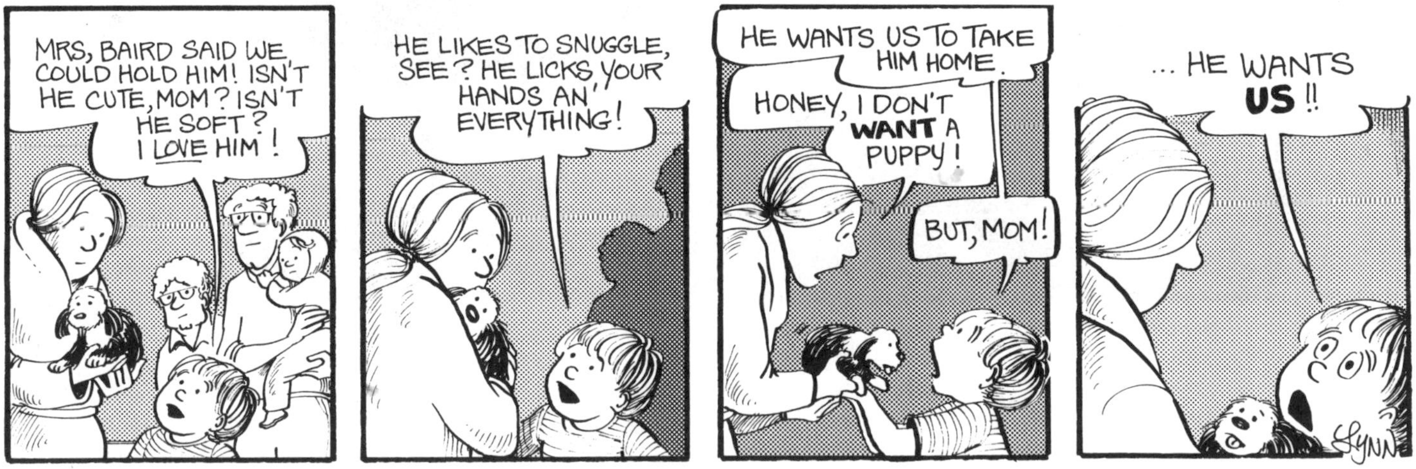
MRS, BAIRD SAID WE COULD HOLD HIM! ISN'T HE CUTE, MOM? ISN'T HE SOFT? I LOVE HIM!
HE LIKES TO SNUGGLE, SEE? HE LICKS YOUR HANDS AN' EVERYTHING!
HE WANTS US TO TAKE HIM HOME.
HONEY, I DON'T WANT A PUPPY!
BUT, MOM!
... HE WANTS US!!
LYNN

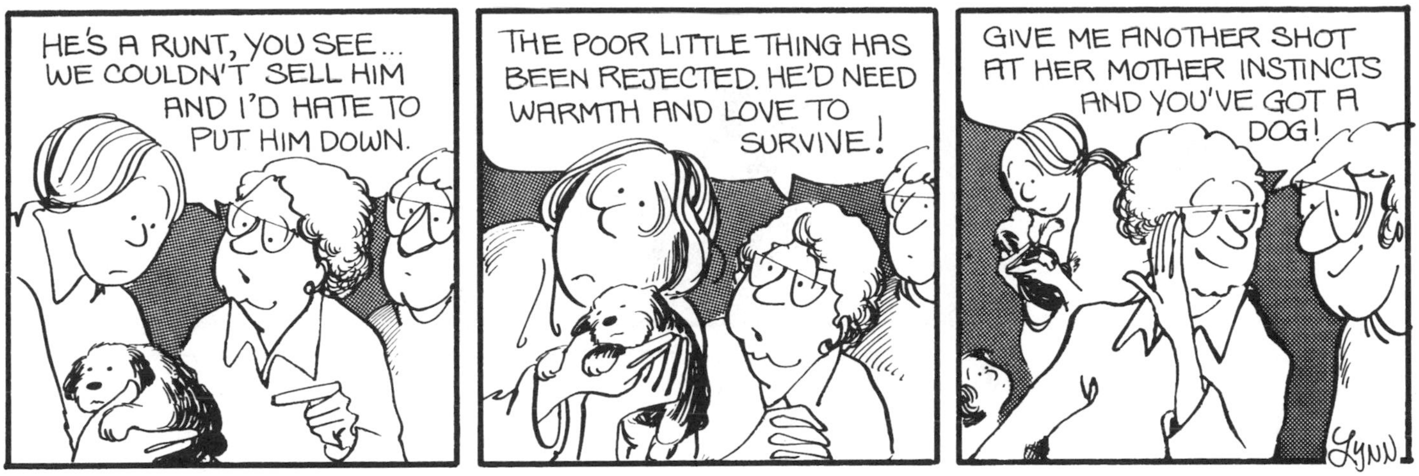
HE'S A RUNT, YOU SEE... WE COULDN'T SELL HIM AND I'D HATE TO PUT HIM DOWN.
THE POOR LITTLE THING HAS BEEN REJECTED. HE'D NEED WARMTH AND LOVE TO SURVIVE!
GIVE ME ANOTHER SHOT AT HER MOTHER INSTINCTS AND YOU'VE GOT A DOG!
LYNN

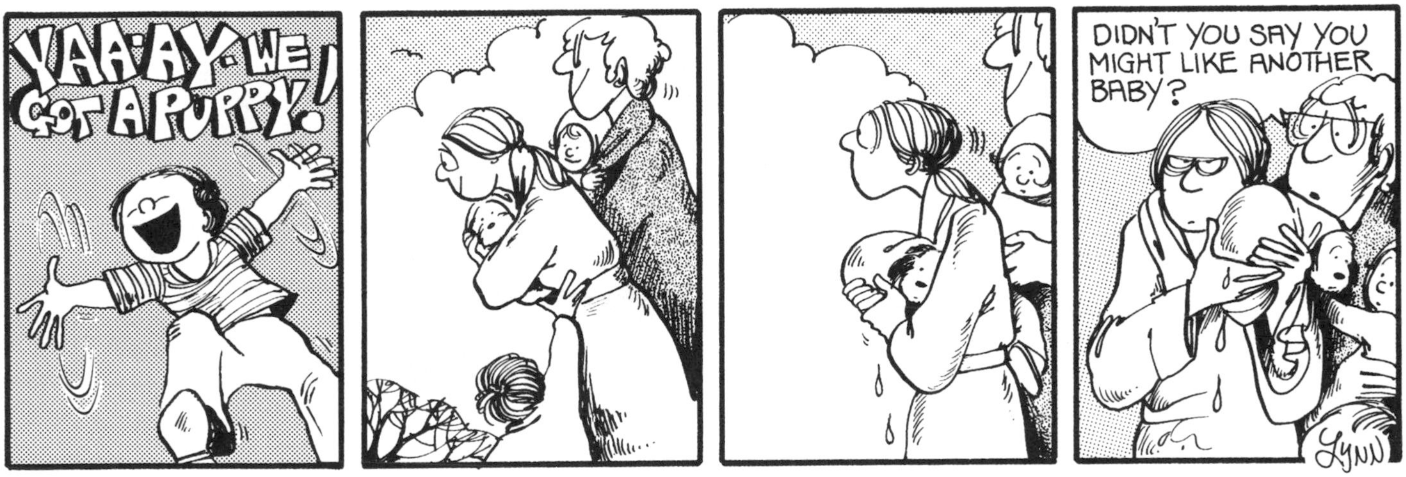
YAA-AY. WE GOT A PUPPY!
DIDN'T YOU SAY YOU MIGHT LIKE ANOTHER BABY?
LYNN

*

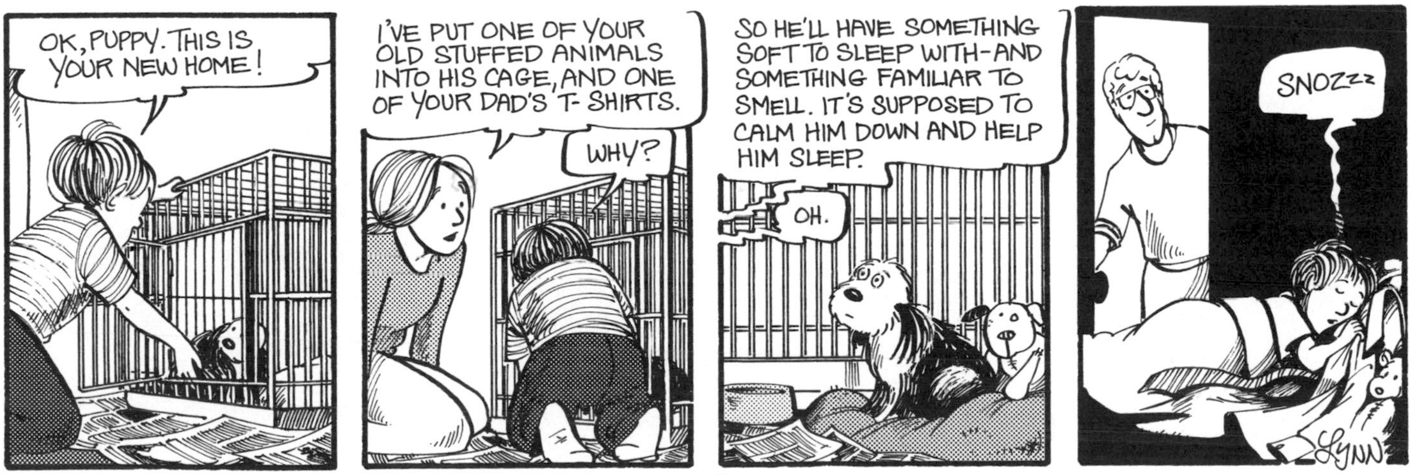
OK, PUPPY. THIS IS YOUR NEW HOME!
I'VE PUT ONE OF YOUR OLD STUFFED ANIMALS INTO HIS CAGE, AND ONE OF YOUR DAD'S T-SHIRTS.
WHY?
SO HE'LL HAVE SOMETHING SOFT TO SLEEP WITH-AND SOMETHING FAMILIAR TO SMELL. IT'S SUPPOSED TO CALM HIM DOWN AND HELP HIM SLEEP.
OH.
SNOZzz
LYNN

My best drawings of Farley were done when "Willy" came to live with us. In downtown North Bay, a pet shop had one of those classic windows full of puppies. I took the kids in—just to look, and we came home with a wriggly black spaniel, much to the chagrin of Dad, who wanted no pets. None. Willy worked his way into our hearts and Farley became alive with attitude, character and charm.

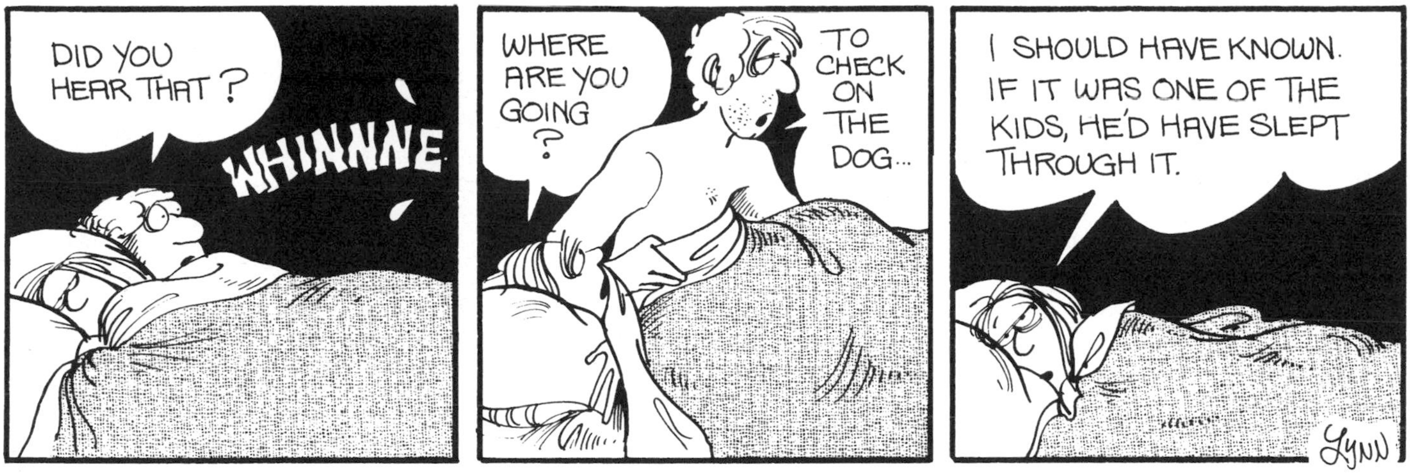
DID YOU HEAR THAT ?
WHINNNE
WHERE ARE YOU GOING ?
TO CHECK ON THE DOG...
I SHOULD HAVE KNOWN. IF IT WAS ONE OF THE KIDS, HE'D HAVE SLEPT THROUGH IT.
LYNN

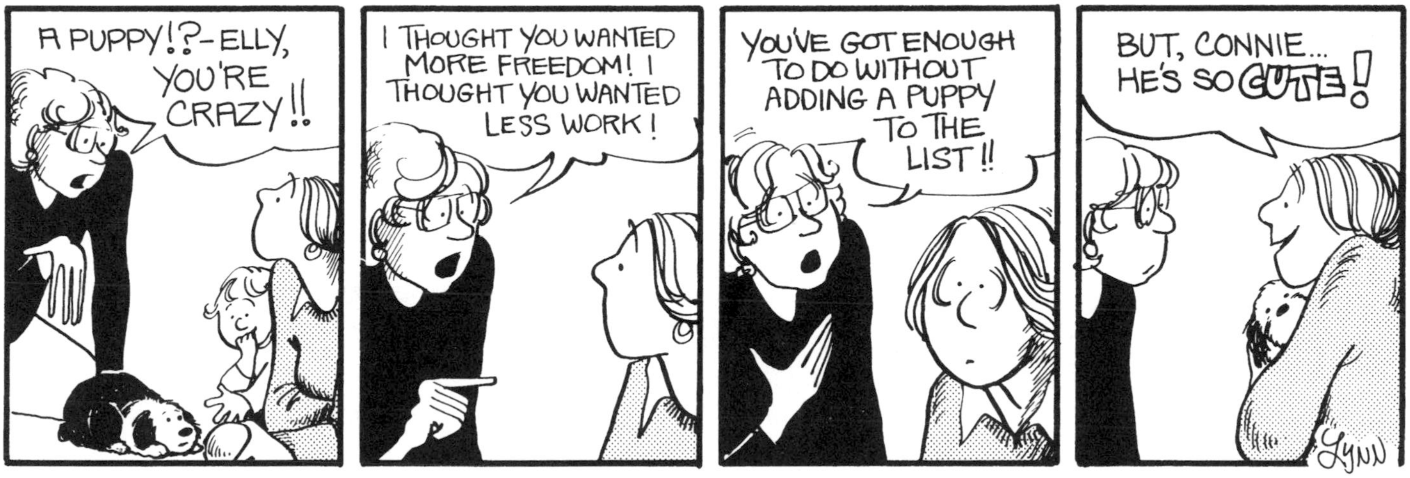
A PUPPY!?-ELLY, YOU'RE CRAZY!!
I THOUGHT YOU WANTED MORE FREEDOM! I THOUGHT YOU WANTED LESS WORK!
YOU'VE GOT ENOUGH TO DO WITHOUT ADDING A PUPPY TO THE LIST!!
BUT, CONNIE... HE'S SO CUTE!
LYNN

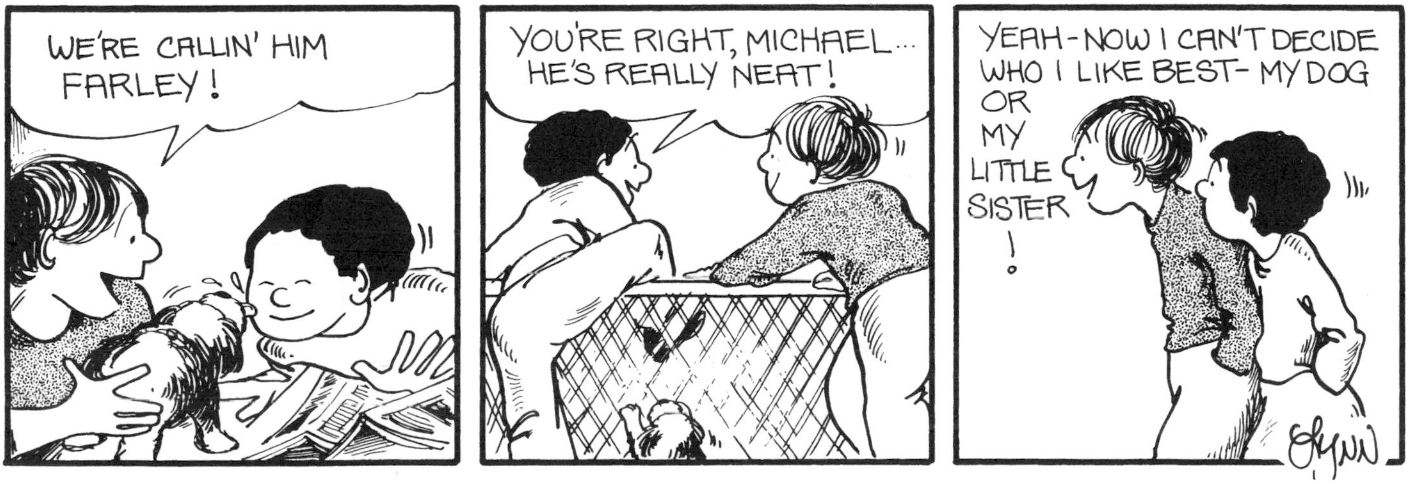
WE'RE CALLIN' HIM FARLEY!
YOU'RE RIGHT, MICHAEL... HE'S REALLY NEAT!
YEAH-NOW I CAN'T DECIDE WHO I LIKE BEST- MY DOG OR MY LITTLE SISTER!
LYNN

*
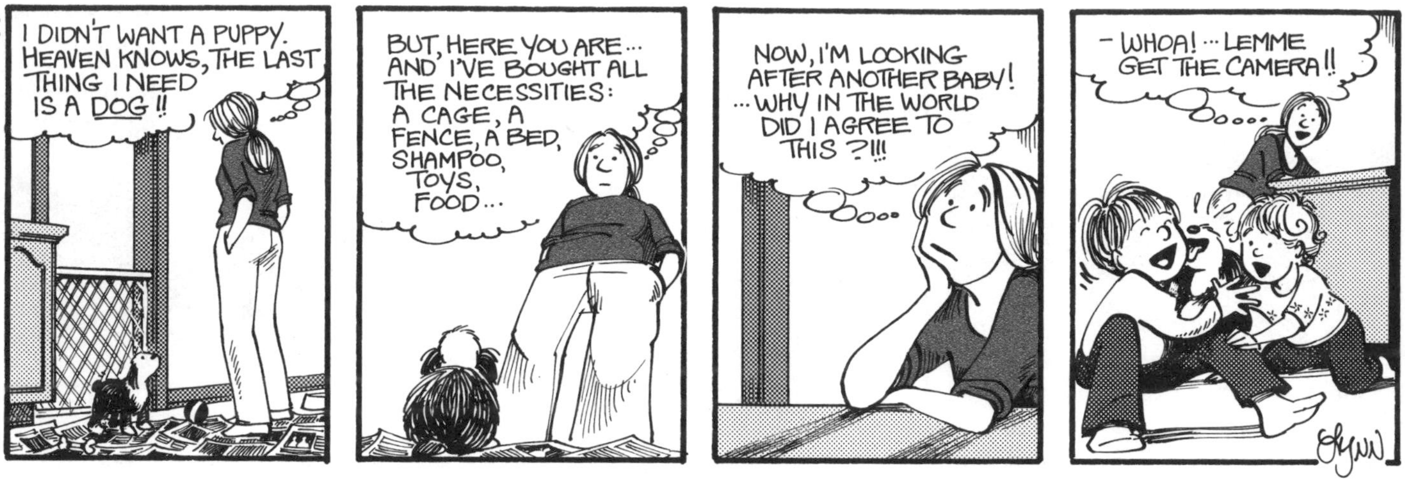
I DIDN'T WANT A PUPPY. HEAVEN KNOWS, THE LAST THING I NEED IS A DOG !!
BUT, HERE YOU ARE... AND I'VE BOUGHT ALL THE NECESSITIES: A CAGE, A FENCE, A BED, SHAMPOO, TOYS, FOOD...
NOW, I'M LOOKING AFTER ANOTHER BABY! ...WHY IN THE WORLD DID I AGREE TO THIS ?!!!
- WHOA! ... LEMME GET THE CAMERA !!
LYNN

*
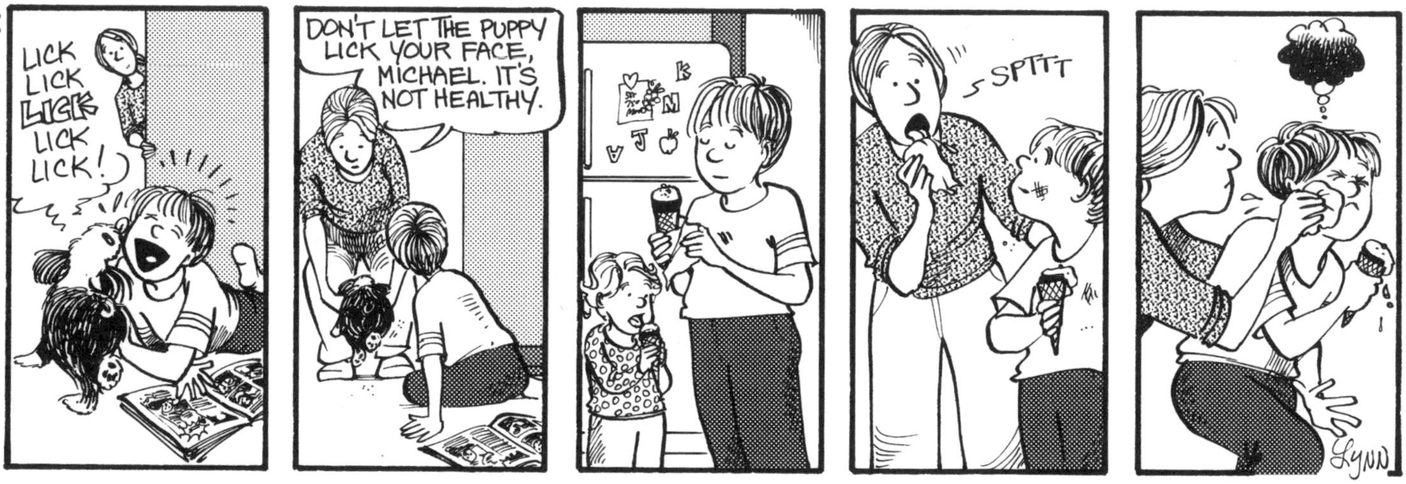
LICK LICK LICK LICK LICK!
DON'T LET THE PUPPY LICK YOUR FACE, MICHAEL. IT'S NOT HEALTHY.
SPTTT
LYNN

*
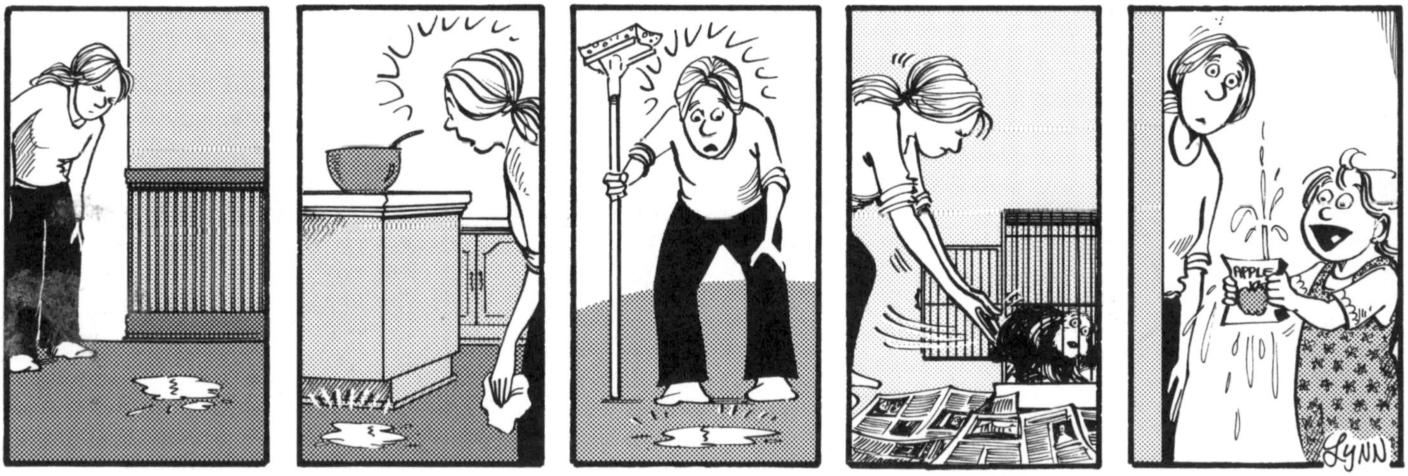
APPLE
LYNN

You never know when a single strip will bring in the mail. So many folks wrote to say they'd frozen while waiting for their puppy to pee that I had to make up a stock reply.

*
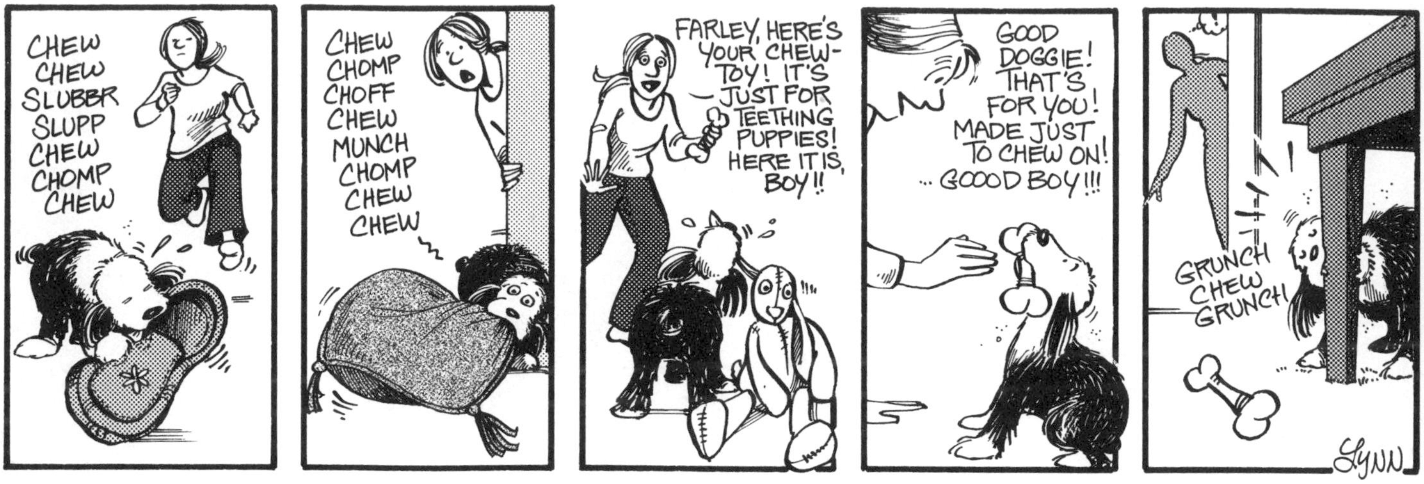
CHEW CHEW SLUBBR SLUPP CHEW CHOMP CHEW
CHEW CHOMP CHOFF CHEW MUNCH CHOMP CHEW CHEW
FARLEY, HERE'S YOUR CHEW-TOY! IT'S JUST FOR TEETHING PUPPIES! HERE IT IS, BOY!!
GOOD DOGGIE! THAT'S FOR YOU! MADE JUST TO CHEW ON! ... GOOOD BOY!!!
GRUNCH CHEW GRUNCH
LYNN

*
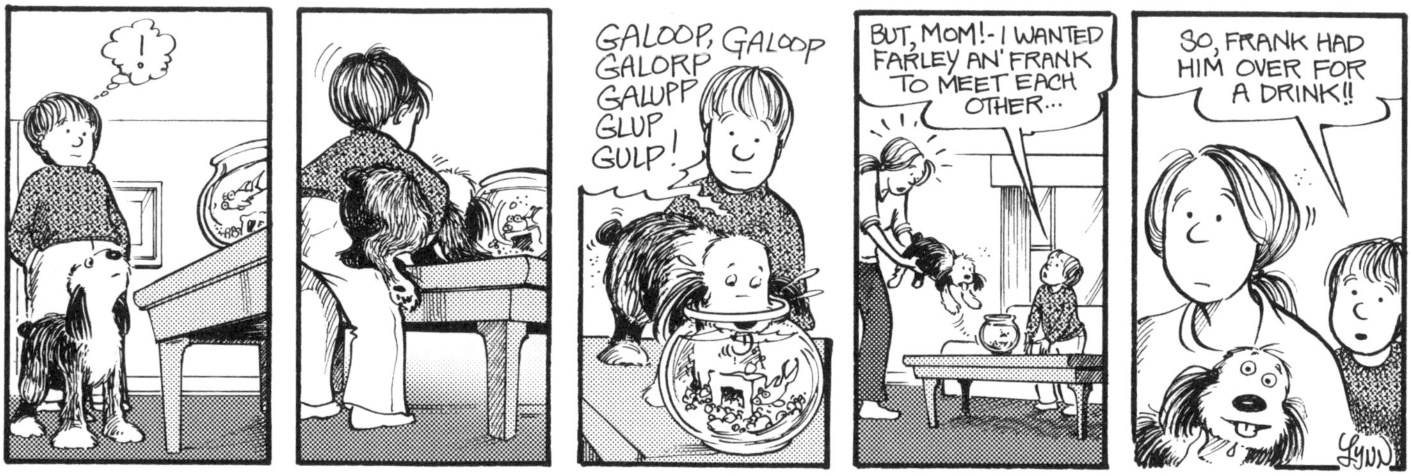
!
GALOOP, GALOOP GALORP GALUPP GLUP GULP!
BUT, MOM! - I WANTED FARLEY AN' FRANK TO MEET EACH OTHER...
SO, FRANK HAD HIM OVER FOR A DRINK!!
LYNN

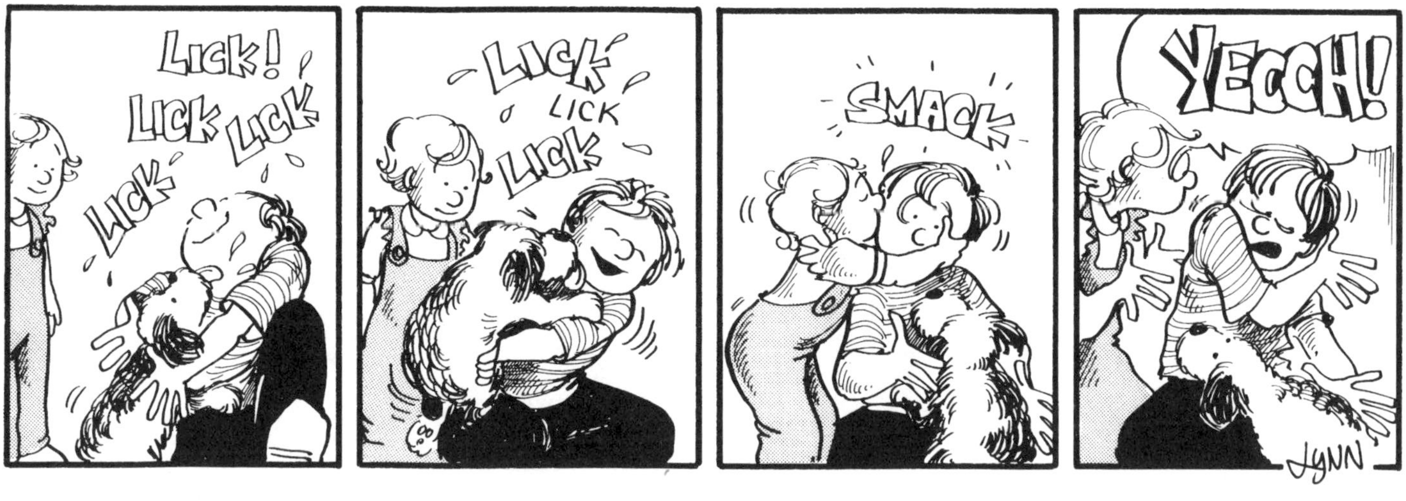
LICK! LICK LICK LICK
LICK LICK LICK
SMACK
YECCH!
LYNN

Few comedians these days are capable of really good humor. They lack the vocabulary, the ethics and the acting skill to entertain an audience with truly funny material. I'm amazed by the laughter that erupts during particularly crude bathroom tirades and I wonder if the audience, too, has lost the ability to detect, appreciate and enjoy real talent. Funny need not be X-rated. Laughter is a gift we all possess. Have we forgotten when to use it? Sure, crude cracks me up, too, sometimes—burps, toots, sex and so on all belong in the mix but, people!—comedy is a craft, a skill, an art form. It's not inhibition that makes a comedian's work smut free, and funny to a diverse and inclusive audience—it's intelligence.

SO RATHER THAN GET A JOB NOW, I'LL PICK UP THE CREDITS I'M MISSING... AND MAYBE GET MY DEGREE!

I JUST WISH I'D TAKEN MY EDUCATION SERIOUSLY— WHEN I HAD THE CHANCE!

LET'S GO, LAWRENCE... SHE KNOWS WE'RE LISTENING.

ONE COOKIE... I ONLY GAVE HER ONE COOKIE.

MOM! SOMETHING'S THE MATTER WITH FRANK!—HE'S SWIMMING UPSIDE-DOWN!

LOOK! HE WASN'T LIKE THAT THIS MORNING—WHAT'S WRONG WITH HIM?

I DON'T KNOW, HONEY.

WHAT ARE YOU DOING?

TAKIN' HIS TEMPERATURE.

I'M AFRAID FRANK'S GONE, MICHAEL.

HE DIED? HOW COME? WHAT HAPPENED?

WELL, I THINK HE MIGHT HAVE BEEN FED A LITTLE TOO OFTEN, AND HIS BOWL NEEDED CLEANING. ...MAYBE WE JUST DIDN'T TAKE CARE OF HIM VERY WELL.

AWWWWHHHHH!!

AMAZING. FRANK HASN'T HAD THAT MUCH ATTENTION SINCE YOU BROUGHT HIM HOME!

~SNIFF~... HE LOOKS SO DIFFERENT, MOM. HE DOESN'T LOOK LIKE FRANK ANY MORE.

HERE. I FOUND A LITTLE COFFIN. LET'S BURY HIM OUTSIDE.

THANKS.

IT'S A JEWELRY BOX. COOL!

THERE. FRANK IS BURIED, NOW.

ISN'T ANYONE GOING TO SAY A FEW WORDS?

BYE-BYE.

When I had Aaron the only training manual I had was the one we bought to train the dog! (The real Farley came well before this job!) At first I actually used some of the suggestions I found in the book. Fortunately, my mom sent me "Dr. Spock." Aaron did do some teething, however, on Milk-Bones.

HONEY - BE GENTLE WITH THE PUPPY! HE'S JUST A **BABY**!

DON'T PICK HIM UP SO FAST - AND DON'T RUN WITH HIM - HE'S JUST A **BABY**!

REMEMBER, BABIES NEED SPECIAL CARE AND SPECIAL TREATMENT. YOU HAVE TO BE EXTRA **NICE** TO A BABY!

PFFTT!

HELLO? - YES... MAY I SPEAK TO THE VET, PLEASE?

DR. SCHELL... I WAS WONDERING HOW LONG IT WOULD BE BEFORE WE COULD FEED OUR PUPPY TABLE SCRAPS.

REALLY?

YOU MEAN I'LL BE FINISHING THE KIDS' LEFTOVERS FOR ANOTHER SIX MONTHS?

WHAT'S THIS - A NIGHT SCHOOL PROGRAM?

UH-HUH, I'M ENROLLING IN A CREATIVE WRITING COURSE!

CREATIVE WRITING!? - EVERYONE'S DOING CREATIVE WRITING. WHY NOT TAKE SOMETHING PRACTICAL?

BELLY DANCING AND GOURMET COOKING, FOR EXAMPLE!

Puns like this are one reason why my work is not translated into many other languages. Expressions and wordplay differ from culture to culture and if this punch line was translated word for word, it wouldn't make sense. Knowing this, perhaps I should have refrained from using such figures of speech, but a good pun (or a bad one) is too hard to resist!

MISS (AHEM) MOREAU IS HERE, DOC!

WHO?

THE BLONDE WITH THE PLAYBOY BODY AND THE SKIN-TIGHT WARDROBE!

...YOU KNOW, THE ONE WITH THE ANTERIOR HYPOPLASIA AND CROSSBITE!

OH, HER!

This is true . . . still, I'm sure he noticed the "Playboy" part.

I'VE BEEN IN THIS BUSINESS FOR A NUMBER OF YEARS NOW, MISS BAKER...

AND DO YOU KNOW HOW HARD IT IS TO CONVINCE PEOPLE I'M A NICE GUY?

IN THIS MODERN AGE, DENTISTRY IS NEARLY A PAINLESS PROFESSION!

SO KINDLY STOP RE-FERRING TO INCOMING PATIENTS AS "THE NEXT VICTIM"!!

I'M EXHAUSTED. I NEED A BEER, A COUCH WITH NO TOYS ON IT ...AND SILENCE!

I HAVE HAD ENOUGH HASSLES TODAY TO LAST A LIFETIME.

MY BACK ACHES, MY HEAD ACHES....BUT I'M HOME WHERE THEY UNDERSTAND.

BOY, IT SURE MUST BE NICE!!

I introduced the subject of creative writing because I sort of want to write a book. I haven't started yet—because I haven't run out of excuses.

HERE'S A COINCIDENCE, —I'LL BE TEACHING THE CLASS YOU'RE IN!

YOU'LL FIND THIS A MOST CHALLENGING PROGRAM!

MANY OF MY EVENING STUDENTS ARE PREPARING FOR A SERIOUS CAREER!

OF COURSE THERE ARE ALWAYS A FEW HOUSEWIVES LOOKING FOR A CHANGE....

HOW WAS YOUR CREATIVE WRITING CLASS?

FINE!

EVERYBODY INTRODUCED THEMSELVES AND WE HAD A DISCUSSION ABOUT DAYDREAMING—WHY WE DO IT AND WHEN.

WE DID FREE ASSOCIATION AND WE TALKED ABOUT THE 6TH SENSE, SUPERSTITIONS, PREMONITIONS AND FATE.

WE DISCUSSED THE COMPLEXITIES OF MEMORY AND HOW IT MIXES WITH THE IMAGINATION.

WOW!

...DID YOU DO ANY WORK?

IS THIS THE REQUIRED READING FOR YOUR NIGHT SCHOOL CLASS?

HMM... ARE YOU SURE THIS IS A COURSE IN CONTEMPORARY ENGLISH?

FLIP FLIP

SURE IT IS. ...WHY?

FLIP FLIP

THERE ISN'T A SMUTTY BOOK IN THE LOT!

289

MICHAEL, DO YOU HAVE YOUR LUNCH? WE'VE GOT TO LEAVE IN 5 MINUTES.

MEET ME RIGHT HERE AFTER SCHOOL. YOU HAVE A HAIRCUT AT 4 O'CLOCK.

RIGHT ON TIME, MRS. PATTERSON, DR. FLETT IS READY TO SEE ELIZABETH.

GOOD! MY EYE EXAM IS IN 40 MINUTES, SO I HAVE TIME TO GO TO THE CLEANERS.

NOW, I'LL TAKE ELIZABETH TO ANNIE'S HOUSE, PUT AWAY THE GROCERIES, GET SUPPER ON AND PICK MICHAEL UP FROM SCHOOL.

PERFECT! NOW TO DROP MIKE OFF WITH HIS DAD AT THE CLINIC, AND I'LL HAVE TIME TO HIT THE GYM BEFORE I GO TO MY WRITING CLASS.

'NIGHT DR. P!- HAVE A GOOD WEEKEND!

YES...THANK GOODNESS FOR MY RECEPTIONIST! —I'VE NEVER MET A WOMAN WHO'S MORE ORGANIZED!!

Dr. Flett was our doctor when Aaron and I lived in Dundas, Ontario. We really liked him, so I used his name in the strip as a way of saying hello. Over the years I've been able to contact lost chums, reunite family members, and thank my teachers by putting their names in the paper. In many ways—this is such a powerful medium!

No. This never happened. When you're thinking up gags, you just focus on what characters are capable of and what might happen. This might have happened to someone—I'm still waiting to find out.

Miss Campbell was the name of my grade two schoolteacher. I thought she was unduly strict and humorless, but when I was promoted to grade three, I cried—I knew I'd miss her.

My mother told me not to play with my food. I told my kids not to play with their food. We let them do it, however, with the hope that a morsel or two will enter the oral cavity and gravitate to the stomach. Hotdogs, though nutritionally questionable are both fun to eat and funny to draw. This is one of my favorite strips.

Farley Mowat (*Never Cry Wolf*)—
one of my favorite Canadian authors.

Shortly after Farley the dog appeared in the strip, I got a letter from Farley Mowat. He said, "I suspect you have named the dog after *me*." I replied, "Your suspicions are correct." He then called to say he wished to extract from me the "royalty" of one original Farley comic strip. I sent him a Sunday—a good one—which he hung on his bathroom wall above the toilet so that "the men could read it." Farley and Claire Mowat continue to send letters at Christmastime—it's an exchange I so enjoy.

FOR BETTER OR FOR WORSE
BY LYNN JOHNSTON
DONG-LE DONGLE DONGG
GIVE
DONG DING DONGLE
DONGLE DING DONGLE
GIVE
MOM? HOW COME THERE ARE SO MANY SANTAS?
WE SAW ONE IN THE MALL, AN' ONE ON THE STREET AN' NOW THIS ONE HERE!
MAYBE THEY'RE **ALL** SANTA CLAUS!
IS THAT EVEN POSSIBLE?!
SURE!
THE JOB OF BEING A SANTA IS PRETTY SPECIAL... IT'S JUST LIKE THE JOB OF BEING A MOM!
.... EVERYONE EXPECTS YOU TO DO EVERYTHING AND BE EVERYWHERE AT THE SAME TIME!!
LYNN

MY BROTHER'S COMING FOR CHRISTMAS, CONNIE!

YEAH, HE'S STILL WITH THE THEATER, STILL PLAYING THE TRUMPET...

MARRIED? NO! - HE LEADS A CRAZY LIFE OF LATE NIGHTS, WOMEN, TRAVELLING! - SOMEHOW HE STILL LIKES TO VISIT US WITH OUR KIDS, DOG AND MORTGAGE!

... I THINK IT CONVINCES HIM HE'S BEEN DOING THE RIGHT THING!

When my brother, Alan (his second name is Philip) entered the story, I had a whole new world of words, attitude and comic imagery to work with . . . and I didn't have to invent a thing.

*

TELL ME ABOUT YOUR BROTHER, ELI. I WANT TO KNOW MORE ABOUT HIM.

WELL...

I KNOW HE'S ATTRACTIVE - I KNOW HE'S A TALENTED MUSICIAN - WITH A GREAT SENSE OF HUMOR...

HE WENT TO SCHOOL IN VANCOUVER, HE'S WORKED ON CRUISE SHIPS, HE'S LIVED IN MONTREAL...

BUT, BEFORE YOU TELL ME ANYTHING ELSE... DOES HE HAVE A GIRLFRIEND?

*

MY BROTHER'S LIFE IS TOO HECTIC FOR SERIOUS RELATIONSHIPS, CONNIE... SO DON'T GET ANY IDEAS.

WHO, ME?!!

I WAS JUST ASKING. IT WAS A MATTER OF INTEREST TO KNOW IF HE WAS "TAKEN" OR NOT...

THE FACT THAT I'M **ALSO** SINGLE IS REALLY A MOOT POINT!

THAT'S DEBATABLE.

MOM? WHEN UNCLE PHIL COMES, WILL HE BRING HIS TRUMPET?

SURE. HE HAS 3 OR 4. HE ALWAYS TRAVELS WITH THEM.

DO YOU THINK HE'LL PLAY?

UH-HUH. HE HAS TO PRACTICE EVERY DAY, SO YOU'LL HEAR HIM A LOT!

COOL!

LOOKS LIKE WE'RE GONNA HAVE A HOUSE FULL OF MUSIC!

MOM? FARLEY JUST CHEWED UP ONE OF LIZZIE'S DIAPERS!

WHY DON'T YOU GET YOUR DAD?

'CAUSE HE'S IN THE WORKSHOP.

THEN DEAL WITH IT YOURSELF!

ME? I CAN'T!

WHY NOT?

SHE'S STILL WEARIN' IT!

I have friends like this. I cherish them. Requests for reprints of this Sunday page came immediately. Big, fat family festivities are fun for everyone but the ones who carry the load.

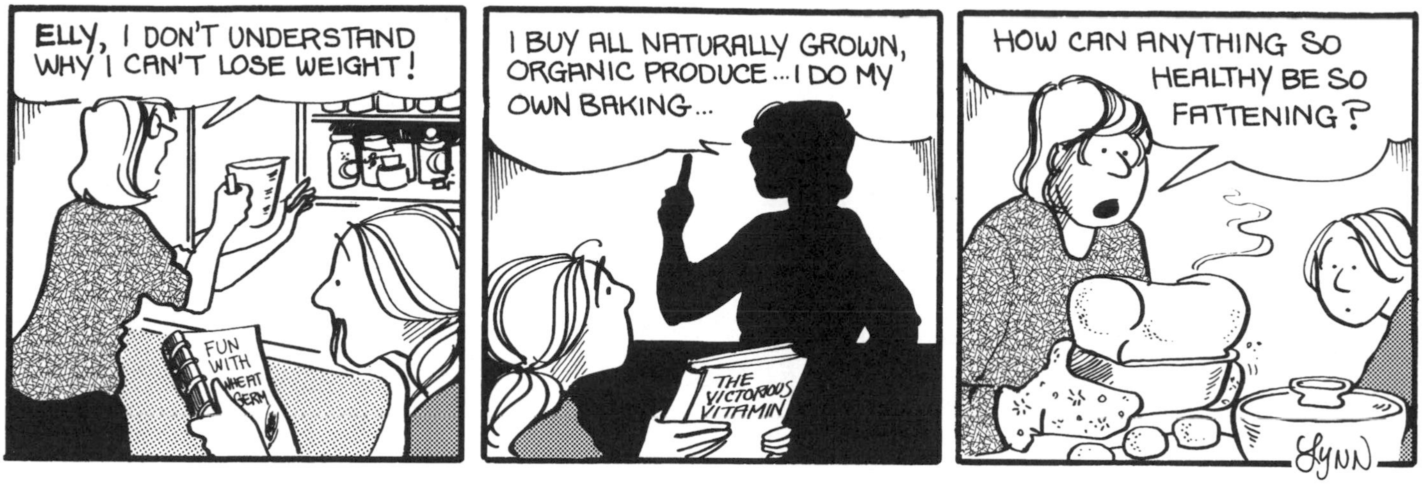
ELLY, I DON'T UNDERSTAND WHY I CAN'T LOSE WEIGHT!
FUN WITH WHEAT GERM
I BUY ALL NATURALLY GROWN, ORGANIC PRODUCE... I DO MY OWN BAKING...
THE VICTORIOUS VITAMIN
HOW CAN ANYTHING SO HEALTHY BE SO FATTENING?
Lynn

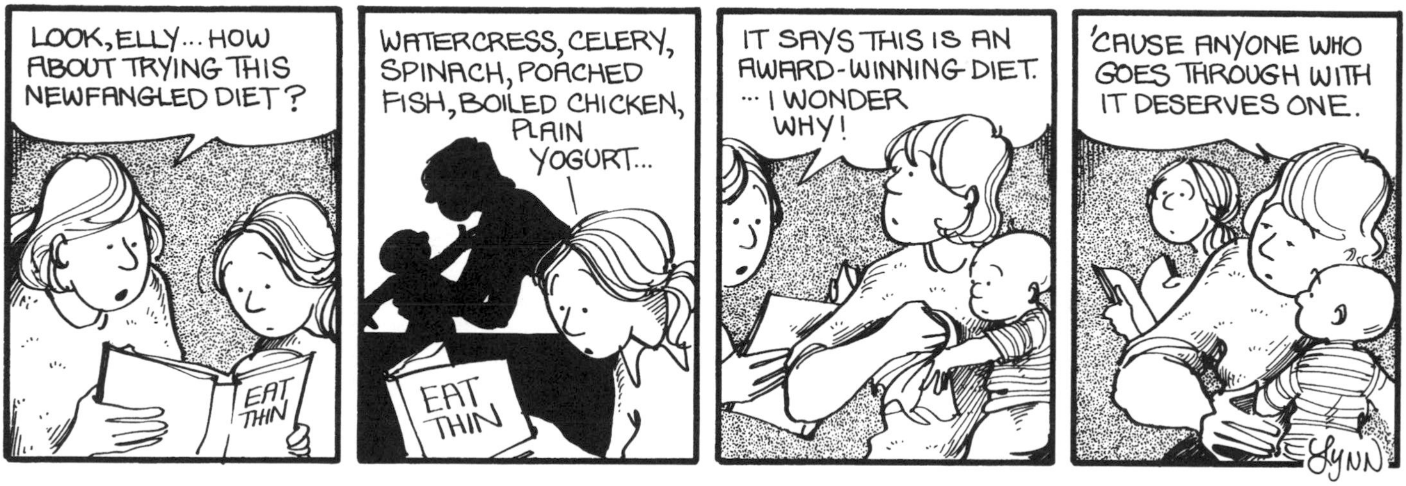
LOOK, ELLY... HOW ABOUT TRYING THIS NEWFANGLED DIET?
EAT THIN
WATERCRESS, CELERY, SPINACH, POACHED FISH, BOILED CHICKEN, PLAIN YOGURT...
EAT THIN
IT SAYS THIS IS AN AWARD-WINNING DIET. ... I WONDER WHY!
'CAUSE ANYONE WHO GOES THROUGH WITH IT DESERVES ONE.
Lynn

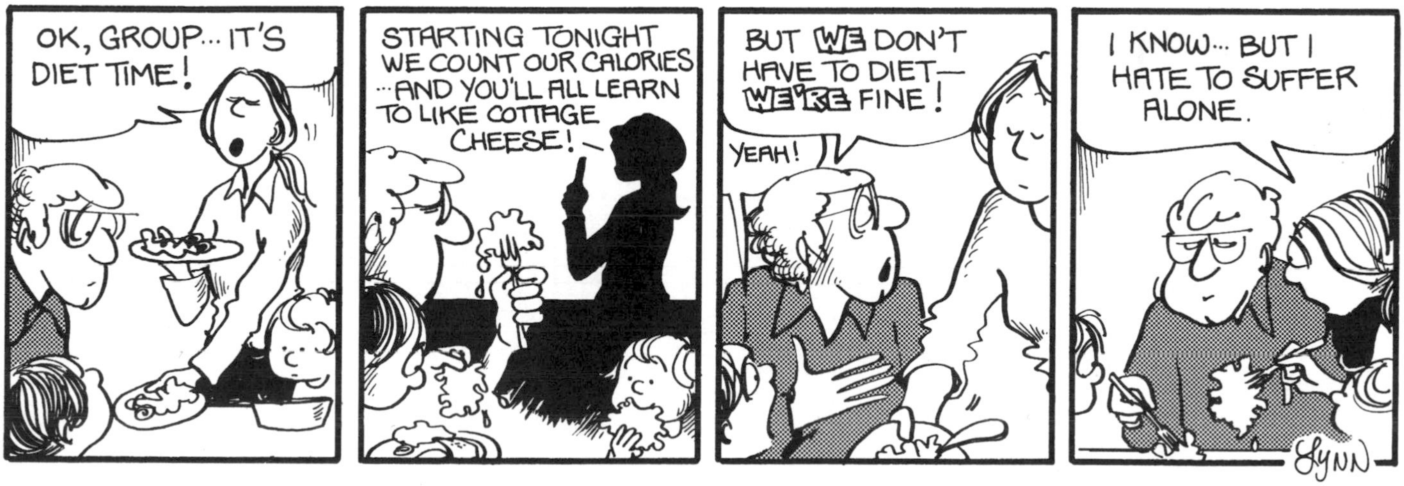
OK, GROUP... IT'S DIET TIME!
STARTING TONIGHT WE COUNT OUR CALORIES ...AND YOU'LL ALL LEARN TO LIKE COTTAGE CHEESE!
BUT WE DON'T HAVE TO DIET— WE'RE FINE!
YEAH!
I KNOW... BUT I HATE TO SUFFER ALONE.
Lynn

My dad objected strenuously to eating "rabbit food." His idea of the perfect meal was bacon, eggs and fried fresh tomatoes. I have to admit, we enjoyed the days when Dad did the cooking—and he later learned to enjoy salads when he finally got dentures that fit.

300

GIRLS ARE WEIRD.

MAYBE NOT **ALL** GIRLS!

YEAH... ALL GIRLS.

I SHOULD KNOW. I'VE GOT A SISTER.

WHAT ABOUT MOTHERS?

YOU'RE RIGHT. GIRLS ARE WEIRD.

GOT ANYTHING FOR THE WIFE YET, JOHN?

NO...

BUT I HAVE SOME IDEAS.

DIAMONDS? PEARLS?

NAH. ELLY'S FAR TOO PRACTICAL FOR THAT STUFF, TED.

I'M THINKING FOOD SEALER. YOU KNOW, ONE OF THOSE WRAPPING GADGETS THAT COVERS LEFTOVERS WITH PLASTIC.

RIGHT...

AND EVERY TIME SHE LOOKS AT VEGETABLES, SHE'LL THINK OF YOU.

A PEARL NECKLACE WOULD BE PERFECT.

ARE YOU SURE?

ABSOLUTELY.

GET HER SOMETHING SIMPLE AND ELEGANT. THAT ONE, FOR INSTANCE, IS QUITE LOVELY.

YES, THAT WILL DO NICELY. CAN YOU GIFT WRAP IT FOR MY FRIEND, PLEASE?

MY PLEASURE.

YOUR PACKAGE, SIR.

UM...THANK YOU.

TRUST ME, JOHN. ELLY WILL BE THRILLED THAT YOU CHOSE AND WRAPPED SOMETHING LIKE THIS YOURSELF!

When I did this, people were still using the term "housewife." Wasn't there a song about "an everyday housewife?"

I have always worked outside the home, but I tried to imagine how it would feel to be Elly Patterson. I would likely have deferred to my husband, apologized for my deficiencies and allowed myself to feel inferior. At least, this was my perception of capable, intelligent women friends, frustrated by "four walls and a phone line."

Today, child rearing is shared by both parents, staying at home (if you can) is preferable and there's no stigma attached to not having a career—other than producing and educating the next generation. After all, isn't that the most important job there is?

MOM! GUESS WHAT! – WE'VE BEEN MAKING SNOWFLAKES!

My brother, Alan, circa 1990.

In his twenties, practicing at the cottage.

My brother is a funny, talented man and a great addition to the strip. I didn't have to make the character up; this is Alan!

As a single and somewhat itinerant musician, Alan came in and out of my life—staying once for a year, and later, just for long weekends and holidays. Aaron loved his company and so looked forward to his Christmas visits.

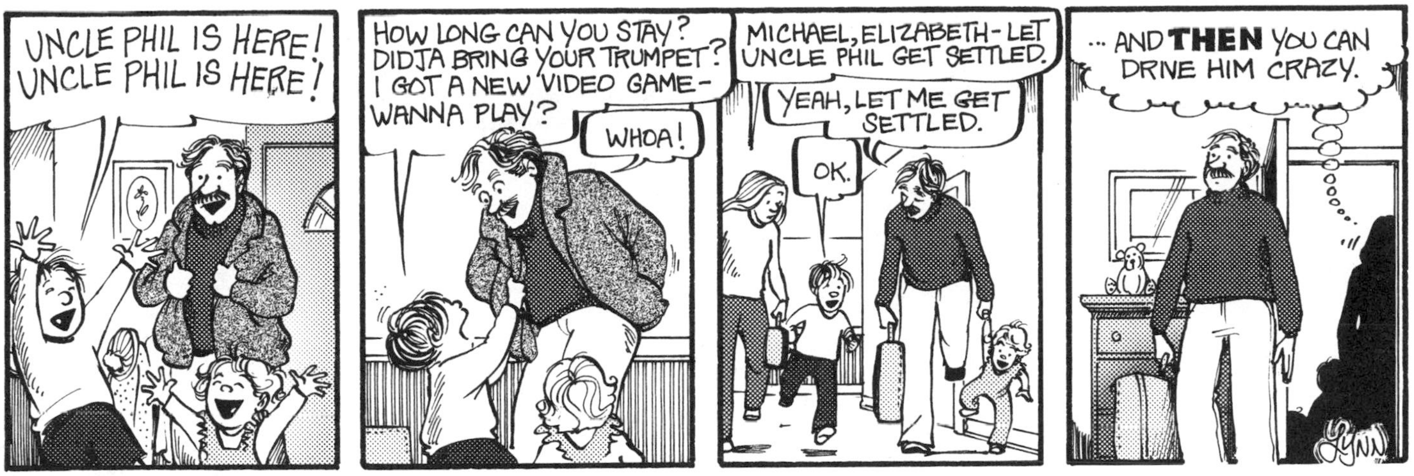
UNCLE PHIL IS HERE! UNCLE PHIL IS HERE!
HOW LONG CAN YOU STAY? DIDJA BRING YOUR TRUMPET? I GOT A NEW VIDEO GAME-WANNA PLAY?
WHOA!
MICHAEL, ELIZABETH- LET UNCLE PHIL GET SETTLED.
YEAH, LET ME GET SETTLED.
OK.
... AND **THEN** YOU CAN DRIVE HIM CRAZY.
Lynn

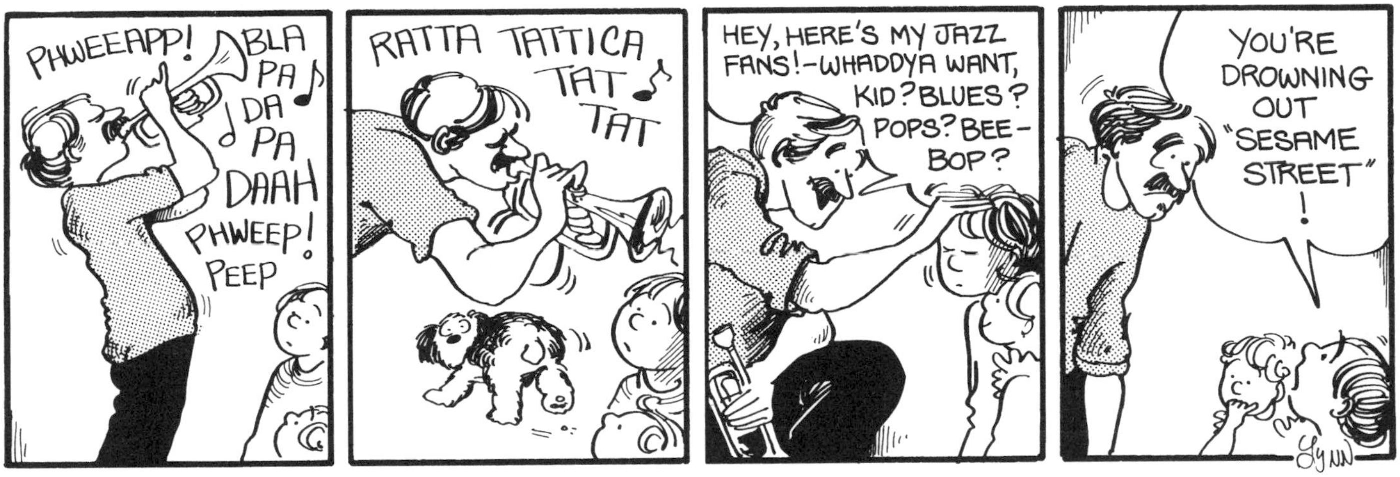
PHWEEAPP! BLA PA DA PA DAAH PHWEEP! PEEP
RATTA TATTICA TAT TAT
HEY, HERE'S MY JAZZ FANS! -WHADDYA WANT, KID? BLUES? POPS? BEE-BOP?
YOU'RE DROWNING OUT "SESAME STREET"!
Lynn

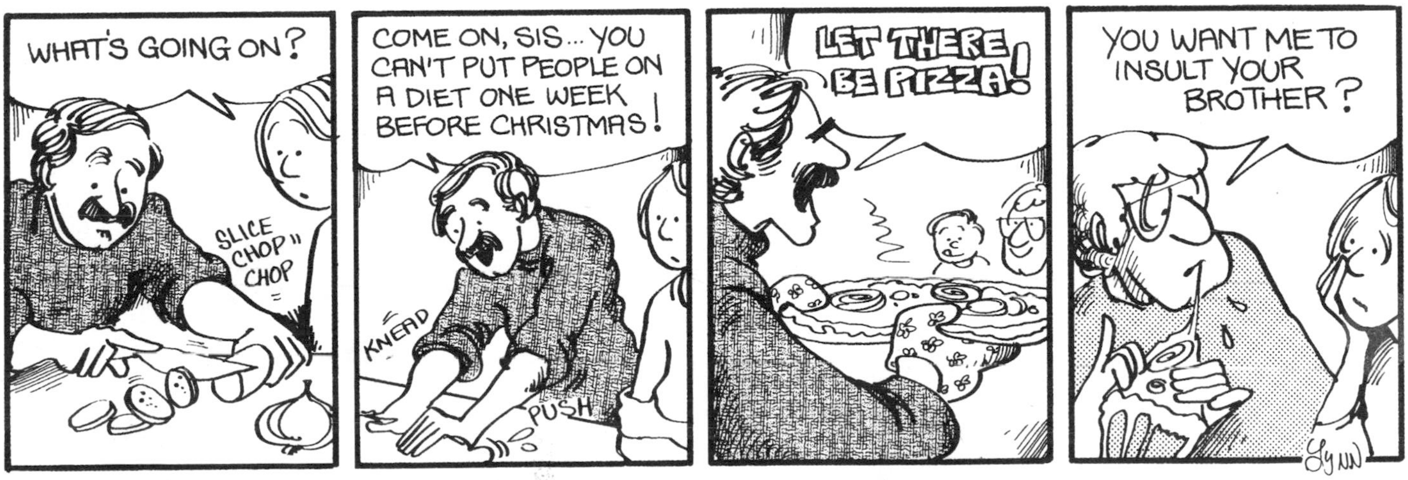
WHAT'S GOING ON?
SLICE CHOP CHOP
COME ON, SIS... YOU CAN'T PUT PEOPLE ON A DIET ONE WEEK BEFORE CHRISTMAS!
KNEAD
PUSH
LET THERE BE PIZZA!
YOU WANT ME TO INSULT YOUR BROTHER?
Lynn

Yes—Mom still does most of the work, but for some strange reason, I find it a pleasure.

Alan—no kids—would rev up my offspring just before bedtime. When they were hyped on adrenaline and running in circles, he'd wonder why they weren't ready for bedtime—and sleep!

I once considered a career in advertising. The problem is—I hate commercials.

I received several e-mails about this one, criticizing me for making Michael "earn" money. They thought he should just get it. I don't get it. The reality is, money is the reward you receive for work—and if parents are a child's most influential teachers, shouldn't we teach them how to work?

*

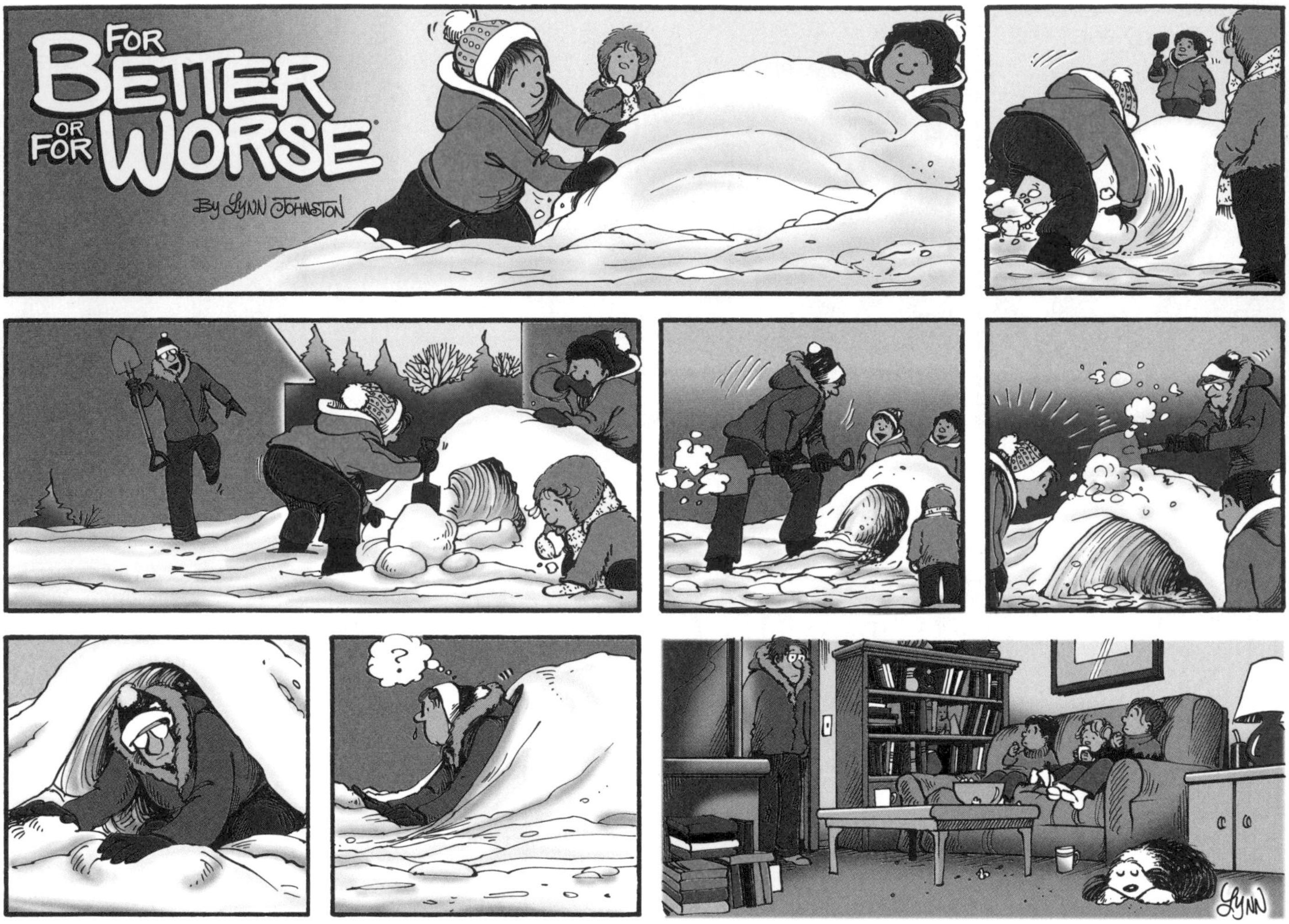
FOR BETTER OR FOR WORSE
BY LYNN JOHNSTON
?
LYNN

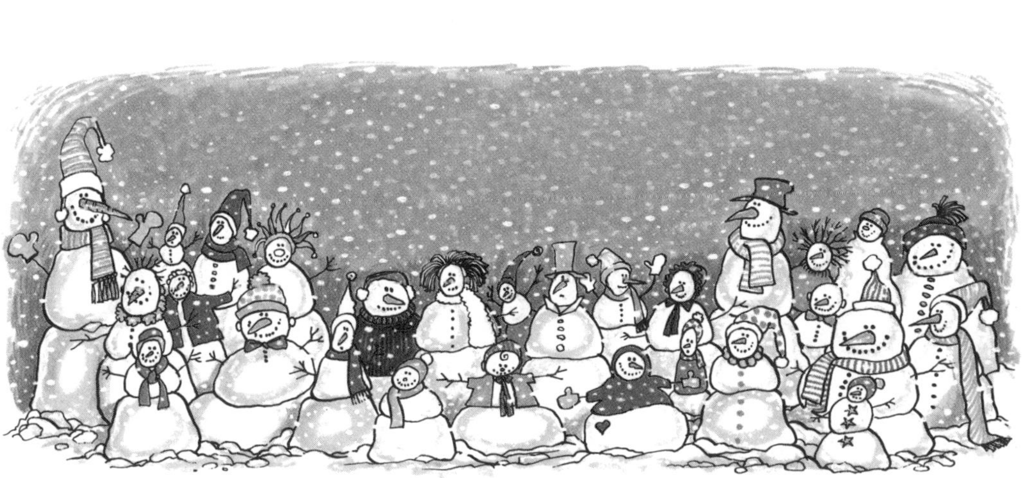

SO- WHEN AM I GOING TO MEET YOUR BROTHER, ELLY?

WHAT'S HE LIKE? TALL? DARK? HANDSOME?

I'LL INTRODUCE YOU, CONNIE... BUT I DON'T THINK YOU AND PHIL HAVE ANYTHING IN COMMON.

HE'S SINGLE, ISN'T HE?

UNCLE PHIL AND I HAD A NEAT TIME SEEIN' SANTA, MOM.

AN' WHEN WE WERE COMING HOME, I ASKED HIM WHAT HE'D LIKE TO GET FROM SANTA.

...MOM?-WHAT'S A BLONDE NUBILE WRAPPED IN CELLOPHANE?

PHILIP!

Word for word . . . this is my brother talking.

BOY, YOUR MOM'S NICE TO TAKE US TO SEE SANTA!

BUT I THOUGHT YOU ALREADY WENT!-HOW COME YOU'RE GOING AGAIN?

I DON'T THINK HE GOT MY WHOLE LIST THE FIRST TIME.

Every Christmas, we looked forward to going out into the woods to cut our tree. Up north, there were acres to choose from. Crown land was everywhere. Late in the summer, we'd tag a good one, and when the time came, we ceremoniously cut it down. Buying a tree from a vendor wasn't an option, so when I did this strip I felt a little smug—knowing that we "bushwhackers" had the real thing.

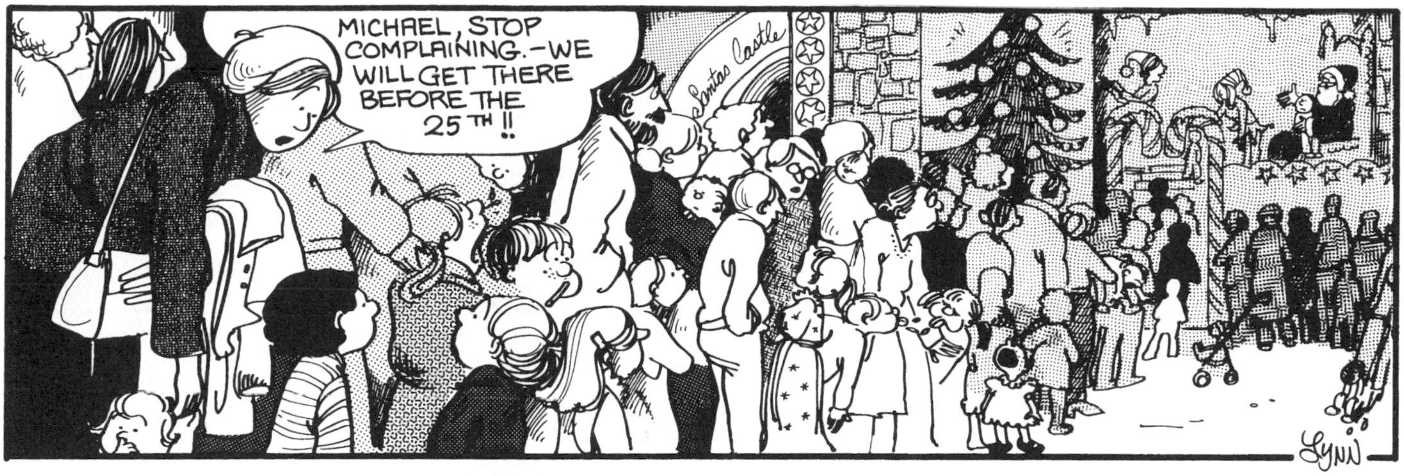
MICHAEL, STOP COMPLAINING.-WE WILL GET THERE BEFORE THE 25TH!!
Santas Castle

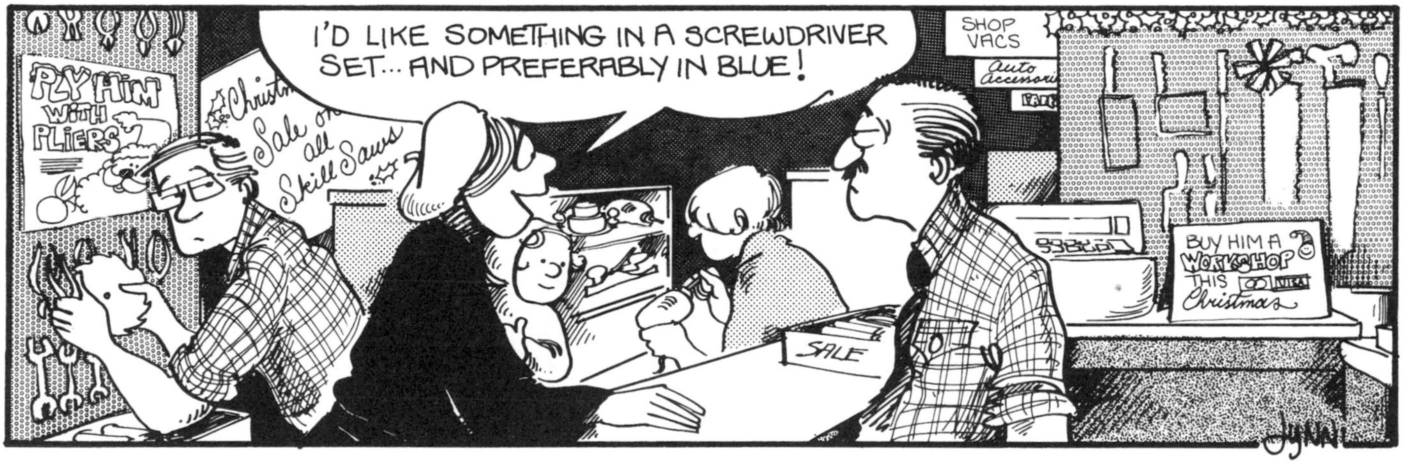
I'D LIKE SOMETHING IN A SCREWDRIVER SET... AND PREFERABLY IN BLUE!
PLY HIM WITH PLIERS
all Skill Saws
SHOP VACS
SALE
BUY HIM A WORKSHOP THIS
Christmas

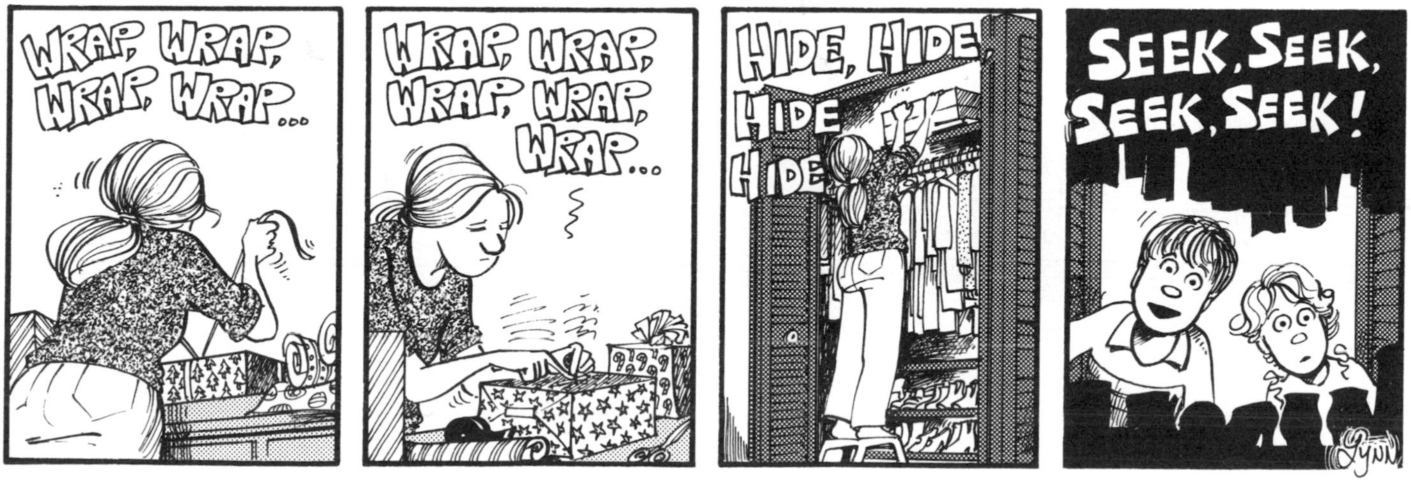
WRAP, WRAP, WRAP, WRAP...
WRAP, WRAP, WRAP, WRAP, WRAP...
HIDE, HIDE HIDE HIDE
SEEK, SEEK, SEEK, SEEK!

Sometimes there's no way to clean off a kid but immersion. Towelettes, facecloths, Kleenex, and spit don't make a dent in the veneer of lunch waste and fuzz that coats the average child's digits. These, of course, go into their mouth along with toys and other household flotsam left lying about. Clean fingers? Not unless it's bath time.

NO WAY! I BET THIS IS THE MONSTER TRUCK I ASKED FOR!!

MAYBE, IF I PULL THE TAPE OFF VE-E-E-E-RY CAREFULLY....

AAGH! IT'S A STUPID COFFEE MAKER!

TAPE, TAPE, TAPE POKE, PUSH, FIX TAPE, POKE

THERE...

THEY'LL NEVER KNOW I TOUCHED IT.

OK, YOU TWO... LISTEN UP.

SOMEONE HAS BEEN SNOOPING AROUND IN ALL THE CLOSETS AND IN THE CRAWL SPACE.

IF YOU ARE LOOKING FOR CHRISTMAS PRESENTS, YOU WON'T FIND ANY — BECAUSE SANTA ONLY BRINGS THINGS TO **GOOD** CHILDREN ON CHRISTMAS EVE!

AND, DON'T FORGET — HE KNOWS WHO'S NAUGHTY AND WHO'S NICE!

NUTS.

SURE I GAVE HIM SOME HINTS, ANNE!

I SAID — BUY ME SOMETHING FRIVOLOUS, AND EXPENSIVE — SOMETHING I CAN SHOW OFF TO MY FRIENDS...

I GUESS IT WAS JUST A FAILURE TO COMMUNICATE...

I WAS THINKING SUEDE COAT — WHILE HE WAS THINKING DISHWASHER.

315

* SO, HAVE YOU INTRODUCED CONNIE TO YOUR BROTHER, EL?

SHE'S BEEN OVER FOR COFFEE BUT NO REAL CONNECTION YET.

SHE'S DYING TO TALK TO HIM — YOU KNOW... ONE ON ONE.

YEAH... I JUST HAVE TO FIND A WAY TO GET HIM OVER TO HER PLACE.

ISN'T MATCHMAKING FUN, ELLY?

IT COULD GET ME INTO TROUBLE, ANNE...

YOU KNOW WHAT THEY SAY ABOUT PLAYING WITH MATCHES!!

YOU TAKING ME TO LAWRENCE'S HOUSE, UNCLE PHIL?

SURE, MAN!

HE'S ON HIS WAY NOW, CONNIE...

PHIL DOESN'T SUSPECT A THING — SO DON'T BE TOO OBVIOUS!

TRY NOT TO WORK "I'M SINGLE" INTO YOUR FIRST SENTENCE.

* LOOK UP INTO THE SKY, LAWRENCE... AN' DON'T LOOK AT ANYTHING ELSE.

WHEN THE SNOW FALLS DOWN TOWARDS YOU, IT FEELS LIKE YOU'RE FLYING UPWARDS, INTO THE SKY, DOESN'T IT.

YEAH.

EXCEPT MY FEET ARE TOUCHING THE GROUND.

FORGET YOUR FEET.

HOW CAN I FORGET MY FEET?

JUST STAND HERE LONG ENOUGH AN' YOU WON'T BE ABLE TO FEEL THEM.

When I started to put Uncle Phil's love life in the strip, Alan was single and hoping to meet someone new. When Phil started seeing Connie, who had a child, Alan began dating a young single mother. Later, when Phil met Georgia, Alan met Joan, who happened to look a lot like Georgia. This was such an uncanny coincidence. Alan asked me not to have Phil and Georgia (nicknamed Geo) get married until he had married Joan, which he did, and then Phil married Geo.

I think I was three. It was early Christmas morning and I had crept into the living room to see if Santa had come. There, under the tree were a zillion packages and I remember sighing and thinking, "They're not all for me."

This is another example of overreaction. In the last panel, Elly could have delivered the same line—with a subtle expression. I was just learning this craft. It took me a while to figure out that less is more.

*

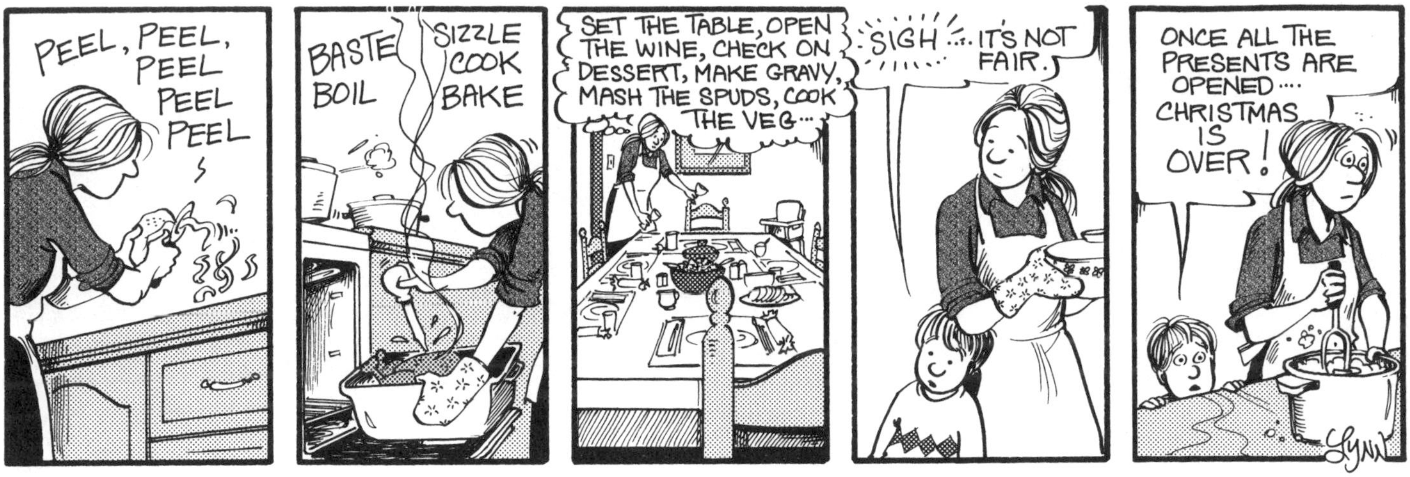
PEEL, PEEL, PEEL PEEL PEEL PEEL
BASTE BOIL
SIZZLE COOK BAKE
SET THE TABLE, OPEN THE WINE, CHECK ON DESSERT, MAKE GRAVY, MASH THE SPUDS, COOK THE VEG...
SIGH... IT'S NOT FAIR.
ONCE ALL THE PRESENTS ARE OPENED.... CHRISTMAS IS OVER!
LYNN

*

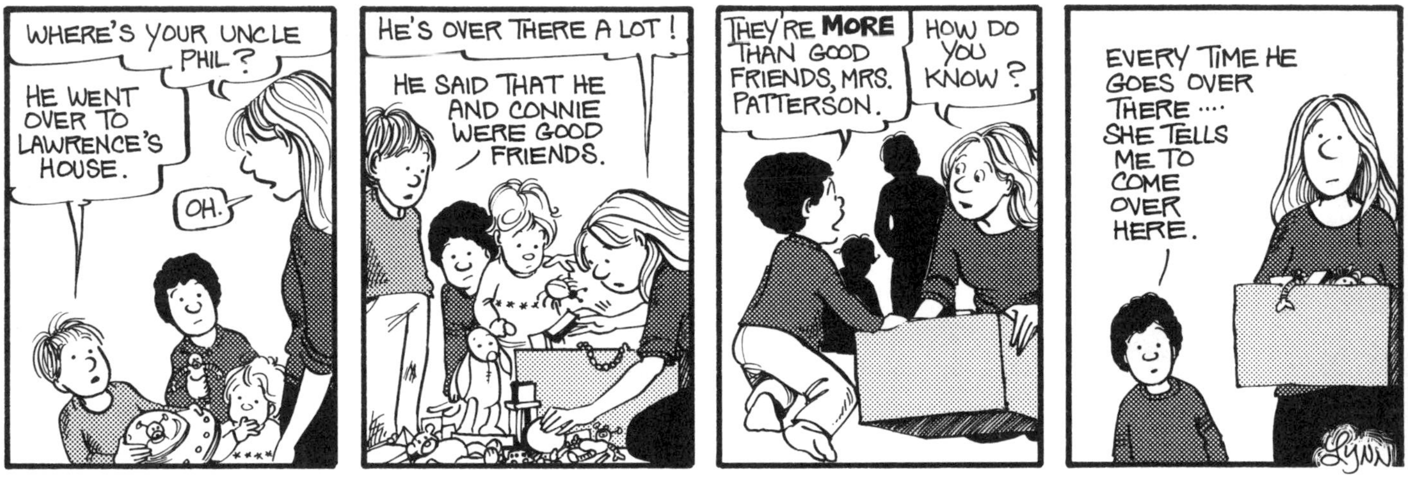
WHERE'S YOUR UNCLE PHIL?
HE WENT OVER TO LAWRENCE'S HOUSE.
OH.
HE'S OVER THERE A LOT!
HE SAID THAT HE AND CONNIE WERE GOOD FRIENDS.
THEY'RE MORE THAN GOOD FRIENDS, MRS. PATTERSON.
HOW DO YOU KNOW?
EVERY TIME HE GOES OVER THERE.... SHE TELLS ME TO COME OVER HERE.
LYNN

*

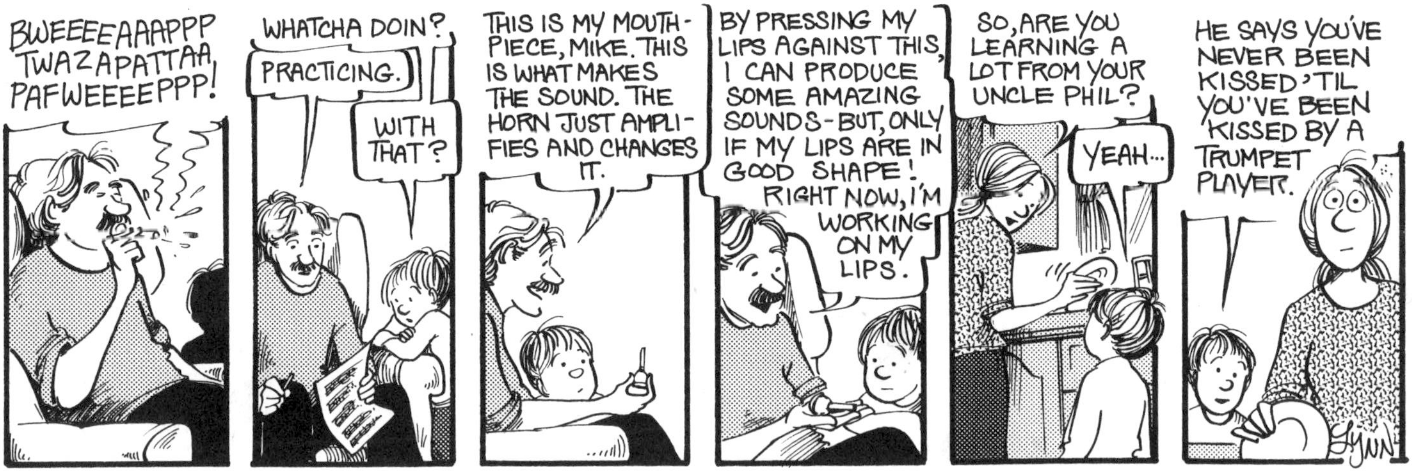
BWEEEEAAAPPP TWAZAPATTAA PAFWEEEEPPP!
WHATCHA DOIN?
PRACTICING.
WITH THAT?
THIS IS MY MOUTH-PIECE, MIKE. THIS IS WHAT MAKES THE SOUND. THE HORN JUST AMPLI-FIES AND CHANGES IT.
BY PRESSING MY LIPS AGAINST THIS, I CAN PRODUCE SOME AMAZING SOUNDS - BUT, ONLY IF MY LIPS ARE IN GOOD SHAPE!
RIGHT NOW, I'M WORKING ON MY LIPS.
SO, ARE YOU LEARNING A LOT FROM YOUR UNCLE PHIL?
YEAH...
HE SAYS YOU'VE NEVER BEEN KISSED 'TIL YOU'VE BEEN KISSED BY A TRUMPET PLAYER.
LYNN

I think Al started playing trumpet when he was nine. He practiced constantly and the exercises he played over and over again still resound in my head, as do great pieces like "Bugler's Holiday" and the "Brandenburg Concerto." I have such respect for professional musicians. To do what they do takes talent and years of serious, dedicated, and hard work!

321

5-4-3-2-1...

HAPPY NEW YEAR!

WELL, GIRL...LOOKS LIKE WE MADE IT THROUGH ANOTHER YEAR!

LET'S GO BACK TO BED, LIZ...THERE'S NOTHING SPECIAL ABOUT TONIGHT AFTER ALL.

* HAPPY NEW YEAR!! YAH HOOOO WOO HOOO HAPPY NEW YEAR!

MICHAEL, WHAT IS GOING ON? IT'S 6 IN THE MORNING AND NOBODY'S UP YET.

I AM!

AN' IT'S A WHOLE NEW YEAR!-I WANNA DO SOMETHING GREAT TODAY! I WANNA DO SOMETHING TOTALLY, AMAZINGLY, PERFECTLY COOL!

BUT... WHAT CAN I DO?

I HAVE AN IDEA.

...LET YOUR PARENTS SLEEP IN UNTIL 8.

* WELL... I WONDER WHAT HAPPENED LAST NIGHT.

DON'T WORRY ABOUT CONNIE, EL—SHE CAN TAKE CARE OF HERSELF.

SHE'S ONE OF MY CLOSEST FRIENDS, JOHN. IF MY BROTHER BREAKS HER HEART,...WHERE WILL THAT LEAVE ME?—I WOULD FEEL SO RESPONSIBLE!

LOOK. ALL YOU DID WAS INTRODUCE THEM. IF SOMETHING GOES WRONG, IT'S NO REFLECTION ON YOU!!

WHAT HAVE I DONE?!

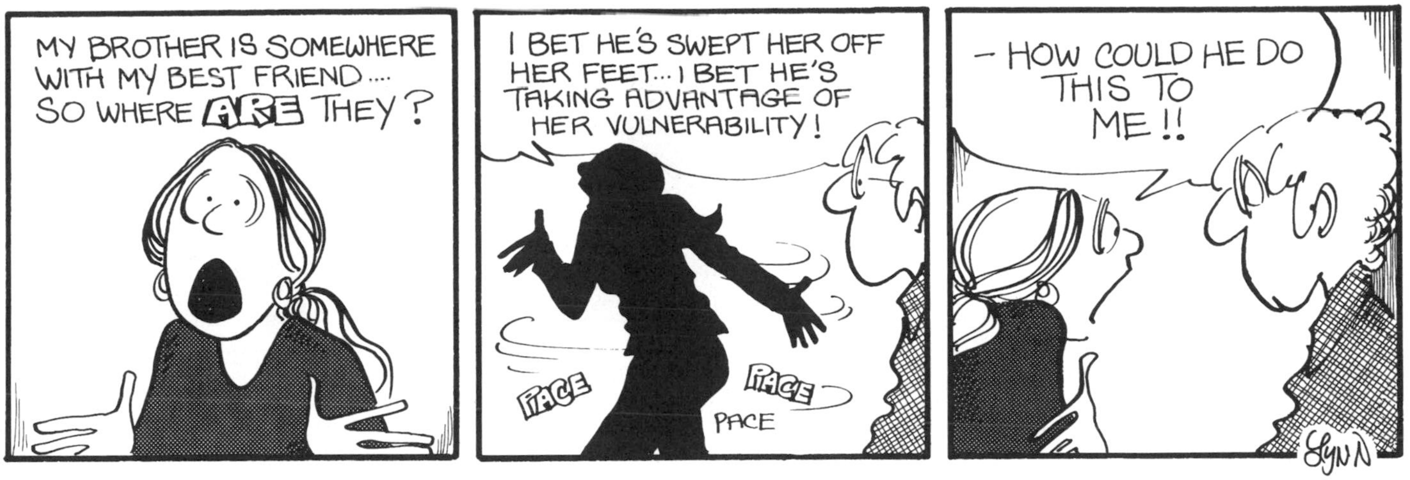
MY BROTHER IS SOMEWHERE WITH MY BEST FRIEND.... SO WHERE ARE THEY?
I BET HE'S SWEPT HER OFF HER FEET... I BET HE'S TAKING ADVANTAGE OF HER VULNERABILITY!
PACE
PACE
PACE
– HOW COULD HE DO THIS TO ME!!
Lynn

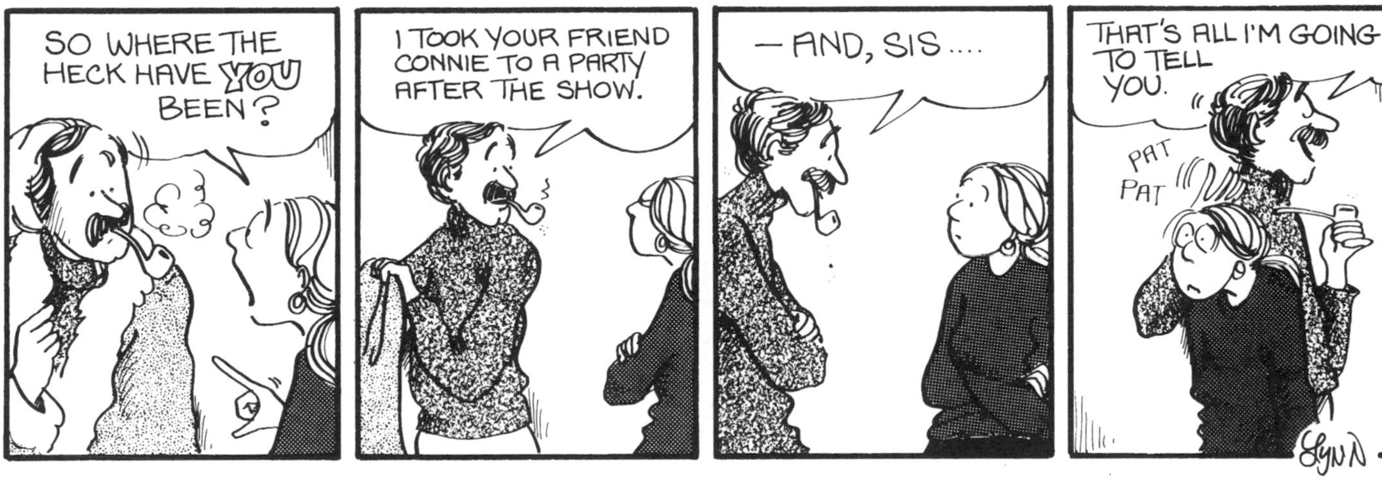
SO WHERE THE HECK HAVE YOU BEEN?
I TOOK YOUR FRIEND CONNIE TO A PARTY AFTER THE SHOW.
– AND, SIS....
THAT'S ALL I'M GOING TO TELL YOU.
PAT
PAT
Lynn

*

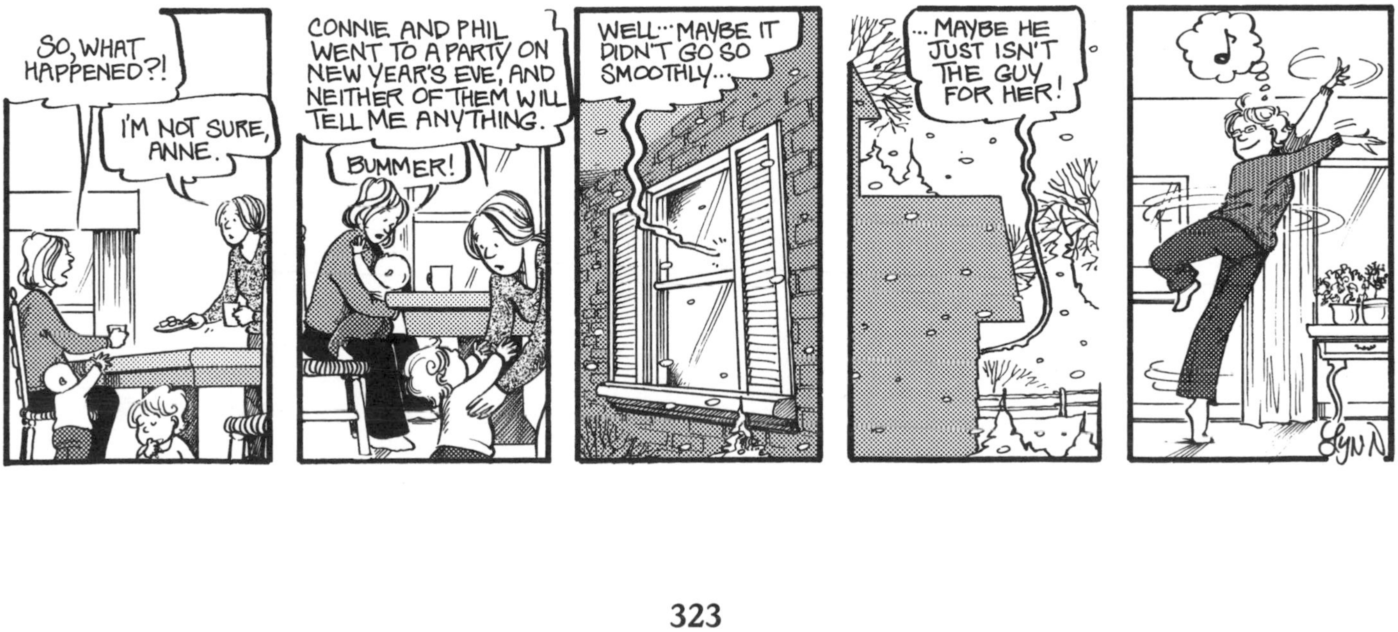
SO, WHAT HAPPENED?!
I'M NOT SURE, ANNE.
CONNIE AND PHIL WENT TO A PARTY ON NEW YEAR'S EVE, AND NEITHER OF THEM WILL TELL ME ANYTHING.
BUMMER!
WELL... MAYBE IT DIDN'T GO SO SMOOTHLY...
...MAYBE HE JUST ISN'T THE GUY FOR HER!
Lynn

Drawing this strip was so much fun. Not only did I get to tease my brother about his occasional quest for a quaff, I got to boot him as well! While inking the last panel, I laughed out loud.

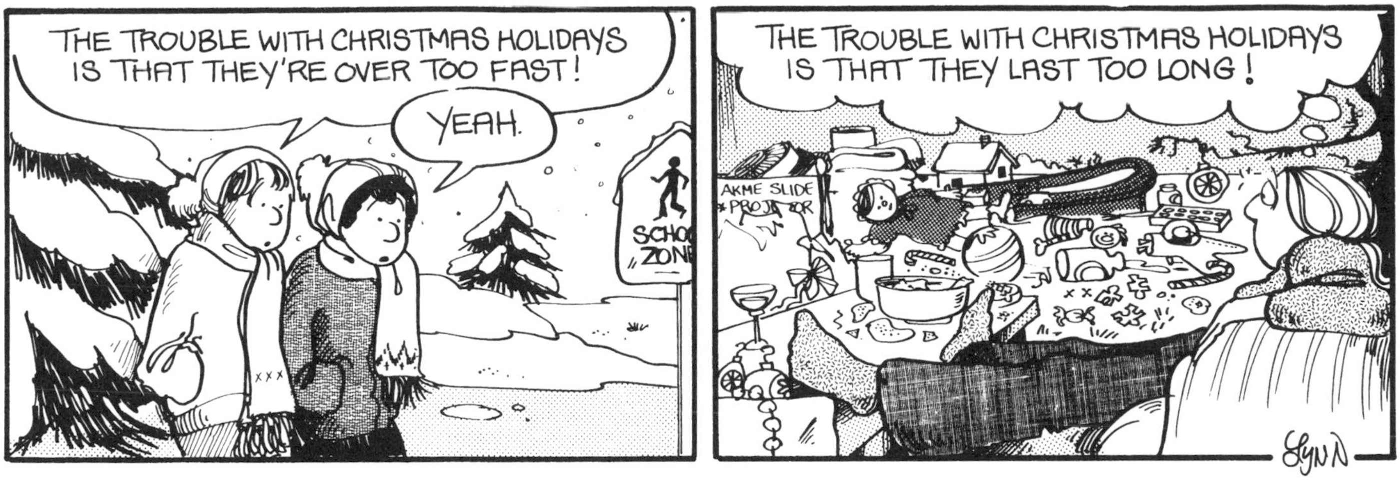
THE TROUBLE WITH CHRISTMAS HOLIDAYS IS THAT THEY'RE OVER TOO FAST!
YEAH.
THE TROUBLE WITH CHRISTMAS HOLIDAYS IS THAT THEY LAST TOO LONG!
AKME SLIDE
Lynn

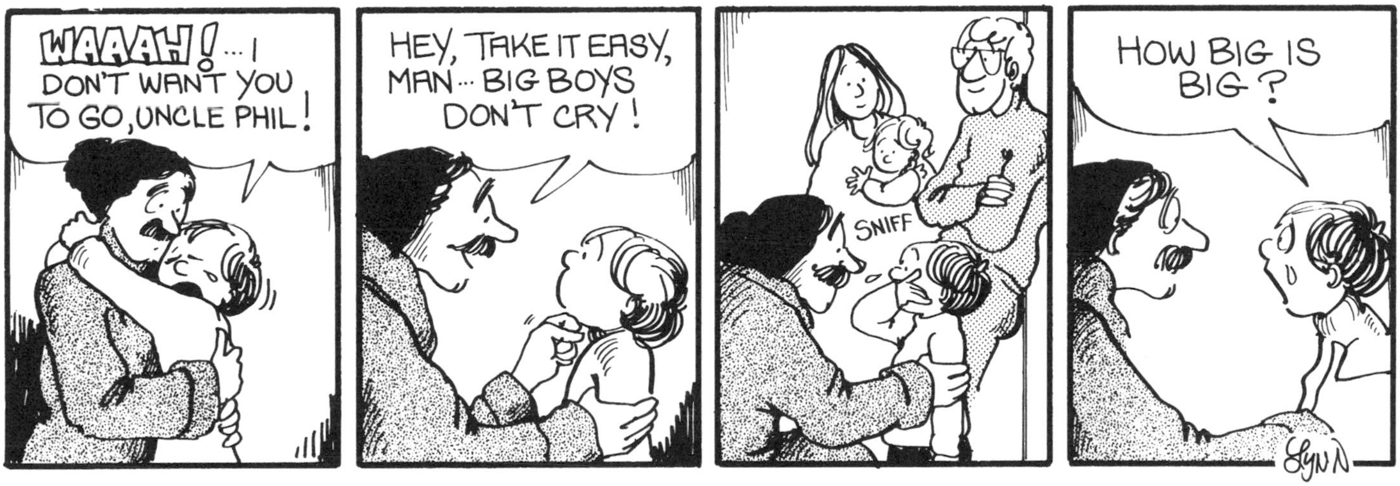
WAAAH!... I DON'T WANT YOU TO GO, UNCLE PHIL!
HEY, TAKE IT EASY, MAN... BIG BOYS DON'T CRY!
SNIFF
HOW BIG IS BIG?
Lynn

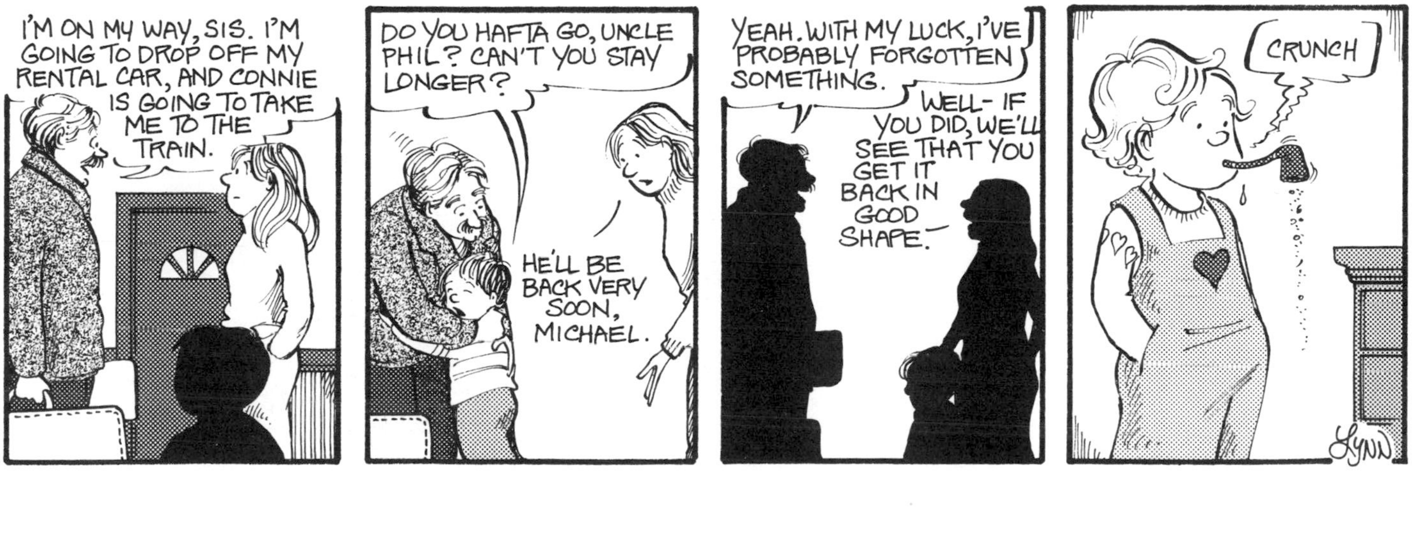
I'M ON MY WAY, SIS. I'M GOING TO DROP OFF MY RENTAL CAR, AND CONNIE IS GOING TO TAKE ME TO THE TRAIN.
DO YOU HAFTA GO, UNCLE PHIL? CAN'T YOU STAY LONGER?
HE'LL BE BACK VERY SOON, MICHAEL.
YEAH. WITH MY LUCK, I'VE PROBABLY FORGOTTEN SOMETHING.
WELL- IF YOU DID, WE'LL SEE THAT YOU GET IT BACK IN GOOD SHAPE.
CRUNCH
Lynn

SO HE'S GONE... TAKEN OFF—JUST LIKE THAT!

IT'S THE STORY OF MY LIFE!—LOVE 'EM AND LEAVE 'EM!

CONNIE—DID MY BROTHER SAY HE LOVED YOU?

OK OK— LIKE 'EM AND LEAVE 'EM THEN.

CONNIE—BE OBJECTIVE.—PHIL IS NOT YOUR TYPE!

HE'S INDEPENDENT, HIS LIFE IS MUSIC AND LATE NIGHTS!—HE PRACTICES AT 3 A.M., HE DOES YOGA!

HE'S NOT A FAMILY MAN—HE'LL NEVER SETTLE DOWN.

YEAH. I GUESS SO.

... BUT OTHER THAN THAT HE'S PERFECT!

I once dated a guy who insisted I didn't really see him—I saw an imaginary image. I was miffed. I told him he was wrong. Of course I saw him; what was he thinking? Mark had blond hair and a thick red beard. One day, he showed up at my door—clean shaven—and I didn't notice.

I'VE GONE AND DONE IT NOW!

CONNIE THINKS MY BROTHER IS THE ANSWER TO HER DREAMS.

SHE REFUSES TO SEE HIM AS HE REALLY IS!

SOMETIMES THAT'S THE KEY TO A SUCCESSFUL RELATIONSHIP.

So many times, I thought I would go off the deep end—but sharing my suffering with an unseen audience saved my sanity. This is another example of "telling it like it is!"

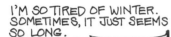

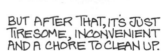

We've all been discouraged from using our strip as a platform. If your work has a serious side, it's hard not to include certain points of view, though—and some of us live with illness such as Alzheimer's, cancer, and diabetes, which finds its way into the mix. The thing is, not to do it often, and if you do—do it well. I have touched on the subject of war and violence a number of times. This is my point of view and I hope I've expressed it well.

Aaron said this and it really made me think. You can learn so much from children—their honesty is to be respected and encouraged.

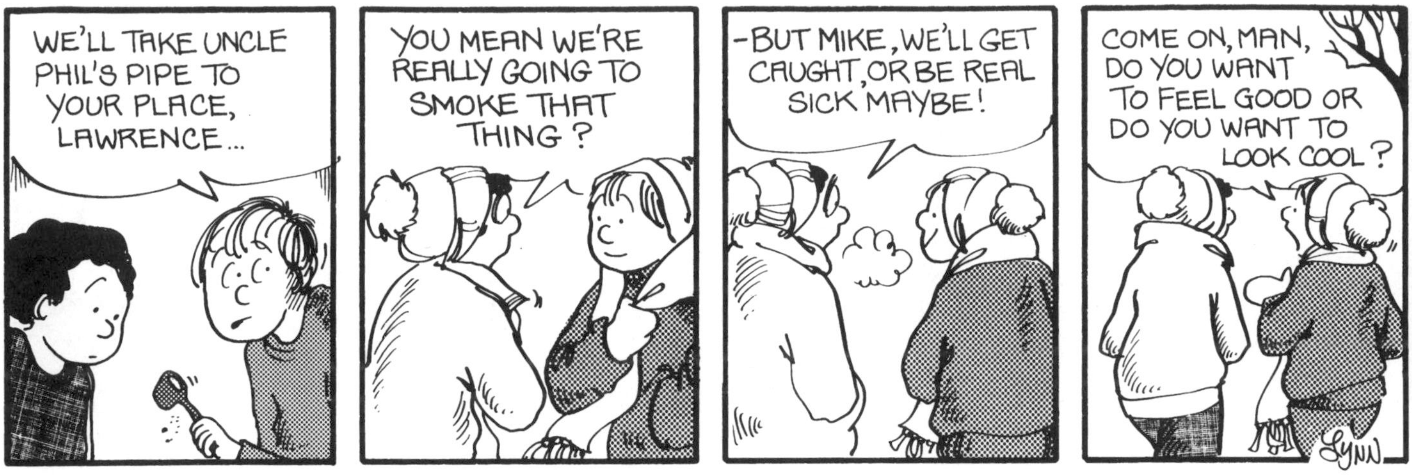
WE'LL TAKE UNCLE PHIL'S PIPE TO YOUR PLACE, LAWRENCE...
YOU MEAN WE'RE REALLY GOING TO SMOKE THAT THING?
-BUT MIKE, WE'LL GET CAUGHT, OR BE REAL SICK MAYBE!
COME ON, MAN, DO YOU WANT TO FEEL GOOD OR DO YOU WANT TO LOOK COOL?
LYNN

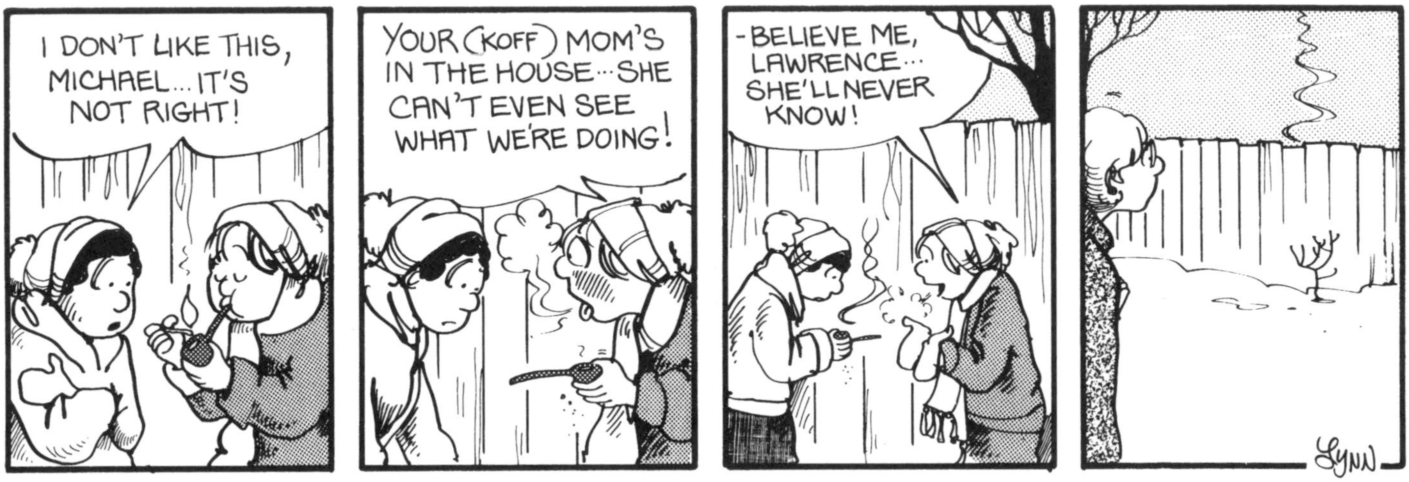
I DON'T LIKE THIS, MICHAEL... IT'S NOT RIGHT!
YOUR (KOFF) MOM'S IN THE HOUSE... SHE CAN'T EVEN SEE WHAT WE'RE DOING!
-BELIEVE ME, LAWRENCE... SHE'LL NEVER KNOW!
LYNN

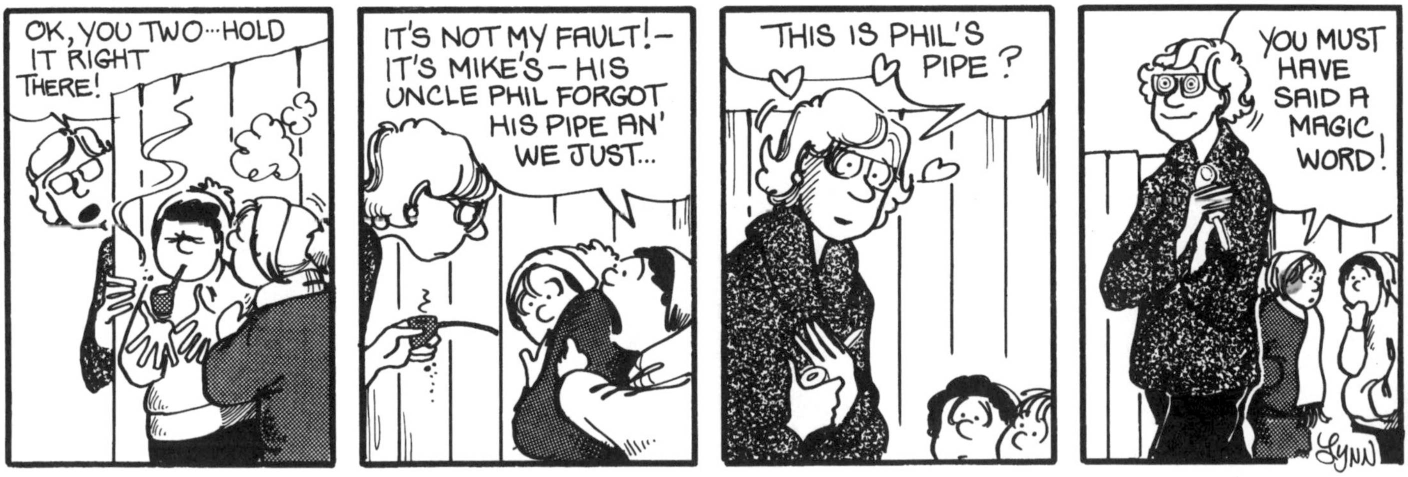
OK, YOU TWO... HOLD IT RIGHT THERE!
IT'S NOT MY FAULT! - IT'S MIKE'S - HIS UNCLE PHIL FORGOT HIS PIPE AN' WE JUST...
THIS IS PHIL'S PIPE?
YOU MUST HAVE SAID A MAGIC WORD!
LYNN

Dad belonged to a barbershop quartet. These guys would practice in our living room every Wednesday night. One of them, a judge, would smoke cigars, leaving large stubs in the ashtray. Alan took one and, together, we smoked the butt until our eyes were bulging and our guts were sore. I don't think I've ever felt so miserable. Mom never got angry. Our taking tearful turns in the bathroom was punishment enough.

331

For some reason, the downspout on my house in Dundas ended halfway down. A good rainfall and melting snow made this a nuisance as kids and dogs, attracted to the fountain, managed to bring most of the water inside.

Kate was our sweet tooth. Getting her to eat veggies was an art. She wasn't nicknamed "cake" for nothing!

WHATCHA WRITING, MOM?

A STORY FOR MY CLASS.

WILL YOU READ IT TO ME?

SURE.

WHAT'S IT ABOUT? AM I IN IT? IS IT ABOUT ME? IS IT A LONG STORY OR A SHORT ONE?

TICKITY-TAP-TAP TAP TICK TAP

TAP TICK TAP

WILL THERE BE PICTURES? HOW MUCH TIME WILL IT TAKE? ARE YOU GONNA...

TAPPITA TICK-TAP TICK TAP

AAAAAU UCHH!!!

LIKE YOU SAID, DAD.... WRITERS ARE TEMPER MENTAL.

OK, I'M READY TO READ MY STORY.

GATHER 'ROUND, GUYS!

LET'S SEE... THIS IS A STORY ABOUT MY CHILDHOOD. UM... LET'S GET THE RIGHT PAGE... UM... ...AHEM...

WHY AM I SO NERVOUS ABOUT READING MY WRITING TO MY OWN FAMILY?!

RELAX, EL!

WE'LL ENJOY IT!

YEAH!

NO MATTER HOW BAD IT IS !!!

THAT WAS A COOL STORY, MOM!

YOU LIKED IT?

I NEVER KNEW YOU PUT A POTATO IN YOUR GRAMPA'S TAILPIPE- OR BOILED A DEAD RACCOON ON YOUR MOM'S STOVE !!

WHOA! YOU DID STUFF YOU'D **NEVER** LET ME DO !

THAT'S WHY PEOPLE WRITE THEIR MEMOIRS **AFTER** THEIR KIDS ARE GROWN.

DINNER'S DONE, KIDS ARE READY FOR BED, MY CLASS STARTS IN 45 MINUTES...

SMAK!

SEE YOU LATER!

WHOA! —THAT WAS A **HOT** KISS!

NOT NOW, JOHN— I'VE GOTTA GO!

YOU'VE GOT A TEMPERATURE! ARE YOU SURE YOU'RE OK?

I'M FINE! ...JUST A LITTLE TIRED, THAT'S ALL.

104°—YOU'RE STAYING HOME.

BUT, I WANT TO GO TO SCHOOL!!!

DAD'S RIGHT, MOM... YOU'RE NOT WELL.

GIVE YOUR MOM A BREAK, GUYS. SHE'S NOT FEELING WELL.

SHE NEEDS TO HAVE A GOOD REST, SO SHE'S GOING TO BED EARLY.

AND, TOMORROW, YOU'RE GOING TO RELAX AND TAKE IT EASY, OK? TOMORROW, YOU'RE TAKING A DAY OFF.

ME, TOO!

I FORGOT! TEACHERS HAVE A PROFESSIONAL DEVELOPMENT DAY TOMORROW.

DON'T WORRY, MOM...

IF WE BUST ANYTHING—WE'LL DO IT QUIETLY.

I'M SORRY YOU'RE NOT FEELING WELL, HONEY.

I TOOK LIZZIE TO THE SITTER, AND MIKE IS IN CRAFT CLASS.

I CAN PICK UP LIZZIE... BUT THERE'S NO WAY I — CAN GET DOWN TO COLLECT MICHAEL.

...SO, THAT MEANS I CAN BE SICK UNTIL 11:45.

Kate once made a sculpture using fake fur, bailing twine and food coloring. She called it *Road Kill*. She got good marks for it, too. That's art!

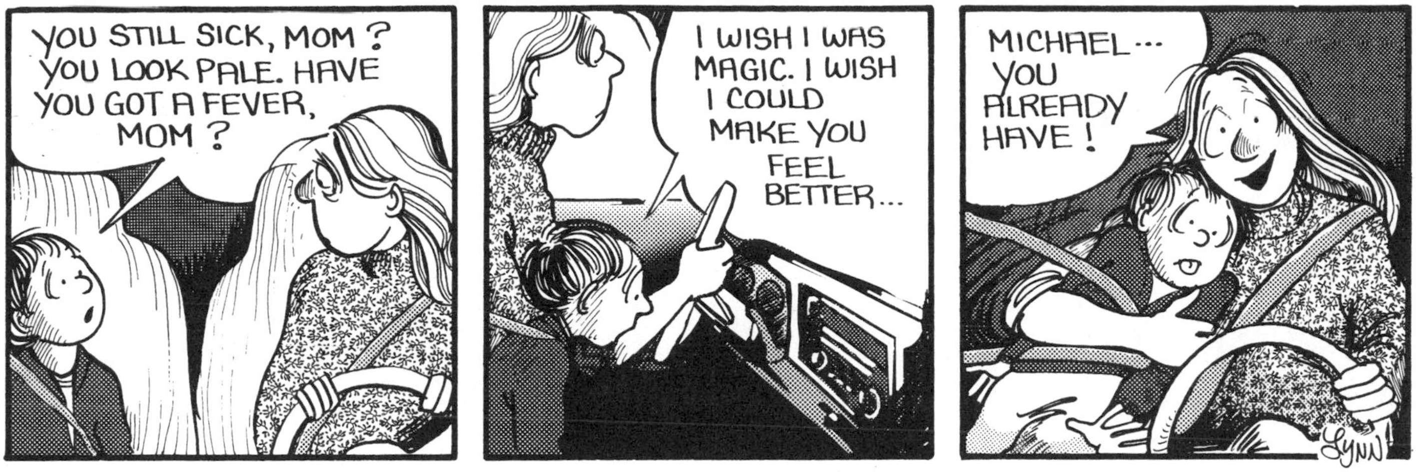
YOU STILL SICK, MOM? YOU LOOK PALE. HAVE YOU GOT A FEVER, MOM?
I WISH I WAS MAGIC. I WISH I COULD MAKE YOU FEEL BETTER...
MICHAEL... YOU ALREADY HAVE!
LYNN

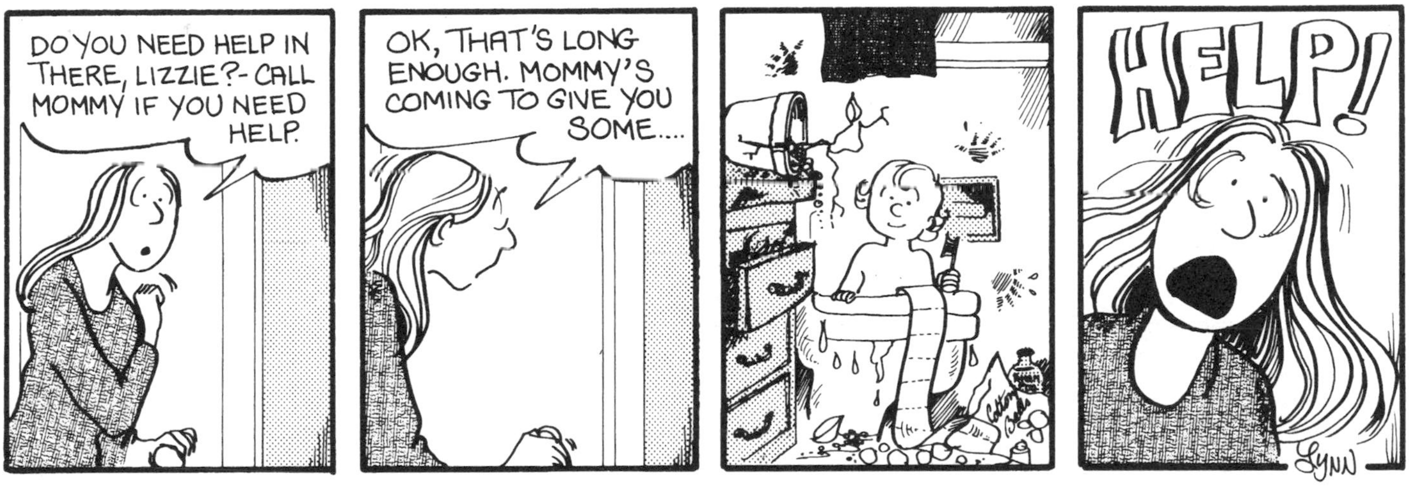
DO YOU NEED HELP IN THERE, LIZZIE?- CALL MOMMY IF YOU NEED HELP.
OK, THAT'S LONG ENOUGH. MOMMY'S COMING TO GIVE YOU SOME....
HELP!
LYNN

*

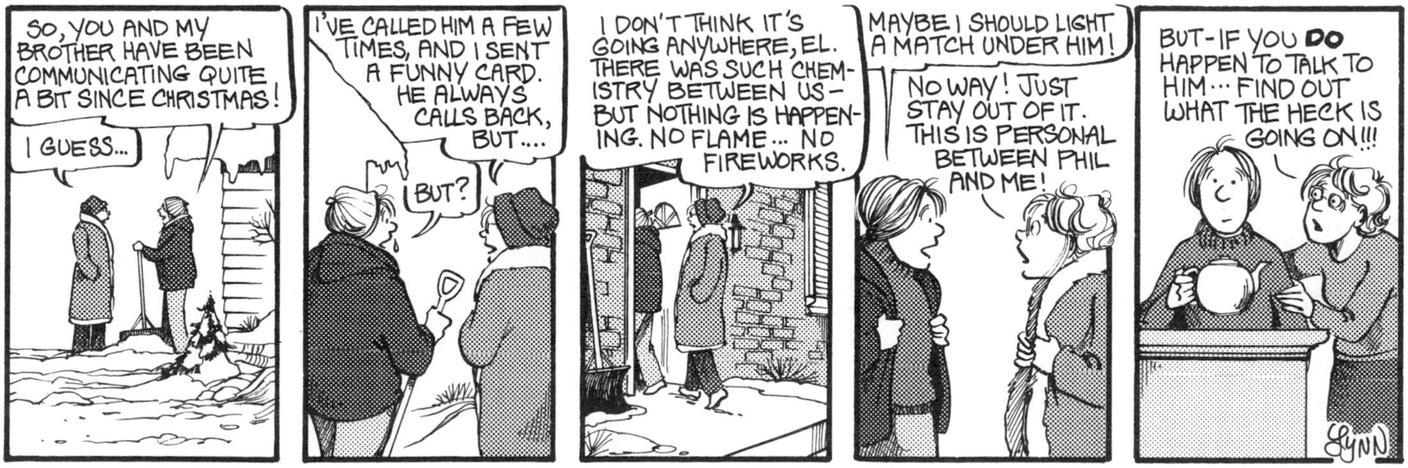
SO, YOU AND MY BROTHER HAVE BEEN COMMUNICATING QUITE A BIT SINCE CHRISTMAS!
I GUESS...
I'VE CALLED HIM A FEW TIMES, AND I SENT A FUNNY CARD. HE ALWAYS CALLS BACK, BUT....
BUT?
I DON'T THINK IT'S GOING ANYWHERE, EL. THERE WAS SUCH CHEMISTRY BETWEEN US- BUT NOTHING IS HAPPENING. NO FLAME... NO FIREWORKS.
MAYBE I SHOULD LIGHT A MATCH UNDER HIM!
NO WAY! JUST STAY OUT OF IT. THIS IS PERSONAL BETWEEN PHIL AND ME!
BUT- IF YOU DO HAPPEN TO TALK TO HIM... FIND OUT WHAT THE HECK IS GOING ON!!!
LYNN

After sending this in to the syndicate, I realized I'd done the same strip before. Different dialogue, same ending.

*

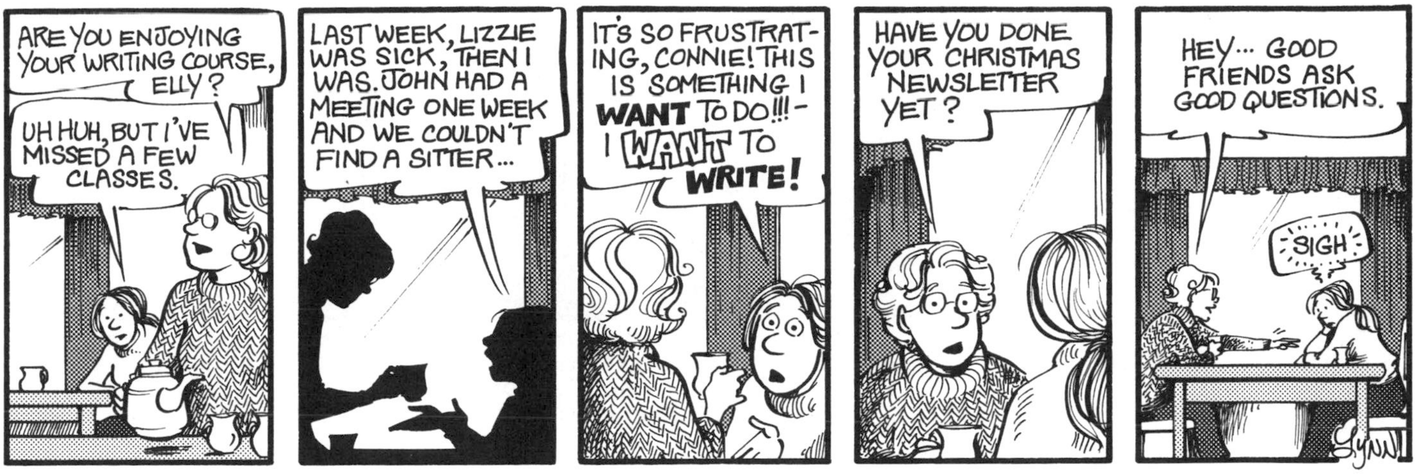
ARE YOU ENJOYING YOUR WRITING COURSE, ELLY?
UH HUH, BUT I'VE MISSED A FEW CLASSES.
LAST WEEK, LIZZIE WAS SICK, THEN I WAS. JOHN HAD A MEETING ONE WEEK AND WE COULDN'T FIND A SITTER...
IT'S SO FRUSTRATING, CONNIE! THIS IS SOMETHING I WANT TO DO!!! - I WANT TO WRITE!
HAVE YOU DONE YOUR CHRISTMAS NEWSLETTER YET?
HEY... GOOD FRIENDS ASK GOOD QUESTIONS.
SIGH
LYNN

*

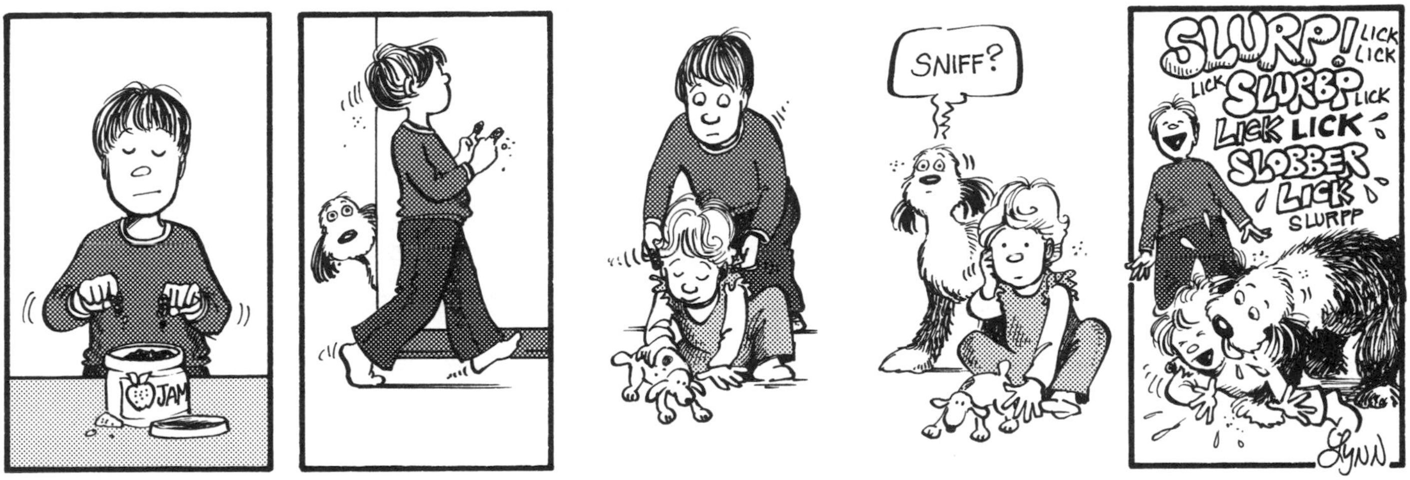
JAM
SNIFF?
SLURP! LICK LICK
LICK SLURBP LICK
LICK LICK
SLOBBER
LICK
SLURPP
LYNN

*

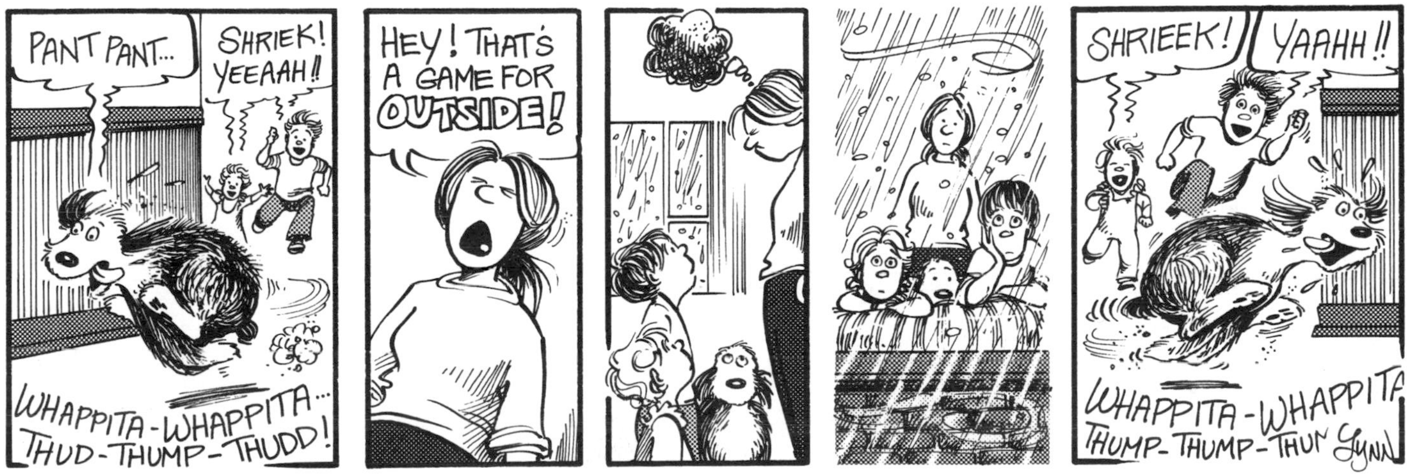
PANT PANT...
SHRIEK! YEEAAH!!
WHAPPITA-WHAPPITA... THUD-THUMP-THUDD!
HEY! THAT'S A GAME FOR OUTSIDE!
SHRIEEK!
YAAHH!!
WHAPPITA-WHAPPITA THUMP-THUMP-THUN
LYNN

The person who coined the phrase "A woman's work is never done" was probably a mother.

I rarely did a series of panels in which the illustrations were almost the same. Occasionally, mind you, this does augment the gag. I enjoyed doing this one.

My friend Kevin has a large, friendly yellow Lab. Oden likes to chew and can grind his way through a big stick in no time. He does have a squeaky toy, however, which despite vigorous squawking abuse, looks virtually new. He treasures it, carries it like a cub, and offers it up to trusted friends only. Despite the negativity in this strip, I do love animals—each one's unique, each one has character. If you ask me, "Are there dogs in heaven?" the answer is, "Of course"—chew toys, footprints, dander, and all.

FOR Better OR FOR WORSE

BY Lynn Johnston

CLICK!

BANG! BLAM!.. COVER ME, JAKE — I'M GOING 'ROUND THE BACK! POW! KABLANG!

AND NOW, HERE'S TONIGHT'S SCIENCE SPECIAL—"FARMS OF THE FUTURE"— WITH YOUR HOST MARK ROADBERRY...

OK, GUYS... BEDTIME!

"YAWN"...I REALLY ENJOYED SPENDING TIME WITH THE FAMILY TONIGHT!

I THOUGHT WE'D FORGOTTEN HOW TO COMMUNICATE!

Lynn

The above strip ran at another time during the 2007 mix of new and old. By scrambling story lines, I gave myself real problems— sometimes the dialogue in an older strip didn't match the new one. If it sounds confusing—it is!!!

In order to draw a dog, you have to *be* a dog! In fact, you have to get into all of your characters. Cartoonists have to be such versatile actors that we often have sore face muscles from making the expressions we draw.

*

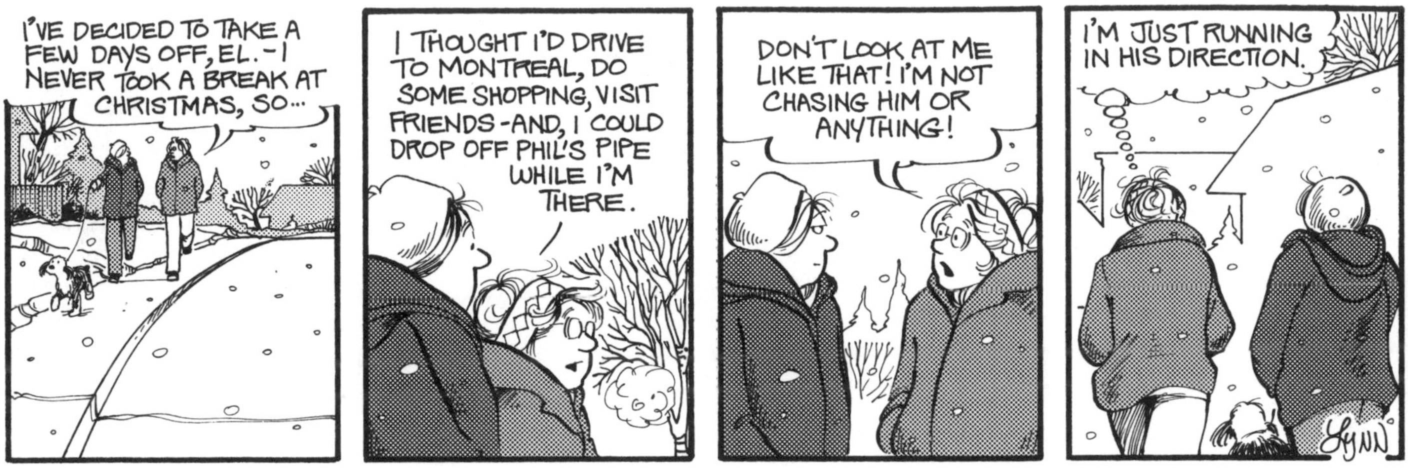
I'VE DECIDED TO TAKE A FEW DAYS OFF, EL. – I NEVER TOOK A BREAK AT CHRISTMAS, SO...
I THOUGHT I'D DRIVE TO MONTREAL, DO SOME SHOPPING, VISIT FRIENDS – AND, I COULD DROP OFF PHIL'S PIPE WHILE I'M THERE.
DON'T LOOK AT ME LIKE THAT! I'M NOT CHASING HIM OR ANYTHING!
I'M JUST RUNNING IN HIS DIRECTION.
LYNN

*

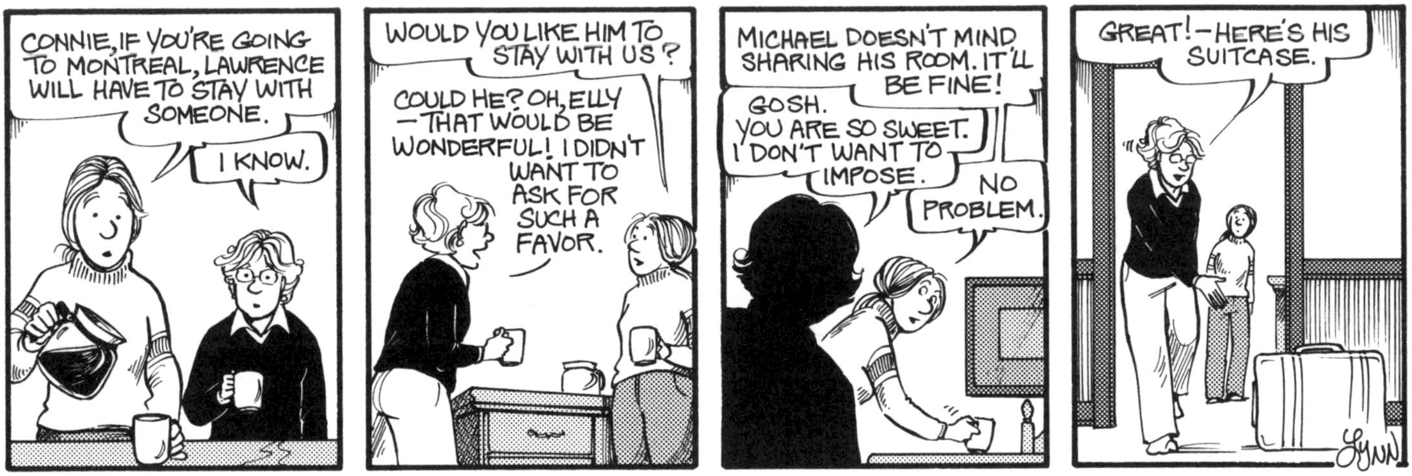
CONNIE, IF YOU'RE GOING TO MONTREAL, LAWRENCE WILL HAVE TO STAY WITH SOMEONE.
I KNOW.
WOULD YOU LIKE HIM TO STAY WITH US?
COULD HE? OH, ELLY – THAT WOULD BE WONDERFUL! I DIDN'T WANT TO ASK FOR SUCH A FAVOR.
MICHAEL DOESN'T MIND SHARING HIS ROOM. IT'LL BE FINE!
GOSH. YOU ARE SO SWEET. I DON'T WANT TO IMPOSE.
NO PROBLEM.
GREAT! – HERE'S HIS SUITCASE.
LYNN

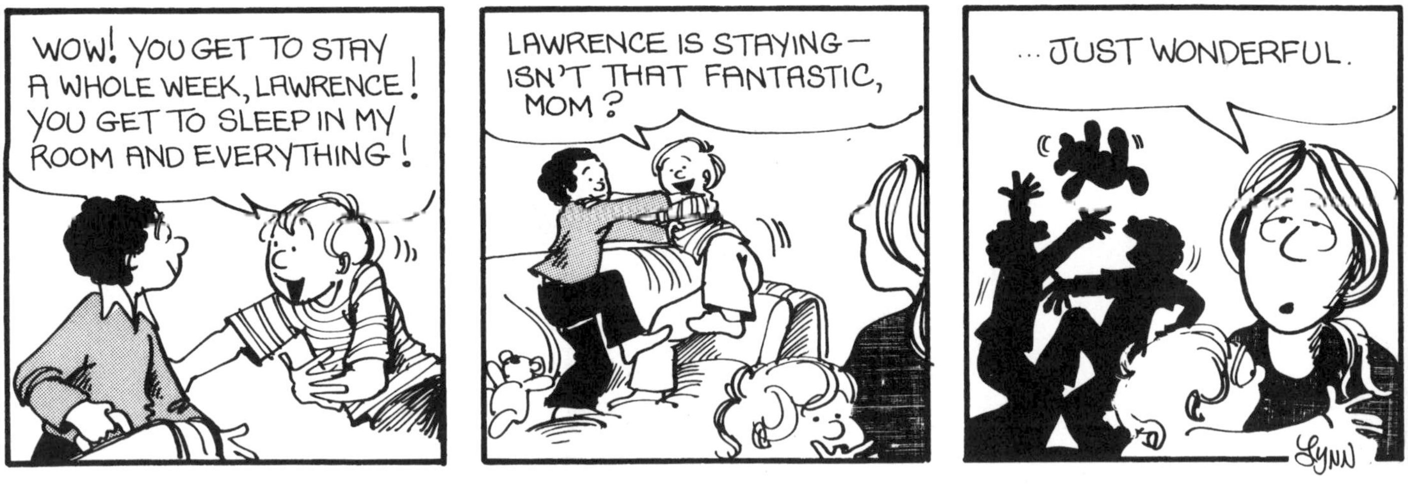
WOW! YOU GET TO STAY A WHOLE WEEK, LAWRENCE! YOU GET TO SLEEP IN MY ROOM AND EVERYTHING!
LAWRENCE IS STAYING – ISN'T THAT FANTASTIC, MOM?
... JUST WONDERFUL.
LYNN

SO, YOU HAVE ANOTHER HOUSEGUEST!

LAWRENCE IS NO TROUBLE, ANNE... AND CONNIE WILL ONLY BE GONE FOR A FEW DAYS.

BESIDES, THE BOYS ARE IN SCHOOL, SO I CAN GET A LOT DONE WITHOUT TOO MUCH INTERRUPTION.

SIGH...I WISH I COULD GET EXCITED ABOUT VACUUMING, THOUGH. NEXT TO WASHING WINDOWS, IT'S THE CHORE I HATE MOST.

IN MY NEXT LIFE, I'M COMING BACK AS A MAN.

NOT ME.

...WITH MY LUCK, I'D COME BACK AS A JANITOR!

YOU BOYS STOP FOOLING AROUND AND GO TO SLEEP!

GIGGLE GIGGLE

OK-THAT'S IT! THIS IS YOUR LAST WARNING!

ONE MORE SOUND AND TWO PEOPLE WILL BE VERY SORRY!

SNICKER OOF! GIGGLE

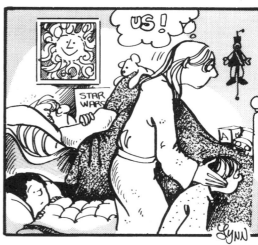

US!

STAR WARS

Aaron played hockey, which meant billets, which meant getting a bunch of boys to sleep. They didn't have to doze off—just cut the noise and stop fooling around. It doesn't happen. Why should it? Staying up is half the fun—and even though Mom's ticked, you know she's gonna make breakfast.

I MISSED RECESS AND I HAD TO WRITE LINES AND I'M NEVER COMING BACK TO SCHOOL — NEVER!

I GOT KICKED OUT OF THE LIBRARY AND I HATE MY TEACHER 'CAUSE IT'S ALL HER FAULT!

WHY?

-- SHE CAUGHT ME MASHING SPITBALLS IN THE DICTIONARY.

I MEET HIM BY CHANCE AS I STROLL DOWN RUE DES FÈVES...

HE SMILES, WE TOUCH, THERE IN THE MIST I LOOK CHILDLIKE... INNOCENT.

I FEEL HELPLESS, WEAK, FEMININE... AND HE I... HONK!

SHADDUP YOU *!!©* MORON!

I redid this strip because I thought it was ugly—Connie wouldn't shout at another driver like this. So when I had the chance, I drew it again. Here are the two strips for comparison.

* I CAN'T BELIEVE I'M DRIVING ALL THE WAY TO MONTREAL TO SEE PHIL RICHARDS.

I MEET HIM BY CHANCE AS I STROLL DOWN RUE DES FÈVES. HE'S SO HAPPY TO SEE ME. HE SMILES. WE TOUCH AND... EMBRACE.

THERE, IN THE EVENING MIST, I LOOK SO YOUNG, SO SWEET. HE GAZES INTO MY EYES. THEN... MY LIPS TASTE THE SALT ON HIS MOUSTACHE...

HONK!

HUMPH! SOME DRIVERS SHOULD PAY MORE ATTENTION TO THEIR DRIVING!!

©

* 114 RUE DES FÈVES. THIS IS PHIL'S APARTMENT.—I'M ON THE STREET WHERE HE LIVES!!

I HAVE TO RETURN HIS PIPE, BUT, WHAT DO I DO?...JUST KNOCK ON THE DOOR? ...I'LL FEEL LIKE AN IDIOT!

OH, WHAT THE HECK! ...THERE'S NOTHING LIKE A LITTLE SURPRISE!

KNOCK KNOCK KNOCK

'ALLO?

When I'm writing a vignette, I am the character. As I walked up to Phil's door in Montreal, in my imagination, a woman answered. This posed a whole series of strips, which I never did, leaving the audience hanging. With the reemergence of the story line, I was able to add a few explanatory quotes and illustrations. Omissions like this were all part of the learning curve.

During the '80s, my sister-in-law was a practicing veterinarian. The diagnosis and the surgery taxed mind and body; the stress of having someone's treasured pet's life in your hands weighed heavily. Like a physician, she had years of training and experience, so when her patient's owners complained about payment—it rubbed her fur the wrong way!

MOM! – LIZZIE'S INTO EVERYTHING!

LAWRENCE AN' I CAN'T PLAY WITHOUT HER GETTING INTO OUR STUFF!

MICHAEL – YOU USUALLY PLAY SO WELL WITH YOUR LITTLE SISTER.

SNIVEL

YEAH, BUT THAT'S WHEN I HAVEN'T GOT A CHOICE!

CONNIE, I DON'T KNOW WHO THE GIRL IS!

LOOK, JUST GO ON DOWN TO THE CLUB AND TAKE IN A SHOW.

CONNIE, THIS IS YOUR PROBLEM AND I REALLY DON'T WANT TO GET INVOLVED!

FAMOUS WORDS. USUALLY SPOKEN WHEN YOU'RE UP TO YOUR NECK IN SOMEONE ELSE'S BUSINESS.

MOM! MOM! – COME QUICK – LAWRENCE JUST HAD A ACCIDENT!!

HE WAS RIDIN' DOWN THE HILL AN' HE SKIDDED ON SOME ICE AN' SMASHED THE BIKE INTO A TREE!

OH, NO! – I HOPE IT ISN'T SERIOUS!

OF COURSE IT'S SERIOUS – IT WAS MY BIKE!

 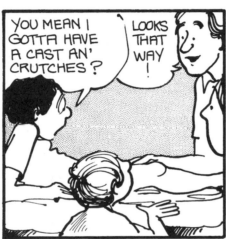 

Nobody broke a leg. This was an opportunity to ask, "What if?" What if I was responsible for a friend's child for a few days and something happened? How would I handle it? What would I do? Questions like this helped to sustain the strip by giving me problems to resolve.

I tried hard to seamlessly integrate old work and new, but after 30 years, I couldn't resist drawing these buildings in detail.

Originally, Connie was to stay with her cousin, which meant more characters and more background art. So I never filled in the blanks. Connie stayed "someplace" where there was a fancy lamp on the bedside table. Continuity was not my strong point.

LOOK, EVERYONE AT SCHOOL SIGNED MY CAST!

AN' I DON'T HAFTA TAKE BATHS FOR A LONG TIME.

I EVEN GET YOUR BED! THIS BROKEN LEG STUFF IS NEAT, MIKE!

TOO BAD IT DIDN'T HAPPEN TO SOMEBODY ELSE.

I'M NOT GOING TO LET FATE SPOIL THINGS. EVEN IF HE IS SEEING SOMEONE, I CAN STILL SEE HIM PER- FORM.

HE WON'T EVEN KNOW I'M THERE. I'LL BE A SECRET, INVISIBLE ADMIRER.

NO, HEH... I'M ALONE. I'M A FRIEND OF SOMEONE IN THE BAND.

IN THAT CASE, WE HAVE ONE SEAT LEFT – RIGHT IN FRONT.

I FEEL FOOLISH. WHAT IF HE SEES ME!

IF HE SEES ME, I'LL DIE!

IF HE SEES ME, I'LL GO NUTS! I'LL GET UP AND LEAVE!

... WHEN'S HE GOING TO SEE ME?!

CONNIE! FAR OUT! TOO MUCH!

SOME GIG, EH?...THE PLACE IS NO BANANA ...BUT THE DOUGH IS COOL.

HANG LOOSE FOR ONE MORE SET AND WE'LL RAP, OK?

...AND HE'S BILINGUAL!

THE WARTHOG GOOD TIMES BOOGIE BAND

NO KIDDING! YOU TAKE OFF FOR A HOLIDAY AND THE KID BREAKS A LEG!

SIS CAN TAKE CARE OF HIM FOR A COUPLE OF DAYS, SO RELAX, OK?

WELL, IT'S BEEN GREAT SEEING YOU. CAN I DROP YOU AT YOUR HOTEL?

NICE. A BRUSH-OFF. BUT NICE.

WHY DID I DO IT? I THREW MYSELF AT HIM! WHY? WHY!

I MADE A FOOL OF MYSELF! - IF ONLY I COULD TURN BACK THE CLOCK!

I'M 35, I'M A MOTHER- AND I'M STILL DOING DUMB THINGS!!

WHO SAYS WE LEARN FROM EXPERIENCE?

"Housewife" again. My mother once hollered, "What do they think—that I'm married to a house?" I'm grateful for changes in our manner of speaking. Stay-at-home mom is harder to say, but it feels better!

I've done this gag twice. Somewhere, there's a Sunday page with almost the same content. I've managed to keep mental track of thousands of punch lines, but somehow this one got lost in the file.

 WELL, I FIGURED OUT SOMETHING THIS WEEK.

 I'M TOO INSECURE! I DON'T NEED A MAN ...I NEED SELF CONFIDENCE! I NEED TO BE HAPPY WITH ME!

 I'M GOING HOME AS A TOTALLY NEW PERSON AND THERE'S ONLY ONE WAY TO DO IT!

 HAVE MY HAIR DYED.

 NERD! CREEP! I HATE YOUR HOUSE! I CAN'T WAIT! THEN GO HOME!

 OK, OK—BREAK IT UP, YOU TWO!

 HANG ON ONE MORE DAY.—LAWRENCE GOES HOME TOMORROW!

 ALREADY?

 HEY, LAWRENCE!— YOUR MOM'S HOME!

 MOM! MOM!

 LAWRENCE!

 MOM?—IS THAT YOU IN THERE?

Here again was my chance to make Connie and Anne look completely different. Connie dyed her hair. With the addition of a simple screen, I had a new character. Trouble is—I kept forgetting to use it. This screen, called Letrafilm, is a patterned adhesive plastic that is stuck on the artwork. By peeling away the excess, areas that I wanted textured or shaded were uniformly filled in. It was an art form all on its own. Thankfully, this tricky process is now done by computer.

ELLY, YOU'VE BEEN JUST GREAT TO US! THANKYOU, THANKYOU!

THANKS FOR TAKING CARE OF LAWRENCE!

I REALLY CAN'T THANK YOU ENOUGH.

BOY...I'D SAY SHE THANKED YOU ENOUGH!

OH, LAWRENCE-I'M SO SORRY I WAS AWAY WHEN YOU WERE HURT!

YOU MUST THINK I'M PRETTY AWFUL.

NO...I THINK YOU'RE AWFUL PRETTY.

BOY. SOME GROWN-UPS NEED A LOT OF UNDERSTANDING!

HOLY COW!- CONNIE?

IT'S THE NEW ME, ELLY! NEW CLOTHES, NEW HAIR, NEW EVERYTHING!

YOU LOOK LIKE A MILLION BUCKS!

LISTEN...I'M FEELING TERRIFIC. LET'S NOT DISCUSS WHAT IT COST.

This strip gives new meaning to the expression "to cut the rug." Fortunately, I made this up. It's just one more fabrication. But certainly somewhere there's a parent looking at this scenario saying, "Whoa! Did this happen to you, too?"

Sticky fingers, sticky faces make kids a lint magnet. Too bad they deposit more grime than they pick up!

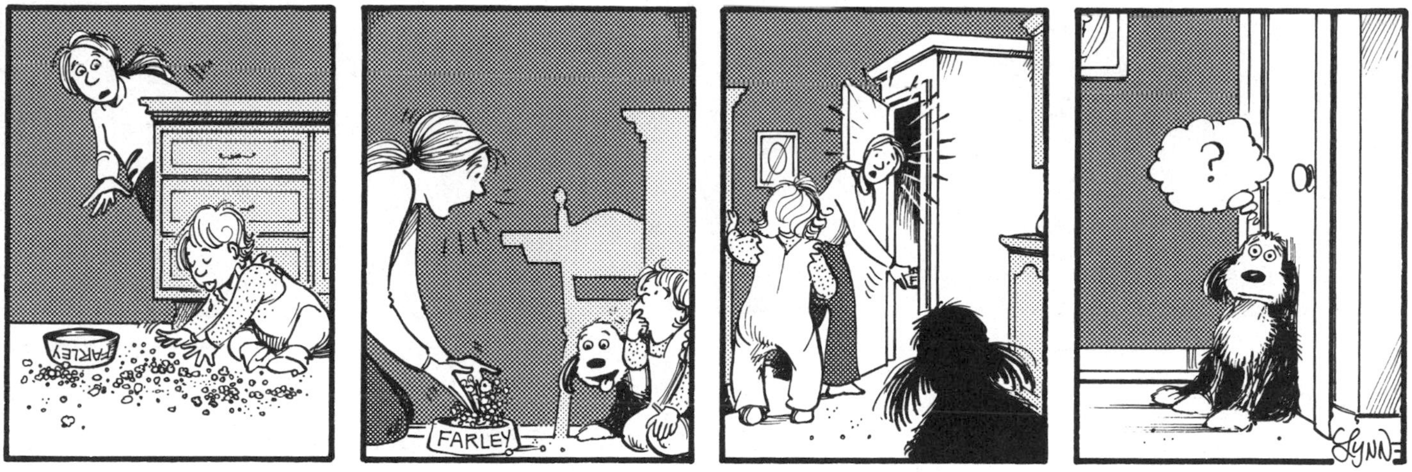
FARLEY
FARLEY
?
LYNN

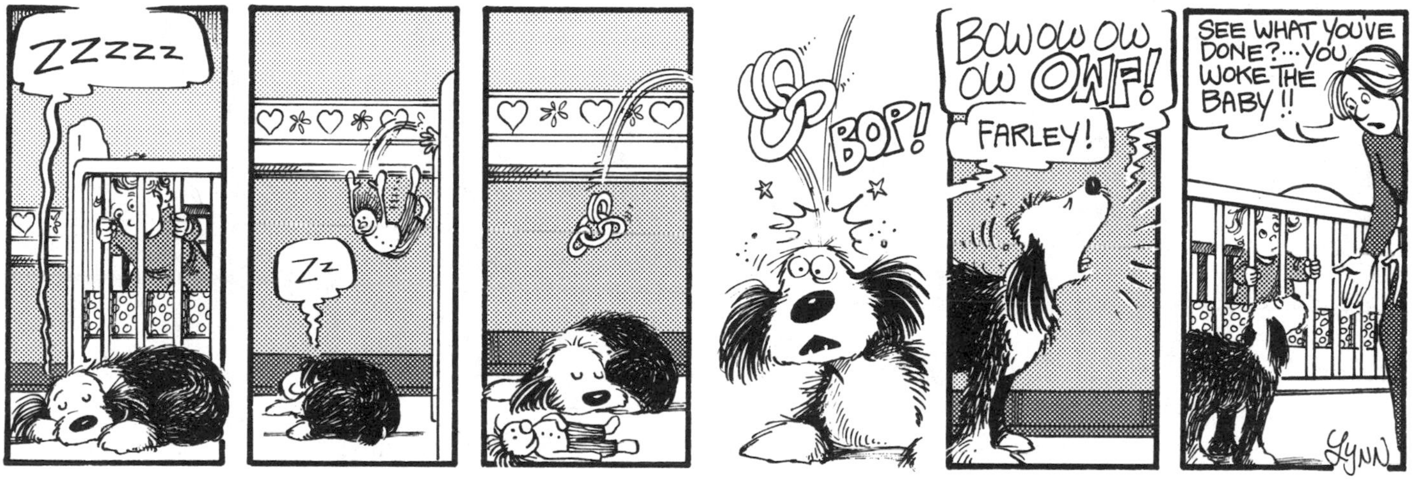
ZZZZZ
Zz
BOP!
BOW OW OW OW OWF!
FARLEY!
SEE WHAT YOU'VE DONE?...YOU WOKE THE BABY!!
LYNN

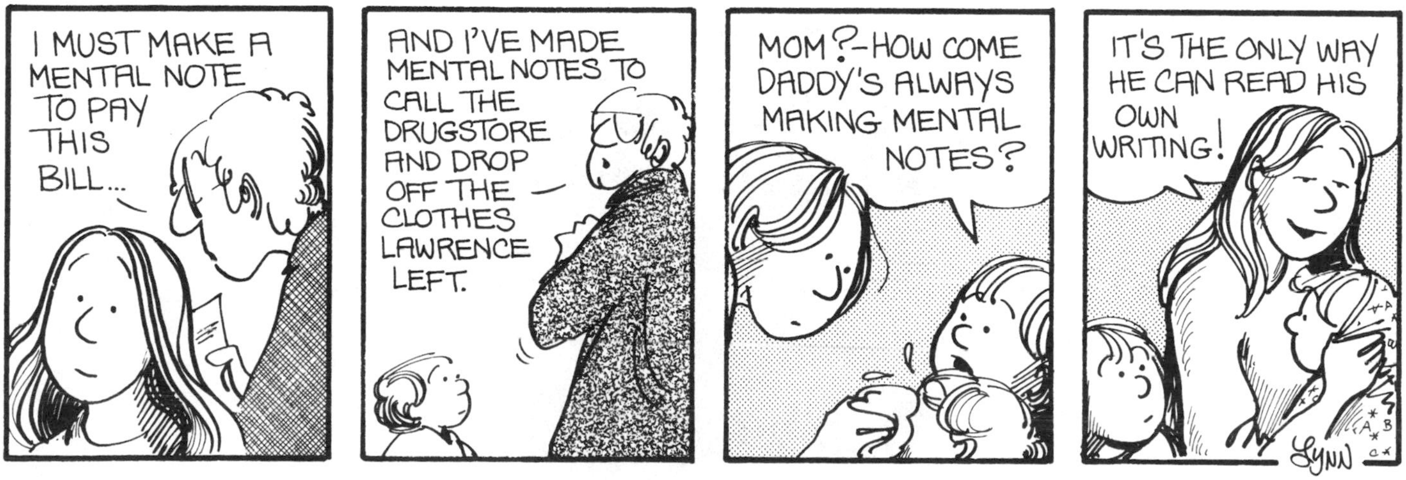
I MUST MAKE A MENTAL NOTE TO PAY THIS BILL...
AND I'VE MADE MENTAL NOTES TO CALL THE DRUGSTORE AND DROP OFF THE CLOTHES LAWRENCE LEFT.
MOM?-HOW COME DADDY'S ALWAYS MAKING MENTAL NOTES?
IT'S THE ONLY WAY HE CAN READ HIS OWN WRITING!
LYNN

Farley wasn't allowed on the couch, the bed or the armchairs. He was a dog, after all, and dogs have their place. It didn't take long to discover that he knew exactly where his place was: When we weren't watching, it was any place at all!

THEY LET ME BE LAWRENCE'S "SPECIAL FRIEND" AT SCHOOL.

I GET TO HELP HIM WITH HIS BOOKS AN' COAT AN' STUFF.

MOM, HOW COME IT HAD TO BE LAWRENCE THAT BROKE HIS LEG?

I THOUGHT THOSE THINGS ALWAYS HAPPENED TO PEOPLE YOU DON'T KNOW!

YOU KNOW WHAT'S GOOD ABOUT US? ... WE TALK TO EACH OTHER!

WE'RE OPEN AND HONEST AND WE LET OUR TRUE FEELINGS OUT.

I CAN'T REMEMBER THE LAST TIME WE HAD A REAL FIGHT!

DO YOU SUPPOSE WE'RE LEADING A DULL LIFE?

This Sunday strip (one of the new ones) received criticism for showing Elly "kicking" the dog. Really, she's pushing him outside with her foot—but folks were hostile anyway. It seems that more people complain about what happens to the pets than what happens to the children!

In grade two, I was smitten by "Jimmy Thompson"—a cute boy who really should have been in grade three. After lunch one day, he agreed to let me look at a snakeskin he'd found in the schoolyard. Wanting to impress "an older man" with my enthusiasm, I leaned in and said, "Wow!"—to which he replied, "Aaaugh! She's got *egg breath*!" Humiliated in front of my friends, I ran off to hide in the girls' washroom—and have been careful with egg breath ever since.

We had a row one night and I banished my husband to a night on the couch. After I'd calmed down, I went into the living room to talk. He was awkwardly pulling his legs into a fitted sheet that he'd taken to sleep in by mistake. He looked so funny. With compassion and forgiveness, I suggested he come back to bed. His response was as shown above, and so was mine!

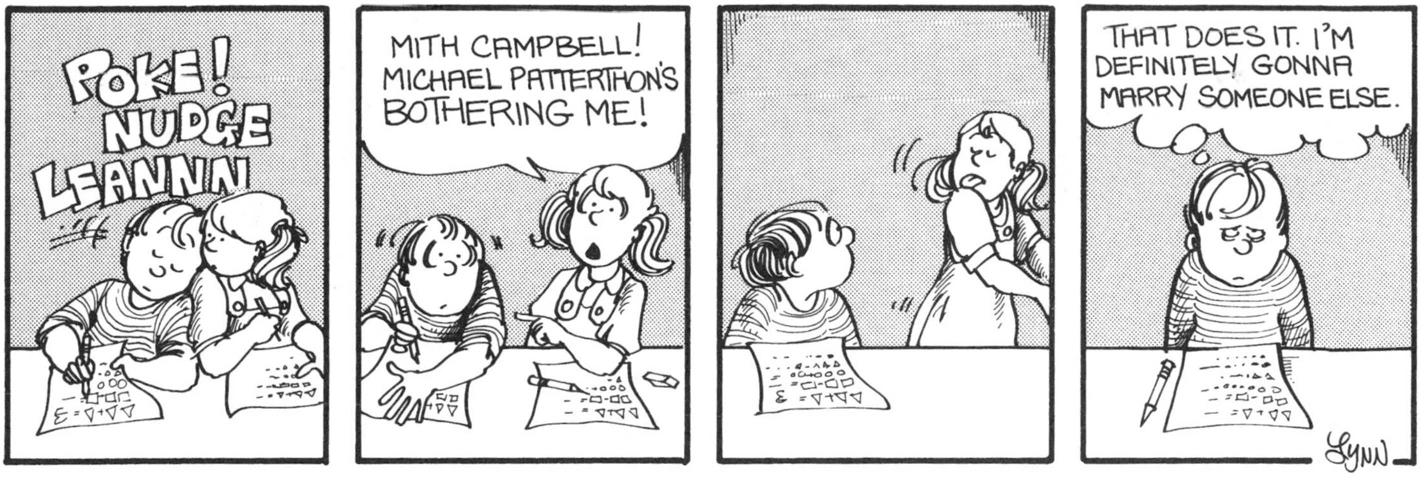
POKE! NUDGE LEANNN
MITH CAMPBELL! MICHAEL PATTERTHON'S BOTHERING ME!
THAT DOES IT. I'M DEFINITELY GONNA MARRY SOMEONE ELSE.
LYNN

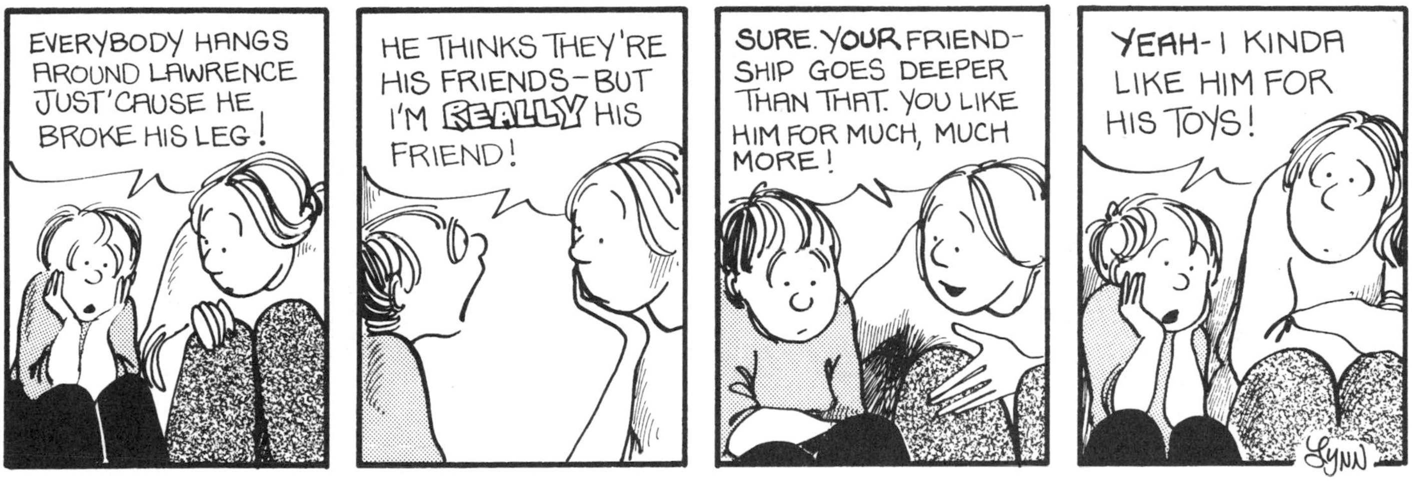
EVERYBODY HANGS AROUND LAWRENCE JUST 'CAUSE HE BROKE HIS LEG!
HE THINKS THEY'RE HIS FRIENDS—BUT I'M REALLY HIS FRIEND!
SURE. YOUR FRIENDSHIP GOES DEEPER THAN THAT. YOU LIKE HIM FOR MUCH, MUCH MORE!
YEAH-I KINDA LIKE HIM FOR HIS TOYS!
LYNN

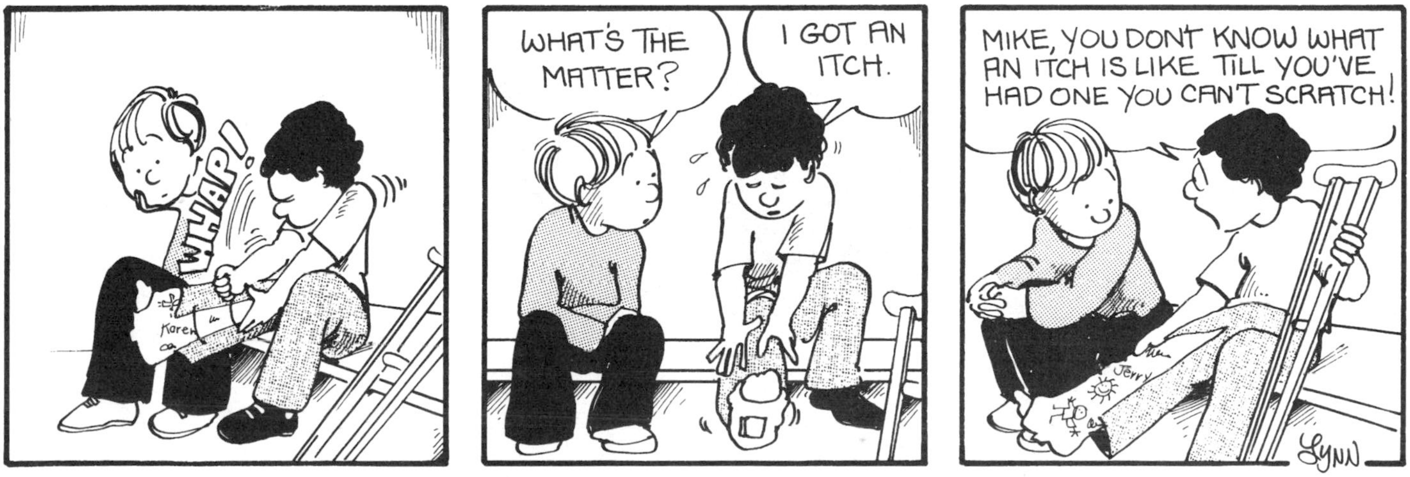
WHAP!
Karen
WHAT'S THE MATTER?
I GOT AN ITCH.
MIKE, YOU DON'T KNOW WHAT AN ITCH IS LIKE TILL YOU'VE HAD ONE YOU CAN'T SCRATCH!
Jerry
LYNN

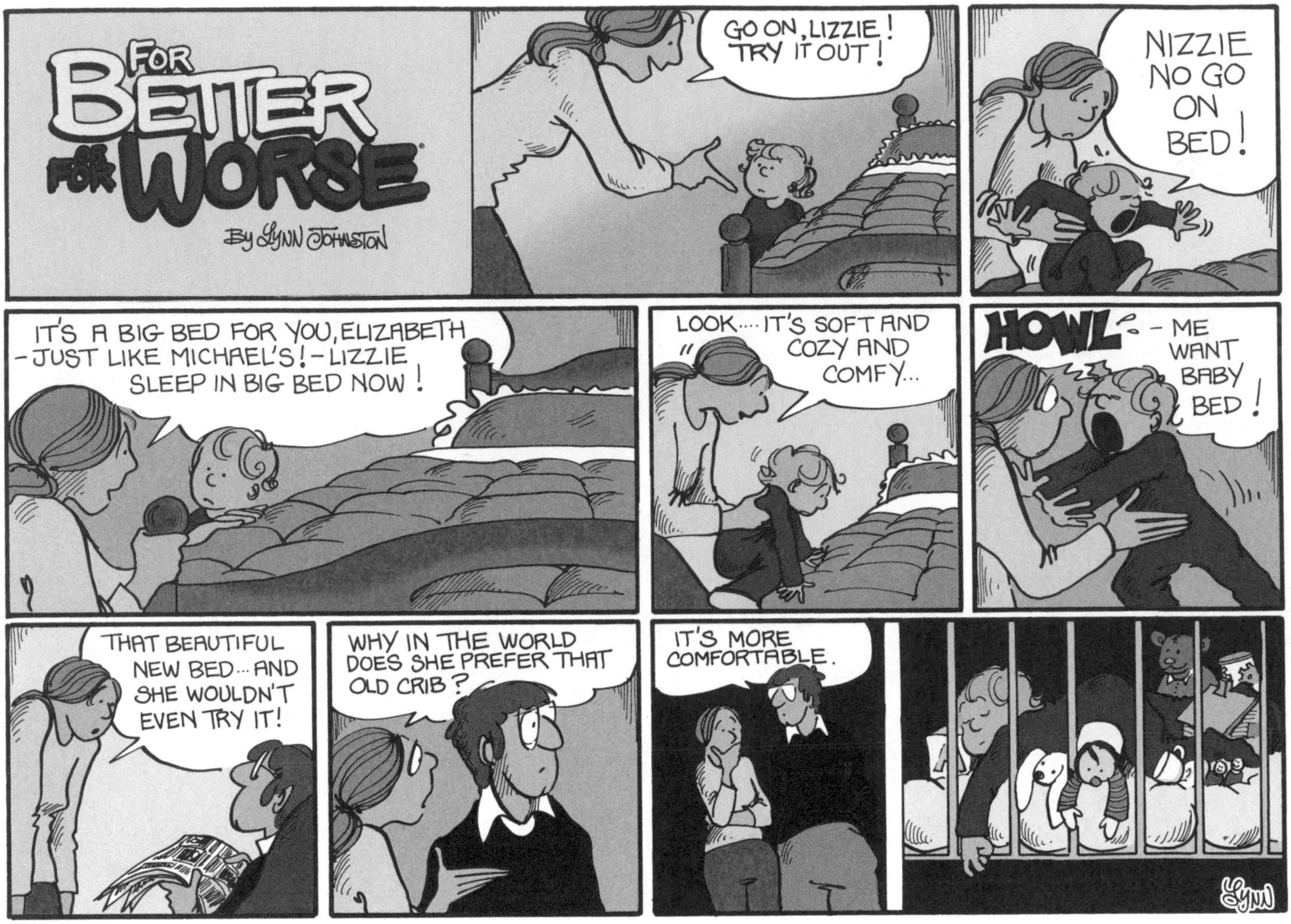

FOR BETTER OR FOR WORSE
By Lynn Johnston
GO ON, LIZZIE! TRY IT OUT!
NIZZIE NO GO ON BED!
IT'S A BIG BED FOR YOU, ELIZABETH -JUST LIKE MICHAEL'S! -LIZZIE SLEEP IN BIG BED NOW!
LOOK.... IT'S SOFT AND COZY AND COMFY...
HOWL
- ME WANT BABY BED!
THAT BEAUTIFUL NEW BED... AND SHE WOULDN'T EVEN TRY IT!
WHY IN THE WORLD DOES SHE PREFER THAT OLD CRIB?
IT'S MORE COMFORTABLE.
Lynn

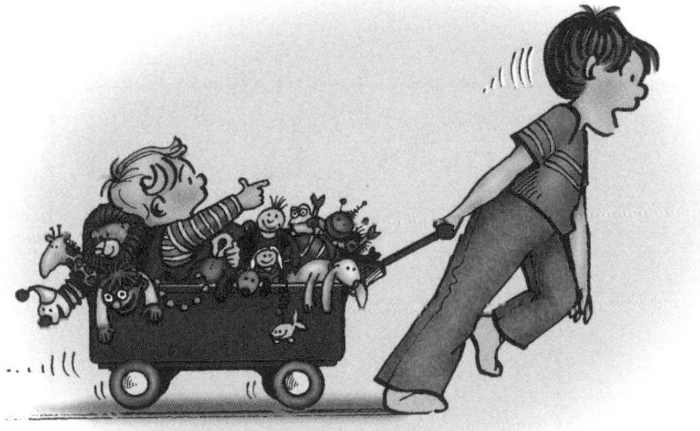

Next to the sink in my laundry room was a pile of mismatched socks. They had been there for years. *A few* months ago, I gave up finding their mates and pitched them out. *A few* days later, you guessed it! I found two of the missing socks! Where did they come from? Where had they gone? If you know, don't tell me. I have my own beliefs.

ELLY, I'M STILL EMBARRASSED ABOUT THE WAY I CHASED YOUR BROTHER.

HE MUST THINK I'M AN IDIOT FOR SHOWING UP ON HIS DOORSTEP LIKE THAT.

HE MUST THINK I HAVE NO CLASS— HE MUST THINK...

WELL, WHAT DOES HE THINK!!?

CONNIE, WHY ARE YOU ALWAYS PREPARED FOR THE WORST?

PHIL THOUGHT YOUR VISIT WAS GREAT. IN FACT HE WISHED YOU COULD HAVE STAYED LONGER.

REALLY?♡

DO ME A FAVOR, EL IF YOU'RE LYING... DON'T LET ME KNOW.

SO, I HEAR THAT LAWRENCE GOT THE CAST OFF HIS LEG TODAY!

YEAH. WE WANTED HIM TO BRING IT IN FOR SHOW AN' TELL.

HE SAYS HIS LEG FEELS FUNNY, BUT HE CAN WALK FINE...

HE JUST WON'T BE ABLE TO KICK ANYONE FOR A WHILE.

I almost did this—which gave me the idea for these strips. It's nice to know that I don't have to suffer for the sake of art.

371

Panel 1: I MUST HAVE LEFT THE KEYS ON THE DRIVER'S SIDE SEAT, MIKE. DID YOU SEE THEM?

UMMM...

SUPER VAC

Panel 2: THEY MIGHT HAVE GONE UP THE VACUUM HOSE.

WHAT DO YOU MEAN "MIGHT HAVE"? WHERE ARE THE KEYS?!!

Panel 3: .... IN THERE.

SUPER VAC

Panel 4: HEY, BUDDY! CAN I USE THAT THING OR ARE YOU HAVING A "RELATIONSHIP"?

Lynn

Panel 5: THANKS FOR BRINGING ME THE SPARE KEYS, EL.

THAT'S O.K. LIZZIE ENJOYED THE TAXI RIDE.

Panel 6: THE ATTENDANT SAID THEY'LL RETURN MY CAR KEYS WHEN THEY CLEAN OUT THE VACUUM SYSTEM.

CAR WASH

Panel 7: I'M REALLY SORRY, DADDY!

Panel 8: DON'T BE MAD AT HIM, JOHN. HE DIDN'T SUCK UP THE KEYS ON PURPOSE... AND, BESIDES, THERE'S A POSITIVE SIDE TO WHAT HAPPENED...

Panel 9: OUR SON WAS WILLINGLY **CLEANING** SOMETHING!!

Lynn

My dad used to take forever in the bathroom. Mom almost banned the bookrack because of him. He'd sit in there 'til his legs fell asleep—with a perfectly good recliner in the front room. Maybe he just liked his privacy. Whatever makes men do this is beyond me, but I believe it sparked the evolution of the multican household. The more, the merrier—especially when you gotta go.

Panel 1: I'D LIKE TO RUN DOWNTOWN FOR AN HOUR OR SO, ANNE— WOULD YOU LOOK AFTER LIZZIE FOR ME? / SURE THING!

Panel 2: WHAT DO YOU HAVE TO DO? / OH... I'M KINDA DOWN IN THE DUMPS, SO I THOUGHT I'D GO SHOPPING.

Panel 3: WHAT KIND OF SHOPPING, SHOES? / NAH. I DON'T NEED SHOES. I'LL PROBABLY GET GROCERIES.

Panel 4: ELLY, BUYING GROCERIES WON'T DO THE TRICK. YOU'VE GOT TO BUY SOMETHING FOR **YOU!** —PROMISE? / OK.

Panel 5: AND IT CAN'T BE EDIBLE UNLESS IT'S CHOCOLATE!

Panel 1: I WASHED SOME OF LIZZIE'S THINGS, ELLY. / THANKS, ANNE!

Panel 2: YOU'RE WONDERFUL! / NO PROBLEM. I ENJOY LOOKING AFTER HER, SO ASK ME ANY TIME.

Panel 3: ARE YOU STILL TAKING THAT WRITING CLASS? / YES, BUT I DON'T HAVE THE TIME TO DEDICATE MYSELF TO WRITING.

Panel 4: HOW MUCH TIME DO YOU NEED? / OH... A YEAR ALONE IN A SPANISH VILLA.

Panel 5: CAN I COME?!!

Panel 1: IT WOULD BE NICE TO RUN AWAY FROM EVERYTHING FOR A WHILE. / YEAH.

Panel 2: WE COULD TAKE A MEDITERRANEAN CRUISE! NO HOUSE TO LOOK AFTER, NO COOKING, NO CLEANING, NO KIDS.... / WHOA!

Panel 3: SPA TREATMENTS, READING ON THE DECK... A COLD MARGARITA, SERVED BY A HANDSOME WAITER... SLEEPING LATE... / AAHHHH

Panel 4: MOM! COME QUICK!

Panel 5: IT'S HARD TO DREAM WHEN YOUR ALARM KEEPS GOING OFF!

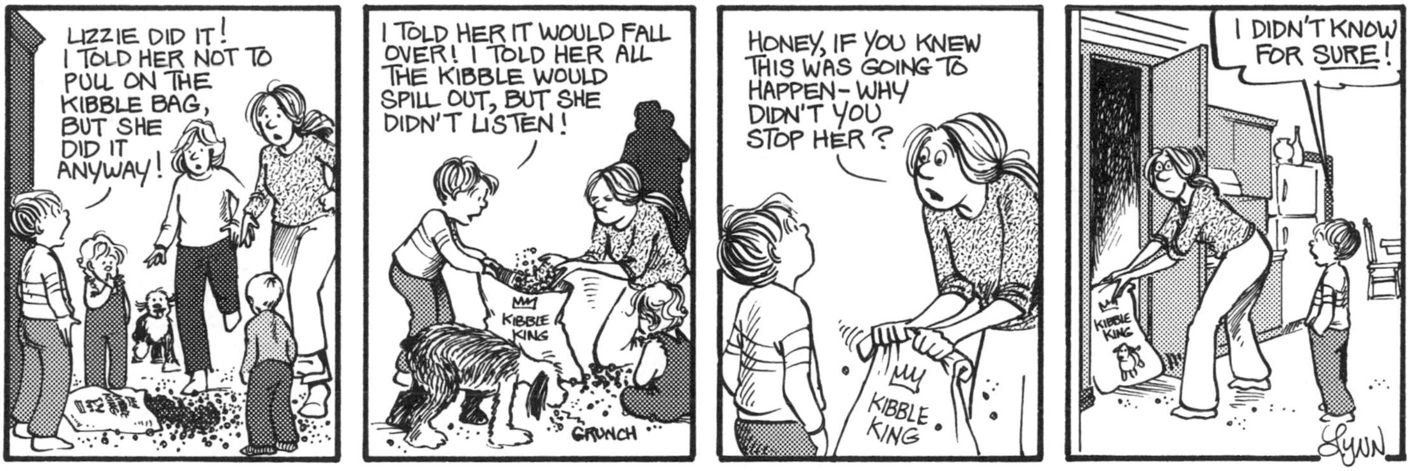
LIZZIE DID IT! I TOLD HER NOT TO PULL ON THE KIBBLE BAG, BUT SHE DID IT ANYWAY!
I TOLD HER IT WOULD FALL OVER! I TOLD HER ALL THE KIBBLE WOULD SPILL OUT, BUT SHE DIDN'T LISTEN!
KIBBLE KING
GRUNCH
HONEY, IF YOU KNEW THIS WAS GOING TO HAPPEN- WHY DIDN'T YOU STOP HER?
KIBBLE KING
I DIDN'T KNOW FOR SURE!
LYNN

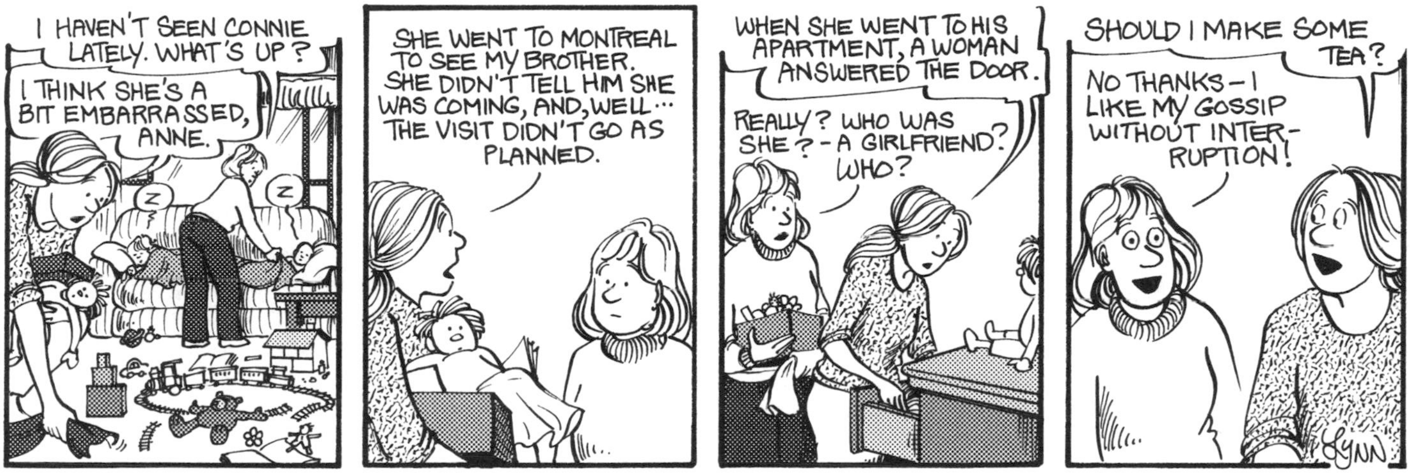
I HAVEN'T SEEN CONNIE LATELY. WHAT'S UP?
I THINK SHE'S A BIT EMBARRASSED, ANNE.
SHE WENT TO MONTREAL TO SEE MY BROTHER. SHE DIDN'T TELL HIM SHE WAS COMING, AND, WELL... THE VISIT DIDN'T GO AS PLANNED.
WHEN SHE WENT TO HIS APARTMENT, A WOMAN ANSWERED THE DOOR.
REALLY? WHO WAS SHE? - A GIRLFRIEND? WHO?
SHOULD I MAKE SOME TEA?
NO THANKS - I LIKE MY GOSSIP WITHOUT INTER-RUPTION!
LYNN

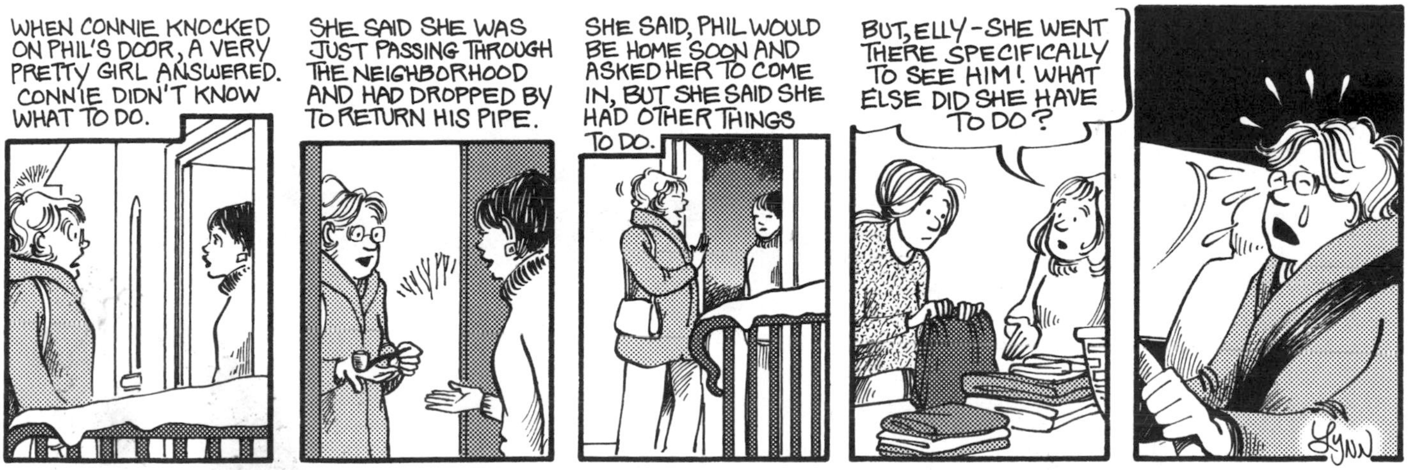
WHEN CONNIE KNOCKED ON PHIL'S DOOR, A VERY PRETTY GIRL ANSWERED. CONNIE DIDN'T KNOW WHAT TO DO.
SHE SAID SHE WAS JUST PASSING THROUGH THE NEIGHBORHOOD AND HAD DROPPED BY TO RETURN HIS PIPE.
SHE SAID, PHIL WOULD BE HOME SOON AND ASKED HER TO COME IN, BUT SHE SAID SHE HAD OTHER THINGS TO DO.
BUT, ELLY - SHE WENT THERE SPECIFICALLY TO SEE HIM! WHAT ELSE DID SHE HAVE TO DO?
LYNN

You can't make this stuff up. You just can't!

SO, IS YOUR BROTHER SEEING SOMEONE, EL?

I DON'T KNOW, ANNE. I HAVEN'T REALLY ASKED HIM.

BUT, HE TOLD ME THE GIRL CONNIE SAW IN HIS APARTMENT PLAYS THE CELLO. HE SAID THEY WERE WORKING ON SOME MUSIC—AND THEY WERE JUST FRIENDS...

DOES THAT MEAN SHE STILL HAS A CHANCE?

MAYBE. I DON'T LIKE TO PRY, BUT I'LL KEEP MY EYES AND EARS OPEN.

WHEN YOU KEEP YOUR EYES AND EARS OPEN ...IT'S HARD TO KEEP YOUR MOUTH CLOSED.

YOU'VE KNOWN CONNIE FOR A LONG TIME.

SINCE UNIVERSITY.

I WAS GOING TO TEACH ENGLISH AND SHE WAS STUDYING RADIOLOGY. SHE WENT OFF TO WORK IN SOUTH AMERICA, AND ME?... WELL... I GOT MARRIED.

CONNIE THINKS MY LIFE IS PERFECT BECAUSE I HAVE A HUSBAND, BUT I ENVY HER 'CAUSE SHE HAS A CAREER.

RAISING KIDS IS A CAREER, EL. ALL YOUR KNOWLEDGE, SKILL AND EXPERIENCE YOU POUR INTO YOUR CHILDREN!

TRUE.

...MAYBE THAT'S WHY I FEEL ...EMPTY SOMETIMES.

CONNIE'S JUST GOING THROUGH ANOTHER ROUGH SPELL. SHE'LL TURN AROUND SOON.

I HOPE!

I WISH MY BROTHER WOULD STOP ANSWERING HER LETTERS, THOUGH. HE GIVES HER HOPE WHEN HE HAS NO INTENTION OF MAKING A COMMITMENT.

WELL, IT'S BETWEEN THE TWO OF THEM, ISN'T IT. REALLY, THIS IS NONE OF OUR BUSINESS.

EXACTLY. IT IS NONE OF OUR BUSINESS.

BUT, LET ME KNOW IF YOU HEAR ANYTHING!

In Lynn Lake, gossip was shared with great prudence. My first experience in this tiny town was at the checkout of the grocery store. The woman at the cash register was downright nasty, and as I exited the store I said to the woman that had been in front of me, "What a witch!" Our house was a ten-minute walk up the road, and as I entered with my groceries, the phone was ringing. It was the cashier from the grocery store, who said, "I hear you called me a witch! The woman you said that to was my sister-in-law!" All I could do was humbly and sincerely apologize.

The key to successful teasing is subtlety. Alan and I were masters of misery when it came to surreptitious slight. We drove each other crazy. For some reason, we're good friends despite years of subtle torment—perhaps it's because we appreciate talent, in any form.

*
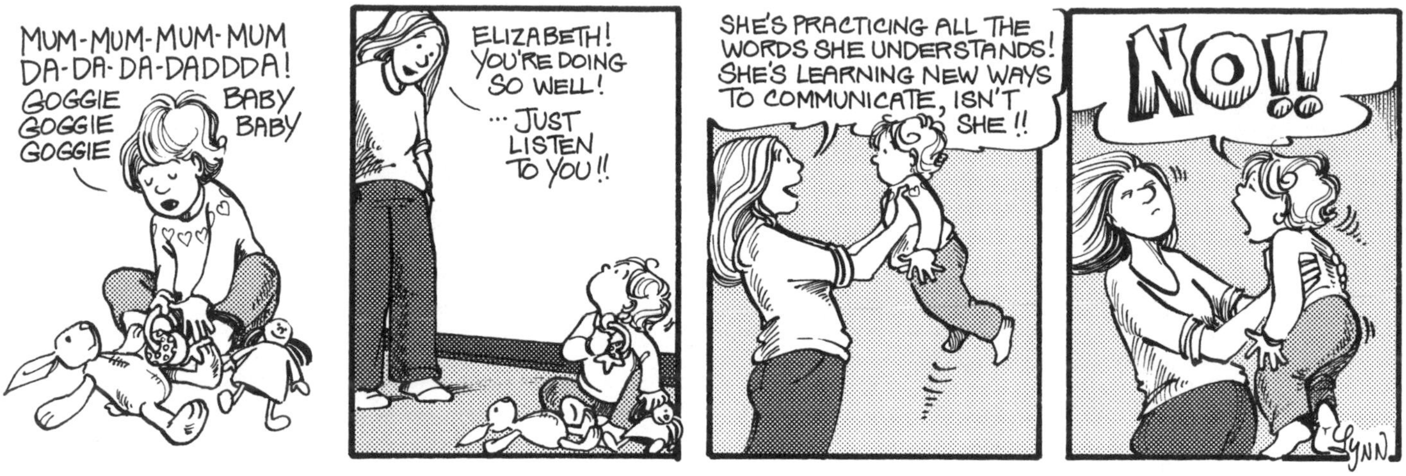
MUM-MUM-MUM-MUM
DA-DA-DA-DADDDA!
GOGGIE GOGGIE GOGGIE
BABY BABY
ELIZABETH! YOU'RE DOING SO WELL!
... JUST LISTEN TO YOU!!
SHE'S PRACTICING ALL THE WORDS SHE UNDERSTANDS! SHE'S LEARNING NEW WAYS TO COMMUNICATE, ISN'T SHE!!
NO!!
LYNN

*
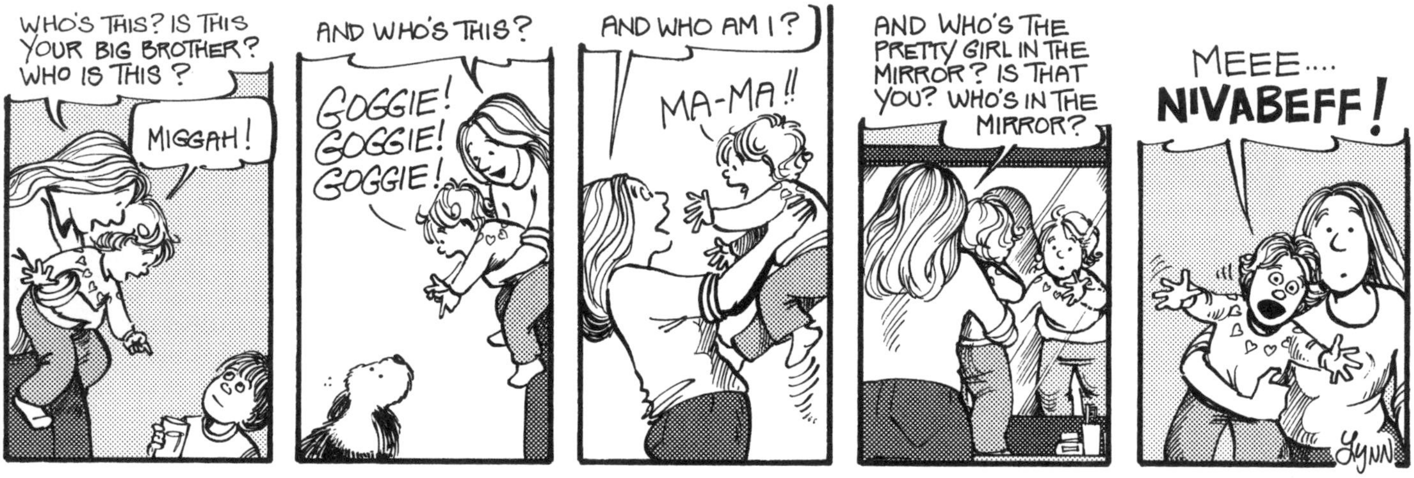
WHO'S THIS? IS THIS YOUR BIG BROTHER? WHO IS THIS?
MIGGAH!
AND WHO'S THIS?
GOGGIE! GOGGIE! GOGGIE!
AND WHO AM I?
MA-MA!!
AND WHO'S THE PRETTY GIRL IN THE MIRROR? IS THAT YOU? WHO'S IN THE MIRROR?
MEEE....
NIVABEFF!
LYNN

*
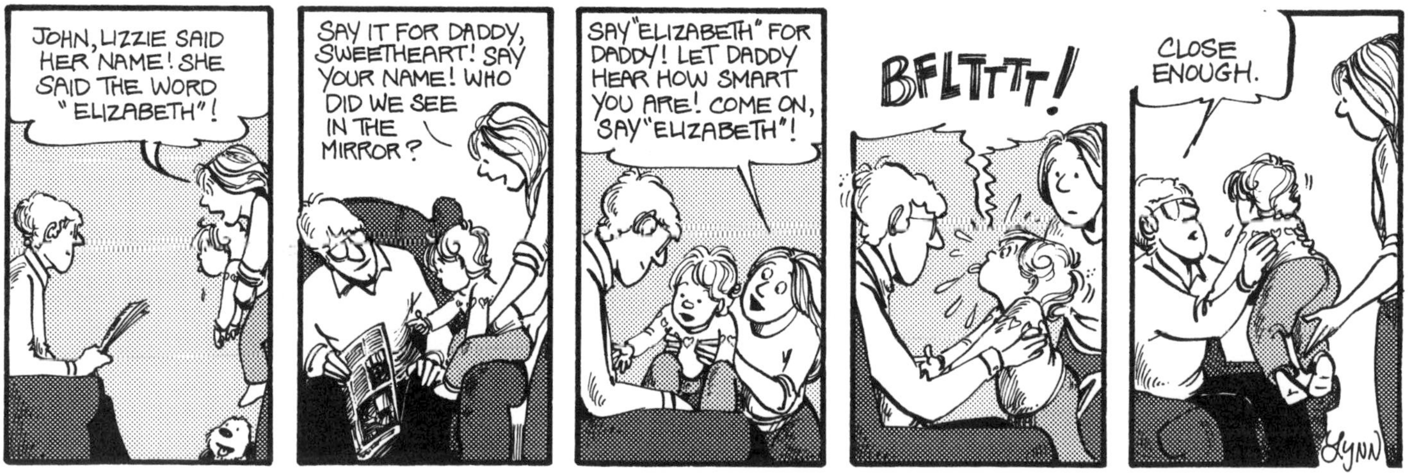
JOHN, LIZZIE SAID HER NAME! SHE SAID THE WORD "ELIZABETH"!
SAY IT FOR DADDY, SWEETHEART! SAY YOUR NAME! WHO DID WE SEE IN THE MIRROR?
SAY "ELIZABETH" FOR DADDY! LET DADDY HEAR HOW SMART YOU ARE! COME ON, SAY "ELIZABETH"!
BFLTTTT!
CLOSE ENOUGH.
LYNN

Never underestimate the power of "donga." I did, and I regretted it.

SHE'S REALLY STARTING TO TALK NOW, ANNE. SHE HAS QUITE A FEW WORDS IN HER VOCABULARY.

SHE KNOWS THE PARTS OF THE FACE, SHE CAN SAY WHEN SHE WANTS TO GO POTTIE...

DOES SHE SAY THE "N" WORD...?

SHE HAS USED THE "N" WORD, BUT SO FAR, SHE HASN'T DIS-COVERED ITS TRUE POTENTIAL.

NO!

ANOTHER DAY, ANOTHER DISCOVERY!

MICHAEL—I ASKED YOU TO PICK UP THESE TOYS AGES AGO!

ARE YOU TWO FIGHTING AGAIN?

LOOK, HONEY... WE CAN ENROLL THE DOG IN AN OBEDIENCE TRAINING CLASS!

OBEDIENCE TRAINING

GREAT... I WONDER IF THEY ACCEPT CHILDREN.

FARLEY'S GOING TO SCHOOL! FARLEY'S SUCH A BIG, BIG BOY!

HE'S GOING TO BE DADDY'S GOOOD PUPPY! HE'S GOING TO DO EVERYTHING DADDY SAYS!

WOULDN'T IT BE JUST AS REASSURING IF HE CALLED ME BY MY FIRST NAME?

382

We used a choke chain to train Farley and a harness to control the kids. When they tell you to "keep them on a leash," they're not fooling!

*

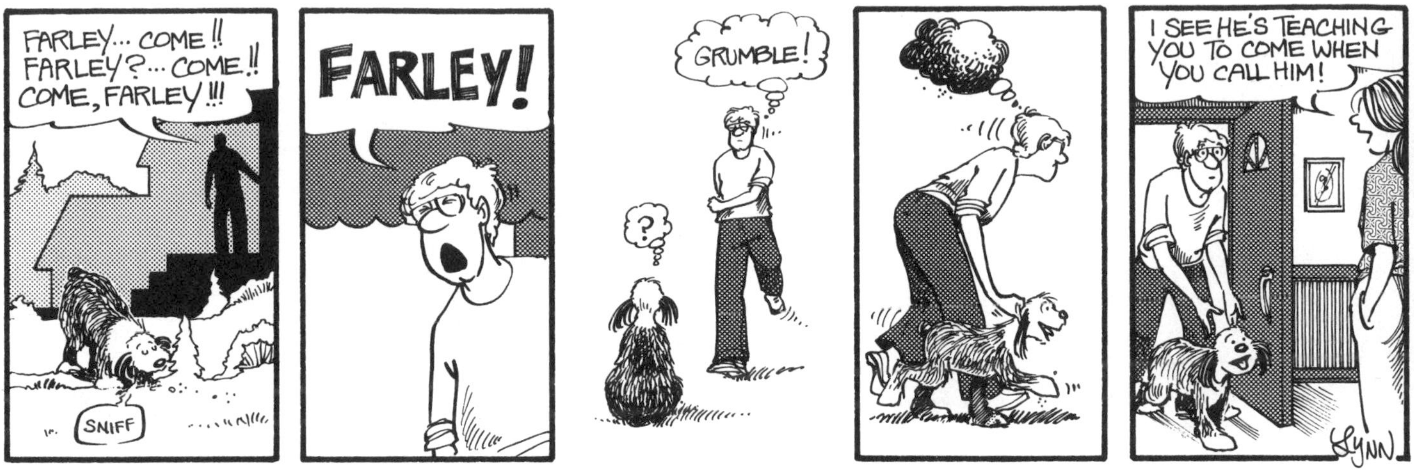

FARLEY... COME!! FARLEY?... COME!! COME, FARLEY!!!
SNIFF
FARLEY!
GRUMBLE!
?
I SEE HE'S TEACHING YOU TO COME WHEN YOU CALL HIM!
LYNN

*

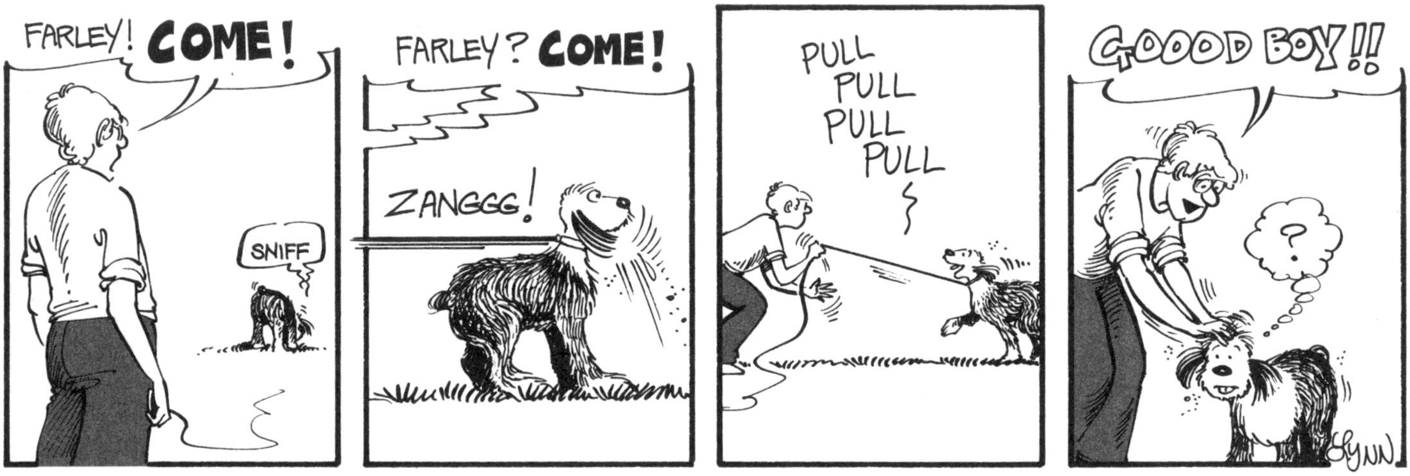

FARLEY! COME!
SNIFF
FARLEY? COME!
ZANGGG!
PULL PULL PULL PULL
GOOOD BOY!!
?
LYNN

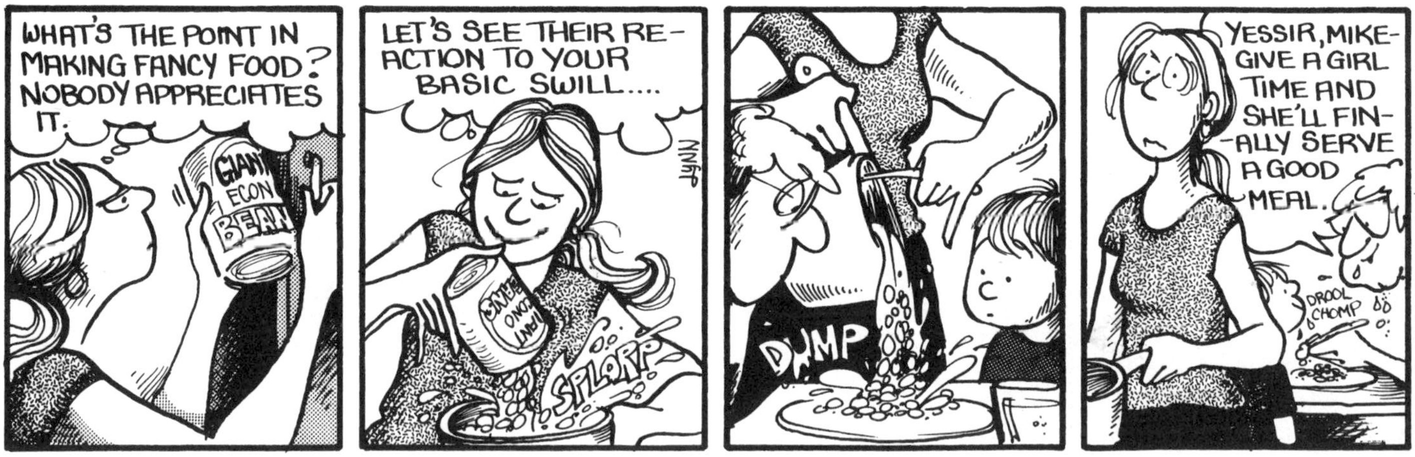

WHAT'S THE POINT IN MAKING FANCY FOOD? NOBODY APPRECIATES IT.
LET'S SEE THEIR RE-ACTION TO YOUR BASIC SWILL....
SPLORP
DUMP
YESSIR, MIKE-GIVE A GIRL TIME AND SHE'LL FIN-ALLY SERVE A GOOD MEAL.
DROOL CHOMP

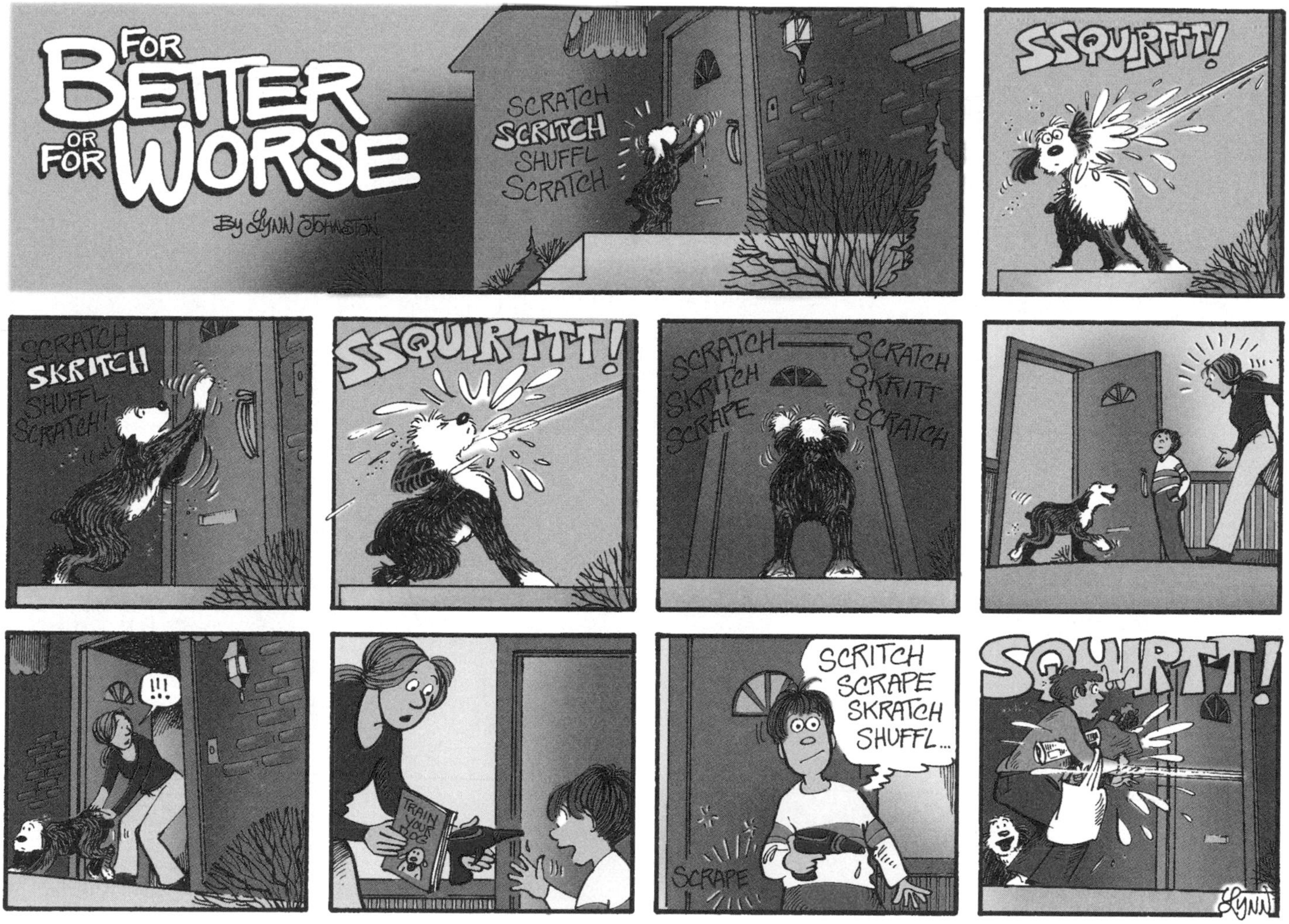
FOR BETTER OR FOR WORSE
BY LYNN JOHNSTON
SCRATCH
SCRITCH
SHUFFL
SCRATCH
SSQUIRTTT!
SCRATCH
SKRITCH
SHUFFL
SCRATCH!
SSQUIRTTT!
SCRATCH
SKRITCH
SCRAPE
SCRATCH
SKRITT
SCRATCH
!!!
TRAIN YOUR DOG
SCRITCH
SCRAPE
SKRATCH
SHUFFL...
SCRAPE
SQUIRTT!
LYNN

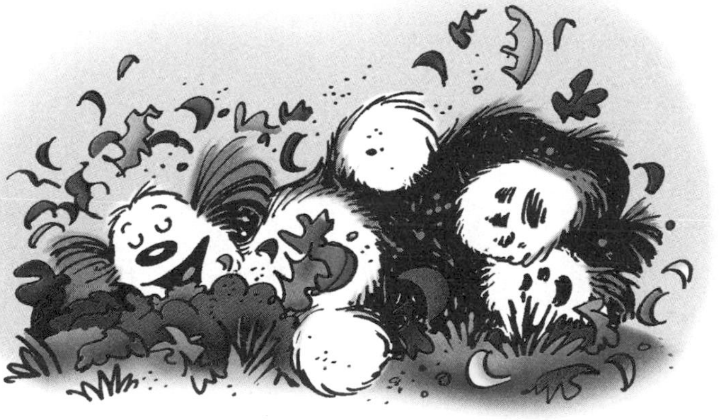

*
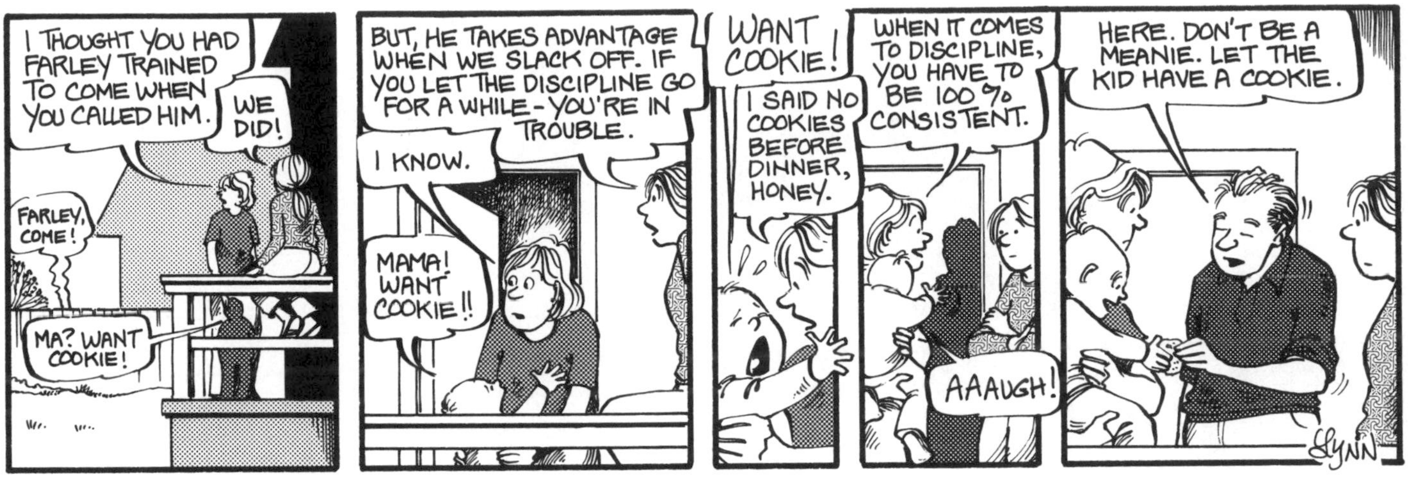
I THOUGHT YOU HAD FARLEY TRAINED TO COME WHEN YOU CALLED HIM.
WE DID!
FARLEY, COME!
MA? WANT COOKIE!
BUT, HE TAKES ADVANTAGE WHEN WE SLACK OFF. IF YOU LET THE DISCIPLINE GO FOR A WHILE - YOU'RE IN TROUBLE.
I KNOW.
MAMA! WANT COOKIE!!
WANT COOKIE!
I SAID NO COOKIES BEFORE DINNER, HONEY.
WHEN IT COMES TO DISCIPLINE, YOU HAVE TO BE 100% CONSISTENT.
AAAUGH!
HERE. DON'T BE A MEANIE. LET THE KID HAVE A COOKIE.
LYNN

*
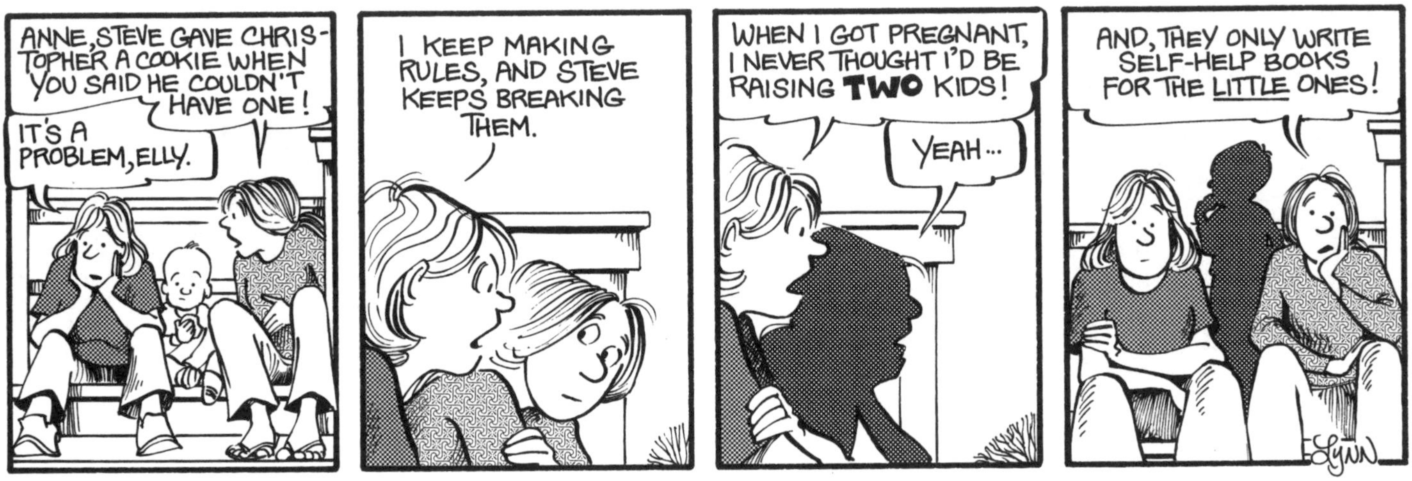
ANNE, STEVE GAVE CHRISTOPHER A COOKIE WHEN YOU SAID HE COULDN'T HAVE ONE!
IT'S A PROBLEM, ELLY.
I KEEP MAKING RULES, AND STEVE KEEPS BREAKING THEM.
WHEN I GOT PREGNANT, I NEVER THOUGHT I'D BE RAISING **TWO** KIDS!
YEAH...
AND, THEY ONLY WRITE SELF-HELP BOOKS FOR THE LITTLE ONES!
LYNN

*
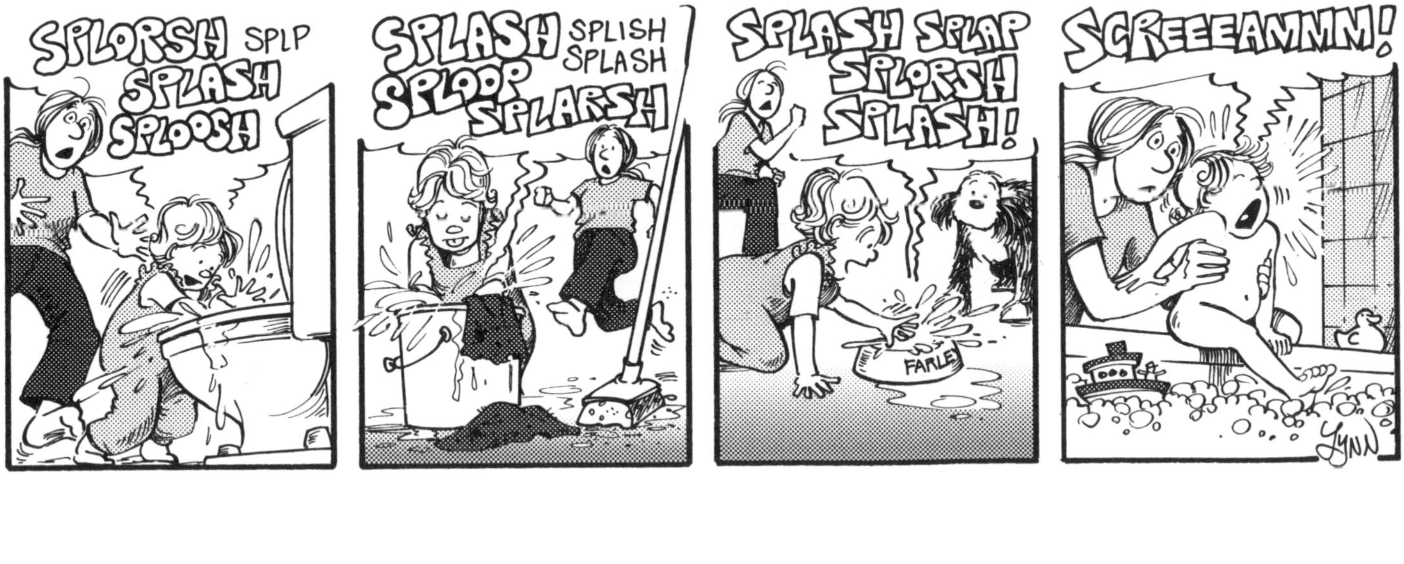
SPLORSH SPLP SPLASH SPLOOSH
SPLASH SPLISH SPLASH SPLOOP SPLARSH
SPLASH SPLAP SPLORSH SPLASH!
FARLE
SCREEEAMMM!
LYNN

I was consistently inconsistent, but I did my best. All you can do is your best, right? Still, in looking back at all the ways I tried to teach and warn, advise and discipline . . . I wonder if I couldn't have done it better?

I was always pleased to see my brother in meltdown mode. In comparison, it made me look good. As the kid most likely to "get it," anything that made my star shine was great news indeed.

FOR BETTER OR FOR WORSE®

BY LYNN JOHNSTON

HONEY, I WANT TO TALK TO YOU!

MICHAEL, YOU'RE A BIG, CLEVER BOY NOW.

DADDY AND I FEEL IT'S TIME WE GAVE YOU SOME GROWN-UP RESPONSIBILITY.

FROM NOW ON, YOUR JOBS WILL BE SETTING AND CLEARING THE TABLE, KEEPING THE SHOE CORNER TIDY AND PUTTING AWAY YOUR OWN LAUNDRY!

I GUESS I REALLY AM A BIG KID NOW!

ELLY! – MICHAEL'S ACTUALLY DOING THOSE CHORES YOU GAVE HIM!

WHATEVER YOU SAID – SURE WORKED!

YEAH. TROUBLE IS – THAT PLOY ONLY WORKS ONCE.

Our hallway bore the "graffiti" of countless comings and goings. Even without a real dog, my kids and their friends managed to add to the decor. For this reason, spring was my least favorite time of year. Summer was better. At least the dirt was dry!

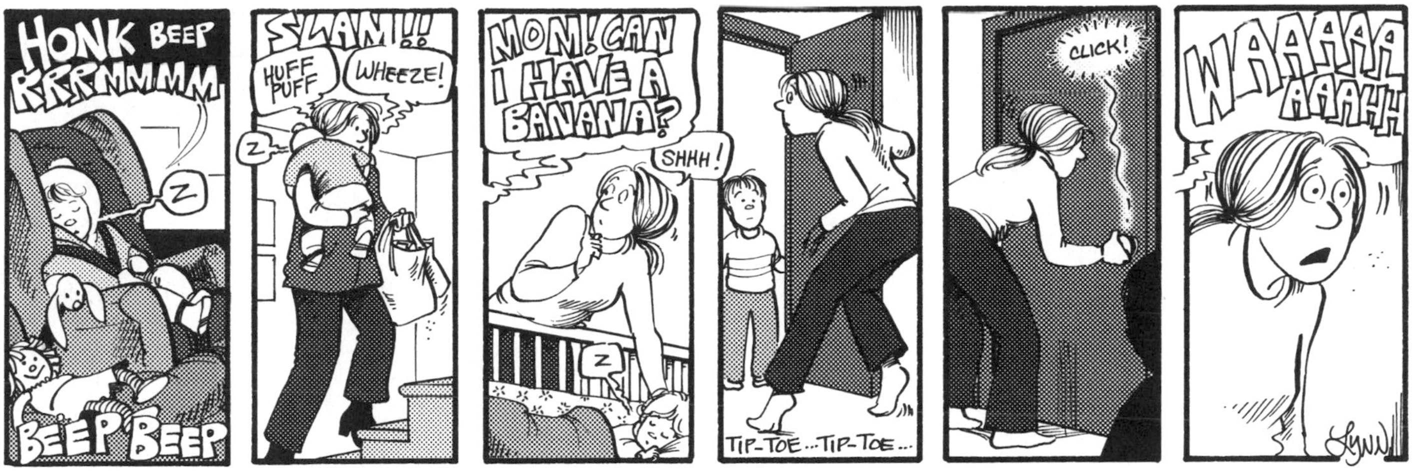

HONK BEEP
KRRMMMM
Z
BEEP BEEP
SLAM!!
HUFF PUFF
WHEEZE!
Z
MOM! CAN I HAVE A BANANA?
SHHH!
Z
TIP-TOE... TIP-TOE...
CLICK!
WAAAAA AAAHH

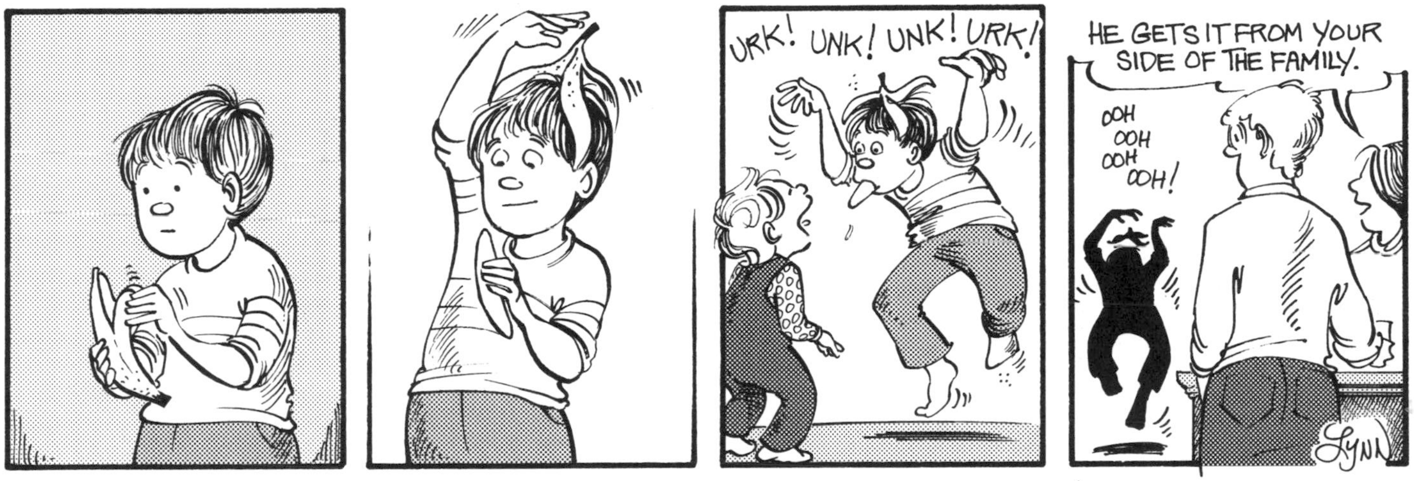

URK! UNK! UNK! URK!
HE GETS IT FROM YOUR SIDE OF THE FAMILY.
OOH OOH OOH OOH!

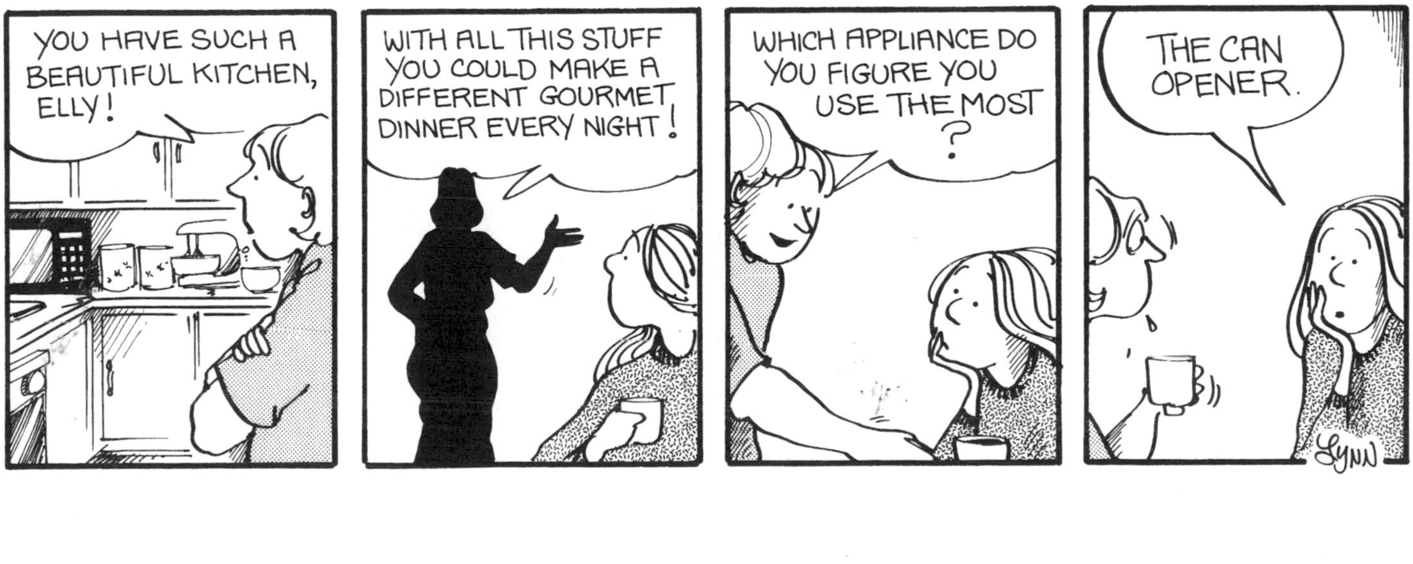

YOU HAVE SUCH A BEAUTIFUL KITCHEN, ELLY!
WITH ALL THIS STUFF YOU COULD MAKE A DIFFERENT GOURMET DINNER EVERY NIGHT!
WHICH APPLIANCE DO YOU FIGURE YOU USE THE MOST?
THE CAN OPENER.

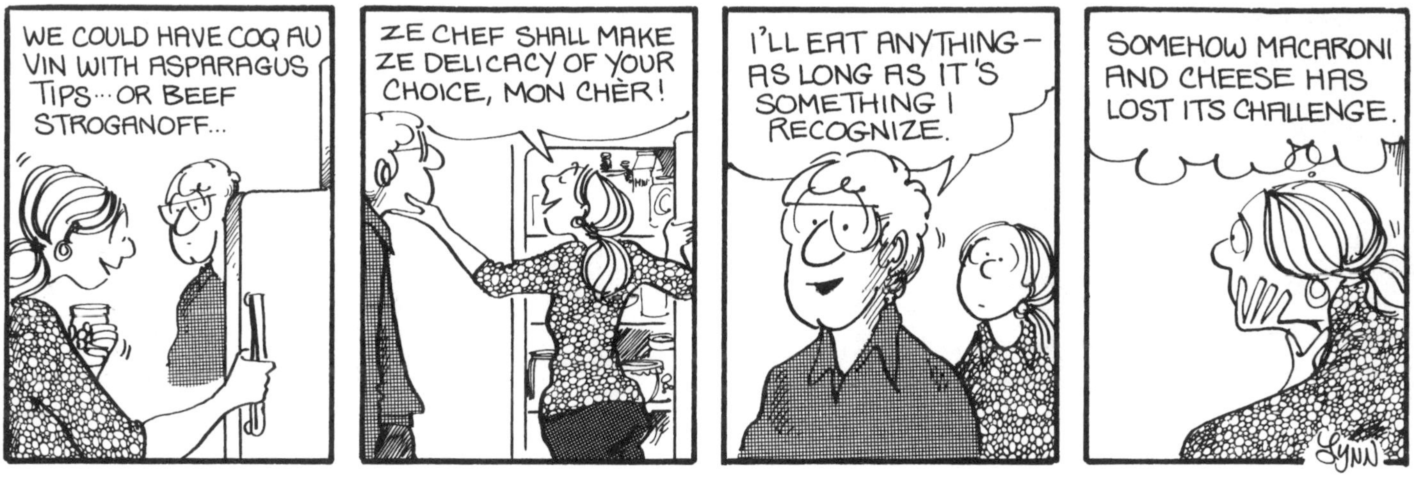
WE COULD HAVE COQ AU VIN WITH ASPARAGUS TIPS... OR BEEF STROGANOFF...
ZE CHEF SHALL MAKE ZE DELICACY OF YOUR CHOICE, MON CHÈR!
I'LL EAT ANYTHING— AS LONG AS IT'S SOMETHING I RECOGNIZE.
SOMEHOW MACARONI AND CHEESE HAS LOST ITS CHALLENGE.
LYNN

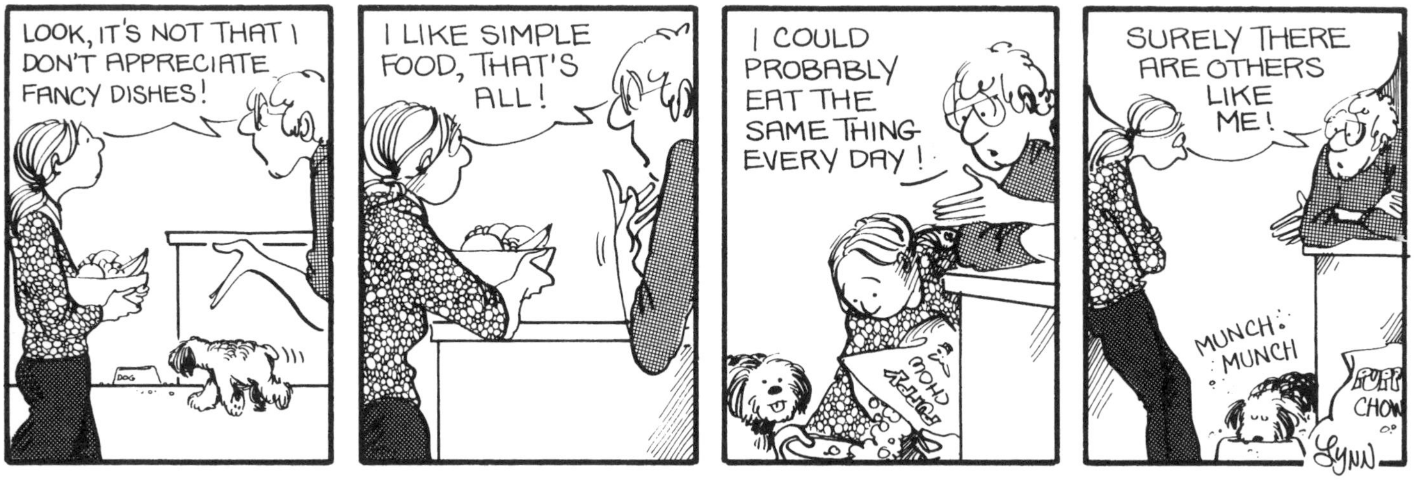
LOOK, IT'S NOT THAT I DON'T APPRECIATE FANCY DISHES!
DOG
I LIKE SIMPLE FOOD, THAT'S ALL!
I COULD PROBABLY EAT THE SAME THING EVERY DAY!
SURELY THERE ARE OTHERS LIKE ME!
MUNCH MUNCH
CHOW
LYNN

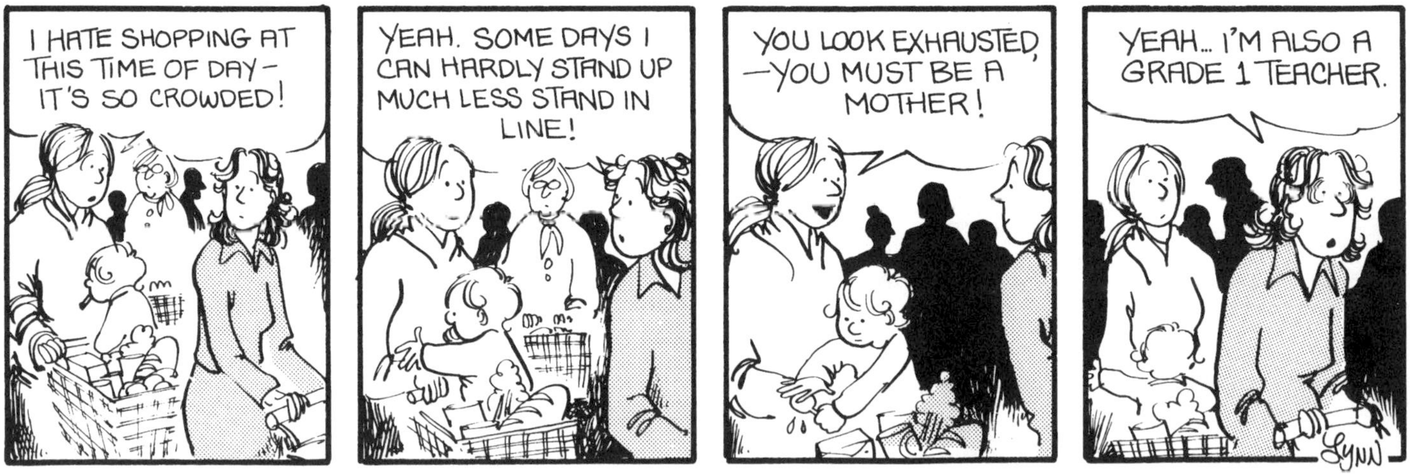
I HATE SHOPPING AT THIS TIME OF DAY— IT'S SO CROWDED!
YEAH. SOME DAYS I CAN HARDLY STAND UP MUCH LESS STAND IN LINE!
YOU LOOK EXHAUSTED, —YOU MUST BE A MOTHER!
YEAH... I'M ALSO A GRADE 1 TEACHER.
LYNN

We had neighbors whose dogs barked all night long. In the far north, sundown took place around two in the morning, so sleep was a problem without the noise. One night, the dogs barked so long we thought we'd go crazy. Then, two shots rang out . . . and silence. We never found out who did it. Nobody really wanted to know. It was a harsh way to solve a problem, but it's a different world up there and justice was often swift, cold and final. You can teach a dog to be quiet. Really, it's a gift and a kindness to the dog!

Wastebaskets do empty themselves. Just wait and somebody will knock them over.

WHATCHA GOT, MICHAEL?

I COLLECTED BOTTLES FOR MR. PERPELUK, AN' HE GAVE ME A WHOLE DOLLAR!

-NOW I DON'T KNOW IF I SHOULD SPEND IT... OR SAVE IT FOR LATER.

LET'S GO TO THE CANDY STORE, AN' I'LL HELP YOU DECIDE!...

I lived for penny candy, and the corner store on Fifth and Lonsdale had a dizzying assortment of goodies. It would take me forever to decide which candies to choose for my hard-earned dime. My all-time favorite was jawbreakers, three for a penny. They turned your tongue black, changed color in your mouth, and tasted like licorice. Nope they don't make 'em like that anymore!

I WANT TWO WHOOPEE BARS, NO... MAKE THAT ONE AN' ONE BOX OF NUM-NUTS...

AN GUM?... YEAH, GUM AN' SOME CHIPS AN' 10 LICORICE WHIPS... ER, NO, 9 AN' A KOO KOO BALL...

FORGET THE KOO KOO BALL... THAT'S TWO WHOOPEE BARS, ONE BANANA ZAP, THREE BUBBLE GUMS...

HERE STAND THE DECISION-MAKERS OF THE FUTURE...

MICHAEL— YOU SPENT THAT WHOLE DOLLAR ON JUNK!

JUNK! YOU CAN'T CALL THIS JUNK... IT'S GOOD STUFF!

KIDS NEED CANDY! IT'S FOOD ENERGY! —THEY SAID SO ON T.V.!

HOW CAN YOU ARGUE WITH THE GOSPEL ACCORDING TO T.V.?

MAAAAAAHH!

THAT IS ENOUGH!!

WHY DON'T WE ALL GO OVER TO THE PARK.

LAWRENCE, GO AND ASK YOUR MOM IF YOU CAN COME WITH US.

I CAN COME. I DON'T HAFTA ASK!

THE RULE HERE IS - YOU ASK FIRST!

OK.

MOM? I'M GOIN' TO THE PARK WITH THE PATTERSONS!

HAVING A PARK DOWN THE STREET IS SO NICE, ELLY.

YES. IT WAS ONE OF THE REASONS WE WANTED TO LIVE HERE.

ME, TOO. THAT AND THE FACT THAT WE'D BE NEIGHBORS!

MMM.

ISN'T IT NICE THAT FATE BROUGHT US TOGETHER AGAIN. WHO KNEW WE'D BE RAISING OUR KIDS TOGETHER, EL? SO MANY PEOPLE LOSE TOUCH AFTER UNIVERSITY.

TRUE!

IT'S AS IF WE WERE LIVING IN SOME KIND OF STORY-BOOK!

YEAH.

...I WONDER WHO "WRITES" THIS STUFF.

CHINGLE-CHIIIME! CHINGLE-CHIME!

IT'S THE ICE CREAM GUY!!

THAT'LL BE 10 BUCKS EVEN, MA'AM.

THERE'S NOTHING LIKE ICE CREAM ON A HOT, STICKY DAY!

EMPHASIZE THE WORD "STICKY."

396

YES, I HAVE BAND-AIDS, BUT WE HAVE TO WASH YOUR HANDS FIRST.

LIZZIE, LET ME WIPE YOUR FACE. MICHAEL, PLEASE PUT ON MORE SUNSCREEN.

DO YOU WANT SOMETHING COLD TO DRINK?

ANYONE WANT A COOKIE?

MAN, THAT BAG HAS EVERYTHING YOU COULD EVER NEED INSIDE IT!

YEAH...

SOMETIMES, I THINK MOMS ARE MAGIC.

Lynn

WELL, I'D SAY IT'S BEEN A VERY SUCCESSFUL DAY.

...THE KIDS WORE OUT BEFORE I DID!!

Lynn

HELLO, BRENDA? CAN YOU BABY-SIT TOMORROW NIGHT?

I KNOW IT'S A SCHOOL NIGHT, BUT WE'LL BE HOME EARLY.

REALLY? THAT'S GREAT!

SHE CAN COME? THAT'S GOOD. —CONSIDERING THAT MIKE'S A HANDFUL, I'M SURPRISED SHE'S SO RELIABLE.

I GIVE HER EXTRA.

...IT'S "DANGER PAY."

Lynn

Aaron was called a nonlinear thinker. I took it as a compliment.

Farley was so hairy he had to be brushed thoroughly at least once a week. Great wads of fine gray fluff came off the brush—enough to spin and knit with. Outside was the best place for the task, and if it was windy, Farley fur flew everywhere. Our neighbor didn't have a laundry line, but she did own a lovely, big, in-ground pool. Now and then, she'd ask me if I knew which tree the "fluff" came from. Before we moved up north, I confessed. It was a tree with a unique bark.

The kids never put gel in Willy's hair, but they did fill it with barrettes, bows and bobby pins. He never complained—he loved the attention.

NIZZIE WAN' COOKIE!

NOT NOW, HONEY. LET'S HAVE SOME BANANA.

NO!!

LOOK! MOMMY'S CUTTING THE BANANA INTO CIRCLES. SEE THE CIRCLES?

GAH?

NOW, WE HAVE A FLOWER! LET'S PUT SPRINKLES ON THE FLOWER. PINK FOR THE PETALS AND BROWN IN THE MIDDLE.

YAH!!

LOOK! PRETTY FLOWER! LIZZIE **EAT** PRETTY FLOWER!

SHRIEK!!!

NIZZIE WANT COOKIE.

WALK, FARLEY! WALK!

AREN'T YOU SUPPOSED TO SAY "HEEL"?

HE JUST RUNS WHEN I SAY THAT! I THINK IT'S BECAUSE "HEEL" DOESN'T MAKE ANY SENSE!

HE DOESN'T SIT WHEN YOU SAY "SIT" OR STAY WHEN YOU SAY "STAY"!

BUT, HE SMELLS WHEN I SAY "SMELL"!

YEAH...

RIGHT NOW,... HE STINKS!

SNIFFF? BLEAH! WHAT **IS** THAT?

I DUNNO!

GROSS! GET HIM AWAY FROM ME!!

I'M GONNA **BARF**! I'M GONNA **HURL**!

LAWRENCE..

IT'S NOT THAT BAD!!!

THAT'S 'CAUSE YOU'RE SNIFFING THE WRONG END!!!

MOM, I WAS WALKING FARLEY AN' HE ROLLED IN SOMETHING GROSS!

NOT AGAIN!

I JUST GAVE HIM A BATH THIS MORNING! IF IT'S NOT ONE OF YOU GETTING DIRTY, IT'S ANOTHER!!!

AND THEN YOU TRAMP IT INTO THE HOUSE FOR **ME** TO CLEAN UP! — I'M SO TIRED OF DOING ALL THE WORK AROUND HERE!..

COOL!

IF YOU JUST LOOK AT 'EM AN' DON'T SAY ANYTHING.... THEY THINK YOU'RE LISTENING!

NOW, I JUST WASHED, DRIED AND BRUSHED THE DOG FOR THE SECOND TIME TODAY.

HE IS NOT TO GO OUT OF THE YARD, OK? HE IS TO STAY ON THE LAWN OR THE DRIVEWAY!

HE IS NOT TO GET WET OR DIRTY.

I PROMISE. ALL HE'S GONNA DO IS STAY IN THE YARD!

!!!

PET SHAMPOO

402

This Sunday page was written and drawn on a day when the newscasts were full of the war in Afghanistan and another fallen soldier was being carried home. I guess there's no money or power in "talking things out."

There are readers who amaze me with their attention to detail and their ability to spot an error or an inconsistency. This book will drive them crazy, as I've broken all the rules! This is far from a complete and consecutive collection of work. Rather it's a story, now seen from a distance; a collection of intertwined ideas, images, and memories put into a form that reads perhaps more easily than the original strip. In rereading this material, I can see just how much personal "stuff" I put out there. Some commentary cut pretty close to the bone, and I wonder if I'd have the courage to do this now!

As stand up comics tend to do, I picked on and criticized myself and my family. Fortunately, I have been forgiven—and we have a rather unique album to refer to—even if it is mostly fantasy. I hope you've enjoyed this collection of new and old.

Readers have told me they feel they've been looking in a mirror, that the Pattersons in *For Better or For Worse* parallel their lives. I must thank all who have written, telling me over and over again—that I am normal. Perhaps, after all these years, it's something I still need to hear!

Lynn